From Economic Crisis
TO REFORM

From Economic Crisis
TO REFORM

IMF PROGRAMS IN LATIN AMERICA AND EASTERN EUROPE

Grigore Pop-Eleches

PRINCETON UNIVERSITY PRESS • PRINCETON AND OXFORD

ISBN: 978-0-691-13503-8

ISBN (pbk.): 978-0-691-13952-4

Library of Congress Control Number: 2008936080

British Library Cataloging-in-Publication Data is available

This book has been composed in Allise, Castellar, Rotis, and Sabon

Printed on acid-free paper ∞

press.princeton.edu

1   3   5   7   9   10   8   6   4   2

FOR KEENA

CONTENTS

ILLUSTRATIONS AND TABLES

LIST OF ABBREVIATIONS

AD	Alianza Democrática
ADIMRA	Asociación de Industriales Metalúrgicos de la República Argentina
ADN	Acción Democrática y Nacionalista
AP	Acción Popular
APRA	Alianza Popular Revolucionaria Americana
BSP	Bălgarska Socialističeska Partija
CDM	Convenţia Democrată din Moldova
CDR	Convenţia Democrată Română
CES	Conferencia Económica y Social
CGT	Confederación General del Trabajo
CMEA	Council for Mutual Economic Assistance
COB	Central Obrera Boliviana
CPC	Confederación de la Producción y del Comercio
CSCE	Conference on Security and Co-operation in Europe
DPS	Dvizhenie za prava i svobodi
EBRD	European Bank for Reconstruction and Development
EFF	Extended Fund Facility
EU	European Union
FSE	Fondo Social de Emergencia
FSN	Frontul Salvării Naţionale
GNI	gross national income
HIPC	Heavily Indebted Poor Countries
HZDS	Hnutie za demokratické Slovensko
IADB	Inter-American Development Bank
ICRG	International Country Risk Guide
IMF	International Monetary Fund
ISI	import substitution industrialization
IU	Izquierda Unida
MAS	Movimiento al Socialismo
MIR	Movimiento de Izquierda Revolucionaria
MNR	Movimiento Nacionalista Revolucionario
MNRI	Movimiento Nacionalista Revolucionario de Izquierda
NEP	New Economic Policy
PCB	Partido Comunista Boliviano

PCRM	Partidul Comuniştilor din Republica Moldova
PDC	Partido Demócrata Cristiano (Chile)
PDAM	Partidul Democrat Agrar din Moldova
PDAR	Partidul Democrat Agrar din România
PDSR	Partidul Democraţiei Sociale din România
PJ	Partido Justicialista
PNŢCD	Partidul Naţional Ţărănesc Creştin Democrat
PPC	Partido Popular Cristiano
PRGF	Poverty Reduction and Growth Facility
PRI	Partido Revolucionario Institucional
PRM	Partidul România Mare
PS	Partido Socialista (Chile)
PSM	Partidul Socialist al Muncii
PUNR	Partidul Unităţii Naţionale a Românilor
SBA	Standby Agreement
SDS	Sayuz na Demokratichnite Sili
SIS	Slovak Intelligence Service
SNS	Slovenská národná strana
STF	Structural Transformation Facility
UCR	Unión Cívica Radical
UDMR	Uniunea Democrată Maghiară din România
VAT	value added tax
VPN	Verejnost' proti násiliu
ZRS	Združenie robotníkov Slovenska

PREFACE

WHEN I STARTED GRADUATE SCHOOL in the fall of 1997, my native country, Romania, was starting to experience the political disintegration of the economic reform efforts initiated with great expectations earlier that year following the long-awaited victory of the anticommunists in November 1996. Even though the International Monetary Fund (IMF) had by then become a household name in Romania (as in much of Eastern Europe) as a central promoter and arbiter of market reforms, I considered the rise and fall of the Romanian neoliberal "revolution" to be primarily a domestic story, and as such paid little attention to the Fund. My intellectual interest in the IMF was sparked a few months later and informed by two very different perspectives: first, Beth Simmons's international political economy course, which emphasized the tight connection between international and domestic political economy; and, second, the increasingly widespread critiques of the IMF as the key promoter of the embattled "Washington Consensus" in the aftermath of the East Asian financial crisis of 1997. As a result, my initial interest was focused on the question—which is still the most frequent reaction I get when telling people that I study IMF programs—of whether IMF interventions were good or bad for developing countries. Even though I had no ideological ax to grind—Romania's disappointing experience with communism until 1989, neo-communist gradualism from 1990–96, and neoliberalism after 1996 was the perfect antidote in this sense—I thought the question was both theoretically interesting and practically important.

Once I started looking more closely at individual IMF programs and at cross-national and cross-temporal differences in program patterns, I realized that analyzing IMF program effects without understanding their politics meant putting the cart before the horse. While the initial intention was to take political science out of the error term (to paraphrase Randall Stone) and, thus, get at the real effects of IMF programs, once I took this step back in the causal chain, I became much more interested in the politics of these programs than in their economic consequences. Situated at the intersection of international and domestic political economy, IMF programs offered a unique opportunity for addressing many of the fascinating and still largely unresolved questions we face when trying to understand the political and economic evolution of less developed countries:

the tension between the interests of the West and the rest in shaping the nature of international financial institutions and transactions; the relative weight of international push and domestic pull in the global wave of market reforms of the last two decades; the scope for partisan politics in the context of globalization and economic crises; the relationship between democratic politics and neoliberal economics in poor countries; and the challenge of policy implementation in countries with weak bureaucracies and unstable politics. Needless to say, none of these dilemmas can be conclusively resolved by simply looking at the politics of IMF programs; however, in this book I do try to advance our understanding of these crucial questions, and I do so through a systematic comparison of three broad episodes of IMF programs spanning two geographic regions (Eastern Europe and Latin America) and more than two decades.

Since this book is the outgrowth of my PhD dissertation at UC Berkeley, much of my intellectual debt goes to my professors and fellow graduate students in Berkeley. First and foremost, the members of my dissertation committee—Beth Simmons, Jim Robinson, Ruth Collier, Ken Jowitt, and Brad DeLong—provided me with an incredibly diverse range of methodologies, ideas, and areas of expertise, which were indispensable for writing a book such as this, spanning multiple regions, subdisciplines, and methodological approaches. In addition to my dissertation committee, I would also like to thank a few of my other teachers from Berkeley, whose advice inside and outside the classroom greatly helped with writing this book: Andrew Janos, Henry Brady, David Collier, Bob Powell, Laura Stoker, Jonah Levy, George Breslauer, Steve Fish, Rui de Figueredo, Barry Eichengreen, Gerard Roland, and Markus Kurtz. At the same time, my graduate school experience was greatly enriched intellectually (as well as personally) by my fellow graduate students. The list of those who deserve credit and thanks for our conversations along the years is likely to be incomplete but here are a few of them: Sebastian Etchemendy, Dwight Dyer, Keena Lipsitz, Scott Gehlbach, Conor O'Dwyer, Thad Dunning, Ben Goldfrank, Ben Bowyer, Naomi Levy, Natalia Ferretti, Sally Roever, and Ken Greene.

I am also grateful to all those who read various parts of the book along the way (sometimes on very short notice) and provided me with encouragement and very helpful feedback: Nancy Bermeo, Miguel Centeno, Dwight Dyer, Sebastian Etchemendy, Anna Grzymala-Busse, Evelyn Huber, John Huber, Bob Kaufman, Markus Kurtz, Evan Lieberman, Carmela Lutmar, Helen Milner, Jonas Pontusson, Randy Stone, Josh Tucker, Jim Vreeland, and Deborah Yashar. Earlier versions of different book chapters were presented and benefited from the comments of participants at various annual meetings of the American Political Science Association and the Midwestern Political Science Association, as well as at talks and workshops at UC Berkeley, Princeton University, Columbia University, Ohio State University, New York University, and Universidad Torcuato Di Tella in Buenos Aires. I would also like to thank John Borland and Aimee Male for reading two versions of the book's introduction (more than a year apart) and helping me make it more readable especially for informed nonacademics. German Lodola, Vicky Murillo, and Randy Stone graciously shared their partisanship and ideology data for the two regions. Tim Waldron and Michael Broache provided competent research assistance. I would also like to thank Chuck Myers for his help and his patience during the review process, and the anonymous reviewers for their extensive and helpful suggestions.

Special thanks go to my brother Cristian (Kiki) for our almost daily conversations on everything from political economy and statistics to international soccer, and for simply being a most wonderful brother and friend.

Words are not enough to express my love and gratitude toward my parents, Renate and Grigore Pop-Eleches. Their unconditional love and devotion for their children have been an inspiration throughout the years. The fact that after giving us their all, they let us wander off across the ocean without a trace of reproach speaks of a selflessness that I hope I will one day be able to emulate. Without them, this book would have never happened, not only because without their encouragement I would have probably studied physics in Romania instead of political science in the United States, but also because during the last month of my book revisions they pampered me with everything from home cooking to round-the-clock child care.

Finally, I want to thank my wife, Keena Lipsitz, to whom this book is dedicated. Since we met early in graduate school, she got to live with me through the whole process from inchoate research idea to dissertation and to book. Whether discussing various ideas, reading, and editing successive versions of book chapters, accompanying me on my many and lengthy research trips to Eastern Europe and Latin America (or putting up with my absences), or simply helping me keep things in perspective at key moments, I could not have asked for a better partner. And speaking of keeping things in perspective, I want to thank our baby daughter, Rica, whose first months on this earth have filled our lives with joy.

From Economic Crisis
TO REFORM

–1–

Introduction

IN THE SUMMER OF 1985, in the midst of the debt crisis, two newly elected Latin American presidents set out to transform the domestic and international political economy trajectories of their respective countries. Despite the shared economic and political challenges facing the neighboring countries of Bolivia and Peru as poor, highly indebted new democracies, the two new leaders moved their countries in opposite directions: in Bolivia Victor Paz Estenssoro ended the country's prolonged economic and political paralysis, and instituted a radical program of orthodox economic reforms, which transformed the country from a regional basket case into an unexpected showcase example of successful neoliberalism and cooperation with the International Monetary Fund. Meanwhile, the newly elected Peruvian president, Alan Garcia, reversed his country's earlier IMF cooperation and initiated a heterodox domestic adjustment program combined with a unilateral debt payment reduction. Even though important elements of Garcia's heterodoxy were also found in Argentina's Austral Plan and Brazil's Cruzado Plan, Peru suffered greater international consequences as its highly publicized break with the IMF ultimately resulted in international economic isolation and high economic costs by the end of the decade.

More than a decade later, newly elected center-right governments in Bulgaria, Romania, and Moldova also set out to redirect their countries' prior economic reform trajectories. While their ex-communist predecessors had not resisted IMF policy advice to the extent of their Latin American counterparts, the electoral victories of openly pro-market coalitions promised to accelerate the pace of IMF-style reforms. These expectations were fulfilled in Bulgaria, where the government of Ivan Kostov pursued a series of remarkably consistent and successful reforms in close and quasi-permanent cooperation with the IMF. Despite their similar goals and starting points, the Romanian and Moldovan reformers were much less successful than their Bulgarian counterparts, as political infighting and lack of bureaucratic expertise contributed to a succession of inconclusive stop-go economic reform efforts. Therefore, the IMF program records of the two countries hardly improved under their pro-market governments, and in Romania the advent of a fully implemented IMF program actually had to wait until after the return to power of the ex-communists in the 2000 elections.

These brief snapshots highlight the tension inherent in the IMF's involvement in developing countries. On the one hand, the IMF's central role in the wave of neoliberal reforms of the last two and a half decades has led some observers to interpret IMF programs as tools for imposing the Western economic agenda on the developing world (Pastor 1989, Stiglitz 2002). On the other hand, these sketches also suggest that the Fund cannot simply impose its agenda on program countries, and that domestic political interests and institutional constraints still matter even in developing countries facing serious economic crises. Therefore, other analysts have suggested that IMF conditionality—the practice of conditioning IMF loans on the implementation of certain economic policies—has played only a modest role in shaping economic reforms (Remmer 1998), serving instead as a political alibi for domestic reformers (Vreeland 2003). These conflicting interpretations, which echo long-standing debates about the nature and implications of IMF conditionality, and about the drivers of neoliberal reforms more broadly, raise a number of important questions: Why and how do economic crises trigger and sustain IMF-backed economic adjustment policies in developing countries? Does the IMF live up to its stated goal of providing impartial policy advice and financial support for troubled developing countries? How do IMF lending patterns reflect the evolving demands of international financial markets and the changing priorities of advanced industrial democracies in the developing world? Under what constellations of domestic interests and institutions are governments more willing to initiate and more capable of implementing IMF-style reforms? How are the pressures of IMF conditionality filtered through the domestic politics of program countries?

More broadly, by focusing on the politics of IMF programs I address a number of central theoretical questions about the increasingly intertwined nature of domestic and international drivers of economic policy making. First, in the tradition of Gourevitch's (1978) "second image reversed" approach, I analyze the influence of the broader trends in the global economy on domestic politics and economic policy choices. In analyzing these international drivers, I emphasize not only the central and continuously evolving role of the IMF in shaping economic policies of developing countries, but also the impact of economic incentives related to international financial markets and the political economy of trade and geopolitical alliances. However, in this book I am equally concerned with how domestic ideology, interests, and institutions in developing countries mediate the powerful economic and political pressures to which these countries are subjected, particularly in economic crisis situations. As such this book builds on earlier analyses of the role of domestic politics in shaping national responses to international crises and pressures (Simmons 1994, Keohane and Milner 1996, Garrett 1998).

Since one of the main arguments of this book is that the interaction between domestic and international political economy is contingent on temporal and geographic context, I address these questions by analyzing evidence from two prominent recent episodes of large-scale economic adjustment under IMF supervision: Latin America during the debt crisis of the 1980s, and Eastern Europe and the former Soviet Union during the post-communist transition of the 1990s. For additional analytical leverage the final part of the book also compares these two episodes to the IMF program patterns in Latin America in the 1990s. This systematic cross-regional and cross-temporal comparison of the politics of IMF programs captures the dramatic geopolitical and economic transformation of the international sphere since the debut of the debt crisis in 1982, and at the same time it highlights the important regional variation in historical and institutional legacies across different parts of the developing world.

At the international level, I show that the IMF's response to economic crises is driven by the changing imperatives of international financial stability and the changing interests of large IMF member countries. Whereas IMF programs during the 1980s debt crisis emphasized austerity measures geared toward the repayment of external debt, IMF conditionality in post-communist Eastern Europe focused more heavily on domestic structural reforms and the international economic and political integration of the former command economies. Moreover, crises in both regions received greater attention from the IMF when they occurred in economically and/or politically important countries. While deviations from technocratic uniformity were driven by both concerns about international financial stability and the narrower political and economic objectives of the Fund's largest shareholders, this book shows that the nature and intensity of such deviations depended on the regional and global crisis context, with systemic concerns playing a greater role during the Latin American debt crisis, and geopolitical considerations being more salient during the post-communist transition.

Domestically, this book shows that economic crisis only triggers economic reforms when international interpretations (such as those of the IMF) of the roots and implications of the crisis resonate with the ideal and material interests of domestic elites and ordinary citizens. The extent of such ideological agreement and the compatibility of democratic politics with IMF-style reforms hinges on the broader regional/global context of a given crisis: during periods of worldwide economic crisis and international ideological contestation—such as the debt crisis of the 1980s in the context of the final decade of the Cold War—IMF interventions are more likely to be regarded as thinly disguised impositions of Western economic interests by significant portions of the elite and the population. In such a political context, economic crises are more likely to trigger divergent partisan policy responses from governments of different orientations, and democracy tends to be at odds with economic adjustment. During periods of global economic expansion and international neoliberal ideological hegemony, the IMF is more likely to be viewed as a technocratic policy adviser. Under such circumstances—as was the case in the ex-communist countries in the 1990s—economic crises trigger nonideological economic adjustment efforts, which are broadly compatible with democratic politics. However, even economic need and ideological agreement do not guarantee the successful implementation of reforms; in addition, governments embarking on IMF-style reforms need to have the bureaucratic capacity necessary to cope with the technical challenges of the reform process and the political capital necessary to weather its political challenges.

The theoretical framework and the empirical tests in this book focus not only on the separate effects of particular factors, such as economic pressures, political interests and institutional constraints but on the interaction between these different elements in shaping the economic reform process.[1] Rather than simply asking whether IMF-style reforms are more likely in countries with financially or ideologically motivated governments or with well-functioning bureaucracies, the book analyzes under what political and institutional circumstances economic crises are more effective triggers of policy change, and, conversely, under what economic circumstances partisanship and bureaucratic capacity matter more for IMF programs.[2] The empirical patterns revealed by this analysis justify not only the emphasis on such interaction effects but also the cross-regional and cross-temporal comparative setup of the book. For example, the analysis shows that economic crises rarely affect developing countries uniformly: Instead, in both regions economic crises were much more likely to trigger IMF programs when they occurred in economically important countries and in countries with well-functioning bureaucracies. Conversely, economic importance and bureaucratic capacity mattered primarily during severe economic crises but were much less important during normal economic environments. The impact of domestic economic crisis intensity also varied as a function of government partisan interests, but

---

[1] For a compelling illustration of the importance of such interactive theoretical propositions, see Franzese's (2002) analysis of policy making in developed democracies.

[2] Earlier work has identified important interaction between partisanship and various domestic institutions such as labor-organizational structure (Alvarez et al. 2001), labor market organization (Boix 2000), central bank independence (Clark et al. 1998, Cusack 2000), as well international constraints (Boix 2000, Garrett 1998). However, the interaction between crisis intensity and partisanship has received much less attention so far.

in this respect the patterns were context-specific: For Latin America in the 1980s, domestic economic crises accentuated partisan policy differences, whereas in Eastern Europe in the 1990s, similar crises instead triggered partisan policy convergence, as political parties discarded their fair-weather policy differences and acquiesced to IMF demands. Partisan crisis responses in Latin America during the 1990s were less clear-cut, but the overall patterns were closer to those of post-communist Eastern Europe, suggesting that the ideological convergence of the 1990s trumped (at least temporarily) the partisan polarization of Latin American politics.

The remainder of this introductory chapter is organized as follows: The next section introduces the analytical framework developed in this book and explains the research design in greater detail. The third section puts the two main crises in comparative perspective, by presenting an overview of the economic and geopolitical background of the Latin American debt crisis and the post-communist transition in both international and domestic terms. The fourth section discusses the theoretical contributions of this book to debates in the international and domestic political economy literatures. The last section lays out the plan of the book and provides a brief chapter summary.

The Analytical Framework

As laid out in more detail in chapter 2, this book analyzes IMF programs as an interaction between the IMF and developing country governments in the context of a number of economic and political constraints at the domestic and international level. Even though IMF programs are negotiated by two primary actors—representatives of the IMF staff and the program country government—the actual dynamics of Fund programs are decisively shaped by the complex web of political and economic constraints under which the two main actors operate. Therefore, to explain the trajectories of IMF programs in the developing world, we must consider a series of analytical steps. First, we have to understand how the nature of IMF conditionality toward a given country is shaped by the competing imperatives of the Fund's multiple agendas. These include ensuring international financial stability, imposing prudent economic policies in program countries, and (occasionally) helping large donor countries pursue their broader economic and geopolitical interests. This international policy environment, combined with the country's financial need and domestic economic imbalances, establishes the broad parameters of what the government *needs to do* to address the demands of the country's economic situation in the context of an IMF program. The partisan interests of the parties and politicians in power affect their interpretation of the country's economic situation and, therefore, shape what the government *would like to do* in the absence of domestic constraints. Finally, governments are constrained domestically in what they *can do* to resolve economic crises. The severity of these constraints depends on the government's ability to overcome potential political resistance from reform opponents, as well as on the capacity and willingness of the state apparatus to implement the government's desired policies.

Research Design

In line with a few recent contributions to the political economy of IMF programs (Stone 2002, Vreeland 2003), this book employs a multimethod approach: The predictions of the theoretical model presented in chapter 2 (and formalized in that chapter's appendix) are tested in subsequent chapters through a combination of cross-country statistical tests (based on twenty-one Latin American/Caribbean[3] and twenty-six Eastern European/former Soviet countries[4]) and comparative case studies of four Latin American countries (Argentina, Bolivia, Chile, and Peru) and four Eastern European countries (Moldova, Slovakia, Bulgaria, and Romania).

The basic theoretical claim of the book is that domestic and external economic crises are not uniform drivers of IMF programs (as much of the prior literature has implicitly assumed) but that economic crises are mediated by politics at both the national and the international level. Therefore, this book departs from prior works by comparing two temporally and geographically bounded country clusters: Latin America during the debt crisis of the 1980s, and the transition economies of Eastern Europe and the former Soviet Union in the 1990s. The final chapter of the book places these two reform episodes into additional comparative perspective by discussing the broad political dynamics of Latin American IMF programs in the 1990s. These comparisons show not only that differ-

---

[3] The criterion for inclusion in the sample was that a country had to be an IMF member (thereby excluding Cuba, for which reliable statistical data were not available in any case) and have a population of at least one million in 1982. The resulting sample included the following countries: Argentina, Bolivia, Brazil, Chile, Colombia, Costa Rica, Dominican Republic, Ecuador, El Salvador, Guatemala, Haiti, Honduras, Jamaica, Mexico, Nicaragua, Panama, Paraguay, Peru, Trinidad and Tobago, Uruguay, and Venezuela.

[4] Since all ex-communist countries were IMF members and had populations above one million, the only transition countries excluded from my sample were Bosnia-Herzegovina and Yugoslavia, for which there was insufficient statistical data in the 1990s. The final sample consisted of the following countries: Albania, Armenia, Azerbaijan, Belarus, Bulgaria, Croatia, Czech Republic, Estonia, Georgia, Hungary, Kazakhstan, Kyrgyzstan, Latvia, Lithuania, Macedonia, Moldova, Mongolia, Poland, Romania, Russia, Slovakia, Slovenia, Tajikistan, Turkmenistan, Ukraine, and Uzbekistan.

ent crisis aspects matter more under certain circumstances (e.g., debt payments during the 1980s in Latin America versus reserves in post-communist Eastern Europe) but that economic crises are interpreted and treated
differently depending on the broader regional and international climate
(e.g., inflation leads to partisan policy divergence in Latin America but to
partisan policy convergence in Eastern Europe).

The comparison of three episodes of IMF programs (in broadly comparable countries) under varying crisis types and crisis "logics" allows me
to trace the changing interaction between economic crisis and political
interests/constraints as drivers of IMF programs and economic reforms.
From this perspective, this book builds on the theoretical insights of earlier studies (Gourevitch 1986, Rogowski 1989), which showed that domestic alliances and policy choices were greatly affected by temporally
specific changes in global markets. Somewhat surprisingly, the more recent literature dealing with IMF programs and the neoliberal reforms of
the last twenty-five years has largely ignored the role of changing temporal
dynamics due to systemic transformations. Similarly, despite the ongoing
theoretical debates about the importance of regions for political science
(Bunce 1995, Schmitter and Karl 1994, Mainwaring and Perez-Linan
2007) and a number of insightful cross-regional comparisons (Greskovits
1998, Haggard and Kaufman 1995, 2007), regional differences have been
generally ignored in the study of IMF programs.[5]

While the specific choice of episodes will be discussed in greater detail
below, I will first lay out the methodological justification for using systematic cross-regional and cross-temporal comparisons, and the potential advantages of this approach over the two most common alternatives: the
single-region approach (Pastor 1987, Stone 2002, 2004) and the multire-
gion and multiperiod sample of IMF programs (Reichmann and Stillson
1978, Thacker 1999, Barro and Lee 2003, Vreeland 2003). To understand
the advantages of this research design, it is useful to consider the implications of having used one of the alternative approaches for the findings
mentioned above. Had the argument been developed by studying only
post-communist Eastern Europe, the book would have concluded that
foreign reserve levels are the crucial driver and higher inflation leads to
ideological convergence. By contrast, the same approach in Latin America
in the 1980s would have yielded very different conclusions, emphasizing
the role of external debt and the partisan policy divergence in response
to inflationary crises. Therefore, a single-region, single-period approach
would run the risk of generalizing on the basis of a specific context to

---

[5] See, for example, Stone and Steinwand's (2008) criticism that much of the IMF literature has ignored the serious heterogeneity of IMF programs and candidate countries.

a broader universe of cases for which the relationship does not hold.[6] Alternatively, this approach can provide valid insights for a particular set of cases but it may not lend itself to some of the comparative insights generated by a systematic cross-regional and cross-period analysis.

The common approach of combining different time periods and regions into one analysis has the potential advantage of providing generalizable results across countries. However, for these results to be meaningful, we have to assume causal homogeneity across time and space.[7] While this may well be the true for Vreeland's (2003) particular concern—the growth effects of IMF programs—for the questions addressed in this book, this approach would have probably found no interaction effects between inflation and partisan orientation (since the two opposite effects would have canceled each other out), missing a crucial aspect of the story.[8] Moreover, pooling requires the use of the same statistical indicators across different episodes, which is precluded by data coverage limitations for several important indicators (such as bureaucratic quality and partisan orientation).

While Eastern Europe and Latin America have been fruitfully compared before in the political economy literature,[9] the choice of the Latin American debt crisis and the post-communist transition as the two main sets of cases for the present analysis was based on several theoretical criteria. First, the two clusters represent the two most extensive episodes of IMF interventions in recent history, which not only signals the prominence of the two crises on the Fund's agenda but also has the advantage of offering significant variation in both dependent and independent variables within each region. Second, the two regions displayed a broad and roughly comparable spectrum of socio-economic development levels, which made them more comparable to each other than each of them would have been to Africa, for example.[10] Third, the Latin American debt crisis and the post-communist transition capture critical junctures in the economic and political development of the two regions in that they involved a massive and costly economic reform push in the delicate political context of democratic transitions.

[6] To Stone's credit, he resists makings such generalizations and emphasizes the potential context specificity of his findings.

[7] For a detailed discussion of the pitfalls of striving for larger sets of cases without regard to causal homogeneity, see Brady et al. 2004.

[8] While this problem can theoretically be addressed by interacting regional/temporal dummy variables with the variables of interest, such an approach would produce a large number of cumbersome triple-interaction effects for many of the key findings of this book.

[9] Greskovits 1998, Weyland 1999, Schamis 2002.

[10] The East Asian crisis was another plausible candidate for comparison but it had the disadvantage of involving a much shorter time period and a significantly smaller number of countries than the Latin American debt crisis and the post-communist transition.

At the same time, however, the two episodes differed significantly along a number of important dimensions, which shaped the political dynamics of IMF programs and of neoliberal economic reforms more broadly.[11] As the following section shows in greater detail, the changes in international financial markets and Western political priorities since the 1980s contributed to important shifts in the agenda of IMF interventions in the developing world. These changes in the international environment, combined with the different roots and nature of the domestic economic crises in the two regions, contributed to different domestic political reactions to neoliberal reform initiatives. Finally, the two regions also differed with respect to their domestic political and institutional landscape, including political parties, interest groups, and state institutions, which led to noticeable differences in the dynamics of reform initiation and implementation.

While these cross-regional differences do not preclude the comparability of the two episodes, they nevertheless suggest that this book's approach of systematic cross-temporal and cross-regional comparisons is more appropriate for studying the political dynamics of IMF programs than the traditional approach of treating IMF programs as uniform treatments across time and space. The inclusion of a third set of cases in the final chapter—Latin America in the 1990s—provides additional analytical leverage by helping identify which of the differences between the initial two clusters are primarily due to temporal changes in the international political economy of IMF interventions, and which are rooted in the domestic socioeconomic and political logics of different regional developmental trajectories.

The case studies in chapters 4, 6, and 7 are nested in the statistical tests of the preceding chapters, and therefore their primary purpose is to provide a more detailed and nuanced analysis of the mechanisms underlying the broad empirical regularities identified by the large-N analysis. In line with Lieberman's (2005) argument about case selection in model-testing (rather than model-building) small-N analysis, the country cases were chosen primarily from among "along-the-line" cases, which fit the theoretical predictions and statistical findings and therefore provide an opportunity for exploring these macro-findings in greater detail. While the book discusses the trajectories of four countries from each of the two regions, the number of cases is actually greater than eight because the significant over-time changes in relevant political and economic variables result in each country providing more than one analytically relevant case to the analysis, thus, Bolivia 1982–85 is a separate case from Bolivia

---

[11] For a more detailed theoretical discussion about the trade-offs entailed in comparing East and South, see Bunce 1998.

1985–89, given that the government change in 1985 resulted in a dramatic change in partisan orientation, and thus offers the opportunity of analyzing two different types of partisan responses to economic crises. Of course, given the fairly large number of resulting cases and the length of the period under consideration, not all cases perfectly fit the model for each of the factors analyzed in the statistical chapters. Such deviations, however, represent an additional benefit of case studies, since they not only remind us of the importance of idiosyncratic factors in shaping political outcomes but can also identify more systematic explanations, which may nevertheless not be suitable for large-N statistical tests (due to data limitations).

The choice of countries for the case studies was guided by two additional methodological criteria. First, I chose cases that jointly capture a large range of the variation in the key drivers of IMF programs discussed in the theoretical chapter and the statistical analyses (King et al. 2001 147–49). For example comparing the IMF programs of a systemically important country like Argentina, with those of marginal countries like Bolivia during and Moldova and in-between cases like Peru and in Bulgaria, helps clarify the mechanisms and implications of preferential treatment during IMF negotiations across regions and time periods. The selected countries also represent a wide range of economic conditions spanning from the catastrophic domestic and external crises in Bolivia during the mid-1980s and in Bulgaria during the mid-1990s to the relative economic stability of Chile since the mid-1980s and Slovakia since the mid-1990s. Furthermore, the case studies capture at least some of the theoretically important variation in regime type (e.g., authoritarian regimes like Chile in the 1980s, semiauthoritarian regimes like Peru and Slovakia in the mid-1990s, and democracies like Argentina and Peru in the 1980s and Bulgaria in the 1990s) and partisan orientations (ranging from leftists like Alan Garcia and nationalists like Mečiar to committed neoliberals like the Kostov government in Bulgaria and successive post-1985 Bolivian governments). Second, since arguments based on cross-country comparisons may suffer from omitted variable bias (King et al. 2001, Brady et al. 2004), cases were also chosen so as to maximize the within-country variation in relevant explanatory variables: For example, the important partisan reorientations experienced by Bolivia and Peru in 1985, Slovakia in 1994, Romania in 1996, Bulgaria in 1997, and Moldova in 1998 and 2001 offer ideal opportunities to study the effects of partisan politics on IMF programs while controlling for most other alternative explanations of IMF programs. Similarly, the rapidly changing economic fortunes experienced by several governments in the eight countries (including the Bulgarian and Romanian ex-communists in 1994–96 and

Argentina and Peru in 1985–88) facilitate within-country assessments of the effects of economic crises.

The Two Crises in Comparative Perspective

In this section I discuss the broad economic and political settings of the Latin American debt crisis and the post-communist transition. The discussion focuses on three broad categories of factors: (1) the international economic and geopolitical environment and its effect on IMF conditionality; (2) the nature and depth of the economic crises experienced by the two regions; and (3) the domestic political and institutional environment in which these crises unfolded.

IMF Conditionality in a Changing International Environment

Since 1982 the mission and the nature of IMF conditionality has been significantly affected by the economic and political transformations related to the spread of globalization and the end of the Cold War. On the economic front, the last two and a half decades have witnessed a rapid rise in international trade, capital movements, and commercial lending, as well as important qualitative changes in the composition of transnational investments. While the 1980s essentially marked the end of the era of bank finance,[12] the 1990s emerged as the "era of equity finance," in which portfolio investments (bonds and equity) and foreign direct investment (FDI) gradually started to displace commercial bank lending, particularly in Latin America and Asia (Eichengreen and Fishlow 1996). The magnitude of these changes has been remarkable: net FDI flows to the developing world increased from $35.7bn in 1991 to $185.4bn in 1999. Net bond financing jumped from $10.9bn in 1991 to $62.5bn in 1996, before declining to $30.3bn in 2000. Net equity flows went from $7.6bn in 1991 to $47.9bn in 2000, despite a temporary decline following the East Asian crisis.[13]

The rising volume and changing nature of international capital flows has affected the Fund's ability to regulate and control international financial markets. During the debt crisis of the 1980s the IMF played a pivotal role as an intermediary between creditors and debtors and extracted significant concessions not only from debtor countries but also from Western commercial banks by threatening to withhold funding unless the banks

---

[12] Following the traumatic experience of the debt crisis, most commercial banks significantly reduced their exposure to developing country debts.
[13] Data from *World Bank* 2001:36.

agreed to a substantial debt rescheduling. By contrast, in the 1990s the rising volume and complexity of international capital flows, amplified at least in part by the Fund's active promotion of financial deregulation, led to a marked reduction of the Fund's ability to control and regulate international financial markets.[14] While the reduced IMF leverage over an increasingly diverse group of international lenders arguably reduced the attractiveness of IMF programs in the 1990s—and even prompted critics to call for closing down the Fund—two other aspects of the international economic and political environment mitigated and possibly reversed these effects. First, the high mobility of capital flows in the 1990s arguably raised the importance of the Fund's seal of approval, particularly for countries with limited or mixed track records in international financial markets. Second, the end of the Cold War triggered an increase in merit-based bilateral and multilateral aid to developing countries, and the IMF's role as a gatekeeper for much of this funding gave it significant leverage over poor, aid-dependent countries (Radelet 2006).

The economic and political priorities of the advanced industrial countries were also quite different both from each other and from previous interventions during the two episodes. Given the high potential impact of the debt crisis and the post-communist transition on crucial Western economic and political interests and the West's control of the majority of IMF voting rights, the IMF interventions in the two program clusters differed from the narrow traditional balance-of-payments approach used in earlier periods. Due to the high degree of exposure of many leading Western commercial banks, the prospect of a massive default on Latin American debt was seen as a serious threat to the stability of the financial systems of the main creditors (Eichengreen and Fishlow 1998).[15] Therefore, Western governments and banks explicitly conditioned the much-needed debt rescheduling on the adoption of strict IMF-led adjustment programs, meant to ensure the continuation of debt servicing by Latin American debtors. Given the primacy of systemic economic concerns on the Western agenda for Latin America during the debt crisis, IMF conditionality showed little concern for domestic social and political consequences, and the resulting austerity measures left little room for "adjustment with a human face" (IADB 1990:3).

Following the collapse of Communism, Western interests in the former Soviet bloc were arguably as much geopolitical as economic in nature.

---

[14] This loss of control was particularly visible in the Fund's widely criticized handling of the East Asian financial crisis of 1997.

[15] While some observers have argued that the prosperity of a few international banks was erroneously equated with the stability of the international financial system (Diaz Alejandro 1985:25), the massive political effort starting with the IMF-led debt renegotiations up to

While the marketization and international integration of the former communist countries undoubtedly coincided with the economic interests of influential Western businesses, the originally envisioned transition from one-party-dominated command economies to liberal capitalist democracies had important geopolitical and ideological repercussions for the shape of the post–Cold War "new world order." Even though the actual progress toward this goal has been much slower and more uneven than initially expected (Pop-Eleches 2007), this vision had significant repercussions on the IMF's role in the region, which differed significantly from the narrow debt repayment focus of Latin American interventions in the 1980s. The first consequence was that the Fund adopted a more politically sensitive approach to IMF conditionality. While this change came at least partly in reaction to harsh criticisms of the Fund's handling of the debt crisis, it was reinforced by the broader geopolitical agenda of the West for post-communist Eastern Europe, which was shaped by several key considerations: (1) security concerns related to the existence of nuclear arsenals in the former Soviet republics as well as the political tensions related to the Yugoslav crises (particularly Bosnia and Kosovo); (2) the geographical proximity between Eastern and Western Europe, which raised the stakes of a complete economic collapse in the former Soviet bloc;[16] and (3) the lingering memories of the Cold War ideological rivalry between East and West, which may have contributed to the temptation to export the full "package" of Western political and economic liberalism to the ex-communist countries, rather than the narrower traditional emphasis on economic liberalism.

Second, in response to criticisms for its failure to respond to evolving financial markets and economic theory advances,[17] in the late 1980s the Fund started to expand its mission beyond the narrow traditional balance-of-payments focus to promote a more comprehensive economic reform agenda for the developing world (Stallings 1992). This focus shift in the Fund's agenda during the late 1980s and early 1990s is illustrated by figure 1.1, which indicates the average number of structural benchmark conditions in IMF programs 1987–99. Thus, particularly during the early and mid-1990s, there was a veritable explosion of structural conditions in IMF programs, which increased eightfold between 1987 and 1997 before starting to decline again in 1998 and 1999.

---

the 1989 Brady Plan indicated the depth of the Western commitment to control the international fallout from the crisis.

[16] According to this logic, political turmoil in Eastern Europe (as proven by the Yugoslav crisis) can easily translate into waves of refugees into Western Europe in addition to the costs of military intervention to avoid a spread of the conflict.

[17] See, for example, Edwards's (1989) sharp critique of the IMF financial programming model.

Figure 1.1: Average Number of Structural Conditions by Program Year

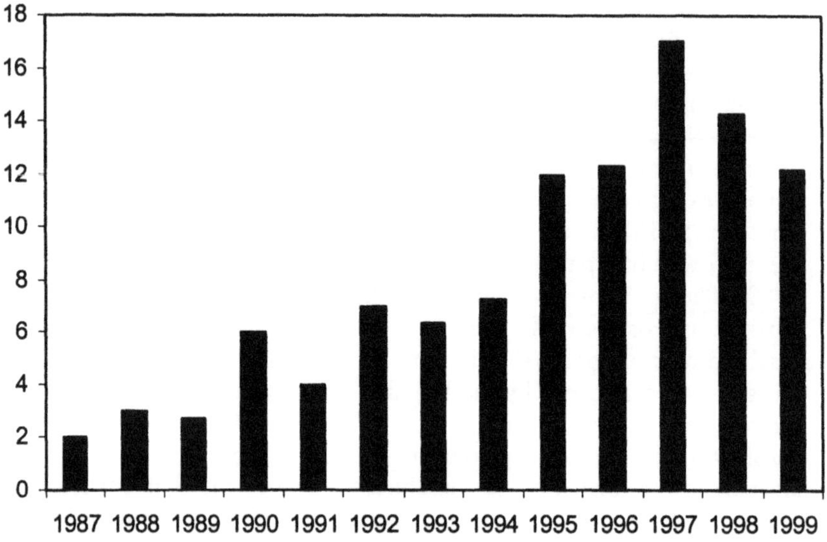

Source: IMF (2001).

The nature of IMF conditionality differed not only temporally but also regionally. Thus, the number of structural conditions in Fund programs involving the former communist countries during the 1990s was consistently and significantly higher than for other regions in the same time period (IMF 2001).[18] On average, transition economies had almost twice as many structural benchmarks in their IMF programs as other countries. This trend was particularly visible starting in 1995, when the average number of structural conditions in IMF programs involving former communist countries jumped to fifteen from about eight in the preceding year and stayed at or above that level for the rest of the decade, whereas in other countries the average number of such benchmarks oscillated between five and ten. Moreover, whereas in the 1980s, structural conditions emphasized exchange rate and fiscal measures (primarily spending cuts), the IMF programs in the transition economies during the 1990s were primarily concerned with tax reforms, privatization, and financial sector reforms, which accounted for more than half the structural conditions during this period (Mercer-Blackman and Unigovskaya 2000:9).

Part of this greater emphasis on structural reforms in IMF conditionality can be traced to the broader economic and geopolitical changes discussed earlier. Thus, the shift in international financial markets toward

---

[18] The East Asian programs of 1997 and 1998 were the only exception to this pattern.

portfolio investment and foreign direct investment placed a greater premium on enacting a broader range of pro-market economic policies (especially privatization and deregulation) than had been required by the relatively indiscriminate bank lending of the 1970s. Moreover, particularly in the transition countries, a rapid dismantling of the large state sector was widely regarded as the best guarantee against a resurgence of political challenges to the liberal world order of the post–Cold War era. However, this transformation was also driven by the theoretical and ideological convictions of the IMF staff, which reflected the ideological ascendancy of neoliberalism in academic and policy circles starting in the 1980s. As Kahler (1989) points out, the traditional dominance of neoclassical prescriptions in stabilization matters was complemented by the gradual intellectual strengthening of its structural policy prescriptions starting in the 1970s, which, however, only gradually started to be applied in practice in the 1980s following the collapse of the import-substitution (ISI) models.[19] While the nature of the adjustment tasks of the 1990s (particularly in the transition countries) may have required complementing monetary and fiscal policy measures with comprehensive structural reforms, this expansion occurred in an area outside the Fund's traditional area of expertise with managing balance of payments crises.[20] While the IMF has since announced an initiative to streamline conditionality by restricting the number of conditions and maintaining only crucial structural benchmarks, there is little doubt that the nature of IMF programs in the 1990s was profoundly influenced by the prominence of structural conditions in IMF conditionality.

The Nature of the Adjustment Challenge

The crises experienced by the two regions during the massive episodes of IMF intervention differed in both their depth and their nature. In terms of their external debt position, Latin American countries were much more vulnerable at the outset of the crisis in 1982. The crisis followed more than a decade of massive lending of recycled oil money by Western commercial banks to Latin America and other developing countries. The wide availability of low-conditionality loans had enabled the Latin American countries to finance their massive fiscal deficits and continue to keep up with the soaring interest payments charged by the commercial banks.

[19] In Eastern Europe, these ideological undertones became particularly clear during the heated debates between neoliberals and market socialists about the appropriate trajectory of the postcommunist economic reforms (Greskovits 1998:29–34).

[20] Given that structural reforms had traditionally been primarily the World Bank's preoccupation, the IMF's expanded reach during the 1990s may explain the increasingly frequent and open tensions between the two Bretton Woods sister institutions.

However, starting in 1979 the recession affecting advanced countries, the rise of interest rates, the lower lending willingness of commercial banks, and the deteriorating terms of trade undermined the ability of Latin American governments to continue with their debt-financed expansionary policies (Eichengreen and Fishlow 1998). Thus, much of Latin American borrowing after 1980 was channeled into maintaining external liquidity (IADB 1990) and by 1982 the net inflow of international loans was insufficient to cover the spiraling interest payments and resulted in the insolvency of the most indebted nations (Brovedani 1985).

By comparison, most of the former communist countries had relatively low debt burdens at the outset of transition: Whereas by 1982, debt servicing accounted for more than 46% of the Latin America's export earnings (and then declined gradually to around 30% by the end of the decade), for the transition economies the corresponding figures fluctuated between 10% and 18% during the 1990s.[21] Similarly, interest payments for the transition economies amounted to less than 1% of GNP before 1994 (and did not exceed 2% at any point during the 1990s), whereas in Latin America interest payments absorbed on average 4.5% of GNP 1982–89. In Eastern Europe (with the notable exceptions of Poland, Hungary, and Bulgaria), the main problem following the collapse of communism was not too much debt, which accounted for only 13% of GNP in 1990, but the extremely low international reserves and very limited access to capital markets.

Despite the severity of the Latin American debt crisis, the initial assessment of the crisis was that the underlying adjustment task was to address the spiraling external payments but did not require a fundamental revision of the region's developmental strategy (Jorge 1985:11). Therefore, it is not surprising that large segments of the population in Latin America were receptive to politicians who blamed the high adjustment costs on the foreign imposition of IMF conditionality, thereby creating a tense and ideologically charged political environment surrounding IMF programs. Meanwhile, at the outset of the post-communist transition, it was much less credible to blame the region's economic woes on the West. Even though neoliberal reforms were not necessarily embraced enthusiastically by post-communist elites and citizens, the IMF nevertheless had the opportunity to play a much more constructive role in the post-communist economic transition by providing the expertise and mobilizing the external funding necessary for a smoother international reintegration. Therefore, we would expect to see fewer political tensions in connection with IMF programs in the post-communist context.

---

[21] The statistical data in this section is based on Global Development Finance (2001 CD-ROM version).

While Eastern Europeans may have had fewer reasons than Latin Americans to distrust the Fund's economic policy advice, their economies and societies suffered much greater disruptions particularly in the early part of the transition. Even though the 1980s were rightfully called "the lost decade" in Latin America, the magnitude of the output loss was much larger in Eastern Europe, where it exceeded 50% of pre-1989 output in many transition countries. Since this economic shock was compounded by the underdeveloped framework of market institutions, ex-communist countries had a significant disadvantage compared to their Latin American counterparts, which could at least depend upon the basic legal and institutional framework necessary for the functioning of a market economy. Therefore, even to the extent that IMF programs emphasized similar policy measures, the economic response to these measures were bound to differ between the two regions, as well as between countries of the same region.[22]

Domestic Political and Social Context

While program initiation may frequently be an elite initiative, the implementation process inevitably involves a broader set of social and political actors. Therefore, we need to analyze the domestic social and political constellations of the two regions, and their likely implications for the politics of IMF programs. At first sight, the two regions are fairly similar in terms of regime type patterns, in that both span a wide spectrum ranging from liberal democracies to semi-authoritarian and authoritarian regimes. Moreover, a significant number of countries in both regions had to tackle the painful and unpopular economic reforms in the volatile political context of democratic transitions, thereby facing similar trade-offs between the political and economic objectives of the new democratic regimes.

Nevertheless, even a cursory overview of the two regions reveals a number of crucial differences in terms of their political and social fabric. At the most basic level, it may be worth remembering that of the twenty-eight former communist countries in Eurasia, only six—Albania, Bulgaria, Hungary, Mongolia, Poland, and Romania—existed in their current geographic form in 1989. Therefore, particularly in the early part of the decade, the overarching tasks of nation and state building complicated

---

[22] For example, tightening domestic credit is likely to have the expected anti-inflationary effect only if state firms face hard budget constraints and banks have the expertise necessary for selective credit allocation. If these conditions are not fulfilled, the measure is likely to "choke" both sick and healthy companies, thereby creating not only unnecessarily deep recessions but also limiting the effectiveness of anti-inflationary policies.

the pursuit of economic reforms in many transition economies (Roeder 1999). Even abstracting from the often disruptive and violent nature of this process in Yugoslavia and the former Soviet Union, the need to fundamentally rebuild state institutions proved to be a formidable challenge for many ex-communist countries, including some of the region's more successful reformers (O'Dwyer 2006, Grzymala-Busse 2007).

In addition to the existence of basic state institutions, the successful conduct of economic policy requires a set of reasonably stable and coherent political organizations representing the interests of relevant social actors. In this respect, too, most Latin American countries had a superior starting point compared to their Eastern European and former Soviet counterparts. While Latin America can hardly be considered the textbook case of consolidated and institutionalized democracy,[23] the spells of authoritarian rule prior to the third wave of democratization were shorter and less totalitarian in Latin America than in the communist regimes in the Soviet bloc (Bunce 1995). Therefore, many Latin American political parties could draw on their pre-authoritarian experience and social constituencies,[24] whereas in the former communist countries (with the partial exception of Poland and Hungary) the only coherent political organizations were the deeply compromised communist parties (Grzymala-Busse 2002). This organizational deficit, which is a lasting legacy of communist rule (Howard 2003), explains the high degree of electoral turnover and political instability in the post-communist countries. While such instability certainly undermines the coherence of economic policy conduct, the vaguely defined ideological platforms of post-communist parties, combined with the reduced maneuvering room between impoverished populations and strict Western conditionality (Innes 2002) have resulted in less radical policy reversals than the more polarized politics of Latin America in the 1980s.[25]

Since the politics of IMF programs are not limited to cabinet meetings and parliamentary debates, it is important to incorporate the role of interest groups in shaping the implementation of IMF-style policy measures. In this respect one must mention several significant interregional differences. In Latin America, labor unions, business associations, and in many cases the army, acted as well-organized interest groups capable

---

[23] See, for example, O'Donnell's (1991) discussion of delegative democracy in Latin America.

[24] Also, several countries (e.g., Colombia, Costa Rica, Venezuela), did not experience authoritarian regimes in more than two decades prior to the outbreak of the debt crisis.

[25] While Frye (2002) shows that polarization has affected economic policies and economic outcomes, policy disagreements focused primarily on the speed and mode of marketization, rather than on raising the specter of a wholesale rejection of the neoliberal economic approach.

of affecting economic policy making both directly, by threatening strikes, coups, or other forms of direct political action, and indirectly, by influencing the agenda of political parties through electoral pressures (Schneider 1997, Schamis 1999, Murillo and Schrank 2005). By comparison, in the ex-communist countries, such interest groups were severely underdeveloped: The business sector was fragmented between an initially well-connected but diminishingly influential group of state-owned enterprise managers; a small number of wealthy oligarchs, whose individual connections did not congeal into stable institutional forms; and a rising number of atomized small entrepreneurs. With a few notable exceptions (such as Solidarity in Poland) labor unions were generally fragmented and continued to suffer from their organizational subordination to the Communist Party apparatus in the decades preceding the collapse of communism. Therefore, transition governments faced less immediate political pressures from reform losers[26] than their Latin American counterparts (Greskovits 1998) but at the same time they suffered from a much higher degree of social "disconnect" (Howard 2003), which hindered the formation of durable reform coalitions and undermined the effectiveness of economic reforms.

Theoretical Contributions

Since IMF programs unfold at the intersection of domestic and international political economy, academic efforts to analyze them have spanned several different disciplines and subdisciplines. Therefore, this book contributes to several different bodies of literature that are concerned with various aspects of the Fund's involvement in the developing world: the international political economy literature on the role of the IMF in international financial markets, and more broadly about the nature of international organizations' behavior in world politics; the comparative political economy literature on the domestic politics of economic reforms in developing countries; and the largely econometric literature on the effects of IMF programs.

International Political Economy of IMF Programs

Scholarly debates about the role of international organizations in global governance have long been concerned with the political implications of IMF lending patterns. The appropriate balance between financial support

---

[26] In fact, as Hellman (1998) argues, post-communist reforms suffered more because of the early transition winners than because of opposition from losers.

and policy adjustment, which is at the very heart of conditional lending, has triggered impassioned and ideologically charged debates; thus, IMF conditionality has been criticized as being too soft,[27] too harsh,[28] or alternatively completely ineffective.[29] This book suggests that the nature and intensity of IMF policy demands vary significantly over time, since they are greatly affected by the broader international economic context. During global financial crises, such as the debt crisis in Latin America, the zero-sum nature of debtor and creditor interests creates significant tensions between the Fund's international policy agenda and the political priorities of developing countries. By contrast, during periods of global economic expansion, such as the financial boom of the 1990s, there is much greater overlap between the interests of debtors and creditors, and IMF programs are less likely to be viewed as painful external impositions by program countries.

Another important theoretical dilemma inherent in IMF lending practices is the trade-off between uniformity and flexibility in the design and enforcement of conditionality. In line with the Fund's mission of technocratically impartial crisis support, IMF conditionality has officially stressed uniformity of treatment at the expense of flexibility.[30] This approach has been criticized from two different perspectives: Some critics have charged that IMF conditionality uses a cookie-cutter approach based on outdated economic principles.[31] Others have pointed out that the IMF applies different strictness standards to different countries as a function of the narrow economic and geopolitical priorities of large Western donors.[32] This latter point taps into the broader debate between realists and institutionalists about the extent to which international organizations pursue public goods or simply serve the narrow interests of their largest shareholders.

Based on the Fund's track record in Latin America and Eastern Europe, this book suggests that the answers to these debates depend to a large extent on the regional and temporal context. From the perspective of flexibility, the comparative evidence suggests a mixed picture: On one hand during the post-communist transition, the Fund paid greater attention to political context and domestic program ownership than during the Latin American debt crisis of the 1980s, where domestic concerns were overshadowed by the emphasis on debt repayment. On the other

---

[27] See, e.g., De Grauwe and Frattiani 1984, Weintraub 1983, Feldstein 2002.
[28] Payer 1974, Koerner 1986, Pastor 1987.
[29] Sachs 1994, Remmer 1998.
[30] Buira 1983, David 1985, Pollack 1991.
[31] Edwards 1989, Stiglitz 2000.
[32] See, for example, Stiles 1991, Killick 1995, Thacker 1999, Stone 2002, Dreher and Jensen 2006.

hand, the much larger number of structural conditions in the IMF programs of the 1990s (especially among the transition economies) suggest a more intrusive approach to conditionality, which was combined with a lower tolerance for heterodox economic policies (as illustrated by the Slovak case in chapter 4).

From the perspective of impartial enforcement, this book confirms that when it comes to IMF programs not all countries are created equal. Unlike earlier works, however, the present analysis differentiates between narrow "realist" and systemic deviations from technocratic impartiality, and shows that the severity of both types of deviations depends on the international context. Thus, during the Latin American debt crisis, systemic concerns about international financial stability predominated and contributed to special treatment for large debtors but only when such countries were facing severe crises. In the context of the international financial boom of the 1990s, systemic concerns were less prominent but preferential treatment in Eastern Europe reflected Western concerns about the region's geopolitical reorientation.

Comparative Political Economy of Economic Reforms

Through its analysis of domestic political dynamics of IMF program initiation and implementation this book addresses a number of broader theoretical questions related to the politics of economic reforms. The book confirms earlier arguments that deeper initial economic crises facilitate the initiation and implementation of market-oriented reforms[33] but it also suggests that the salience of different crisis aspects depends on the broader regional and temporal context; whereas inflationary crises contributed to IMF program initiation and implementation during the Latin American debt crisis and the post-communist transition, the same was not true for Latin America in the 1990s. Similarly—as one would expect—debt service payments played a greater role during the debt crisis than during the 1990s, while reserve levels were more salient in cash-strapped Eastern Europe than in Latin America.

Moreover, both the statistical tests and several of the cases discussed in this book (e.g., Bolivia in 1982–85, Peru in 1987–89) suggest that countries often fail to implement reforms despite experiencing long periods of severe economic crisis. By themselves, economic crises are not sufficient to trigger reforms in the absence of governments willing and able to use these crises as catalysts for decisive economic policy changes. The theoretical emphasis on the temporal and regional variation in the interaction

---

[33] See, for example, Stallings and Kaufman 1989, Nelson, 1990, Rodrik 1994, Haggard and Kaufman 1995, Remmer 1998.

between economic crises and domestic politics engages the broader debate about the importance of partisan differences on economic policy making in the context of globalization. While this question has attracted a fair amount of scholarly attention, most studies have focused on advanced industrial countries,[34] and their findings about the temporal dynamics of partisan differences have been contradictory.[35] More recently, a few studies have shown that partisan politics has affected the trajectories of neoliberal reforms in both Latin America (Remmer 1998, Murillo 2002, Murillo and Schrank 2005) and Eastern Europe (Appel 2004, Frye 2002). However, none of these studies engage in explicit cross-regional and cross-temporal comparisons of partisan political dynamics, and they do not address the crucial theoretical question about the interaction between partisanship and crisis intensity in driving economic reforms. Moreover, partisanship has played a relatively marginal role in statistical analyses of IMF programs with the notable exception of Stone (2002).[36]

In contrast, I find that partisan politics do matter but that their salience and temporal evolution vary by region: in Latin America the ideologically polarized reactions to the IMF interventions of the 1980s were followed by a significant decline in partisanship during the 1990s and renewed polarization since 2001. Meanwhile, ideology played a relatively modest role in Eastern Europe in the 1990s, and there is no clear sign of a rebirth of a more assertive left along Latin American lines. More importantly, I show that partisan differences do not have a uniform effect on IMF programs but instead depend on context-specific interactions with the intensity of the economic crisis. Thus, if there exist alternative ideologically based crisis interpretations and solutions (such as during the Latin American debt crisis) then partisan differences are exacerbated by economic crises. Meanwhile, if the Fund's monopoly on crisis management solutions is largely unchallenged (as it was during the Washington Consensus of the 1990s) then partisan differences are more likely to be abandoned in the face of economic emergencies (as occurred in both Eastern Europe and Latin America after 1990). Moreover, partisan differences also depend on the nature of the crisis, with some crises (such as low

[34] See inter alia Alvarez et al. 1991, Simmons 1994, Garrett 1998, Bernhard and Leblang 1999, Pierson 2001, Huber and Stephens 2001, Kwon and Pontusson 2005, Milner and Judkins 2005.

[35] Thus, Pierson 2001 and Huber and Stephens 2001 find that the effect of government partisanship has declined since the 1970s with respect to social policy outcomes, whereas Kwon and Pontusson 2005 show that partisan effects increased from the 1970s to the mid-1990s but then declined dramatically afterward.

[36] Vreeland's 2003 argument about conditionality-seeking governments highlights the importance of domestic political interests, but he uses fiscal deficits rather than government orientation as an indicator of domestic political will, which suggests that his results should not necessarily be interpreted in partisan terms.

liquidity) less likely to trigger ideological disagreements than other more contentious economic problems (such as high debt service burdens).

This book also addresses the question of whether democratic politics and neoliberal economic reforms are compatible. Much of the work drawing on the experience of the 1980s noted that authoritarian regimes had generally been more successful in implementing reforms,[37] while others questioned the ability of democracies to overcome the popular resistance toward the high short-term costs of economic reforms (Przeworski 1991). On the other hand, several studies of the post-communist transition have emphasized the positive correlation and reinforcing nature of political and economic reforms in the former communist countries.[38] The present analysis confirms that democracy was hard to reconcile with IMF-style reforms during the Latin American debt crisis but was no longer an obstacle in Latin America in the 1990s and even improved the program implementation prospects in East European countries. These different outcomes can be traced to differences in how economic crises were perceived by elites and citizens: In Latin America the roots of the debt crisis were widely perceived as being of an external nature, which resulted in a lower willingness to bear the economic costs of adjustment policies and made it much more difficult for governments to implement reforms in a democratic context. Meanwhile, in Eastern Europe the domestic roots of the economic crises were much less disputed, and, therefore, voters were more likely to support or at least tolerate neoliberal reforms despite their considerable short-term costs.

Econometric Assessments of IMF Program Effects

The group of studies most directly concerned with IMF programs has grown out of policy concerns about the economic, political, and social repercussions of IMF programs, and has focused primarily on econometric assessments of program effects. Despite the steadily growing number of such studies, the evidence from the various large-N analyses has so far been largely inconclusive and contradictory. The only relatively robust finding of this literature is that IMF programs are generally effective in terms of one of their primary tasks: improving the overall balance of payments position of program countries.[39] However, with respect to other

---

[37] See Kaufman and Stallings 1989, Sheahan 1987. On the other hand Remmer's (1996) analysis of Latin America has argued that authoritarian regimes had no advantage over their democratic counterparts in terms of either political stability or economic performance.

[38] Fish 1998, Bunce 1999, but see Kurtz and Barnes 2002.

[39] See, for example, Gylafson 1987, Khan 1990, Pastor 1987, and Killick 1995. For some other studies, however, these improvements failed to reach statistical significance (Edwards 1989, Goldstein and Montiel 1986).

significant repercussions, such as program effects on inflation,[40] economic growth,[41] savings rates, and income inequality,[42] findings have generally been contradictory or inconclusive.

While this book is not directly concerned with econometric assessments of IMF program effects, its approach nevertheless has important implications for this literature. First, the book's emphasis on the politics of IMF programs should help correct for the fact that many of these studies "relegate the discipline of political science to the error term" (Stone 1999:4). While a number of recent works have started to address this issue,[43] a recent review of the literature emphasizes that our understanding of the politics of IMF lending is still tentative and rudimentary (Steinwand and Stone 2008).

Second, compliance with IMF conditionality has been consistently low,[44] and even though this has been widely acknowledged,[45] the large-N "IMF effects" literature has largely ignored the different degrees of compliance with IMF programs.[46] But ignoring the politics of program compliance is the logical equivalent of trying to assess the effectiveness of a drug without asking whether or not the patient took the prescribed drug, and what his/her reasons were for taking or not taking it. The present analysis of the economic and political drivers of compliance not only contributes to a better theoretical understanding of IMF programs but may also help with the design of politically more feasible IMF programs. Political feasibility and program completion are particularly important since, as Joel Hellman (1998) has argued in the case of transition economies, partial reforms may actually produce worse results than avoiding reforms altogether.

Finally, the explicit cross-temporal and cross-regional comparative analytical approach of this book questions the implicit assumption of

---

[40] Thus, Stone (2002) and Donovan (1982) found statistically significant improvements in the inflation records of program countries, but most other studies were inconclusive (Khan 1990, Killick 1995, Gylafson 1987, etc.), and Pastor 1987 actually detected a statistically significant increase of inflation for Latin American IMF programs.

[41] Przeworski and Vreeland 2000 and Vreeland 2003 find that IMF programs result in significant economic contractions but earlier studies in the yielded much weaker results (Pastor 1987, Goldstein and Montiel 1986, Killick 1995).

[42] See, for example, Pastor 1987, Heller et al. 1988, and Loxley 1984, though more recent work by Vreeland 2003 finds that IMF programs result in higher inequality.

[43] See, for example, Thacker 1999, Stone 2002, Vreeland 2003.

[44] Less than half of Latin American programs in the 1980s were fully implemented and the former communist countries in the 1990s fared no better.

[45] Reichmann 1978, Heller 1988, Edwards 1989, Killick 1995.

[46] More recently, a few studies have started to pay closer attention to compliance patterns (Edwards 2001, Ivanova et al. 2003) but the political dynamics of compliance are still significantly understudied.

much of the IMF-effects literature that IMF programs can be considered uniform treatments across space and time. Returning to the earlier medical analogy, this book shows that the nature of the treatment has changed over time (as IMF conditionality has evolved in response to the changing international economic and political environment), and that even similar treatments can provoke very different results depending on patient-level characteristics, such as domestic partisan politics or the quality of bureaucratic institutions.

Structure of the Book

The book is structured as follows: Chapter 2 develops a theoretical model of IMF program initiation and implementation, which builds on a formal model (presented in the appendix) and provides a systematic analysis of how the interaction between the IMF and program country governments is affected by key parameters of the domestic and international environment. The model yields a series of hypotheses that specify a number of important interaction effects between different domestic and international drivers of IMF programs and provide the basis for a more nuanced and targeted empirical analysis in the statistical and case study chapters.

The empirical part of the book is divided into three sections. The first section explores the international dimension IMF programs during the Latin American debt crisis and the post-communist transition. It analyzes how developing country governments respond to external crises and international market incentives, and how the Fund's response to such crises is influenced by systemic concerns for international financial stability and by the narrower economic and geopolitical concerns of large IMF donors. The comparison illustrates how the changes in the international context between the debt crisis of the 1980s and the post–Cold War "Washington Consensus" of the 1990s led to important variations in the economic and political dynamics of IMF programs in the two episodes. Chapter 3 presents the statistical results of the drivers of IMF program initiation, design and compliance in twenty-one Latin American and Caribbean countries 1982–89 and twenty-six ex-communist countries 1990–2001. The case study evidence from four Latin American (Argentina, Bolivia, Chile, and Peru) and two Eastern European countries (Moldova and Slovakia), which is presented in chapter 4, illustrates the statistical findings from the preceding chapter, and provides a more detailed account of the opportunities and constraints faced by the countries of the two regions as a function of their economic and geopolitical status.

The second section focuses on the domestic politics of IMF program initiation and implementation during the two main crisis episodes. Chapter 5 analyzes the statistical patterns of the complex interaction between economic crises, partisan concerns, and institutional constraints that drive the dynamics of IMF programs. Chapter 6 revisits the six cases discussed in chapter 4 and adds a paired comparison between Romania and Bulgaria.

The third section (chapter 7) broadens the scope of the comparative analysis developed in chapters 3–6 by focusing on the political dynamics of IMF programs in Latin America 1990–2001. Since this third cluster of programs represents a combination between the international political and economic environment experienced by the ex-communist countries in the 1990s and many of the domestic economic and political characteristics of Latin America in the preceding decade, this comparison provides better analytical leverage for understanding the roots of the important differences in the political economy of IMF programs discussed in the preceding chapters.

The final chapter synthesizes the theoretical contributions and empirical results of the book, not only for understanding the politics of IMF programs but for more broadly understanding the political economy of neoliberal economic reforms in the developing world. The conclusion also discusses the policy implications of these findings for the design of more politically feasible IMF programs, in the context in which, despite a number of recent calls for its demise, the IMF is likely to remain a key intermediary between developed and developing countries in the context of increasingly complex international financial markets.

$-2-$

A Theoretical Approach to IMF Program Initiation
and Implementation

AT FIRST GLANCE, the dynamics of IMF program initiation and implementation are deceptively simple. To set the process in motion, a government facing balance-of-payments difficulties has to approach the IMF with a request for a loan. To get access to funding, the borrowing country government, in close consultation with IMF staff, drafts a letter of intent, which specifies a set of policies designed to redress the country's financial imbalance. The letter includes a series of specific quantifiable goals, a timetable for achieving these goals, and the amount of IMF financial assistance that is tied to the achievement of program targets. Once the program is approved by the IMF Board of Directors, it enters into force and moves to the second stage: implementation. The national authorities of the program country (with varying degrees of technical assistance from IMF staff) design and implement policy measures intended to fulfill the program targets upon which the disbursement of IMF credit tranches is conditional. The IMF staff periodically reviews the progress and the compliance with program targets and based on its assessment decide to either approve the disbursement of a credit tranche, or to withhold the funds until targets have been met or renegotiated. Such program suspensions may be temporary if the country manages to catch up with program targets, or alternatively, the program can go off track and be suspended entirely.

The technocratic nature of most practical steps during IMF program initiation, implementation, and evaluation seems to imply a fairly depoliticized process in line with the Fund's neutral mandate of helping countries "correct maladjustments in their balance of payments without resorting to measures destructive of national or international prosperity" (IMF 1947, v). While many of the crucial decisions regarding IMF programs are indeed of a technical nature and are often made during closed-door meetings between technocrats, political consideration are nevertheless present—and often highly significant—at various critical junctures of IMF program initiation, design, and implementation. To understand why IMF programs often deviate from the technocratic "ideal type," it is important to recall that these programs do not occur in a vacuum but are deeply embedded in a complex web of economic and political interests at both the domestic and international levels. Thus, the IMF attempts to balance the economic priorities arising from its role as an international lender of last resort and overseer of international financial stability with the more specific economic and geopolitical interests of its largest shareholder countries and its own bureaucratic interests. Meanwhile, the governments of potential program countries are influenced in their decisions not only by their domestic and international economic priorities but also by political and bureaucratic constraints on the range of feasible economic policy options. The discussion below provides a more detailed justification for the individual components of this theoretical framework and shows how the framework can be applied to explain the changing dynamics of IMF program initiation and implementation.

The first the part of the chapter situates IMF programs at the intersection of international and domestic political economy and identifies how this broader environment informs and constrains the preferences and choices of the two main protagonists—the Fund and the program country government. The second part of the chapter builds on this framework of preferences to show how the interaction between the Fund and the program country government shapes the political dynamics of IMF program initiation and implementation. While the key elements of this theoretical approach are formalized in the appendix, the discussion in this chapter presents the intuition behind the formal model in nonmathematical terms, and derives a number of theoretical predictions about the economic and political drivers of IMF programs, which will be tested in the subsequent empirical chapters.

The Theoretical Framework: Actors, Preferences and Context

According to their mission, IMF programs provide the institutional setting through which countries experiencing economic crises can obtain the financial support and policy advice necessary to help them address their economic troubles. At the most basic level, IMF programs involve two main actors—the government and the IMF—who bargain over funding and policy reforms. However, since both the main actors are ultimately involved in two-level games,[1] their preferences and strategies are affected by the priorities of additional actors, such as the domestic opposition (for the program country government), and large Western shareholder

[1] For the theoretical basis of two-level games, see Putnam 1988.

governments and the international financial community (for the IMF). As a result, the simple initial IMF program equation—addressing economic crises through a combination of policy adjustment and financial assistance—is ultimately shaped by a complex set of political factors at both the domestic and the international level.

While acknowledging that no single theoretical framework can do full justice to the wide range of factors influencing the politics of IMF programs, I will nonetheless try to capture several crucial dimensions of the economic and political interests of the IMF and its interlocutor governments during program initiation and implementation. Using as a starting point the centrality of economic crisis as a driver of IMF programs, the theoretical discussion in this chapter identifies several domestic and international factors that mediate the link between economic crisis and IMF-style reforms. At the international level, I argue that crises in developing countries do not simply trigger technocratically uniform funding and conditionality packages from the IMF. Instead, the Fund balances the policy imperatives of this "equal treatment" principle with other (potentially conflicting) priorities such as its systemic responsibility for international financial stability or the narrower economic and geopolitical interests of its main shareholders. Nor are there reasons to expect that domestic economic policies simply mirror the "objective demands" of economic crises. Thus, ideological convictions may significantly affect the government's interpretation of the roots and the solutions to a given crisis. Moreover, even to the extent that the government agrees with the Fund's basic policy prescriptions, its ability to react in a manner consistent with IMF program requirements may be severely affected by domestic political opposition and by its limited bureaucratic capacity to implement coherent economic policies. The following section lays out in greater detail the main economic and political priorities of the Fund and developing country governments, and thereby sets the stage for a more systematic understanding of how "objective" economic crisis imperatives are mediated by political interests and institutional constraints. The basic economic and political dynamics of IMF programs are outlined in figure 2.1.

The International Dimension of IMF Programs

In order to understand the different motivations underlying IMF lending to developing countries, it is important to briefly consider the Fund's overall position in the international financial architecture. Since the demise of the Bretton Woods fixed exchange rate system in the early 1970s, the Fund's most prominent role has been as an intermediary between the governments of developing countries, which accounted for the vast majority of IMF programs in the last three decades, and a variety of economic and

Figure 2.1: Analytical overview

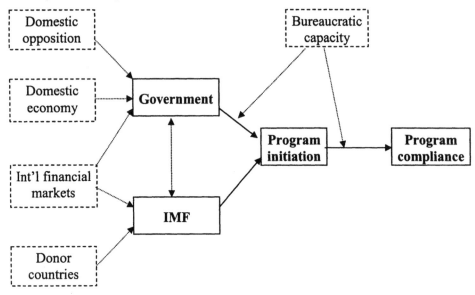

political interests from advanced industrial democracies, which contribute most of the IMF's financial resources through their IMF quotas. Given the different interests of these multiple constituencies, the Fund's vaguely worded original mission—to help countries enact adjustment policies "without resorting to measures destructive of national or international prosperity" by "making the general resources of the Fund temporarily available to them under adequate safeguards"—is inevitably open to contradictory interpretations. Not surprisingly, depending on one's ideology or economic and political interests, it is possible to come up with fundamentally different interpretations about the nature of "adequate safeguards," or about the appropriate balance between the potentially conflicting goals of national and international prosperity.

Given the inherent ambiguity of the Fund's mission and the genuine tension between its different objectives, the actual patterns of IMF lending provide a useful testing ground for competing theoretical approaches to international relations. From a realist perspective, international organizations simply reflect the interests of powerful nation-states,[2] and therefore IMF lending should be shaped by the power differential inherent in the Fund's governance structure, which assigns vote shares in rough proportion to the size of financial contributions and is therefore heavily skewed

[2] Mearsheimer 1994, Strange 1996.

in favor of advanced industrial nations. However, the realist approach can be critiqued from several perspectives; thus, from an institutionalist perspective,[3] large powers may be willing to forfeit part of their narrow self-interest in order to allow international organizations like the IMF, to provide global public goods such as international financial stability. From a liberal point of view,[4] one could argue that state interests in the context of IMF programs should not be viewed as unitary but rather as reflecting the interests of shifting coalitions of domestic actors. Finally, from the point of view of principal-agent models (Vaubel 1991, Lake 1996), IMF lending decisions could simply reflect the narrower logic of bureaucratic self-interest and institutional survival.

The theoretical framework developed in this chapter starts from the assumption that the motivations underlying IMF lending behavior represent a combination of the theoretical ideal types described above, and that the relative weight of different motivations is likely to depend greatly on the particular context of a given intervention. Therefore, the crucial question is not so much which theory is right and which one is wrong, but under what circumstances we are more likely to witness particular types of motives in the Fund's conditionality approach. While this question ultimately has to be answered empirically in subsequent chapters, the purpose of this chapter is to set up a theoretical model that captures the key elements of the different theoretical possibilities and provides a set of empirically testable predictions about the observable implications of the Fund's different motivations.

THE TECHNOCRATIC IDEAL

The logical starting point for analyzing the drivers of IMF lending is the Fund's technocratic mission to provide technical and financial assistance to countries experiencing economic crises (especially balance-of-payments difficulties). From the perspective of the Fund's official principle of "political neutrality" (Guitian 1981, Polak 1991), we should expect to see a straight-forward link between economic crises and IMF lending. In line with the Fund's role as international lender of last resort, IMF programs should be more frequent in situations characterized by severe economic crises, when private lenders are unlikely to risk extending additional loans. From the perspective of the formal model developed in the appendix, the IMF's responsiveness to economic crises simply means that the Fund's utility from extending a loan rises as a function of the country's financial need—in other words, the Fund should be more eager to lend to needier countries.

---

[3] Baldwin 1993, Keohane and Martin 1995.
[4] See, for example, Moravcsik 1997.

However, even from a purely technocratic standpoint, the Fund's responsibility to assist troubled economies has to be balanced against several competing considerations. First, IMF lending has to counter the moral hazard problem inherent in the existence of a lender of last resort, which may give countries incentives to pursue irresponsible economic policies because they count on being bailed out once they get in trouble. Second, given the Fund's limited resources and the explicit stipulation that its financial support is supposed to be temporary, the IMF has to "think like a bank" and ensure that its loans will be repaid by the program countries. Finally, since IMF lending is often insufficient to cover the financing need of developing countries, its responsibilities include the mobilization of additional funding from third-party lenders (Stone and Steinwand, 2008). For such catalytic effects to occur, third-party lenders (especially those from the private sector) have to regard the Fund's seal of approval as a credible signal of a country's policy trajectory. For all these reasons the Fund has to make its financial support conditional on "adequate safeguards," that is, the adoption of economic policies that ensure that the Fund's resources are appropriately used and reduce the likelihood of such crises recurring in the future. In practice, these safeguards take the form of program conditions that specify policy targets that the country has to achieve in order to be able to access IMF funding. From a strictly technocratic perspective, these targets should be roughly similar (though not necessarily identical) across different programs, and the IMF should punish countries whose policies deviate significantly from program targets. To capture this logic in the context of the formal model, the Fund's utility is assumed to decline as a function of the shortfall between the policy target and the actual policy outcome, and once the shortfall reaches a certain threshold, the Fund stops the disbursements of funds to the country. To the extent that the Fund is willing to forgive deviations from program targets (e.g., by approving condition waivers), a narrow technocratic perspective would require that such exceptions should only apply during extreme economic crises, when the costs associated with softer conditionality may be outweighed by the Fund's responsibilities as a lender of last resort.

Before discussing the various deviations from this technocratic model, it is important to point out that even this narrow conception of IMF conditionality is not completely immune to criticism and divergent interpretations. At the most fundamental level, radical critics of the Fund (e.g., Payer 1974, Swedberg 1986) have pointed out that even in its purely technocratic version, IMF conditionality is politically biased in favor of a particular type of society—an internationally open market economy with weak labor movements. From this perspective, the Fund's policy advice, which is firmly rooted in neoclassical economics, is not simply technical in nature but also deeply ideological (even though its proponents may not recognize it as such). But the technocratic credibility of the Fund's economic policy prescriptions has also been questioned from a number of different perspectives, which are less concerned with the inherent ideological nature of IMF lending. Thus, a number of observers have criticized the Fund's insistence on using its outdated financial programming model in an international context that no longer fit the original assumptions of the model (Buira 1983, Edwards 1989, Pereira da Silva 2001), while Stiglitz (2000) went even further by questioning the competence of IMF staff, which he famously characterized as "third-rank students from first-rate universities." A related line of criticism is directed at the Fund's tendency to ignore country-specific circumstances and apply an inflexible "cookie-cutter" approach, which ultimately undermines the effectiveness of its advice (Buira 1983, Stiglitz 2000). Finally, the relative balance between conditionality and funding in IMF programs has been attacked from both sides, for example Sachs (1994) argued that the Fund's approach to Russia should have included more funding and less stringent conditions, while Feldstein (2004) raised the opposite critique about the IMF policies toward Argentina before 2001.

Obviously such debates have important implications for the effectiveness of IMF programs, because if the Fund's policy advice is widely considered to be either ideologically biased or technically flawed, it is likely to affect the attitudes of the Fund's interlocutors in developing countries. However, from the perspective of the theoretical debates discussed earlier, what matters more is whether or not the Fund's particular vision of "economically correct" policy adjustment is actually applied evenly to different types of potential client countries. In other words, the immediate question is not whether the Fund's treatment is appropriate and helpful, but whether or not different countries receive the same type of treatment.

WITH A LITTLE HELP FROM MY FRIENDS: THE PREFERENTIAL TREATMENT OF WESTERN ALLIES

Whatever disagreements analysts of IMF programs may have on specific aspects of conditionality, few would disagree that the use of IMF funding to reward the political allies of large Western shareholders undermines the credibility and effectiveness of the Fund.[5] Yet, in recent years there has emerged substantial empirical evidence linking a country's geopolitical proximity to the Fund's Western shareholders with a variety of types of preferential treatment by the IMF, including more frequent access to IMF lending (Thacker 1999), more generous loans (Barro and Lee 2002, Oatley and Yackee 2004), fewer program conditions (Dreher and Jensen

---

[5] For eloquent arguments in this sense, see especially Thacker 1999 and Stone 2002.

2006), and less severe punishment for noncompliance (Stone 2004). On the other hand, Bird and Rowlands (2001) have argued that the overall explanatory power of such political exceptionalism is relatively modest and highly sensitive to the timing of the program.

The practical implications of political interference with IMF lending practices are likely to be deleterious for a number of reasons; thus, Stone (2002, 2004) shows that the governments of privileged countries correctly anticipate weaker punishments for noncompliance and therefore deviate more from the tenets of conditionality. Therefore, the practice not only leads to inconsistent policies in privileged countries but to the extent that it is sufficiently widespread, it precludes the use of scarce IMF funds in economically more justifiable programs. To make matters worse, politically motivated preferential treatment undermines the Fund's credibility in international financial markets (thereby weakening catalytic effects) and it makes the IMF vulnerable to critiques from developing countries, where opponents of IMF-style policies can point to the double standard inherent in the Fund's unequal enforcement of policy conditionality.

In light of all these disadvantages, why would the Fund's largest shareholders condone (and even promote) a practice that undermines the IMF's ability to provide the very public good for which it was created? The answer to this puzzle, which Stone (2004) characterizes as a strategic game with commitment problems, is that in line with realist views of international organizations, the Fund's main principals cannot resist the temptation to use IMF lending to pursue their narrow national interests. Despite its systemic costs, the practice has the advantage of leveraging the resources of any given country[6] and it allows Western governments to reward their allies without having to undergo the domestic public scrutiny associated with direct foreign aid. In turn, the IMF staff, whose salaries and job security depend on keeping the key shareholders satisfied, are unlikely to resist such pressures for preferential treatment, even if the resulting programs cannot be fully justified from a technocratic perspective.

The present analysis is less concerned with the question why the Fund's largest shareholders are unable to solve their commitment problem in order to improve the effectiveness of IMF lending. As a result, the formal model does not explicitly model the strategic calculations underlying the decision of Western shareholders to pressure the IMF for preferential treatment of their allies. However, the utility function of the IMF in the formal model allows for the possibility that in addition to its official mandate as a crisis lender, the Fund benefits from lending to certain privileged

---

[6] Even the United States, which as the largest IMF shareholder contributes almost 18% of its resources, essentially gets a fivefold multiplier on its own investment if it succeeds to channel money to its allies via IMF lending.

countries. While this assumption reflects the logic of realist power politics, this book's research design and empirical approach adds an important neoliberal component in that it tests the influence of multiple Western interests (including not only geopolitical orientation but also economic ties) and consciously allows for the possibility that the salience of certain types of interests will depend on the specific temporal and geographic context of a given IMF intervention.

TOO BIG TO FAIL: SYSTEMIC IMPORTANCE AND ITS IMPLICATIONS

While the discussion above, along with much of the academic literature on preferential lending, has focused on "realist" national interest-based deviations from technocratic impartiality, it is important to consider an additional source of preferential treatment, which is more difficult to classify as either political or technocratic. This source, which is more compatible with institutionalist theoretical expectations, is rooted in the systemic responsibilities of the IMF, which on occasion may justify the Fund bending the rules in favor of economically important countries. To understand why this may be the case, we need to go back to the *Articles of Agreement*, according to which the IMF is charged with promoting international monetary cooperation and facilitating the expansion and balanced growth of international trade. Since both of these objectives can be jeopardized by economic crises in developing countries with large overall debt and trade flows, the Fund's concerns in such situations are no longer simply directed at helping an individual member country but at preventing broader regional or global contagion effects. In this case, preferential treatment no longer simply reflects narrow political interests trumping technocratic rationality but rather is the result of a trade-off between two international public goods: the unbiased provision of conditional crisis lending and policy signals (Masson and Mussa 1997) and the promotion of international financial and economic stability.

The different logic of these two types of preferential treatment is captured in the formal model, which includes separate parameters for narrow "realist" and broader systemic importance in the Fund's utility function. Since systemic threats are predicated on the existence of severe crises in sufficiently large economies, the formal model captures this intuition by including a multiplicative interaction term between systemic importance and crisis severity in the utility function of the IMF. In other words, the Fund's utility from lending to developing countries should be higher if the country in question is both economically troubled and sufficiently large for its troubles to reverberate beyond its borders. By contrast, as discussed earlier, Western pressures for special treatment of their economic/political allies are likely to reflect primarily their narrow realist priorities, which are not necessarily related to the extent of the crisis experienced by the country in question.

However, politics is not—and cannot be—entirely absent from systemically motivated preferential treatment. Thus, the process of deciding what amounts to a systemic threat is at least partially driven by politics; for example, the Fund's sweeping interventions during the debt crisis of the 1980s were justified by concerns about the international fallout of a default by Latin American debtors, but critics have charged that international financial stability was erroneously equated with the prosperity of a few large Western commercial banks (Jorge 1985). Along similar lines, Gould (2003) has shown that the Fund's policy priorities are often excessively influenced by the interests of private international creditors. Even to the extent that one could objectively assess the systemic threats posed by a given country's default, balancing these costs against the moral hazard risks posed by soft lending practices is ultimately a political question whose resolution depends on the relative political influence of competing economic and partisan interests in the Fund's large shareholder countries.

THE FUND AS A SELF-INTERESTED AGENT

While so far I have focused on the tension between different types of private and public goods pursued by large IMF shareholders, it is important to keep in mind that the relationship between IMF staff and its member countries is at least to some extent subject to the problems identified by principal-agent theories. Since principals are inherently limited in monitoring agent behavior, and since such problems are exacerbated in the case of international organizations by the existence of multiple principals and multiple layers of delegation (Nielson and Tierney 2003), it is reasonable to assume that IMF lending does not simply reflect the interests of its principals but also the narrower self-interest of its staff. In fact, several prior studies (e.g., Vaubel 1991) have identified systematic evidence that IMF lending is driven at least in part by bureaucratic concerns about institutional survival and resource maximization.

Since the present study is not directly concerned with the strategic dimension of the principal-agent relationship between member countries and IMF staff, I do not explicitly model this relationship within a principal agent framework. Instead, the Fund's utility function includes a budget constraint, which captures the notion that the relative utility of the Fund from a given loan should be higher when a larger part of its resources are not being used in other countries. Moreover, it is possible that the Fund's lending utility is affected by its own funding cycles, given that prior IMF staff have incentives to use a larger proportion of resources prior to the periodically scheduled board meetings, which decide whether and by how much member countries will increase their financial contributions to the Fund via higher country quotas. In line with Vreeland and Przeworski's (2000) statistical findings, the formal model assumes that these constraints only apply during the initiation phase but not in the implementation phase.[7]

INTERNATIONAL FINANCIAL MARKETS AND ADDITIONAL FUNDING SOURCES

Since the Fund's direct lending often covers only a fraction of the financing need in program countries, the success of IMF programs depends on their ability to mobilize additional funding from third parties. The empirical evidence on the effectiveness of IMF programs in mobilizing catalytic funding is mixed: While Marchesi (2003) found that IMF programs facilitated debt reschedulings, Rodrik (1997) identified a positive effect on bank lending, and Bird and Rowlands (1997, 2001) found some evidence of higher official lending associated with IMF programs, other studies found weak or even negative effects (Ozler 1993, Edwards 2000).[8]

Even the brief review above suggests that at least in theory IMF programs may trigger additional funding from a variety of sources; in the past, multilateral assistance (especially from the World Bank) as well as certain bilateral loans have been conditioned on prior IMF approval of a country's policy approach. Moreover, IMF signals can affect a variety of private lending decisions, ranging from commercial bank loans and rescheduling to FDI and portfolio investment. However, the present study is not directly concerned with the question of whether and under what conditions IMF programs trigger additional funding from different sources but only with the possibility that governments may expect these programs to have positive or negative financial implications beyond direct IMF funding. As a result, the theoretical model developed here does not endogenize catalytic effects[9] but treats them as exogenous parameters, which could (but do not necessarily have to) influence the government's policy calculus.

---

[7] This assumption also makes sense from the perspective of IMF bookkeeping, since funds committed to ongoing programs are excluded from the "uncommitted usable resources" category on the IMF balance sheet.

[8] Some of these inconsistencies may be due to the fact that catalytic effects vary significantly by different types of countries: Thus, Bird and Orme 2002 found generally positive effects in middle-income countries but negative effects in the poorest countries, while Mody and Saravia 2003 found that IMF programs did trigger greater private capital flows in countries with intermediate economic conditions but the effects were weaker (and even reversed) in countries with very poor or very good economic situations.

[9] For an interesting theoretical model dealing with this question, see Corsetti et al. 2003. A similar logic also underlies Stone's (2002) discussion of lending credibility, even though he is not directly concerned with catalytic finance.

IMF Programs and Domestic Politics

Even though external pressures from the IMF and international financial markets constrain the policy options of governments in developing countries, IMF programs cannot be properly understood simply as external impositions on powerless and compliant domestic actors. Governments can and do avoid the dictates of IMF conditionality even in situations where purely financial considerations would have predicted a much more accommodating stance by the government in question. Meanwhile, other governments enter IMF programs for domestic political reasons even if their economic circumstances do not require IMF assistance (Vreeland 2003). To understand when and why this happens, we need to analyze how the domestic economic and political environment affects the relative costs and benefits of IMF program participation for the governments in question.

BEGGARS CAN'T BE CHOOSERS: ECONOMIC CRISES AS PROGRAM DRIVERS

From a purely technocratic perspective, the logical starting point for understanding the domestic drivers of IMF program initiation and implementation closely mirrors the earlier analysis of international dynamics. Since IMF programs are intended to assist governments in redressing economic imbalances and to provide financial assistance to countries with limited outside funding options, we should expect economic crises to figure prominently among the reasons why governments would subject themselves to the rigors of IMF conditionality. Indeed, existing studies have repeatedly pointed to the strong empirical link between a variety of economic crisis indicators and IMF programs.[10] Even Vreeland (2003), who argues that governments sometimes desire IMF conditionality for domestic political reasons, found that classical indicators of external financial need (such as low reserves) were important predictors of IMF program initiation.

The most obvious causal mechanism linking economic crisis to IMF program initiation is that governments facing severe external payment difficulties, low reserves, and limited access to international financial markets have few alternatives other than to seek funding from the IMF and other international financial institutions. While such external financial crises are at the core of the Fund's mission as an international lender of last resort, governments have also entered IMF agreements to deal with pressing domestic economic problems, especially inflationary crises (Bird 1995, Santaella 1996, Stone 2002). One important reason for this link is

---

[10] See, for example, Bird and Orme 1986, Cornelius 1987, Bird 1995, Knight and Santaella 1997.

that the external funding obtained in conjunction with IMF agreements can help governments finance fiscal deficits in noninflationary ways[11] and thereby fight inflation even without fully addressing the underlying fiscal imbalances. From this perspective, both external and domestic economic crises should contribute in similar ways to IMF program initiation and implementation, as governments facing more critical situations stand to benefit more from IMF financial assistance. This expectation is reflected in the government's utility function in the formal model, which is assumed to be a monotonously increasing function of the country's economic crisis intensity. While the theoretical model does not differentiate between domestic and external drivers of financial need, the empirical tests in chapters 3, 5, and 7 use a variety of crisis indicators to capture the relative importance of different types of crises as catalysts of IMF programs.

The discussion so far has largely assumed that governments resort to IMF programs only to the extent that their need for IMF funding is sufficiently intense to overcome the potential costs associated with IMF conditionality. However, it is worth briefly mentioning another possible mechanism through which economic crises may trigger IMF programs; thus, several analysts (Drazen and Grilli 1993, Williamson 1994) have argued that deep crises can help create a societal consensus in favor of reforms, while at the same time weakening the economic and political benefits of previous rent-seeking activities. Vreeland (2003) goes one step further and uses fiscal deficits as a proxy of the government's "desire" for IMF conditionality rather than as an indicator of economic crisis. From this perspective, IMF adjustment policies are no longer an external imposition but rather reflect a shift in the inherent reform preferences of domestic political actors. While I agree that the policy preferences of domestic politicians are crucial for understanding IMF programs, my theoretical approach differs from Vreeland's in the sense that I do not assume—as Vreeland implicitly does—that domestic economic crises are uniformly interpreted by domestic actors as requiring IMF-style adjustment policies. Instead, as I will elaborate below, these crisis reactions are mediated by the partisan policy preferences of the government and the opposition.

PARTISAN CONSIDERATIONS

The classical trade-off inherent in IMF programs is that governments sacrifice part of their policy-making freedom in return for the financial benefits associated with successful IMF programs. However, the actual costs of this sacrifice to different governments largely depend on how their a priori policy preferences compare to the orthodox economic policy re-

---

[11] For an argument along these lines, see Sachs's (1994) criticism of the Fund's insufficiently generous financial support for Russia's stabilization efforts in the early 1990s.

quirements of IMF conditionality. For example, for ideologically committed neoliberals, such as the Pinochet government in Chile, the adoption of IMF-style economic policies requires only minimal adjustments from an ideological point of view, since the government would have preferred similar policies even in the absence of an IMF program. On the other hand, a similar IMF program may provoke significant (and possibly insurmountable) "cognitive dissonance" for leftist governments whose unconstrained policy ideal point is very far from the Fund's.[12]

Partisan differences in policy preferences can be driven by two related but nevertheless distinct factors: partisan ties and ideological convictions. Partisan ties refer to the propensity of politicians to pursue policies that will favor the economic interests of their core social constituencies. For the purpose of this analysis, ideology is defined as a system of ideas about how the world works, and politicians subscribing to certain ideologies should be expected to interpret economic crises through the analytical lens of their respective ideologies and to propose policy solutions that fit this model. For the most part, these two facets of partisan orientation tend to overlap and produce similar types of expected policy prefersences; thus, parties with leftist political ideologies tend to draw most of their political support from low-income sectors and often have close institutional ties to organized labor. This overlap implies that such parties should be less eager to adopt IMF programs both because the Fund's neoliberal economic theories may conflict with their own ideological views and because IMF-style adjustment policies tend to be more costly for organized labor and the poor (Vreeland 2003). Nonetheless, the examples of the Argentine Peronists and the Polish Solidarity in the early 1990s suggest that strong institutional ties to organized labor can coexist with economic neoliberalism, while most communist successor parties in Eastern Europe had weak ties to organized labor. Therefore, the empirical tests will differentiate between these two sources of partisan differentiation.

In an extension of the formal model, I also explore the possibility that the salience of partisan preferences is not constant but is affected by the type and severity of the economic crisis. From this perspective, the government's response to economic crises no longer hinges only on the question of whether the benefits of program participation outweigh the government's partisan disutility due to conditionality. Instead, economic crisis intensity now also affects how much the government cares about having to implement policies that deviate from its partisan ideal point. Depending on the nature of ideological convictions and the partisan ties of

---

[12] In the context of the formal model, this intuition is captured by including a monotonic decline in government utility as a function of the difference between its own ideal point and the policies required as part of the IMF agreement.

governing politicians, the policy impact of partisan differences could be either diminished or reinforced by severe economic crises. While the formal model does not endogenize the nature of these partisan crisis dynamics, its theoretical contribution lies in the fact that it provides a basis for exploring different patterns of interaction between crisis intensity and partisan political preferences, which have been ignored by earlier work.

DOMESTIC POLITICAL AND INSTITUTIONAL CONSTRAINTS

Since IMF programs usually require adjustment measures with profound socioeconomic and distributional consequences, their initiation and implementation often become the focal point of domestic political debates between the government and a range of potential reform opponents in the national parliament and in the broader society. The political stakes of these debates are extremely high, and there are numerous instances of governments losing power as a result of the economic and political fallout surrounding either the implementation or the rejection of IMF conditionality.[13] As a result, the theoretical model has to allow for the possibility that the government's policy choices in the context of IMF programs would also depend on the political orientation of the opposition. Rather than explicitly modeling the strategic nature of this political interaction, the formal model captures this intuition by including the opposition's preferred policy ideal point in the government's utility function.

However, even a cursory look at the domestic politics of economic reforms suggests that the relative influence of the preferences of the opposition is mediated by domestic political factors. Given that regime type has figured prominently in political explanations of IMF-style economic reforms (e.g., Kaufman 1989, Remmer 1994, 1998) one obvious factor to consider is the openness of the political process. Rather than assuming that democracy either facilitates or undermines IMF programs, the model simply assumes that greater openness accentuates the importance of the political preferences of the opposition in the government's overall policy calculus. Moreover, since the formal model does not explicitly model elections or other specific institutional features of democratic politics, the parameter capturing the government's responsiveness to the preferences of other political actors can also be interpreted along slightly different lines. For example, we should expect governments to be more responsive to the median voter in periods immediately preceding elections, while in the postelectoral honeymoon period governments may be more insulated from such popular demands. Alternatively, the intuition can also be ap-

---

[13] Thus, whereas Peruvian voters punished Belaunde's AP for its close cooperation with the IMF, five years later they ousted Alan Garcia's APRA in 1990 as a response to a crisis provoked to a large extent by his complete rejection of IMF conditionality.

plied to parliamentary politics, where we would expect governments with tenuous parliamentary support to be more accommodating toward opposition preferences than governments with comfortable majorities and weak opponents.

Finally, the government's ability to initiate and implement IMF programs hinges not only on financial incentives and political muscle but also on the sheer capacity of the state apparatus to design and execute a coherent policy program. The successful and timely initiation of an IMF program requires a reasonably competent group of government experts and sufficiently reliable economic data to establish and negotiate feasible performance criteria in cooperation with the IMF staff. Since IMF conditionality usually only sets broad policy parameters for the country, the government has to develop a more detailed plan for fulfilling IMF policy targets, such as specific areas of expenditure cuts or strategies for raising new tax revenues. Once such a detailed blueprint is in place and has been promulgated into law (via parliamentary vote or executive ordinance/ decree), the government still faces the significant hurdle of ensuring the timely implementation of the program targets by the different levels of the bureaucratic apparatus. As a consequence, in countries with weak and ineffective bureaucratic institutions, even an ideologically committed and financially desperate government may not be able to ensure the adequate design and execution of a successful IMF program.

From Preferences to Outcomes:
Negotiating Program Initiation and Implementation

Whereas the preceding section has analyzed the key components affecting the policy preferences of the IMF and the governments of program countries, we still have to address the question of how these various interests interact in the context of an IMF program to produce the wide range of initiation and implementation patterns observed in reality. To answer this question I developed a formal model of the interaction between the Fund and the government in the context of IMF programs. The model is presented in greater detail in the appendix. For the purpose of the present discussion I will merely outline the key elements of this model, and then turn to a discussion of the theoretical predictions derived by solving this model.

The model revolves around two main actors—the government and the IMF—who bargain over funding and policy reforms. The primary goal of the two actors is to maximize their overall utility, whose main components were discussed in the previous section. There are two main stages to the model: program initiation and program implementation. During program initiation, the government decides whether or not to approach the IMF to negotiate a program. If the government does not approach the IMF or if the two sides cannot agree on mutually acceptable program parameters, then nothing happens and both the IMF and the government get their status quo payoffs.[14] If the two sides reach an agreement, they establish a set of program parameters consisting of a certain funding commitment M_p conditional on the fulfillment of a set of policy targets q_p. Once the program parameters are set, the game moves to the second stage—implementation.

During program implementation, the government decides on a policy target q_0, and a policy outcome is realized, which reflects the original target as well as any implementation shortfalls (see below). The IMF observes the outcome q^* of the government's policy choice (but not the government's intended target, which is private information), and then decides whether or not to disburse the promised amount of funding to the government. Third-party lenders (private or official) then react to the Fund's signal by either extending additional credit to the government (in the case of IMF approval) or by withdrawing existing credits (in the case of IMF disapproval of a country's policies). In practice, this game is repeated several times during the duration of a program, given that IMF disbursements are generally made on a quarterly basis. I do not explicitly model the repeated-game aspect of IMF programs; however, I will discuss how target fulfillment at a given stage affects the model parameters for the next period, and implicitly the chances of future compliance.

To understand the economic and political drivers of IMF programs, let us briefly trace the key decisions of the two main actors in the context of this game-theoretic framework. Following the logic of backward induction, we have to start with the Fund's decision whether or not to disburse the promised funding based on the observed policy outcome of the government's implementation efforts. Since the IMF does not disburse partial credit tranches to reward partial implementation, this decision is dichotomous: The Fund will disburse the committed funds as long as the policy deviations from program targets are sufficiently small to be outweighed by the benefits to the Fund from lending to a given country. These benefits, which include the contribution of such loans to either public goods (such as international financial stability) or the narrower interests of large shareholder countries, define thresholds of policy deviations, which the Fund is willing to tolerate before cutting off access to funding. In line with the earlier discussion, these thresholds are both time- and country-specific,

---

[14] In practice the status quo payoffs are only achieved if the failed negotiations between the Fund and the potential borrower government are secret. If they are not, the country may incur audience costs, as discussed below.

since they reflect the changing mix of economic and political factors driving IMF deviations from uniform treatment of program countries.

In a world where governments have full control over policy implementation and full information about the Fund's tolerance for policy deviations, their task during implementation boils down to deciding which of the two following options yield the highest overall utility: The first option involves implementing the "minimum acceptable" policy for which the IMF would still disburse funding, while the second option is to simply stick to their status quo policy, which it would have chosen in the absence of conditionality. Depending on the nature of the status quo policy (which is a function of the government's partisan preferences and domestic political constraints), this choice may be above or below the Fund's minimum threshold and could therefore result in either successful compliance or program failure.

During program initiation, the government has to assess the relative costs and benefits of entering an IMF program by comparing the utility of its optimal policy choice during implementation to the utility of avoiding an IMF program altogether and implementing its status quo policy. The intuition behind this choice is relatively straightforward: If during implementation the government can secure IMF funding by implementing its status quo policy, then it will always prefer to enter an IMF program, since this means getting funding for the policies they would have wanted to pursue anyway. This scenario arguably captures the logic of much of Chile's involvement with the IMF, especially after 1985. If, however, the government's optimal choice during implementation is to pursue status quo policies without securing IMF funding, then the government would choose not to enter such a program at all, which would allow it to avoid the costs associated with the negative signals inherent in program breakdown. Finally, if the optimal implementation-stage strategy involves the "minimum acceptable" policy, then the government has to weigh the financial benefits associated with successful compliance against the partisan and/or domestic political costs of adopting an economic policy that differs from its preferred status quo policy. The final step in the backward induction sequence is the Fund's decision about what kind of program details to offer a given country. In making this decision, the Fund has to weigh the opportunity costs of committing large amounts of funding to any given program against the possibility that more generous funding will result in greater compliance incentives for the government and more successful program implementation.

The discussion above suggests that under the current assumptions of the model we would not expect to observe program failure because governments would be able to foresee when program implementation is not in their best interest, and therefore avoid such programs altogether.

However, in reality IMF programs do fail fairly regularly; as will be discussed in chapter 3, less than half of the Latin American and Eastern European programs in the last two decades were fully implemented. The theoretical model developed so far can be adapted in a number of ways to account for the possibility of program failure. Below I will briefly discuss the intuition of how different model assumptions can be relaxed to capture different sources of incomplete program implementation.

One reason why it could be rational for a government to sign an IMF agreement, which it will eventually fail to implement fully, is that in reality, IMF programs are actually repeated games in which the government sets policy targets and the IMF withholds or disburses funding several times over the course of a program. Since key elements affecting the government's policy choice may change over the course of the program, it is quite possible that the net benefits of compliance could change sufficiently in later stages of the program to where an initially attractive IMF program is no longer worth implementing; for example, if during the early stages of the program the government complies with conditionality and receives IMF and third-party funding, the government's financial need may be lower in subsequent stages, which would reduce the government's incentives to comply with program conditions. A similar effect would occur if the social costs of reforms radicalize the antireform opposition, thereby raising the political costs of reforms to the point where they outweigh the benefits of IMF funding. Finally, if a change in government occurs during an IMF program, and the new government is less reformist than its predecessor, then it is possible that the new government would be willing to bear the financial costs of noncompliance in order to fulfill its partisan priorities.

An alternative approach to understanding program breakdown focuses on the implications of the government's incomplete control over policy outcomes. Since most IMF programs occur in countries with significant limitations on state capacity and bureaucratic expertise, the actual outcomes of government policies may differ significantly from the original intentions. The resulting policy deviations may undermine the government's ability to fulfill program targets even if the government has every intention of complying with IMF conditionality. As the formal model in the chapter 2 appendix illustrates, the lack of policy precision due to weak bureaucratic institutions affects not only the actual realization of the government's policy intentions but can also affect the initial policy choice. To see why this is the case, consider a government whose optimal policy choice would be to implement the "minimum acceptable" policy, which is just barely sufficient to secure IMF funding. Under imprecise policy implementation such a strategy runs the risk (proportional to the degree of institutional uncertainty) of resulting in an actual policy outcome below the Fund's minimum threshold, in which case the government achieves the worst of both worlds in that it implements a suboptimal policy (from a domestic political perspective) while at the same time being denied access to IMF finance. As a result, the government will either receive a lower expected payoff for the same amount of policy effort, or it will have to set much more ambitious targets in order to ensure that it will meet program conditions even in the event of imperfect policy execution. Whatever the government's choice, it is clear that in the presence of policy execution uncertainty, the overall utility of compliance with IMF conditionality declines in comparison to the status quo, which means that we should expect more frequent program breakdown as well as less frequent IMF programs in countries with weak bureaucratic institutions.

Another source of uncertainty, which may contribute to program failure, is that governments may not know precisely how the IMF evaluates their country's economic and political importance. While this aspect of IMF lending is not explicitly modeled in the formal model in the appendix, the basic intuition of this mechanism is straightforward: Since neither the IMF staff nor its most influential shareholders would openly admit that different standards are applied to the programs of certain privileged countries, the extent of preferential treatment is likely to be subject to a great degree of uncertainty and speculation. In fact, the Fund and its main principals may purposely choose to maintain a certain dose of uncertainty in order to extract greater policy concessions from such privileged countries. However, this strategy may backfire, since the governments of such countries may overestimate their economic and political clout and thereby implement insufficient reforms, which fail to clear even the less stringent standards imposed by the Fund in such situations.

Theoretical Predictions

This final section presents the main empirical predictions of the theoretical model developed in this chapter. These predictions are based on the comparative statics of the formal model developed in greater detail in the appendix. Predictably, many of the model predictions reflect the assumptions about the preferences of the main actors, which were discussed and justified in the previous section. What the analytical exercise of formalizing these intuitions adds to the earlier discussion is an explicit emphasis on the role of interaction effects among the economic and political drivers of IMF programs. In theoretical terms, the emphasis on mediating factors is crucial for understanding how the "objective" pressures of economic crises are filtered through political and institutional constraints at both the domestic and the international level. These interaction effects are also important in that they suggest specific testable hypotheses for the empirical chapters and emphasize the nonlinear nature of many program drivers.

While some of the predictions discussed below may be considered intuitive in retrospect, this feature does not necessarily detract from the theoretical utility of the formal model, which was used to derive them. First, intuition depends greatly on the vantage point of the individual observer, and as such the same prediction may be obvious to some analysts but surprising to others. Second, it is important to distinguish between *ex ante* and *ex post* intuitive predictions: While the former category consists of predictions about factors that are widely recognized to have certain effects (such as balance-of-payments crises as IMF program drivers), the latter would include nontrivial hypotheses, which have not been discussed by the prior literature even though they make intuitive sense in retrospect. Finally, even for straightforward predictions, whose derivation would not have required a formal model, such a model may provide a useful framework for the systematic analysis of multicausal phenomena such as IMF programs.

The International Political Economy of IMF Programs

In line with the Fund's official role as crisis manager and international lender of last resort, the formal model predicts that from the Fund's perspective greater financial need should invariably be associated with higher initiation and implementation rates. This prediction reflects the expectation that the IMF may show greater lenience toward countries experiencing extreme crises, in order to avoid the disruptions associated with a possible default. However, not all crises are created equal; thus, the model predicts that the extent of this crisis-driven lenience should be greater in economically important countries than in their smaller counterparts. While this prediction constitutes a deviation from the principles of technocratic uniformity in the IMF's crisis reactions, it can be justified by its systemic responsibility for international financial and economic stability.

With respect to preferential treatment in IMF lending, the theoretical predictions depend on the nature of a given country's claim to special status. When the claim is based on the country's political and economic ties to key Western IMF shareholders, then the model predicts greater IMF lenience toward the respective country regardless of the intensity of the crisis. At the implementation stage, such lenience implies that for any given level of deviation from program targets we should observe less frequent program breakdown in Western economic and political allies. However, since governments are aware of the perks associated with preferential status, they are likely to adjust their policies in accordance with the Fund's expected lenience, which means that the aggregate compliance levels in such privileged countries may not necessarily be higher than for regular program countries. However, the effects of such alliances should be much more obvious for program initiation, since politically motivated lenience inevitably translates into an improved balance between the financial benefits and the policy adjustment costs inherent in IMF programs. Therefore, to the extent that such political interventions by large IMF shareholders occur, we should expect Western allies to be more frequent IMF clients, irrespective of the intensity of the economic crises they experience.

When preferential treatment is due to the country's systemic economic importance, the model predicts that the effect of economic size should be mediated by crisis intensity: Thus, if a large developing country experiences extreme financial need, the likelihood of preferential treatment should be higher than if the same country faced moderate economic difficulties, which are less likely to threaten international financial stability. In fact, if the crisis is sufficiently mild, the systemic benefits of lending to a large country may actually be outweighed by the greater opportunity cost of such a loan given the Fund's limited financial resources. As in the case of narrow, politically motivated deviations from technocratic uniformity, we should expect to see clearer empirical differences during program initiation than during implementation, since in the latter, the Fund's greater lenience toward systemically important countries may be counteracted by the government's greater propensity to deviate from program targets.

While the formal model predicts different patterns of program initiation and implementation depending on the predominant logic of IMF lending—technocratic uniformity, political pandering, and systemic concerns—the question about which particular consideration plays the most important role ultimately has to be answered empirically in the following chapters. Nonetheless, we can use our knowledge about the nature of the different crisis episodes to make some predictions about the temporal and regional variation of these patterns. In particular, we would expect systemically based exceptionalism to play a greater role during the Latin American debt crisis, where international financial stability was significantly threatened by a possible default of the region's largest debtors. By comparison during the 1990s, economic crises in the largest Eastern European and Latin American countries could still trigger justified concerns about regional repercussions but their global systemic implications were limited by the much more dispersed nature of foreign debt after 1990. On the other hand, geopolitical concerns should be more salient during the post-communist reorientation of the former Soviet bloc and in Cold War–era Latin America than in Latin America in the 1990s.

The predicted effects of third-party lending in conjunction with IMF programs depend on the type of incentive to which program participation is linked. Thus, the promise that successful program completion may help unlock previously unavailable funding opportunities from either private or official sources should act as an incentive for both higher compliance and more frequent program initiation, since catalytic finance increases the attractiveness of IMF programs. However, if poorly implemented programs trigger the loss of some previously accessible funding sources—for example because private lenders react to this negative signal by raising interest rates—then the model predicts higher compliance but *less frequent* initiation. The intuition behind this prediction is that governments will be more cautious about entering IMF programs if by doing so they run the risk of losing financial support from creditors who may interpret an incomplete program as a worse signal than no program at all.

Even though the formal model does not distinguish between different sources of supplemental funding triggered by IMF programs, earlier work (e.g Bird and Orme 2002) suggests that the magnitude and relative composition of such catalytic finance varies significantly across different countries and time periods. With respect to private lending, the catalytic effect of IMF programs should be most noticeable in countries with intermediate access to international financial markets but is likely to be weaker in desperate situations (where no amount of IMF signaling can convince private lenders to risk their funds) and in countries whose strong credit position does not require IMF reinforcement. The relative importance of the Fund's role as a gatekeeper of official lending is more ambiguous: On one hand, countries with the most limited access to private lending are the most dependent on multilateral and bilateral loans, but on the other hand much of the assistance to such countries tends to be of a humanitarian nature, and therefore less likely to be tied to IMF conditionality.

Dealing with the Home Front: Economic Crises and Domestic Politics

From a technocratic standpoint, economic crises—both domestic and external—should increase the likelihood of IMF program initiation and implementation. As governments experience deeper economic troubles, their greater dependence on direct and indirect funds associated with IMF programs makes these programs more attractive. This intuition is captured by the positive relationship between financial need and the probability of program initiation and implementation in the formal model. Of course, even extreme financial need is no guarantee for successful IMF programs, since the economic benefits may be outweighed by political considerations or institutional constraints; thus, the model predicts that program initiation and implementation are likely to suffer if IMF conditionality is strongly at odds with the partisan preferences of the government or the opposition, or if weak institutional capacity undermines the government's ability to implement reforms effectively.

However, the model's implications are not limited to the prediction—implicit in the assumptions about the government's priorities—that economic crisis may not be enough to overcome domestic political obstacles. Instead, the model predicts that the very impetus provided by economic crises will be mediated by these domestic political and institutional constraints. In other words, similar crises may trigger very different policy reactions depending on the government's willingness and ability to formulate crisis responses in line with IMF economic adjustment expectations. Thus, if the government ideologically disagrees with the Fund's crisis diagnosis, then it is conceivable that its policy preferences will diverge further from those of the IMF as the crisis intensifies. If this partisan radicalization is sufficiently pronounced, then a worsening crisis may actually reduce the likelihood of IMF-style reforms, as their economic benefits are overshadowed by their political costs. An alternative reason why similar economic crises may trigger very different policy responses is suggested by the nature of the interaction between institutional weakness and financial need in the formal model: As the government's ability to execute its policy intentions declines, its response to economic crises weakens. This failure to tackle even pressing economic crises is not only due to weaker implementation (which may lead to program failure even when the government is genuinely trying to comply), but also to the fact that such governments may be less willing to even try to initiate demanding reforms, since the likelihood of failure is so high.

With respect to partisan considerations, the model also suggests a more nuanced picture than the straightforward initial assumption that governments prefer policies close to their partisan ideal point. In the basic model, which assumes that the intensity of the government's partisan policy preferences is constant, the model does indeed predict that right-leaning governments should be more likely to initiate IMF programs irrespective of crisis intensity. This logic is similar to Vreeland's (2003) argument that some governments want to have IMF conditions imposed as an excuse for pursuing their domestic political agenda.

However, if we relax this "constant partisanship" assumption and allow the intensity of partisan preferences to vary as a function of crisis intensity, the model suggests two possible partisan scenarios with very different implications for the politics of IMF programs. In the first scenario, partisan policies differ greatly across parties at low crisis intensity levels but during severe crises the policy preferences of both the right and the left converge as domestic actors broadly agree with the Fund's crisis diagnosis. This *crisis-driven partisan convergence* can be interpreted as evidence of the weakness of the left's ideological convictions and partisan ties, and therefore should be more likely to occur during the neoliberal hegemony of the 1990s. Alternatively the convergence may be simply due to the fact that some crises do not lend themselves as easily to divergent ideological interpretations. In the second scenario, *crisis-driven partisan divergence*, partisan differences are accentuated during crisis situations, as the right initiates IMF-style reforms, while the left fails to do so. This difference may either be due to the fact that the Fund's crisis diagnosis is compatible with the ideological convictions of the right but not the left, or because the left is less sanguine about enacting IMF-style austerity measures, which tend to hurt its traditional constituents, such as the poor and organized labor. Such partisan divergence should be more likely in situations where the nature of the economic crisis is open to divergent interpretations, and where party platforms are anchored by fairly strong ideological beliefs and partisan ties. On both counts, this effect should be more likely in Latin America during the 1980s, given the hotly debated roots and consequences of the debt crisis and the greater ideological diversity prior to the end of the Cold War.

Unlike the uniform effect of political openness implicitly assumed by much of the literature, the model suggests that the effects of greater political competition are mediated by the relative partisan preferences of the government and the opposition. If the government favors greater reforms than the opposition or the median voter, then factors associated with greater societal input—such as greater democracy or impending elections—are expected to undermine the prospects of IMF programs. If, on the other hand, the government is more reluctant to follow IMF policy prescriptions than the opposition or the general population, then greater political openness may actually promote the initiation and implementation of IMF programs. This variation should be observable not only as a result of the different political constellations of different countries within a region but also across the three different crisis episodes. Since popular resistance toward IMF-style adjustment policies was arguably the strongest during the debt crisis, we should expect democratic politics to be harder to reconcile with Latin American IMF programs in the 1980s than for the interventions in the following decade.

Conclusion

This chapter has developed a theoretical framework for analyzing the politics of IMF program initiation and implementation. The framework captures a wide range of domestic and international factors that affect

the preferences and constrain the actions of the two main protagonists—
the IMF and the program country government—during their interactions
in the context of IMF programs. The second part of the chapter discussed
the theoretical predictions of a formal model, which incorporates a number of crucial facets of the process of IMF program initiation and implementation. The model, which is presented more formally in the appendix,
yields a series of testable hypotheses about how IMF programs are affected by economic crises, partisan preferences, the domestic institutional
features, and the IMF's different economic and political priorities.

A crucial aspect of the analysis presented in this chapter is that the
effects of individual factors are not necessarily additive but emerge from
the complex interaction between "objective" economic crises, the intentions of political actors (e.g., the partisan orientations of the government
and the opposition), the particular institutional and structural features of
the domestic political economy (e.g., the intensity of political competition
and the partisan cohesion of key political actors), and the country's financial and geopolitical position in the world at a given point in time.
Most importantly, the theoretical model suggests that the link between
economic crises and IMF program initiation and implementation is mediated by political and institutional factors at both the international and
the domestic level. From an international perspective, we should expect
the Fund to react more decisively and show greater flexibility in response
to economic crises in systemically important countries, which may have
greater regional or global repercussions. The domestic response to economic crises should be stronger for governments that for partisan reasons
agree with the Fund's crisis diagnosis and are sufficiently bureaucratically
capable and politically secure to implement the demanding requirements
of IMF adjustment programs.

APPENDIX to CHAPTER 2

Statistical Indicators and Methods

One of the main challenges of testing any theoretical model—and particularly formal models—is to find the appropriate empirical measures to capture the theoretical concepts discussed in the model. While the discussion in this chapter has already pointed to a number of potential measures, this appendix will provide a more systematic overview linking the theoretical concepts to the indicators used in the following statistical and case study chapters. The key indicators are also summarized in table 2.1.

Dependent Variables: IMF Program Indicators

In line with the theoretical framework, the dependent variables in the statistical tests capture three relevant dimensions of IMF programs: program initiation, program design, and program implementation and enforcement. For program initiation, I use a dichotomous measure indicating whether a given country has signed a new Standby (SBA) or Extended Fund Facility (EFF) program with the IMF at a given point in time. The data was coded on the basis of monthly information published in the *IMF Survey.*

For program design, the formal model allows for the IMF to adjust either the size of the loan or the nature of program conditions. Since the amount of IMF funding available to a given program is based on the country's IMF quota,[15] the most straightforward indicator of IMF financial largesse is the annualized share of the quota committed in support of an SBA or EFF program. Unlike the relative size of IMF loans, the toughness of program conditions is much harder to compare consistently across countries. Even if program targets were publicly available for all programs, it would be virtually impossible to establish how tough a given target (or combination of targets) is in a given economic situation. Therefore, the present analysis focuses on a more easily comparable aspect of IMF conditionality: the number of structural conditions and total conditions contained in a given post-communist IMF program 1993–98.[16] Un-

---

[15] Except under extraordinary circumstances, members can only borrow up to 100% of the quota annually and up to 300% of the quota cumulatively.

[16] The data, which draws on the Fund's internal program monitoring database (MONA) as published in Ivanova et al. 2002, is unfortunately not available prior to 1993, which means that the current analysis cannot be extended Latin American programs of the 1980s.

TABLE 2.1
Overview of Theoretical Concepts and Statistical Indicators

Theoretical concept	Model symbol	Indicators	Latin America 1980s	Latin America 1990s	Eastern Europe 1990s	Source
Prog initiation		New program	✓	✓	✓	IMF + author
IMF funding	M_p	Loan size/IMF quota	✓	✓	✓	IMF + author
Prog. targets	q_p	# total conditions			✓	Ivanova et al. (2003)
		# structural conditions			✓	Ivanova et al. (2003)
		Program waivers			✓	Ivanova et al. (2003)
Compliance	Pr (comp)	Active program	✓	✓	✓	IMF + author
Financial need/crisis	μ	Reserves/imports	✓	✓	✓	IFS
		Interest payments/GDP	✓	✓	✓	GDF
		Inflation	✓	✓	✓	IFS/EIU
		Fiscal balance	✓	✓	✓	IFS
		Growth	✓	✓	✓	WDI
Signals/ side benefits	S_n, S_p	Country credit score	✓	✓	✓	IIS
		EU integration tier			✓	Author, Pacek et al. (2009)
		Official lending	✓			GDF
		Debt rescheduling		✓		GDF
Narrow econ/pol. importance	p_{pol}	UN voting	✓	✓	✓	US State Dep't
		UN voting change	✓	✓	✓	US State Dep't
		Imports from EU,US	✓	✓	✓	DOTS
Systemic importance	p_{sys}	Debt size	✓	✓	✓	GDF
		Total imports	✓		✓	WDI
Partisan orientation of gov't and opposition	$q_{gov} q_{opp}$	Ex-communist/ nationalist			✓	Author
		Ideology	✓	✓	✓	Coppedge (1997), Stone (2002), Lodola & Queirolo (2005)
		Labor based party	✓	✓		author Roberts (2002); Murrillo & Shrank (2005); author
Inst uncertainty	k	Bureaucratic quality	✓	✓		ICRG
		Quality of governance and public administration			✓	NIT + author
Political constraints	S	Regime	✓	✓	✓	Polity
		Veto points	✓	✓	✓	Henisz
		Seat share of largest gov't party	✓		✓	Author
		Post-election period	✓		✓	Author
		Pre-election period	✓	✓	✓	Author

less there is a trade-off between the number and the difficulty of program conditions, it is reasonable to expect that programs with a large number of conditions will be tougher to implement.

The third dimension—program implementation—is captured by two measures. The first is a dichotomous measure indicating whether a given program was active (i.e., the government had access to IMF funding) in a given time period.[17] This measure of compliance does not capture the extent to which a given country fulfilled the specific policy targets of the IMF agreement,[18] only whether or not the IMF considered the overall policies to have been sufficiently compliant to warrant the stamp of IMF approval. However, this potential bias in favor of politically privileged countries should be mitigated by the inclusion of controls for the sources of such exceptionalism, which are discussed below. Moreover, the measure is consistent with the approach to conditionality proposed by the formal model, which specifically incorporates the role of politically driven "softness" in the enforcement of IMF conditionality. The second indicator—the number of program waivers approved by the Fund within a given program—is a more direct measure of the extent to which the IMF is willing to deviate from strict technocratic standards to ensure the successful completion of a program. While such waivers are important for program flexibility in situations where circumstances beyond the government's control make it difficult to fulfill the original program targets, they are also potential mechanisms for political interference, since they allow unpunished deviations from IMF conditionality. Unfortunately, data for this indicator, based on Ivanova et al. (2003), were only available for postcommunist programs 1993–98 and therefore do not allow for cross-temporal and cross-regional comparisons.

Independent Variables: Economic and Political Drivers

Building on the theoretical discussion in chapter 2 and the key parameters of the formal model, I will briefly discuss the choices for the statistical indicators used to test the theoretical hypotheses about the drivers of IMF programs.

---

[17] Since IMF-funding disbursements are closely tied to the fulfillment of IMF conditionality countries eligible for IMF funding through an SBA or EFF agreement were coded compliant with IMF conditionality. Because for precautionary programs, nondisbursement does not automatically imply noncompliance, this data was supplemented by country-specific information from the IMF country desks, EIU Country Reports, and Ivanova et al. 2003.

[18] Unfortunately, there is not enough publicly available data to allow for a cross-country comparison of target fulfillment. Moreover, even if such data were available, it would still be extremely difficult to control for potential variations in the toughness of the program conditions across countries.

ECONOMIC CRISIS AND FINANCIAL NEED

The first main category of explanatory variables consists of indicators of financial need and economic crises, which figure prominently in the book's theoretical framework and in the previous literature. Although the formal model treats financial need uniformly, the statistical tests differentiate between external and domestic economic crises. I use two different external crisis indicators, which have been frequently employed in the IMF literature: the amount of interest payments as a share of GDP, which captures the financial burden of foreign debt service, and the level of foreign reserves in months of imports,[19] as a proxy of a government's liquidity concerns. Given the IMF's concern for balance-of-payments crises, some of the tests also include a measure of the change in foreign reserves (in the preceding quarter) as a proxy of the temporal trend in a country's liquidity position.

In line with a number of earlier studies (Santaella 1986, Remmer 1996, Stone 2002), the statistical tests use the level of consumer price inflation as the main indicator of domestic economic crises. Compared to alternative measures, inflation has the theoretical advantage of being the most visible and politically salient aspect of economic crisis and the practical advantage of being easier to measure consistently across countries and time periods[20] and, therefore, a more reliable measure for cross-country tests. A closer look at the literature, however, suggests that even with respect to inflation, there is little consensus as to what constitutes a crisis. Thus, Bruno and Easterly (1995) identify inflation levels above 40% as harmful for growth—a threshold also used by Milner and Kubota (2005)—while Ghosh and Stevens (1998) have set this threshold much lower. Meanwhile, other analysts have emphasized the crucial role of hyperinflation (Weyland 1998), while much of the literature (e.g., Stone 2002) treats inflation as a continuous variable. The present analysis relies primarily on logged inflation levels but it also briefly analyzes the effects of different time lags and threshold specifications. Despite data limitations mentioned above, I also used two additional measures of domestic economic crises: First, following Vreeland (2003) I used lagged budget deficit (as a % of GDP) to capture hidden structural problems that have not yet been reflected in inflation. Second, in line with Tornell (1998) and

[19] Following Milner and Kubota 2005, I also tested a variety of threshold indicators of crisis, but these produced weaker results than the continuous measures presented below.

[20] For example, fiscal deficit statistics suffer because of the reliance of some governments on quasi-fiscal deficits to achieve better official budget statistics, growth rates have a hard time accounting for large unofficial sectors, and unemployment statistics are notoriously unreliable due to country-specific differences in accounting procedures and reporting incentives.

Milner and Kubota (2005), I used lagged GDP change as a proxy of over-all economic performance.

Unlike the straightforward link between external crisis indicators and financial need, the relationship between domestic crises and the demand for IMF funding is somewhat more complicated in the sense that IMF funds are at best a partial fix for the domestic imbalances reflected by fiscal deficits and inflation. However, as Sachs (1994) argued in the case of Russia, the direct and indirect funding mobilized by the IMF could go a long way in helping governments finance their fiscal deficits in noninfla-tionary ways. Similarly, an inflow of external funding could provide an important economic growth impetus by promoting productive invest-ments. A second validity concern is raised by the fact that inflation may be a symptom of some of the very reform measures promoted by the IMF, especially in the context of price liberalization in the ex-communist coun-tries. To counter the danger of reverse causation, I have tested the effects of longer lags (of up to four quarters) prior to program initiation, which yield similar (or even stronger) results and therefore suggest that inflation indeed captures economic crisis rather than early reform effects. For simi-lar reasons, during implementation I use pre-program inflation as a crisis indicator, so as to avoid the risk of incorporating program effects.

SYSTEMIC AND GEOPOLITICAL IMPORTANCE

In line with the theoretical discussion, I differentiate between indicators of systemic importance, and narrower economic or geopolitical factors, which induce large shareholders to lobby the Fund for preferential treat-ment of a certain country. Earlier studies have used a variety of indicators (including GDP and IMF quota) to capture the size and implicitly the systemic importance of a given country. For the present analysis, however, the more appropriate measures are those that directly capture those as-pects of a country's size that have a direct bearing on the Fund's systemic responsibilities. Therefore, the statistical tests use logged indicators of total external debt and total imports,[21] which reflect a country's impor-tance in international financial markets and trade.[22]

Among the indicators of narrow "realist" deviations from techno-cratic impartiality, one can distinguish three subtypes. First, to capture geopolitical concerns, I used two indicators: To test whether Western al-

[21] I obtained similar results using alternative measures, including short-term debt and total trade as well as global shares of trade and debt (results omitted).

[22] The measures are lagged by a year to avoid the possibility of reverse causation, since IMF programs may affect overall debt and import levels. Since the two measures are highly correlated (at .8 or higher), model specifications only include one of the two indicators to reduce multicollinearity concerns.

lies get preferential treatment, I used the degree of agreement between a program country and the United States across all votes in the preceding United Nations General Assembly voting session.[23] Several models also include the change in voting record agreement compared to the preceding year, in order to test Thacker's (1999) hypothesis about the importance of relative movements toward the U.S. position.[24]

The second type of indicator taps into the economic interests that may motivate large member states to pressure IMF staff for preferential treatment of certain developing countries. Unlike the systemic measures, which capture overall international economic importance, these indicators reflect the intensity of bilateral economic ties, particularly a country's imports from the United States or other Western industrial countries (Bird and Rowlands 2001, Barro and Lee 2002, Stone 2004). Given the economic and political context of the two regions analyzed in this book, I focus on the imports of a given country from the United States and the European Union.

Finally, I also tested the importance of a number of alternative drivers of preferential treatment, including foreign aid disbursements (following Stone 2002, 2004), population size, and geographic proximity to advanced industrialized countries. While plausible arguments can be made to justify each of these measures, they suffer from a number of drawbacks and generally produce modest results, and are only briefly mentioned in the analysis.[25]

PARTISAN ORIENTATION

Determining the partisan ideal points of the government and the opposition is difficult because measures of partisan orientation do not travel well across regions and time periods. To measure the government's ideological orientation, in Latin America I build on Coppedge's (1997) expert-survey-based party classification scheme, which scores parties from 0

---

[23] I obtained similar results using a measure that only considers key UNGA votes (Thacker 1999) but ultimately I agree with Barro and Lee's (2002) argument that the decision about which votes to count as "important" introduces an unnecessary degree of arbitrariness in the coding. Nor were the results affected if I used the affinity scores in UN voting advocated by Gartzke (2000).

[24] In addition to proximity, I also tested whether geopolitical importance affects IMF lending. Following Dreher et al. (2006) I used membership in the UN Security Council as a proxy of such importance. However, the results were rather modest and are not discussed in the book due to space constraints.

[25] For example, foreign aid has the advantage of capturing the directly expressed political preferences of Western donors, but it is less useful for differentiating between economic and geopolitical sources of such preferences, and—if it is sufficiently generous and unconditional—bilateral aid may actually reduce a country's need for IMF funding.

(right) to 4 (left).[26] For the purpose of this study, Coppedge's scheme has the distinct advantage of using pre-electoral statements and policy positions as a basis for the score, which reduces the danger that party ideology scores may be affected by post hoc knowledge of policy choices (including IMF program participation).[27] For multiparty governments, the coalition's ideology score was calculated as a weighted average of individual party scores using seat shares. A similar approach was taken to calculate the ideological orientation of the opposition.

While no similarly extensive expert-survey was available for Eastern Europe,[28] I used Stone's (2002) ideology measure, which scores post-communist governments on a 21-point scale from −10 (left) to +10 (right). Unfortunately Stone's coverage stops in 1999 and was not available for opposition parties. Since several scholars have also argued that the traditional left-right divide is less useful in the post-communist context (Tismaneanu 1996, Tucker 2006), most of the statistical tests used a dichotomous political orientation measure, which was obtained by coding political parties in the region along one of the key fault lines of postcommunist politics—whether a given party is a communist successor party. Moreover, I have also tried to capture a peculiar type of party (in countries like Slovakia, Croatia, and Belarus) whose leaders, while not necessarily former top communist officials, pursued a nationalist/populist political agenda that is at odds with IMF-style reforms. Since statistical tests did not reveal significant differences between ex-communists and nationalists/populists, or between reformed and unreformed ex-communists,[29] the statistical tests presented in the following chapters use a composite category of *anti-reform parties*, which includes both ex-communists and nationalists/populists.

Finally, in line with a well-established literature in Latin America (Collier and Collier 1991, Roberts 2002, Levitsky 2003, Murillo and Schrank 2005), I will also analyze the implications of an alternative source of partisan political preferences, which are not necessarily rooted in ideology but in the institutional ties of certain political parties to organized labor. Building on Roberts (2002) and Murillo and Schrank (2005)

[26] Since Coppedge's data does not extend past 1995 and does not include all the Central American and Caribbean countries in my sample, I have coded the missing countries and years using data from Lodola and Queirolo (2005) and various secondary sources (especially Nohlen 1993).

[27] In the one instance where this may nevertheless have happened—the scoring of the Argentine PJ as center-right between the 1989 and 1991 elections—I recoded the party as center-left, given its pre-electoral criticisms of IMF-style reforms.

[28] The Benoit-Laver (2005) expert survey does cover most of the countries in my post-communist sample but it does not cover the time period analyzed here.

[29] For the importance of this distinction, see Grzymala-Busse 2002.

I coded Latin American governments as being labor-based if they included a party with established institutional ties to major labor unions in a political party system characterized by Roberts (2002) as *labor-mobilizing*. [30] Meanwhile in Eastern Europe, with the exception of Poland (and to a lesser extent Bulgaria and Hungary), there were no comparable institutional ties between labor unions and major political parties (Robertson 2004), and, therefore, a similar measure of labor-based parties would make much less sense in the post-communist context.

Since a number of the theoretical predictions about the role of political constraints depend on the relative policy preferences of the government and the opposition, I used the above partisan measures to construct a *partisan difference* variable. For the ex-communist countries, partisan difference takes a value of 1 if the government is less reformist than the opposition, 0 if their partisan positions are similar (either both the government and the opposition are pro-reform, or both are anti-reform), and −1 if the opposition is more pro-reform than the government. In Latin America partisan difference was calculated by subtracting the partisan orientation score of the opposition from that of the government, thereby yielding a scale from −4 (a right-wing government facing a left-wing opposition) to +4 (for cases with the opposite political constellation).

POLITICAL CONSTRAINTS

The formal model conceptualizes political constraints as any institutional or situational factor that impels the government to pay greater attention to the policy preferences of the opposition. The most obvious institutional feature of this kind is regime type, which has figured prominently among the domestic political explanations of IMF program dynamics (Remmer 1994, Bird and Rowlands 2001, Stone 2004) and of economic reforms more broadly (Kaufman and Stallings 1989, Haggard and Webb 1994). In this analysis I use the *Polity regime score*, which captures the institutional dimension of political regimes[31] and is calculated as the difference between its democracy and autocracy score to produce a 21-point scale.

Beyond regime type, the analysis also considers a number of alternative measures of political constraints. First, to capture Tsebelis's (1995) argument about the importance of veto players as obstacles to policy change, I used Henisz's (2000) measure of political constraints, which codes the number and relative alignment of veto players in the executive, legislative,

---

[30] Roberts (2002:15) defines these systems on the basis of peak trade union density and union concentration.

[31] Polity's emphasis on institutional features such as executive constraints makes it more relevant for the study of IMF programs than the political and civil rights measured by Freedom House. However, the results were not substantially affected by the use of alternative democracy measures.

judiciary, and subfederal entities to construct a proxy of the "feasibility of policy change." Second, I used the parliamentary seat share of the largest governing party as a proxy of a government's power over the opposition. Arguably, this measure is preferable to the total seat share of the government, since it penalizes the much more unstable coalition governments, which may have larger overall seat shares but are often weakened by coalitional conflicts. Third, given the ongoing debates about the policy effects of electoral cycles[32] and earlier findings about the importance of honeymoon effects in tackling economic crises (Weyland 1998), I coded the three quarters leading up to a legislative or presidential election as a pre-electoral period and the four quarters following an election as a post-electoral period. These two measures are intended to capture the idea that during the honeymoon following electoral victories even a democratic government has more leeway to ignore the policy demands of the opposition, whereas in pre-electoral periods governments are expected to pay greater attention to the political preferences of the median voter and the opposition.

INSTITUTIONAL UNCERTAINTY AND BUREAUCRATIC QUALITY

As laid out in the theoretical framework, IMF programs face significant technical challenges and therefore their success hinges at least in part on the effectiveness of bureaucratic institutions. Somewhat surprisingly, this important aspect of the reform process has been ignored almost completely by earlier statistical work on the subject, perhaps because of the scarcity and problematic nature of many cross-country governance indicators (Kurtz and Schrank 2006). To measure this concept for the transition countries I use the *governance and public administration* scores from *Nations in Transit* from 1993 to 2001.[33] Since similar scores are not available for Latin America, I used annual *bureaucratic quality* scores from the *International Country Risk Guide (ICRG)*, which have been also used by a number of previous studies (Knack and Keefer 1995, Adsera et al 2000).[34]

IMF SIGNALING

The formal model allows for the possibility that the Fund's decision to extend or withhold funding can serve as a signal to third-party lenders, and can thereby trigger additional benefits or costs. While significant debates persist about Fund's ability to mobilize additional lending from pri-

---

[32] For an extensive critical review of these debates, see Franzese 2002b.

[33] Since no scores were available for 1990–92, I have coded the variable for these years by adjusting the scores for 1993 for the changes in governance and public administration discussed in the 1995 edition of *Nations in Transit*.

[34] Geographic coverage for many ex-communist countries was limited before 1998, which undermines the utility of ICRG scores for Eastern Europe.

vate sources (Ozler 1993, Sachs 1994, Rodrik 1997, Edwards 2000) as well as its ability to coordinate with other official lenders (Tussie and Botzman 1992, Bird and Rowlands 2001), what matters for the current analysis is not whether such effects actually occur but whether governments act as though they may occur. Chapters 3 and 7 test a variety of potential indicators of such signaling effects. Given that Mody and Saravia (2003) found that private catalytic effects only occurred for countries with intermediate economic conditions, I test this hypothesis by using a quadratic specification of country credit ratings published on a biannual basis by *Institutional Investor*, based on a survey of financial managers from seventy-five to one hundred top international banks. For private lending, I also tested the effects of short-term debt (as a % of GDP), since both positive and negative IMF signals should be particularly crucial for countries with high exposure to such volatile funding. Another potential side benefit of IMF programs is suggested by Marchesi's (2003) findings that the Fund facilitated debt rescheduling in developing countries. Unlike with other economic indicators, the tests follow Bird and Rowlands (2001b) in using current rather than lagged values of rescheduled debt as a predictor of program initiation. Even though, technically, debt renegotiation agreements occurred after a program was announced, the implicit (and often explicit) link between IMF approval and debt concessions certainly played an important role in driving Latin American governments into IMF agreements.

For official lending effects I use lagged indicators of official, multilateral, and World Bank lending (as a % of GDP) in the preceding year as a proxy of the importance of such funds for a given country. In Eastern Europe, in line with earlier studies emphasizing the important incentives of European integration (Kurtz and Barnes 2002, Jacoby 2004, Vachudova 2005), I tested whether the promise of additional benefits in conjunction with EU membership provided additional incentives to initiate and implement IMF programs. Following Pacek et al. (2009), I divided ex-communist countries into three categories: front-runners, second-tier candidates, and long shots.

CONTROL VARIABLES

The statistical models presented in the following chapters also included several control variables that did not explicitly capture any theoretical concepts discussed in chapter 2, but that may nevertheless affect IMF programs according to earlier findings. In line with a number of prior findings about the role of recidivism in IMF lending (Conway 1994, Bird 1995, Bird et al. 2004), the initiation-stage regressions in the three episodes include an *IMF program history* indicator, which reflects the frequency of past involvement of a given country with the IMF. While the statistical models do not include country dummies (since many of the variables of interest vary primarily across rather than within countries), this program history indicator should reflect other medium-term unobservable drivers of IMF program initiation and implementation, and therefore reduce the potential omitted variable bias inherent in cross-national regressions. To control for possible economic or political shocks at the regional/international level, all the regressions include year dummies (not reported). Finally, the regressions also control for GDP/capita in the preceding year as a proxy of overall economic development levels, since a number of earlier studies (e.g., Vreeland 2003) have found it to be a significant predictor of IMF program dynamics.

Methodological and Statistical Considerations

The statistical tests presented below rely on quarterly data instead of the yearly statistics employed by most large-N studies of IMF programs.[35] This approach facilitates a more fine-tuned understanding of the short-term dynamics of IMF programs, which usually last between twelve and eighteen months and have quarterly disbursements. Since both economic and political conditions can vary substantially over the course of a year, much of the crucial short-term variation is likely to be washed out in tests employing yearly data.

For the analyses of program initiation and compliance, which have dichotomous dependent variables, I used random effects time-series cross-sectional logistic regressions.[36] Following Beck and Katz (2001), I did not include country dummies in the models since doing so would have resulted in the loss of a large portion of the observations for countries with all positive or all negative outcomes, and because cross-country variation is theoretically and substantively important. However, as mentioned earlier, the inclusion of the prior IMF engagement indicator should capture some of the potential unobserved heterogeneity across countries. To deal with temporal dependence, all the statistical models include a non-event duration measure and cubic time splines as recommended by Beck et alia (1998).

---

[35] There are, however, a few exceptions (e.g., Stone 2002, 2004 uses monthly data).

[36] One alternative would be to use bivariate probit models with partial observability along the lines of Przeworski and Vreeland 2000 and Vreeland 2003. However, as Steinwand and Stone (2008) point out, the validity of such tests relies heavily on the justification for the identifying assumption—i.e., of factors that only affect one of the two actors. Given the strategic nature of the interaction between the two protagonists in the present analysis, such identifying assumptions are likely to be debatable. For example, while economic size works primarily through the Fund's decision to give large countries preferential treatments, the governments of such countries are aware of these considerations, and are therefore likely to adopt different strategies than their smaller counterparts (e.g., by attempting to extract addi-

To analyze loan size, which is continuous but left-censored, I performed a box-cox transformation to ensure normality and then used time-series cross-sectional OLS regressions with panel-corrected standard errors, correcting for panel heteroskedasticity. For the number of structural and total program conditions in a given program, which are count variables with overdispersion, I used negative binomial regressions with robust standard errors.[37] Finally, for the number of waived program conditions, which is a count variable with more than a third of zero-value observations, I used zero-inflated Poisson regressions clustered by country and with Huber/White robust standard errors.[38]

The statistical tests rely heavily on interaction effects, which play an important role in testing several key theoretical predictions discussed in chapter 2. Since interaction effects are difficult to interpret by simply looking at regression coefficients (Braumoeller 2003, Brambor et al. 2006), I report relevant substantive effects and significance levels (using conditional standard errors) for different values of the modifier variable. Moreover, for a few crucial interaction effects I present graphs plotting the predicted effects of different independent variables based on the results of the statistical models.[39] To illustrate the statistical effects of both crisis intensity and economic/political importance indicators, the graphs show predicted probabilities rather than marginal effects of individual variables. However, the value range for which these findings are statistically significant is indicated as shaded areas in the graphs and is also discussed in the text.

Unlike much of the existing literature, which uses data pooled across multiple regions and time periods, the data for this analysis are pooled within but not across the three clusters of cases: Latin America (1982–89), Latin America (1990–2001), and Eastern Europe and the former Soviet Union (1990–2001). Given the regional and temporal variations in the geopolitical and systemic priorities of the Fund's major shareholders, this focus on temporally and geographically more restricted sets of cases facilitates causal homogeneity within clusters and structured comparisons across the clusters.

---

tional concessions). For the current data, the results of bivariate probit models with partial observability were indeed highly sensitive to even minor changes in identifying assumptions.

[37] Both the Poisson goodness-of-fit test and the likelihood-ratio tests of the overdispersion parameter indicate quite clearly that the negative-binomial model is preferable to a simple Poisson model.

[38] The highly significant Vuong statistic indicated that zero-inflated Poisson is preferred to regular Poisson models. Meanwhile, likelihood ratio tests suggested that negative binomial regressions were not preferable to Poisson regressions. However, the overall findings were not affected by the choice of estimation method.

[39] Since neither *SPost* in Stata nor *Clarify* support time-series cross-sectional models, the graphs were created in Excel using the predicted probabilities and conditional standard errors calculated from the regression results.

However, one needs to be careful about comparing regression results across different samples of cases. Given that the sample for Latin America in the 1980s is smaller than for Eastern Europe and Latin America in the 1990s, one concern is that sample size differences could limit the comparability of standard errors (though not of regression coefficients). However, since the sample size differences are fairly small (e.g., roughly 20% between Latin America in the 1980s and Eastern Europe in the 1990s) their effects on standard errors are sufficiently small to where they are unlikely to affect the overall statistical significance of the findings, especially since the analysis does not make strict use of traditional significant thresholds in interpreting the results. The more serious concern is about how to compare results for variable such as bureaucratic quality or partisan orientation, which are measured differently across regions (either due to data availability or for theoretical reasons). Such coding differences obviously reduce the immediate comparability of regression coefficients, but I would argue that the gains in validity more than compensate for this loss.

Since countries are not randomly selected into IMF programs but choose to (or have to) initiate programs for a variety of economic and political reasons, the statistical analysis of IMF program implementation has to deal with the problem of selection bias. The present analysis uses Heckman's (1979) approach of including the inverse Mills ratio obtained from the selection equation as an additional control variable in the main model of interest. However, this approach requires the identification of instruments, which affects selection into a program but not the likelihood of compliance. For the compliance regressions in chapters 3, 5, and 7, I considered two instruments. The first—the average number of countries covered by an IMF agreement among a given country's neighbors—captures the contagion effects inherent in waves of policy reform (Kopstein and Reilly 2000, Elkins and Simmons 2004). These neighborhood effects, which help explain a government's decision to enter an IMF program but not necessarily its ability to follow through with implementation, played a significant role in predicting program participation during the Latin American debt crisis and the post-communist transition, but were only marginally significant (at .1) in Latin America in the 1990s. Since diffusion effects were a weaker instrument for program participation in Latin America in the 1990s, I used an additional instrument for the regressions in chapter 7: In line with the discussion about the role of budget constraints for the Fund's program initiation calculus, I found that during the two years following an IMF quota increase, Latin American countries were significantly more likely to be engaged in an IMF program but there was no effect on implementation.

-3-

Changing Crisis "Recipes": The International Drivers of IMF Programs

SINCE IMF PROGRAMS OCCUR at the intersection between domestic and international politics, the logical starting point for understanding their political dynamics is the broader international political economy context in which these programs occur. Building on the analytical framework developed in the preceding chapter, I focus on the role of external crises as IMF program drivers and on the international political and economic interests that mediate the effects of these crises. Drawing on statistical evidence from two of the most prominent episodes of crisis-driven economic adjustment in recent history—the Latin American debt crisis and the post-communist transition—the chapter shows how external financial need and relations with international financial markets shape the program initiation and implementation incentives of governments in the developing world. Moreover, the chapter analyzes the relative importance of different drivers of the Fund's policy agenda, including its role as an international lender of last resort, its systemic concerns for international financial stability, and pressures from Western shareholders for preferential treatment of geopolitically or economically important countries.

In line with the theoretical discussion in the previous chapter, the analysis focuses on several different aspects of IMF lending in developing countries: the timing of program initiation, aspects of program design (such as loan size and number of conditions), and, finally, program implementation and enforcement. The chapter devotes a separate section to each of these aspects and shows how IMF programs in the two regions were affected by international political and economic constraints and incentives. For each aspect of IMF lending, the analysis will test the predictions of the theoretical model for two broad groups of international drivers: First, I show how external financial need and a country's broader standing in international financial markets shape the likelihood of IMF program initiation and implementation. The second set of questions concerns the extent to which IMF lending conformed to the principle of technocratic impartiality during the two program episodes and whether any deviations from this principle were driven primarily by systemic concerns for international financial stability or by the narrower economic and political interests of large IMF shareholders.

The systematic cross-regional and cross-temporal comparison of IMF programs in this chapter offers a useful testing ground for the theoretical framework proposed by this book. On one hand many of the basic parameters of IMF lending have changed relatively little over successive decades, and should be reflected in the program dynamics of both episodes: First, the financial vulnerability of developing countries should be expected to play a major role in both regions; second, the Fund's signaling role to third-party lenders should continue to matter in the context in which direct IMF lending is rarely sufficient to meet the financing needs of developing countries; and finally the unequal power of different member countries within the IMF, combined with the powerful temptation of donor countries to leverage this power to pursue their economic and political interests, should be reflected in deviations from the technocratic impartiality ideal in the Fund's treatment of different program countries. Nonetheless, within the constraints of these broad parameters, we should expect to see significant variation in the nature of the economic and political interactions that shaped IMF programs during the two episodes. Thus, given the specific economic threats posed by the debt crisis, we should expect foreign debt to play a more decisive economic and political role during Latin American IMF programs in the 1980s than in Eastern Europe a decade later. Meanwhile the post-communist transition should be expected to bring other types of considerations to the forefront, in line with the geopolitical reorientation of the region following the end of the Cold War. Similarly, the changing patterns of official lending and the contrast between the private lending bust of the 1980s and the subsequent financial boom of the 1990s should be reflected in a change in the Fund's signaling role in mediating between developing countries and third-party lenders. These differences do not imply that the two episodes are too different to be meaningfully compared—on the contrary, it is by comparing IMF programs in different international contexts that we can establish which aspects of IMF lending appear to be intrinsic features of the Fund's institutional logic and which simply reflect the ever-evolving nature of international financial markets and crises.

The Drivers of IMF Program Initiation

During the eight years between the "official" debut of the debt crisis in 1982 and the end of the decade, the twenty-one Latin American and Caribbean countries included in the present analysis initiated forty-three high-conditionality IMF programs and spent an average of 36% of the time covered by a program. Beneath these regional aggregates, however, there is large variation across countries and time periods. Whereas in early 1982, prior to Mexico's insolvency announcement, only three of the countries in the region (Costa Rica, Jamaica, and Uruguay) were involved in IMF programs, a year later the number of programs had quadrupled and by the end of 1983 two thirds of the countries in my sample had committed to an IMF program. Following this initial "shock treatment" for what was initially regarded a short-term crisis with short-term solutions, the number of programs decreased at first rather slowly (to ten by late 1985), then declined all the way to four "usual suspects" (Argentina, Chile, Jamaica, and Mexico) in mid-1987 before climbing rapidly again to ten programs by the end of 1989.

Even by the high standards of the Latin American debt crisis, the Fund's role in the post-communist transition was remarkable in its ubiquity. Only two of the twenty-six transition countries—Slovenia and Turkmenistan—did not have a single IMF program since the collapse of communism in the region. The remaining twenty-four countries managed to "collect" a remarkable seventy-four high-conditionality programs between 1990 and 2001, ranging from a single program in Albania, Belarus, and Tajikistan to seven programs in Latvia and Romania.

The international drivers of program initiation are summarized in figures 3.1a and 3.1b, which illustrate the substantive effects of the main statistical findings in tables 3.1a and 3.1b. These findings are discussed in greater detail below.

"Beggars Can't Be Choosers": Financial Need and Program Initiation

Why did so many Latin American and Eastern European governments subject themselves to the rigors of IMF conditionality and thereby forfeit a large part of their policy-making freedom? As discussed in the theoretical chapter, previous studies suggest that the logical starting points for answering this question are the external economic crises, which frequently confront vulnerable developing economies. In fact, according to the IMF *Articles of Agreement*, financing need due to unfavorable developments in a country's balance of payments or international reserves position constitutes a necessary condition for the use of Fund resources in the context of a Standby Arrangement or similar program. When facing such crises, countries are more likely to turn to the IMF both to take advantage of the Fund's direct lending and because IMF programs have the potential to unlock additional funds from third parties, which use the signals provided by IMF involvement to judge a country's creditworthiness. Therefore, in line with the predictions of the theoretical model, we should ex-

Figure 3.1a: Substantive effects of program initiation—Latin America (1982–89)

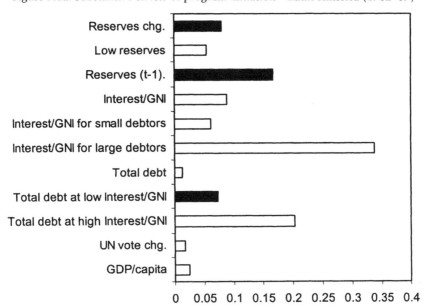

Note: Effects represent change in initiation probability for a change in the variable of interest from the 10th to the 90th percentile. Negative effects are marked as black bars.

pect to see more frequent program initiation and better compliance in countries with high levels of financial need, and where successful compliance with IMF conditionality promises to unlock substantial additional benefits beyond the relatively modest direct loans provided by the Fund. This straightforward analysis linking external crises to IMF programs represents an empirical starting point for subsequent discussions, which pay closer attention to how crisis effects are mediated by both domestic and international politics. In particular, I will show how program initiation is affected by liquidity concerns, external debt service, and by a number of different linkages between developing countries and the global economy.

LIQUIDITY CRISES

Given the centrality of balance-of-payments crises to the Fund's mission, both the absolute levels and the relative changes in international reserves provide a good litmus test for a country's financial health and its likely dependence on IMF lending. The weaker a country's liquidity position, the higher the danger that even a short-term negative trade shock or capi-

Figure 3.1b: Substantive effects of program initiation—Eastern Europe (1990–2001)

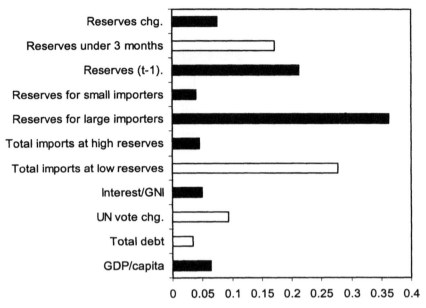

Note: Effects represent change in initiation probability for a change in the variable of interest from the 10th to the 90th percentile. Negative effects are marked as black bars.

tal outflow could result in the inability of the government to honor its outside financial obligations. Afflicted countries not only experience significant short-term economic trauma as a result of insolvency but their long-term development prospects are likely to suffer from future restrictions in international capital market access. Moreover, Western concerns about the international spillover effects of such financial crises were one of the principal reasons for the establishment of the IMF as an international lender of last resort.

In terms of liquidity, the ex-communist countries averaged a threateningly low 2.2 months worth of foreign reserves in the 1990s, well below the level of 3 months of imports that is generally regarded as the minimum threshold for a comfortable reserve position. This weakness was largely a legacy of the communist system with its continuous shortage of hard currency and was exacerbated in the case of the former Soviet republics by an arrangement whereby Russia assumed the bulk of the debt and the foreign reserves of the Soviet Union. Hence, the other former Soviet republics emerged at independence with practically no hard currency reserves and faced an uphill battle to build up their reserve position in the context of a foreign trade oriented primarily toward other ex-communist (and equally hard-currency-starved) countries in the early transition period. Even though the average reserve position of the countries in the region improved gradually over the course of the twelve transition years under analysis (from less than 1 month of imports in early 1993 to about 3.5 months in late 2001), only Hungary, Poland, and oil-rich Turkmenistan had international reserves in excess of four months of imports for most of the transition period.

By contrast, during the 1980s the regional average for the Latin American and Caribbean countries in my sample was about 4 months of imports but declined from a peak of 4.6 months in mid-1986 to around 3 months by late 1989. Subregional differences were even larger than among transition economies, with South American countries (particularly Venezuela, Chile, and Paraguay) having consistently higher reserves than most Caribbean and Central American countries, whose reserves fell below the critical level of two months of imports for most of the decade. Moreover, the changing fortunes of Argentina, Peru, Brazil, and Colombia were reflected in the large temporal variation in their reserve levels in the 1980s. Nonetheless, reserve shortfalls were less acute in Latin America than in Eastern Europe a decade later, and, therefore, one would expect them to play a less important role as drivers of IMF programs.

The statistical results in tables 3.1a and 3.1b confirm the theoretical predictions about the importance of liquidity crises for program initiation in both regions. While international reserves were statistically significant (at .01) and substantively important in both regions, the liquidity effects were nonetheless larger in cash-strapped Eastern Europe than in Latin America (see figs. 3.1a and 3.1b). The greater impact of low reserves in Eastern Europe becomes even clearer when comparing the results for a dichotomous specification of *Low international reserves* in model 2, which uses three months of imports as a threshold for financial distress: Among ex-communist countries such crises were substantively and statistically significant (at .001), whereas in Latin America they had only marginally significant effects (.1 one-tailed).

With respect to balance-of-payments crises, model 3 indicates that the effects of *changes in international reserves* compared to the prior year were substantively similar across the two regions, but the results were much more statistically significant in Eastern Europe (.001) than in Latin America (.1 one-tailed). In part, the lower sensitivity of Latin American countries to both levels and changes in foreign reserves could be due to their more comfortable overall liquidity position. However, as we will see in the following subsection, this effect may also reflect the fact that even

TABLE 3.1A
International Drivers of Program Initiation—Latin America (1982–89)

	(1)	(2)	(3)	(4)	(5)	(6)	(7)
Reserves (t-1)	−.28**			−.25*	−.28**	−.28**	−.32**
	(.10)			(.11)	(.10)	(.10)	(.10)
Low international reserves		.63#					
		(.43)					
Reserves (t-5)			−.25*				
			(.10)				
Chg reserves			−.23#				
			(.14)				
Interest/GNP	.88*	.86*	.86*	.56	.86*	.90*	−.41
	(.41)	(.39)	(.40)	(.46)	(.40)	(.42)	(.69)
Total debt	−.06	.03	.01	.24		−.01	−1.96*
	(.26)	(.25)	(.27)	(.32)		(.30)	(.89)
Quality of bureaucracy	.34#	.26	.28	.64*	.21	.32#	.51#
	(.24)	(.23)	(.23)	(.30)	(.24)	(.24)	(.27)
Regime	.03	.03	.03	.02	.04	.03	.04
	(.04)	(.04)	(.04)	(.04)	(.04)	(.04)	(.04)
Gov't ideology	−.30*	−.34*	−.31*	−.37*	−.27#	−.29#	−.22
	(.18)	(.18)	(.18)	(.19)	(.19)	(.19)	(.19)
Inflation	.29#	.30*	.28#	.22	.38*	.30#	.38*
	(.18)	(.18)	(.18)	(.24)	(.20)	(.19)	(.20)
IIS Credit Rating				.16#			
				(.08)			
IIS Credit Rating (squared)				−.004**			
				(.001)			
Imports from US					.19		
					(.19)		
UN voting					.04	.02	
					(.05)	(.05)	
Chg. UN voting						.02	
						(.06)	
Total debt* Interest/GNP							1.07*
							(.47)
IMF Program History	2.32*	2.97**	2.62*	2.93*	2.72**	2.41*	2.41*
	(1.03)	(.98)	(1.03)	(1.16)	(1.03)	(1.06)	(1.02)
GDP/capita	.09	.00	.06	.03	.07	.08	.14
	(.13)	(.13)	(.13)	(.17)	(.13)	(.14)	(.14)
Observations	495	495	495	490	495	495	495

Logistic regression coefficients with standard errors in parentheses (# −10%; * −5%; ** −1%—one-tailed where appropriate)

TABLE 3.1B
International Drivers of Program Initiation—Eastern Europe (1990–2001)

	(1)	(2)	(3)	(4)	(5)	(6)	(7)	(8)
Reserves (t-1)	−.59**			−.48**	−.60**	−.57**	−.64**	.79
	(.16)			(.17)	(.15)	(.16)	(.16)	(.65)
Low international reserves		2.32**						
		(.54)						
Reserves (t-5)			−.60**					
			(.18)					
Chg reserves			−.57**					
			(.20)					
Interest/GNI	.50	.49	.49	.73#	.54	.42	−.06	.48
	(.43)	(.43)	(.43)	(.45)	(.42)	(.44)	(.63)	(.42)
Total debt	.14	.13	.14	.08		.13	.00	
	(.13)	(.13)	(.13)	(.14)		(.14)	(.18)	
Quality of governance	.67*	.41#	.66*	.72*	.61*	.52*	.73*	.71*
	(.28)	(.26)	(.28)	(.28)	(.29)	(.31)	(.29)	(.28)
Regime	−.03	−.00	−.04	−.04	−.03	−.01	−.04	−.02
	(.05)	(.05)	(.05)	(.05)	(.05)	(.06)	(.05)	(.05)
Anti-reform gov't	−.21	−.30	−.20	−.28	−.26	−.08	−.21	−.07
	(.36)	(.36)	(.36)	(.37)	(.35)	(.37)	(.36)	(.36)
Inflation	.26*	.37**	.25*	.32*	.27*	.23#	.24#	.33*
	(.14)	(.14)	(.14)	(.14)	(.14)	(.14)	(.14)	(.14)
IIS Credit Rating				.25*				
				(.11)				
IIS Credit Rating (squared)				−.004*				
				(.002)				
Imports from EU					.23*			
					(.11)			
UN voting					.02	.02		
					(.02)	(.02)		
Chg. UN voting						.06*		
						(.02)		
Interest/GNI*Total debt							.30	
							(.25)	
Total imports								.42**
								(.16)
Imports* Reserves (t-1)								−.15*
								(.07)
IMF Program History	1.42	1.20	1.47	.32	1.31	1.54	1.33	1.40
	(1.06)	(1.05)	(1.09)	(1.14)	(1.06)	(1.06)	(1.07)	(1.07)
GDP/capita	−.21	−.13	−.20	−.22	−.36#	−.23	−.24	−.25
	(.16)	(.15)	(.16)	(.17)	(.19)	(.18)	(.17)	(.17)
Observations	622	626	614	622	609	586	622	622

Logistic regression coefficients with standard errors in parentheses (# −10%; * −5%; ** −1%—one-tailed where appropriate)

relatively comfortable reserve levels were dwarfed by the massive external obligations faced by many Latin American debtors.

Despite their healthier international reserves position, Latin American and Caribbean countries experienced a much more precarious external debt situation than their ex-communist counterparts. The regional debt/ output ratio in Latin America rose from 38% in late 1981 to 65% in 1987 before declining to 49% in late 1989 with several countries—including Bolivia, Jamaica, Nicaragua, Panama, and Costa Rica—weighed down by debts ratios exceeding 100% of GNI. By comparison, foreign debt accounted for around 15% of output of the former communist bloc at the start of the transition, with only three countries—Bulgaria, Hungary, and Poland—experiencing debt ratios in excess of 30%. Meanwhile, most of the newly independent states of the former Soviet Union emerged debt-free at independence due to the aforementioned agreement whereby Russia assumed most of the reserves and external obligations of the Soviet Union. However, by 1999, Eastern European debt ratios had reached an alarming regional average of 60% of GNI before declining to a more manageable 46% in late 2001.[1] While several countries—such as Hungary, Bulgaria, and Russia—had inherited substantial foreign debts from the 1980s and struggled with payment crises at various points of the transition, the region overall was less affected by the specter of massive debt defaults that had haunted Latin America a decade earlier.

More importantly from the point of view of IMF programs, Latin America's predicament was even worse with respect to interest payments, which accounted for 4%–5.5% of gross national income (GNI) 1981–88 before declining to around 3% in 1989. In several countries, including Bolivia during its paralyzing crisis in 1982–4, but also in Chile and Jamaica in the mid-1980s, interest payments exceeded 10% of GNI, thereby putting governments in the difficult position of choosing between harsh austerity measures or losing control over fiscal deficits and inflation. Meanwhile, the Eastern European regional interest/GNI ratio averaged less than 1% prior to 1996, with only Hungary and Bulgaria experiencing interest burdens in the 4%–5% range that had been the norm in Latin America in the 1980s. Despite the ex-communist bloc's rapidly rising debt, only 2% of the region's GNI was transferred abroad as interest payments by late 2001, though a few countries—most notably Moldova

[1] Even more so than in Latin America, this increase in post-communist relative indebtedness occurred at least in part due to the severe economic contraction of the early 1990s. However, even in absolute terms the overall debt owed by countries in the region more than doubled from 1990 to 2000.

and Kyrgyzstan—had reached interest payment levels of 5% of GNI by 2001, which are alarming given the two countries' low development levels. The comparison between the two regions yields very similar conclusions when using alternative measures of debt burden: Thus, Latin American debt-servicing expenses averaged the equivalent of thirty months worth of export earnings, almost five times higher than the regional average for Eastern Europe and the former Soviet Union.

The higher prominence of debt-servicing pressures in Latin America is reflected in the statistical evidence in tables 3.1a and 3.1b. According to model 1, interest payments played a greater role in IMF program initiation in the heavily indebted Latin American countries than in their postcommunist counterparts: The effects of higher *interest/GNI* were substantively large[2] and statistically significant (at .05) in Latin America, whereas in Eastern Europe the substantive effects were only half as large and statistically insignificant.[3] These findings confirm the predicted importance of external financial need during IMF program initiation, but they also reveal some interesting regional variation in the salience of different types of crises, as reserves mattered more in Eastern Europe while debt burden played a greater role in Latin America.

ACCESS TO INTERNATIONAL CAPITAL MARKETS
AND OTHER THIRD-PARTY LENDERS

In the volatile relationship between developing countries and international financial markets, the IMF fulfills two important functions meant to address two different types of market failure: The first is related to the Fund's role as an international lender of last resort and involves the provision of loans to countries with no (or very limited) access to alternative sources of credit in order to address their balance-of-payment difficulties. The second role of the IMF—as a judge of developing countries' economic policies—is meant to facilitate international lending by reducing the informational asymmetries in international financial markets and the information costs for lenders. While the Fund's effectiveness in mobilizing additional private lending remains disputed (Ozler 1993, Rodrik 1997, Edwards 2000), the seal of IMF approval can also facilitate a country's access to official lending, given that multilateral loans (especially from the World Bank) as well as some bilateral aid are explicitly linked

[2] As illustrated in fig. 3.1a, in Latin America the effects of interest payments, while weaker on average that those of reserves, were stronger than those of other liquidity indicators (such as low reserves and reserve changes).

[3] Similar (but slightly weaker) regional results were also obtained using alternative debt burden measures such as debt service as a % of exports and total debt as % of GDP (results omitted).

to compliance with IMF conditionality. The relative weight of these IMF functions (and implicitly of the motivations for program initiation and implementation) differs significantly with a country's position in international financial markets: For countries with minimal prospects of private capital market access (such as Moldova in the mid 1990s), the main lure of IMF programs lies in the promise of direct IMF funding, which along with other linked multilateral lending can account for most of the external financing available to such governments. In such cases, however, the signaling benefit is likely to be limited, since even careful compliance with IMF conditions is unlikely to give them access to private capital markets in the short to medium term. At the other extreme are countries (such as Latvia and Estonia in the late 1990s) with ready access to private lending: To the extent that such countries enter IMF programs, they tend to do so on a precautionary basis (often choosing not to draw on available IMF funds), which suggests that they largely rely on the Fund for its signaling role. Finally, countries with intermediate standing in international finance (such as Romania and Bulgaria for much of the 1990s) stand to benefit from both the direct funding and the potential positive signals of successful IMF program to private and official lenders. Moreover, prior work suggests that to the extent that private catalytic effects of IMF lending exist, they tend to occur in such intermediate cases (Mody and Saravia 2003), where IMF signals may tip the balance of international creditworthiness in either direction.

As a result, as discussed in the appendix to chapter 2, different degrees of access to private capital markets capture a mix of financial need and signaling, which means that the theoretical predictions of the formal model depend on the relative importance of the two elements in a given situation. Thus, to the extent that the Fund's main function is that of lender of last resort, we should expect program initiation to decline monotonically with greater access to private capital markets. If, on the other hand, signaling is the primary motivation for program initiation, then IMF programs should be more frequent in countries with medium to medium-high capital market access. Since the relative mix of motivations for program initiation depends on both the nature of countries analyzed and the broader international financial context, the discussion will start with a brief comparison of capital market access in the two episodes before analyzing its impact on IMF programs.

Figure 3.2 illustrates the broad temporal trends based on the regional average in credit ratings during the two crises. Even this rough measure captures the remarkable and abrupt "fall from grace" of Latin American debtors following Mexico's default in mid-1982, followed by a relative stabilization in 1985–88 and a renewed decline in 1989 despite the "official" end of the debt crisis heralded by the Brady Plan. However, the

Figure 3.2: Credit ratings—regional averages

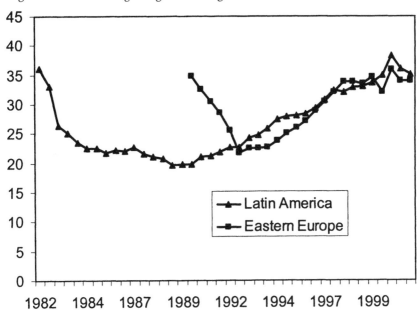

decline was not uniform across countries; thus, some of the region's largest debtors (Brazil, Argentina, Mexico, and even neoliberal poster-child Chile) suffered dramatic declines of 25 or more points on the 100-point IIS scale, whereas less indebted countries (such as Panama, Trinidad-Tobago, and Paraguay) held up better. Finally, a group of Caribbean and Central American countries started out from a much lower base and therefore also experienced much smaller declines.

At first glance, judging by figure 3.2, the early transition years also witnessed a substantial decline in credit ratings for the former communist countries, as financial markets became aware of the economic mess left behind by the communists in countries like Bulgaria and Romania. However, much of the decline in the regional average is due to the inclusion starting in 1992 of a large number of newly independent states whose economic and political woes, combined with their short international track record, yielded many low credit ratings and produced a regional average comparable to that of Latin America in the throes of the debt crisis.[4] However, unlike the extended credit malaise that plagued

---

[4] In fact a properly weighted regional average would yield even lower results, since several of the region's worst performers were not even included in the IIS ratings until the late 1990s.

Figure 3.3: Credit ratings and IMF program initiation

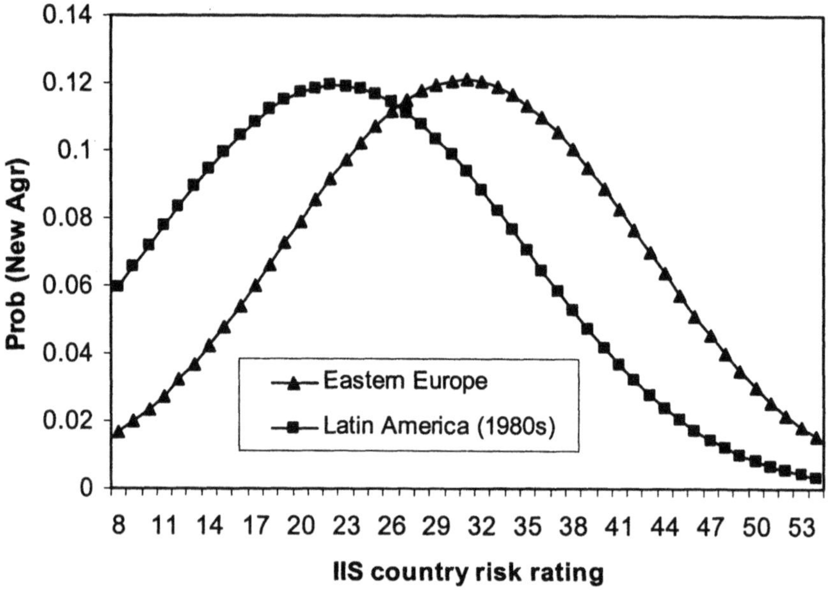

Source: Institutional Investor

Latin America in the 1980s, the post-communist transition witnessed a gradual but substantial improvement in credit ratings, as increasing numbers of countries managed to gain access to commercial lending in international markets. Much of this growth, however, was driven by a few star performers—especially Poland, Slovenia, and the three Baltic states—whereas elsewhere the journey toward global finance was slower and more prone to temporary reversals (e.g., in Russia, Romania, and Bulgaria), and had barely started in the poorer parts of the Balkans and the former Soviet Union.

How did capital market access affect IMF program initiation during the two crisis episodes? Figure 3.3 based on the results in model 4 of tables 3.1a and 3.1b reveals an inverse quadratic relationship between credit ratings and program initiation: In both Latin America and Eastern Europe the most likely IMF program candidates were countries with intermediate-level credit ratings. This pattern is consistent with the signaling hypothesis, which predicted that IMF programs should be most attractive to the borderline cases, for which access to international capital markets was possible but by no means certain. Meanwhile, the financial need hypothesis receives weaker support, given that program participation declines significantly among countries with the worst credit ratings, for which the Fund's lender-of-last-resort function should be the most important. Nonetheless, the importance of direct IMF funding should not be dismissed entirely as a program participation incentive: For both regions the likelihood of initiation declined substantially for countries with comfortable credit ratings and easy access to alternative (and usually cheaper) sources of private credit, which may help explain the ability of countries like Trinidad-Tobago, Colombia, and Venezuela to avoid the IMF until the late 1980s, as well as the petering out of the initially intense IMF involvement of countries like Poland, Hungary, and the Czech Republic by the mid 1990s. Moreover, the decline of participation rates for countries with far from reassuring credit ratings (especially in Latin America) suggests that at least part of the initiation incentives were linked to direct IMF funding (and possibly other official lending).

While the overall relationship between credit ratings and IMF program incidence was remarkably similar for the two regions, figure 3.3 nonetheless reveals some interesting differences. Eastern European countries were significantly more likely to resort to IMF programs at higher levels of international credit ratings than their Latin American counterparts. This finding may be due to the desire of transition countries to reassure international capital markets by entering precautionary IMF programs but also reflects the more sober reality that during the debt crisis most Latin American governments only resorted to the IMF when they had few other alternatives. The stronger role of financial need in the context of the commercial credit freeze of the 1980s is further supported by the greater propensity of program initiation in the lower range of the credit rankings in Latin America compared to Eastern Europe (according to fig. 3.3).

For other potential indicators, the role of signaling as an incentive for program initiation received much weaker empirical support.[5] Thus, countries with high levels of short-term loans were not more likely to initiate IMF programs in either region, which suggests that such programs were not widely used to reassure short-term investors. In fact, the (albeit statistically insignificant) negative effect suggests that the potential negative signals associated with IMF programs may have served as a disincentive for program initiation. Nor was there statistical evidence to support the role of lending coordination between the IMF and other official lenders as a driver of IMF programs: Neither World Bank nor overall multilateral or official lending (as a % of GDP) emerged as significant predictors of program initiation, which suggests that any coordination among lenders is sufficiently weak to be counterbalanced by substitution effects between different types of lending. Finally, in the post-communist context, the promise of EU integration appears to have played a modest role during program initiation, as none of the integration wave dummies reached statistical significance (results omitted).

---

[5] Results were omitted for space reasons.

Political and Economic Importance and IMF Program Initiation

While the preceding sections have shown that on average program initiation is significantly more likely in countries experiencing various types of external vulnerability and financial crises, the discussion now turns to the complicated and contentious issue of the extent to which all crises receive equal treatment by the Fund. As discussed in chapter 2, this question involves testing the predictions of three ideal case scenarios of IMF lending: The first, *technocratic impartiality*, requires the IMF to treat all its members by the same technocratic standards, and would therefore predict that external crises should trigger the same responses from the IMF irrespective of when and where the crisis takes place. Moreover, under this scenario, we should observe no systematic differences in program access as a function of the country's international economic and political standing. The second scenario, *narrow interest-based preferential treatment*, involves certain countries receiving easier access to IMF lending due to pressures by large IMF shareholders on behalf of their economic and/or political allies. However, this scenario makes no specific predictions about the interaction between crisis intensity and economic/political importance, which means that preferential treatment could occur uniformly across a wide range of economic situations, or that it could be limited to either low- or high-crisis intensity situations. Finally, I consider the role of a third possible scenario—*systemically motivated preferential treatment*. Unlike the narrow interests driving the second scenario, these deviations can be justified on the basis of the Fund's systemic responsibility to ensure international financial and economic stability. Under this scenario, systemically important countries (e.g., large debtors or large markets) may receive preferential access to IMF funding during severe economic crises in order to avoid broader regional and global contagion effects of such crises. Therefore, we should observe a positive interaction effect between systemic importance and crisis intensity, which implies that the IMF should be more responsive to crises in large countries but should not extend special favors during periods of low/moderate financial distress.

Given that the previous section has already established the overall importance of external crisis as a program driver, proving the first scenario involves disproving the other two; in other words, the extent of technocratic impartiality is inversely proportional to the extent of narrow and/or systemic preferential treatment revealed by the tests of the last two scenarios. On the other hand, the two types of preferential treatment are not necessarily mutually exclusive in the sense that the IMF may grant favors to both systemically important countries and to economic/political allies of its large shareholders. Nonetheless, given the Fund's budget constraints during periods of high demand for IMF financial support, there may be a tradeoff between the two types of preferential treatment, which means that "frivolous" preferential treatment should be more frequent in situations where the broader international environment is more permissive, such as during the financial boom of much of the 1990s. Finally, it is important to remember that the relative weight and nature of such deviations from technocratic impartiality should be expected to vary across time and space in line with the changing demands of international financial markets and large IMF shareholders. In this respect, the systematic cross-temporal and cross-regional comparison used in this chapter provides an ideal testing ground for the shifting priorities of IMF lending.

PRIVATE FAVORS: PREFERENTIAL TREATMENT FOR WESTERN ALLIES DURING PROGRAM INITIATION

As discussed in the chapter 2 appendix, earlier work has identified a number of different proxies of economic and/or political importance, which may contribute to a country receiving preferential treatment by the IMF. While at the end of this section, I will briefly discuss the findings with respect to several other indicators, the present discussion focuses primarily on two of the most prominent aspects of linkages between developing and developed countries: geopolitical alliances and bilateral economic ties.

Since Thacker's (1999) influential article, the link between geopolitical orientation (as reflected in voting patterns in the UN General Assembly) and IMF conditionality enforcement has become one of the key "stylized facts" about the high politics of IMF lending (Stone and Steinwand 2008). However, while Thacker had identified temporal variation in the strength of these effects, the link between geopolitical context and the impact of UN voting patterns on IMF programs has not been explicitly addressed. In this context, the two episodes discussed in this chapter offer an interesting variation in context: On one hand, the Latin American votes of the 1980s were still cast in the "logic" of the Cold War competition between the United States and the Soviet Union, while the postcommunist voting occurred in the unipolar world of the 1990s. On the other hand, the United States' assertive stance toward geopolitical adventures in the Western Hemisphere may mean that the stakes of Latin American UN votes were lower than those of the West's erstwhile Cold War enemies in Eastern Europe and the former Soviet Union.

Even a brief look at the UN voting trends in the two regions reveals some interesting patterns. First, with the partial exception of the early 1990s, the UN voting records of Eastern European countries were much more closely aligned to those of the United States than the corresponding votes of Latin American countries in the 1980s.[6] Second, significant cross-country variation existed with both regions and broadly confirmed conventional wisdom about geopolitical alignments: in Latin America, Nicaragua was (unsurprisingly) among the least compliant, while Chile, Colombia, and a few Central American countries were closest to the United States. In Eastern Europe, the key dividing line was between Eastern Europe and the former Soviet Union. Finally, temporal trends were much stronger and clearer among the transition countries, which experienced a strong convergence with U.S. voting until 1995, followed by a renewed divergence in the late 1990s particularly for Russia and several other ex-Soviet republics.

The regressions in tables 3.1a and 3.1b suggest that preferential treatment of Western geopolitical allies during program initiation only occurred in post-communist Eastern Europe but not during the Latin American debt crisis: Thus, according to model 5 a U.S.-friendly UN voting record was at least a marginally significant predictor of initiation in Eastern Europe (.1 one-tailed) but not in Latin America. Moreover, judging by the results in model 6 of the two tables, Thacker's finding about countries being rewarded for moving politically closer to the United States is confirmed for Eastern Europe (significant at .01) but not for Latin America. These findings suggest that Western concerns with the geopolitical reorientation of the former Soviet bloc were more salient than U.S. concerns with its Western Hemisphere "backyard" even before the end of the Cold War.

In terms of bilateral economic ties, the statistical tests in this section focus on a given country's imports from the regional hegemon (the United States for Latin America and the EU for Eastern Europe) given that trading patterns confirm gravity models of trade whereby countries tend to trade more with geographically close partners.[7] The most striking cross-regional difference in trade patterns is their temporal evolution during the time periods in question: Whereas the hardships of the debt crisis meant that Latin America's imports from the West declined noticeably in the early- to mid-1980 before making a modest recovery at the end of the decade, Eastern Europe's post-communist trade reorientation translated into steadily rising imports from the EU, which suggests that we should expect greater bilateral trade effects on IMF lending in Eastern Europe. In terms of intraregional differences, Mexico was by far the largest market

---

[6] These cross-regional differences declined but did not disappear when comparing the two regions in the 1990s, a finding that raises some interesting questions about the reliability of this indicator in cross-regional analyses.

[7] However, the results do not change significantly for different trading partners (see the electronic appendix).

for U.S. goods and services, followed by Brazil and Venezuela at roughly a third of Mexican levels. Meanwhile in Eastern Europe, Poland was the largest market for EU exports, followed by Russia (prior to the 1998 crisis), the Czech Republic, and Hungary, and at some distance by Slovakia and Romania.

As predicted by Eastern Europe's ascendance as a growing market for Western goods, model 5 confirms that large importers of EU goods and services had noticeably easier access to IMF lending (significant at .05) though the results were not particularly large in substantive terms. Meanwhile, in Latin America, the effects of higher U.S. imports were positive but fell far short of statistical significance, which suggests that trade considerations played a modest role in the high politics of IMF lending during the Latin American debt crisis. For other potential indicators of economic and political importance, I found no additional evidence of preferential treatment in either region; thus, higher levels of bilateral aid (from a variety of donors) were not linked to easier IMF access, nor was there evidence that countries with larger populations or in closer geographic proximity to advanced industrial countries benefited from preferential treatment.

THE PRICE OF STABILITY: SYSTEMICALLY MOTIVATED PREFERENTIAL TREATMENT DURING PROGRAM INITIATION

While the analysis so far has identified some statistically significant but substantively moderate evidence for narrowly motivated preferential treatment in Eastern Europe, the evidence was much weaker for Latin America in the 1980s. However, the lack of such "frivolous" interference during the debt crisis does not necessarily mean that IMF conditionality during the debt crisis lived up to the technocratic impartiality principle. Given the threat posed by the potential default of Latin American debtors, it is possible that Western interests during this episode were simply more concerned with international financial stability, in which case we should expect to see preferential treatment patterns reflecting systemic rather than bilateral political and economic concerns.

Before discussing the statistical evidence for systemically based preferential treatment, it is useful to provide a brief overview of the two regions with respect to the two key indicators of systemic economic importance discussed in the appendix to chapter 2: total external debt and total imports. As discussed earlier, foreign debt was clearly the dominant Western concern in 1980s Latin America, and this concern is justified by the much greater total debt of the region, which amounted to $310bn in late 1981, almost twice as large as the corresponding debt of the ex-communist countries ($156bn) in late 1989. Because the survival of the highly exposed U.S. and British banks was the crucial concern of Western governments during the 1980s, the much larger threat to international financial stability posed by a possible debt repudiation by Latin American debtors becomes even clearer when we compare the total debt owed to commercial banks, which was three times higher in Latin America ($169bn in 1982) than in the former Soviet bloc ($55bn in 1989). By 2001 the combined debt of the transition economies had more than doubled to $381bn but only 30% of this debt was owed to commercial banks, reflecting the diversification of international capital flows during the 1990s. Somewhat surprisingly, after eight years of austerity and stagnation brought about by the debt crisis, the overall debt of the Latin American and Caribbean countries increased by another 50% to reach $475bn in late 1989, and even commercial bank debt had grown by 30% over the same time period.

In Latin America the largest debtors throughout the decade were Mexico, Brazil, and Argentina, which accounted for almost two thirds of the region's debt and were therefore the most likely candidates for preferential treatment. Of the other Latin American countries, arguably the only ones with potentially worrisome overall debt levels were Venezuela and to a lesser extent Chile (at least in the early 1980s). In Eastern Europe, the most important debtor was by far Russia, which had assumed the foreign debt of the Soviet Union and accounted for roughly 45% of regional debt in 1993, followed by Poland, whose debt made up another third of post-communist public debt even after the country's successful debt reduction negotiations in 1989. At the start of the transition, the only other Eastern European countries with significant foreign debt were Hungary and, to a lesser extent, Bulgaria. Despite the rapid growth of foreign debt over the course of the 1990s, the top rankings remained unchanged with the exception of Bulgaria being overtaken by Ukraine and the Czech Republic, none of which, however, amassed sufficient public debt to raise serious concerns among Western creditors.

Developing countries matter to the world economy not only as debtors but also as potential markets—hence their increasingly widespread designation as *emerging markets* in the 1990s. This aspect was particularly important in Eastern Europe, as the dramatic westward trade reorientation of the ex-communist countries created significant opportunities for international businesses to reach tens of millions of consumers in previously untapped markets. By comparison, Latin American imports declined for much of the 1980s at least in part due to pressures from the West and the IMF for countries to adjust exchange rates and curb domestic demand in order to raise the foreign currency necessary to honor their high external obligations. Therefore, differences in market size are expected to play a greater role in the politics of IMF programs in Eastern Europe than in Latin America.

In Eastern Europe, Russia started out as by far the largest importer, followed by Kazakhstan, Ukraine, and Poland. However, as trade in the former Soviet space declined and East-Central European countries grew at a much faster rate during the 1990s, by the end of the decade Poland had almost tied Russia in market size (around $50bn per year), with Hungary and the Czech Republic following closely behind (in the $30–35bn range), and Ukraine, Romania, Slovakia, and Slovenia the only other countries over the $10bn mark in 2000. Meanwhile in Latin America during the 1980s, the two largest overall markets for foreign goods and services were Brazil and Mexico, followed at some distance by Venezuela, and even farther behind by Argentina, Colombia, and Chile.

The statistical results in table 3.1a and 3.1b provide clear evidence that program initiation during the Latin American debt crisis and the post-communist transition was affected by systemically driven deviations from technocratic impartiality. However, unlike the implicit assumption of earlier studies, large debtors and markets were not uniformly more likely to enter IMF agreements than their smaller counterparts; thus, the coefficients for total debt in both regions failed to reach statistical significance (see models 1–3). Instead, in line with the predictions of the systemic argument, economically important countries had an easier time securing IMF programs when facing severe economic crises, as suggested by the strong interaction effects between size and crisis indicators in models 5 and 6 for the two regions. Since these interaction effects, which are crucial for understanding systemic preferential treatment, are difficult to read off of regression coefficients (especially for logit models), I illustrate the key findings graphically below.

Figure 3.4a illustrates the results of model 7 in table 3.1a by plotting the predicted probabilities of program initiation for Latin American countries during the 1980s as a function of the interest payment burden for a small debtor (set at the 10th percentile of the debt distribution in the sample) and a large debtor (set at the 90th percentile).[8] The graph reveals very different trajectories in the likelihood of program initiation as a function of the systemic importance of their overall debt; thus, whereas for the smallest debtors, higher interest payments were only a modest (and statistically insignificant) driver of initiation, for the largest debtors the effect was substantively large and statistical highly significant (at .001). In other words, IMF programs during the debt crisis were much more likely in situations where domestic concerns about honoring external obligations were reinforced by IMF concerns about systemic stability. This

---

[8] The other independent variables were set at their means/medians, and the horizontal axis in the graph captures the 5th to the 95th percentile of the logged interest payment burden of the countries in the sample.

Figure 3.4a: Debt, interest burden and initiation—Latin America (1982–89)

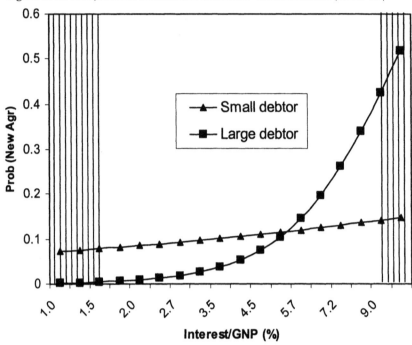

Note: Statistical significance for predictor variable: continuous line (p < .05), dotted line (p > .05). Statistical significance for modifying variable: shaded area (p < .05).

finding may explain the frequent presence of the region's largest troubled debtors—Mexico, Argentina, Chile (and to a lesser extent Brazil)—on the IMF program country roster of the 1980s, as well as the Fund's willing-ness to endorse heterodox stabilization efforts in Brazil and Argentina, despite the tensions between these policy packages and the standard pre-scriptions of IMF orthodoxy. Furthermore, figure 3.4a suggests that while large Latin American debtors received preferential access to IMF lending when facing serious crises (significant at .05 one-tailed), the effect disap-peared at moderate debt burdens and was even reversed in low-crisis situ-ations, where large debtors were actually less likely to enter an IMF agreement (significant at .05). Similar (but slightly weaker) interaction effects were obtained by using other proxies of economic importance (such as total imports, size of IMF quota or of GDP).[9]

---

[9] These results are omitted here for space reasons.

Despite the lower salience of foreign debt in the post-communist transition, model 7 in table 3.1b reveals a similar positive interaction between debt size and interest payment burden during Eastern European IMF program initiation. As in the Latin American case, interest payments mattered much more for larger debtors but as expected the effects were substantively weaker and only achieved statistical significance for the largest debtors (above the 80th percentile of debt size). Similarly, the effects of debt size were weaker in Eastern Europe; even though at high interest payment burdens (above the 75th percentile), the initiation odds were noticeably higher for large debtors (significant at .05 one-tailed), at low interest burdens, debt size was unimportant (but did not turn significantly negative as in Latin America).

For Eastern Europe, we can observe similar patterns for alternative measures of systemic economic importance and crisis intensity. Thus, according to model 8 in table 3.1b, there was a negative interaction between *total imports* and *foreign reserves*, which suggests that the Fund responded more decisively to liquidity crises when they occurred in large markets with greater potential repercussions for regional or global trade. As illustrated by figure 3.4b, low reserve levels were much more likely to result in IMF programs in countries with large markets; thus, for large markets (90th percentile), lower reserves were associated with a much higher likelihood of program initiation (significant at .001), while in small markets the effects were substantively modest and statistically inconclusive. As predicted by the systemic exceptionalism hypothesis, however, size was associated with greater IMF presence only in situations of extreme economic duress (significant at .05), that is, when large countries were at risk of suffering serious liquidity crises. As in the case of debt in Latin America, the trend was reversed in low-crisis situations, as economically important countries were actually less likely to initiate IMF programs when their foreign reserves were at reassuring levels.[10] Meanwhile in Latin America the interaction between reserves and imports was negligible, which reflects the lower salience of trade and liquidity crises during the debt crisis.

These findings confirm the importance of systemically motivated deviations from the principle of equal treatment during the debt crisis and the post-communist transition. Economically important countries had easier access to IMF funding but only when facing economic crises that were sufficiently severe to threaten broader international repercussions in the absence of IMF interventions. When not facing imminent crises, however, large countries were actually less likely to be involved with the

---

[10] However, the effect was only marginally statistically significant (at .1 for reserves above the 95th percentile).

Figure 3.4b: Market size, reserves, and initiation—Eastern Europe (1990–2001)

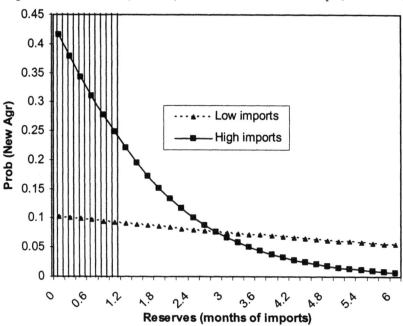

Note: Statistical significance for predictor variable: continuous line (p < .05), dotted line (p > .05). Statistical significance for modifying variable: shaded area (p < .05).

IMF. This somewhat surprising finding may reflect the fact that small countries are more dependent on the Fund's seal of approval during non-crisis situations since private lenders are less likely to expend resources to monitor the economic policies of small markets and therefore rely more heavily on IMF signaling.[11] However, this reversal also suggests an alternative conception of preferential treatment: Since IMF programs entail significant sovereignty costs, which are probably higher for large countries, the lower incidence of IMF programs in these countries during low-crisis environments may simply reflect their greater willingness and ability to resist the policy pressures associated with IMF conditionality. Seen from this perspective, economically important countries benefit both by being able to avoid IMF programs when not facing imminent economic pressures and by having fast-track access to IMF agreements when required by economic circumstances.

[11] This mechanism arguably explains the high incidence of precautionary IMF programs in the Baltic republics in the late 1990s despite their fairly healthy reserve positions and private capital access.

Economic and Political Drivers of IMF
Program Funding and Conditions

In addition to their relative timing, IMF programs differ along at least three other important parameters: the relative size of the committed funding, the range and depth of the policy conditions attached to the program, and the severity with which conditionality is enforced and deviations are punished. Since, as we have seen, not all countries and crises are created equal, the resulting differences in the bargaining positions of program countries vis-à-vis the IMF should also be reflected in cross-country variations in program funding and conditionality. From a systemic point of view, we should expect to see larger relative loans and laxer conditionality when economically important countries face significant crises. Meanwhile, if IMF programs are simply used by large shareholders to bestow favors on their allies, funding differences may be unrelated to crisis severity but simply reflect such bilateral ties.

Even though the centrality of direct funding to the success of IMF programs continues to be the subject of considerable debates, most governments do approach the Fund at least partly for the traditional purpose of obtaining temporary support for balance-of-payments difficulties. For such governments a larger monetary commitment from the IMF can provide much needed relief from international and domestic financial pressures, and in extreme cases can provide a political life raft for governments facing severe crises. Since countries are not obliged to draw on an existing loan commitment, larger loans should be preferable even for governments whose primary reason for program initiation is to have policy conditions imposed from the outside,[12] since larger loans provide a more credible "alibi" with respect to domestic political audiences. Unlike program initiation, which is a joint decision of the IMF and the government, the amount of funding committed to a given program is largely a decision of the Fund, and therefore reflects the economic and political priorities of the IMF (and its largest shareholders).

At first glance it appears as though the Fund was more generous during the debt crisis: Thus, the average Latin American IMF program was allotted 76% of the country's IMF quota, significantly more than the 43% committed for the typical Eastern European program in the 1990s. This difference may reflect the greater demands on IMF resources in the 1990s due to the rapid rise in the number of worldwide IMF programs. How-

---

[12] See Vreeland's (2003) argument that some governments seek IMF conditionality in order to weaken domestic political opposition to economic reforms, which the government wanted to pursue anyway.

TABLE 3.2
Drivers of Program Design and Enforcement

	Latin America		Eastern Europe				
	(1)	(2)	(3)	(4)	(5) #	(6)	(7)
	Loan size	Loan size	Loan size	Loan size	# structural conditions	# total conditions	# waivers
Total debt	.09#	.13*	.07*	.01	−.32*	−.17*	.18#
	(.06)	(.07)	(.04)	(.06)	(.15)	(.07)	(.14)
UN voting (t-1)	−.02*	−.02*	−.004	−.004	.03	.02#	.04**
	(.01)	(.01)	(.005)	(.005)	(.02)	(.01)	(.01)
Interest/GNI	−.06	−.09	−.10	−.08	−.08	−.13	−.10
	(.11)	(.12)	(.09)	(.09)	(.26)	(.18)	(.33)
Reserves (t-1)	−.04	.04	−.05#	−.18*	−1.01**	−.43**	−.04
	(.03)	(.07)	(.03)	(.08)	(.30)	(.16)	(.09)
Inflation (t-1)	−.01	.00	.10**	.08**	−.09	−.10*	.11
	(.04)	(.04)	(.03)	(.03)	(.07)	(.05)	(.10)
Regime	.016	.01	.025*	.02*	−.07#	−.04#	.04
	(.014)	(.01)	(.011)	(.012)	(.04)	(.03)	(.04)
Gov't ideology	.03	.02	−.04	−.04	.36	.03	.12
	(.04)	(.04)	(.07)	(.07)	(.35)	(.12)	(.37)
Quality of bureaucracy/ governance	−.06	−.05	−.03	−.01	.09	.16	−.72**
	(.07)	(.07)	(.06)	(.06)	(.21)	(.12)	(.27)
IMF Program History	−.34*	−.33*	−.23	−.27	−1.09#	−.82*	.97
	(.17)	(.17)	(.21)	(.21)	(.59)	(.40)	(.67)
GDP/capita	.02	.03	.04	.03	−.47**	−.34**	.29#
	(.03)	(.03)	(.04)	(.04)	(.17)	(.09)	(.15)
Total debt*Reserves		−.03#		.04#	.34**	.15**	
		(.02)		(.03)	(.09)	(.05)	
Total # conditions							.01**
							(.00)
Observations	44	44	72	72	44	44	264
R-squared	.77	.77	.61	.63	.21	.15	N/A

Standard errors in parentheses # significant at 10%; * significant at 5%; ** significant at 1%—one-tailed where appropriate

ever, these higher funding levels probably produced few real benefits to Latin American citizens, since most of the funds left the country almost immediately in the form of debt service payments.

Table 3.2 provides an overview of the economic and political drivers of IMF loan size (as a share of the quota) in the two episodes. Somewhat surprisingly, external economic vulnerability does not translate into substantially greater IMF generosity; thus, whereas lower reserves are at least marginally associated with larger loans in both regions (weakly significant at .1 one-tailed), higher interest payments appeared to have no discernible impact on IMF loan size. Among the economic crisis indicators, the only clear effect was the positive impact of higher inflation on loan size in Eastern Europe but there was no similar effect in Latin America.

To see how financial need is mediated by political considerations let us turn to the effects of economic and political importance indicators. As suggested by the positive and marginally significant effects of debt size in models 1 and 3, economically important countries received somewhat more generous loans in both regions. While one could argue that offering larger loans to countries like Brazil or Russia can be justified on systemic grounds, according to systemic stability theory such preferential treatment is only justifiable in extreme crisis situations.

According to the interaction effect in model 2, the systemic threat inherent in the Latin American debt crisis was once more reflected in preferential lending patterns: At comfortable reserve levels, small and large debtors received similar and statistically indistinguishable relative loan amounts, whereas in intense crisis situations large debtors secured noticeably larger loans (significant at .05 one-tailed). Moreover, lower reserves translated into larger loans for large debtors (.05 one-tailed) but not for systemically unimportant countries. In Latin America, similar interaction effects also occurred for other indicators of systemic importance (e.g., total imports) and economic crisis (e.g., interest payments). In Eastern Europe the picture was reversed and differences in IMF generosity were noticeable only in low-crisis situations; thus, judging by the positive interaction effect between debt size and reserves in model 4, large debtors received substantially more generous loans at high reserves (significant at .01) but during liquidity crises loans for smaller countries "caught up" and were statistically indistinguishable from those of systemically important countries. This practice cannot be justified as providing a global public good, since international financial stability would be better served if IMF largesse would occur in situations of serious financial need. Instead they are arguably reflective of a more narrowly motivated preferential treatment toward certain important countries, particularly Russia (Stone 2002).

In terms of other narrow interest-based drivers of loan size, the effects were generally modest in both regions. Thus, U.S. allies did not receive larger loans and in fact the effects of UN voting pointed in the wrong direction (especially in Latin America). Narrow economic interests also played a negligible role in driving IMF financial generosity toward the countries of the two regions, as a variety of bilateral trade measures failed to produce significant results. Alternative measures of "special status" potential, such as foreign aid and population size were also insignificant.

The only exception worth mentioning is the positive effect of regime type in Eastern Europe, which suggests that the IMF was more generous toward post-communist democracies. In Latin America, the effect was also positive but was substantively much smaller and failed to reach statistical significance, a finding that foreshadows the lower priority of democracy on the IMF agenda during the debt crisis, which will be discussed in chapters 5 and 6. Finally, the weak effects of *government orientation* in both regions suggest that there is no evidence of an ideological bias in IMF lending (at least when it comes to loan size).

Program Conditions

As discussed in the appendix to chapter 2, efforts to assess the relative toughness of IMF programs are significantly limited by the scarcity of data, and as a result the present discussion is limited to analyzing the number of conditions imposed in IMF programs from the ex-communist countries 1993–98. To the extent that the number of structural and total conditions is indicative of how demanding a given program is, the results offer at least some tentative evidence that economic crises affected IMF programs in a highly uneven fashion. Thus, in both models 5 and 6 we find a strong positive interaction effect between reserve levels and total debt, which is compatible with the predictions of systemic preferential treatment; thus, for large debtors, liquidity crises (i.e., lower reserves) were associated with a substantial decline in the number of structural and overall program conditions (significant at .01) but for less important countries greater financial distress actually resulted in programs with more conditions (significant at .001). In other words, liquidity crises appear to have strengthened the bargaining power of systemically important countries, while weakening that of most other IMF clients.

Meanwhile, there was no statistical support for narrowly motivated preferential treatment, in the sense that the coefficient for UN voting actually pointed in the wrong direction, and bilateral trade and aid indicators did not matter either (results omitted). Two domestic factors did, however, appear to affect program design: First, democracies received marginally fewer program conditions (.1 two-tailed), thereby confirming the pro-democratic bias in IMF lending to post-communist Eastern Europe. Second, *GDP/capita* was negative and significant (at .05 two-tailed), suggesting that the proliferation of structural and overall conditions occurred primarily in the Fund's poorest clients, which may reflect the Fund's attempt to compensate for the weak domestic capabilities of the governments of many poor countries.

Program Compliance

The preceding two sections have shown that Latin American and East European IMF programs were initiated at least in part in response to external financial crises, but that the Fund's response to these crises also reflected the reality of large differences in the political and economic importance of the countries in the two regions. However, program initiation and design only represent the first stages of the long and difficult economic adjustment process under IMF auspices. Compliance with IMF conditionality has been rather patchy; in both Latin America and Eastern Europe, countries involved in IMF programs were "in good standing" about two-thirds of the time. For the former communist countries slightly less than half of the IMF programs were completed in more or less their entirety, about one-fifth went off track early in the program and around a third either slipped in the later stages of the program or recovered after suffering some temporary setbacks. For Latin America the corresponding compliance record was slightly worse, with around two-fifths of programs completed, about a quarter significantly but not fully completed, while a third of programs went off track during their early stages. Given the high costs of partial reforms (Hellman 1998), this uneven implementation record is important for both theoretical and practical reasons.

As discussed in chapter 2, the implementation process should also reflect the tension between the technocratic imperatives of IMF lending and the temptation of large IMF shareholders to use these programs in the pursuit of narrow economic or political objectives. Thus, on one hand compliance should reflect the extent to which the government's economic policies meet the commitments assumed as part of the IMF program. As discussed earlier, this technocratic perspective would predict more conscientious implementation in countries confronting severe external crises since their governments have stronger financial incentives to adopt policies in line with their IMF commitments. In practice, however, this technocratic calculus may be affected by political considerations; while the domestic aspect of this political dimension will be discussed in chapters 5–6, from the perspective of the current discussion we are primarily concerned with the extent to which the Fund's enforcement of conditionality departs from technocratic impartiality for either systemic or narrow "realist" reasons.

Program Waivers: The Politics of Uneven Enforcement

Given that program compliance patterns reflect the actions of both government efforts and IMF rigidity, it is useful to focus briefly on a program aspect that is more clearly driven by the Fund's choice of how strictly to enforce conditionality, namely the number of program waivers given to individual countries within a given IMF program. The Fund can waive one or more program conditions in situations where circumstances beyond the government's control make it difficult to fulfill the original program targets. While such waivers are important for program flexibility in an unpredictable international environment, they can also be used to allow certain countries to get away with deviations from IMF conditionality without having to pay the price of noncompliance.

The correlates of program waivers in Eastern Europe, presented in model 7 of table 3.2, confirm the importance of political criteria in postcommunist IMF programs. Thus, large debtors received significantly more waivers, and since these deviations were not limited to extreme crisis situations,[13] they cannot be justified in purely systemic terms. In terms of narrow "realist" drivers of program waivers, the positive and significant (at .01) effect of *UN voting* suggests that Western allies were more likely to get a break when encountering implementation setbacks.[14] Combined with the Fund's preferential treatment of democracies with respect to loan size and number of conditions, this finding suggests that the West used IMF lending to support its broader strategy of promoting the political reorientation of its erstwhile ideological rivals. While the success of this transformation may be considered a global public good, it arguably falls outside the Fund's institutional mission, and as such constitutes a nonsystemic deviation from technocratic impartiality.

Drivers of Compliance

FINANCIAL NEED

As in the case of initiation, external financial need should be a predictor of program compliance, since countries in more precarious external financial situations should be more dependent on the funding and signaling benefits associated with program implementation.

The statistical results in table 3.3 largely confirm the importance of external financial need during implementation but they also reflect the different economic priorities of the two crises. Thus, in line with the exigencies of the debt crisis, model 1 suggests that in Latin America higher interest-payment burdens were associated with much greater IMF program compliance, and the effect was both statistically significant (at .001)

---

[13] Interaction effects were negligible between total debt and reserves and negative between total debt and interest payments (results omitted).

[14] On the other hand neither bilateral aid nor bilateral trade had a significant impact (results omitted).

TABLE 3.3
International Drivers of Program Compliance

	Latin America					Eastern Europe				
	(1)	(2)	(3)	(4)	(5)	(6)	(7)	(8)	(9)	(10)
Reserves (t-1)	−.20*	−.27*	−.29*	−.21*	−.23*	−.48*	−.32#	−.60**	−.59**	−.58
	(.11)	(.13)	(.12)	(.12)	(.12)	(.19)	(.18)	(.21)	(.19)	(.39)
Interest/GNP	2.03**	1.99**	2.81**	2.02**	.08	−.23	−.84	−1.71*	−1.58*	−.23
	(.57)	(.56)	(.62)	(.55)	(.71)	(.59)	(.63)	(.81)	(.68)	(.57)
Total debt	−.06	−.19	−.36		−4.19**	−.27	−.64**	−.26		−.33
	(.32)	(.32)	(.30)		(1.27)	(.21)	(.22)	(.24)		(.30)
Quality of bureaucracy/ governance	.31	.59#	.35	.07	.59#	.37	.19	.41	.65*	.37
	(.33)	(.34)	(.33)	(.34)	(.33)	(.44)	(.36)	(.51)	(.36)	(.40)
Regime	−.061#	−.10*	−.05	−.04	−.04	.18*	.14#	.13	.16#	.18*
	(.046)	(.05)	(.05)	(.04)	(.05)	(.09)	(.08)	(.09)	(.08)	(.08)
Gov't ideology	−.22	−.18	−.25	−.24	−.21	.06	−.25	.28	.05	.09
	(.20)	(.19)	(.20)	(.20)	(.20)	(.48)	(.47)	(.53)	(.49)	(.48)
Inflation (t-1)	.59#	.37	.57	.55#	.81*	.19	.14	.16	.22	.19
	(.36)	(.32)	(.37)	(.32)	(.37)	(.19)	(.19)	(.22)	(.20)	(.20)
IIS Credit Rating		.22#					.07			
		(.13)					(.17)			
IIS Credit Rating (squared)		−.005#					−.000			
		(.003)					(.003)			
Official funding/GDP				−.17*						
				(.08)						
EU first tier								4.29**		
								(1.44)		
EU third tier								.26		
								(1.20)		
Imports from US				.28						
				(.25)						
Imports from EU									.10	
									(.18)	
UN voting				.04					.06#	
				(.06)					(.04)	
Total debt* Interest/GNP					2.14**					
					(.63)					
Total debt* Reserves										.02
										(.12)
Inverse Mills ratio	3.99**	4.36**	3.85**	3.89**	4.27**	2.84**	2.91**	2.78**	2.98**	2.91**
	(.86)	(.97)	(.85)	(.83)	(.90)	(.63)	(.61)	(.60)	(.65)	(.64)
Observations	255	251	255	255	255	404	404	404	404	404

Logistic regression coefficients with standard errors in parentheses # significant at 10%; * significant at 5%; ** significant at 1%—one-tailed where appropriate.

Figure 3.5a: Substantive effects of program compliance—Latin America (1982–89)

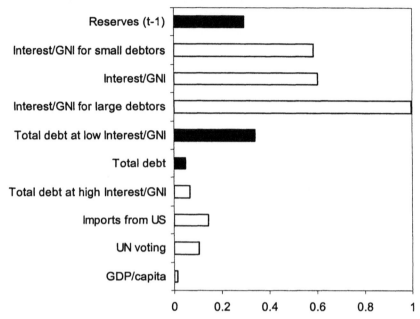

Note: Effects represent change in compliance probability for a change in the variable of interest from the 10th to the 90th percentile. Negative effects are marked as black bars.

and substantively large (see figure 3.5a). Meanwhile, in Eastern Europe the effect of higher interest payments was much weaker and actually pointed in the "wrong" direction.

Post-communist governments were nonetheless significantly affected by external financial considerations in their implementation "calculus": model 6 in table 3.3 indicates that countries with more comfortable reserve positions were much less likely to comply with IMF demands (significant at .01). By comparison, immediate liquidity concerns played a more modest role in Latin America, as indicated by the weaker substantive and statistical significance of *international reserves* in model 1 in table 3.3. This difference may reflect the fact that even relatively healthy reserve levels were weak guarantees of financial solvency in Latin America, given the much greater burden of foreign debt servicing.

The implementation dynamics of IMF programs in the two regions also differed significantly in terms of the implications of varying degrees of credit-worthiness. While the most likely program initiation candidates in both regions had been countries with intermediate credit scores, the

Figure 3.5b: Substantive effects of program compliance—Eastern Europe (1990–2001)

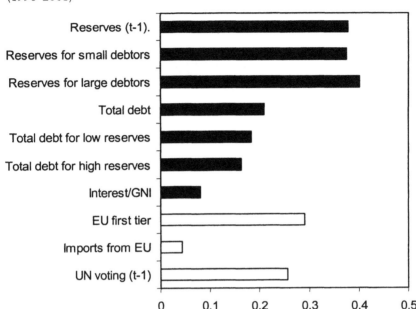

Note: Effects represent change in compliance probability for a change in the variable of interest from the 10th to the 90th percentile. Negative effects are marked as black bars.

results in figure 3.6 (based on models 2 and 7 in table 3.3) reveal an interesting divergence during implementation, which reflect the important implications of the differences in international context for the two IMF program episodes.

In Latin America compliance was highest among middle range countries, which had better capital markets prospects than the basket cases at the low end of the IIS rating scale, but were more dependent on IMF funding than the countries with high credit ratings. By contrast, among the transition economies, the likelihood of compliance increased monotonically with better credit ratings, and the effect was strongest in the upper ranges of the IIS rating scale. On the one hand, this difference may be due to the greater frequency of precautionary programs in Eastern Europe discussed earlier, since governments only enter precautionary IMF programs if they are reasonably confident that they can complete them (and hence reap the signaling benefits associated with compliance). On the other hand, the difference also reflects the greater relative importance of direct IMF lending in Latin America in the context in which the utility

Figure 3.6: Credit ratings and compliance

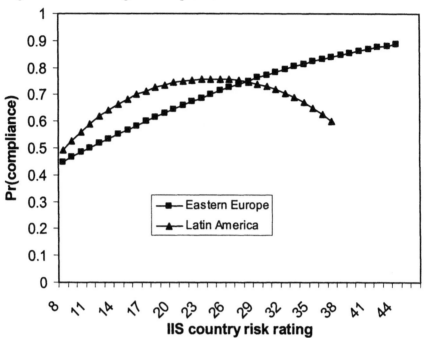

of IMF signaling to private capital markets was undermined by the wide-spread reluctance of private lenders to extend additional loans to this troubled region.

However, as discussed earlier, compliance with IMF programs can serve as a signal not only for private lenders but also for official funding sources. To the extent that official lenders explicitly and consistently condition their support on IMF approval, such coordination could greatly strengthen the Fund's leverage over program countries but the extent of coordination and the relative attractiveness of such linked benefits are likely to depend on the temporal and regional context. In Eastern Europe the golden goal of EU integration provided both substantial incentives and stringent economic conditionality, part of which was closely tied to the achievement of economic stabilization and structural reforms that also figured prominently on the IMF agenda. While the earlier analysis showed that likely EU candidates were not more likely to initiate IMF programs, model 8 indicates that such countries were significantly more likely to comply an existing IMF program (significant at .01). This finding suggests that the fears about the negative EU integration repercussions of an IMF program breakdown served as a significant additional implementation incentive in Eastern Europe. By contrast, in the absence of a similar regional integration project, in Latin America official lending did not play a similar catalytic role; in fact, according to model 3 in table 3.3, countries with greater reliance on official lending were less likely to comply with IMF programs (marginally significant at .1 two-tailed). This somewhat surprising finding suggests that in the absence of effective coordination between official lenders (see e.g., Tussie and Botzman 1992) program countries may consider different official lenders as potential substitutes, which lowers their dependence on any given lender and reduces compliance with IMF conditionality.

ECONOMIC AND POLITICAL IMPORTANCE DURING IMPLEMENTATION

In light of the earlier evidence of preferential treatment during program initiation and design, one might reasonably expect similar patterns at the implementation stage, as political pressures on the IMF to extend funding to economically and politically important countries may supersede technocratic concerns about the long-term credibility of conditionality. However, as suggested by the theoretical discussion, countries with greater political leverage are likely to be aware of their special status, and may, therefore, pursue economic policies that deviate significantly from program targets, thereby triggering the suspension of the program despite the Fund's greater leniency. This logic is supported by prior work on post-communist IMF programs (Stone 2002) that found that large countries (especially Russia) were at least as likely to be punished for IMF noncompliance as their smaller counterparts, but that their punishment spells were shorter, thereby allowing a faster return into the fold of the IMF.

Turning to the statistical evidence, the implementation-stage patterns do not reveal significant deviations from technocratic uniformity due to the economic and geopolitical interests of large IMF shareholders. Thus, in Latin America both higher *U.S. imports* and closer *UN voting* records were associated with better compliance records during the debt crisis but the results failed to reach statistical significance. In Eastern Europe, EU imports had no impact on implementation but the UN voting record was positive and marginally significant (.1 one-tailed), in line with the greater role of geopolitics in post-communist IMF programs. Other potential indicators of special status—such as bilateral aid from various donors—were not associated with higher compliance, and even pointed in the wrong direction (results omitted).

Compared to the uniformly weak evidence for narrow interest-based preferential treatment, support for systemic exceptionalism varied greatly by region. In Latin America, in line with the international threat posed by the debt crisis, implementation patterns once again confirm that severe crises triggered different responses in countries of different systemic impor-

Figure 3.7a: Debt, interest burden, and compliance

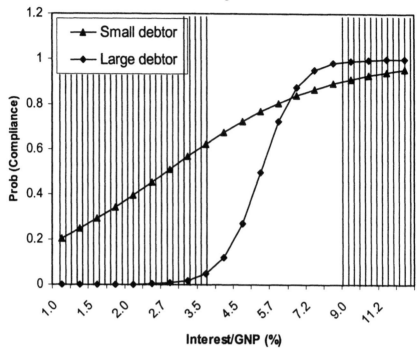

Note: Statistical significance for predictor variable: continuous line (p < .05), dotted line (p > .05). Statistical significance for modifying variable: shaded area (p < .05).

tance: Figure 3.7a (based on the interaction effect in model 5 in table 3.3) shows that at low interest-burden levels small Latin American debtors had a much better compliance record than their economically more important counterparts (significant at .01) but for the latter compliance improved more dramatically with higher interest burdens. Therefore, at very high levels of interest payments (above 10% of GNP) large countries actually had a compliance advantage over smaller countries (statistically significant at .05) in line with the expectations of systemic preferential treatment.[15] Similar (but slightly weaker) interactions were found using alternative crisis and systemic importance indicators, such as reserves and total imports (results omitted). These interaction effects suggest that during the Latin American debt crisis systemically important countries did not receive pref-

[15] However, the difference was small in substantive terms (see fig. 3.4a) because under such financial duress predicted compliance probabilities were very high for all types of countries.

Figure 3.7b: Debt, reserves, and compliance—Eastern Europe (1990–2001)

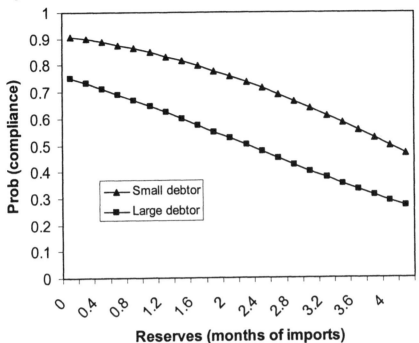

Note: Statistical significance for predictor variable: continuous line (p < .05). Modifier variable was not statistically significant.

erential treatment in relatively low-crisis environments, and were in fact more likely to get "punished" by having credit tranches withheld. However, in serious crisis situations compliance levels in large countries "caught up" and even exceeded those of their smaller counterparts, which suggests that under such circumstances concerns about the regional and global consequences of an economic collapse superseded the competing concerns about maintaining the credibility of IMF conditionality.

By contrast, among the transition countries, systemically important countries did not have an implementation advantage under any economic circumstances; indeed, judging by figure 3.7b based on the interaction effect in model 10 in table 3.3, reserves mattered equally for small and large debtors, and debt size was negative (and barely missed statistical significance) for low/medium reserve levels. This compliance deficit of large transition countries is surprising considering the earlier findings about the larger loans and the higher frequency of waivers granted to privileged countries. In other words, greater IMF flexibility toward policy deviations by systemically important countries does not mean that such countries can deviate from program targets with impunity. However, the costs of such punishments were probably mitigated by the prompter initiation of IMF programs in response to financial distress, a conclusion that is broadly compatible with Stone's (2002) findings that larger countries are more likely to get punished but suffer shorter punishment spells than their smaller counterparts.

Conclusion

The statistical evidence presented in this chapter confirms the importance of external financial crises as drivers of IMF programs in Latin America and Eastern Europe. Moreover, in both regions, IMF programs appear to have been driven not only by the promise of direct funding from the IMF but also by the expected signaling benefits of IMF policy approval for third-party lenders. However, in line with the theoretical approach advanced by this book, the chapter has shown that the effects of such crises and policy signals are not uniform but rather depend on the nature of the broader international economic and political context and on the particular position of a given country in the global economy. The policy repercussions of external financial crises do not simply reflect the economic adjustment efforts of program country governments but also the nature of the Fund's push, which in turn hinges on the importance of a given crisis to large Western shareholders (for either systemic or narrower interest-based reasons).

In response to the pressing Western concerns with international financial stability and the survival of leading commercial banks, the IMF interventions in Latin America were primarily targeted at avoiding the outright default of the Latin American countries, and especially of the region's largest debtors. The emphasis on debt repayment is reflected by the clear statistical evidence in this chapter about the crucial role of the debt service burden as a driver of the IMF program initiation and implementation. The deviations from technocratic impartiality in IMF lending also reflected the centrality of systemic concerns on the agenda of the Fund and its largest shareholders; thus, under normal economic circumstances large debtors did not benefit from preferential treatment, and in fact may have been less likely to initiate and implement IMF programs. However, when facing severe external crises, which may have jeopardized broader regional and international stability, such systemically important countries benefited from faster program initiation, more generous loans, and more forgiving program design/enforcement. The fact that external crises mattered much more for program initiation and implementation in large countries confirms that IMF programs reflect not only the demand by the recipient country but also the Fund's supply-side considerations. While the Fund's concern with large debtors is justified by its systemic mandate as a guardian of international financial stability, its rather weak and inflexible response to financial distress in small countries raises more troubling questions about the way the IMF served its smaller constituents during the Latin American debt crisis. On the other hand, the Fund's focus on systemic priorities also meant that IMF programs during the debt crisis show very little evidence of narrow economic or geopolitical interference with IMF lending by its largest shareholders.

While external financial need was also a key driver of post-communist IMF programs, the main concern of Eastern European governments was not debt repayment but gaining access to hard-currency credits to overcome the critically low foreign reserve levels inherited from the communist period. As a result, transition countries were more likely than their Latin American counterparts to initiate and implement IMF programs once they had (re)gained access to private capital markets. The lower international financial threat posed by the post-communist transition is reflected in the more inconsistent empirical support for the systemic exceptionalism hypothesis in Eastern Europe; while in terms of program timing and program design (number of conditions) preferential treatment for large economies was indeed limited to extreme crisis situations, the same cannot be said about loan size and program waivers, where size-based favoritism occurred even when economic conditions did not warrant such exceptions. Moreover, Western geopolitical allies had easier access to IMF programs and were more likely to receive program waivers, suggesting that IMF conditionality was at least partly subordinated to the broader Western goal of promoting the geopolitical reorientation of the former Soviet bloc.

Therefore, despite the numerous similarities in IMF program dynamics revealed by this chapter, the Fund's role in the two regions differed in important ways, which are reflected in both in its interactions with individual countries (chapter 4) and in the domestic politics of IMF programs (chapters 5 and 6). Given the zero-sum nature of debt repayment during the Latin American debt crisis, the Fund's attempts to mediate between Western lenders and Latin American debtors were inevitably bound to generate significant domestic and international political tensions about the appropriate distribution of adjustment costs. In such an international context, IMF conditionality was more likely to be regarded as a Western imposition on structurally disadvantaged developing countries despite the fact that the Fund's deviations from technocratic impartiality were justifiable in terms of preserving international financial stability, which is a global public good and one of the Fund's core missions. By contrast, during the post-communist transition, the more favorable international financial context of the 1990s lending boom meant that the IMF had the opportunity to play a much less controversial role as a reform "coach" for countries eager to (re)gain access to international financial markets. Even though IMF programs in Eastern Europe were neither universally welcomed nor uniformly implemented, they nevertheless largely eschewed the zero-sum nature of the international distributional conflicts that had marked the politics of IMF-style reforms during the Latin American debt crisis.

−4−

Navigating External Crises: Case Study Evidence

To complement the statistical findings about the international drivers of IMF programs, this chapter provides a more detailed account of the role of external financial need and economic/geopolitical importance in shaping the interactions between the IMF and individual Latin American and Eastern European countries. Among the Latin American countries, the chapter traces the trajectories of Argentina, Peru, Bolivia, and Chile, four cases that illustrate a variety of IMF interactions, ranging from showcase cooperation in Chile and post-1985 Bolivia, to frequent involvement and patchy compliance in Argentina, and outright rebellion in post-1985 Peru. In Eastern Europe, the surprisingly close IMF relations of Moldova illustrate the powerful draw of IMF funding and legitimacy for economically and politically vulnerable countries, while the more conflictual relationship between the Mečiar government in Slovakia and the Fund demonstrates that even extreme financial need is not a sufficient condition for IMF program initiation and implementation, especially in the context of the tight constraints on acceptable economic policies imposed by IMF conditionality in the mid-1990s.

These brief case studies, whose domestic aspects will be analyzed in more detail in chapter 6, serve two main purposes: First, they illustrate how financial need affected the initiation and implementation of IMF programs across a broad range of situations whose international contexts differed with respect to the size and importance of the country, as well as regional and temporal variations of IMF conditionality. Thus, the chapter contrasts the trajectory of Argentina, one of the region's largest debtors, to that of more marginal countries like Bolivia or Peru, and confirms the more active involvement of the IMF in countries considered pivotal to international financial stability. The contrast between Mečiar's Slovakia and Garcia's Peru on the one hand, and Alfonsín's Argentina on the other, suggests that size also mattered with respect to the severity with which anti-Western rhetoric and deviations from economic orthodoxy were punished by the Fund.

Second, the cases contribute to a richer understanding of the complex international dynamics of IMF programs by discussing country-specific factors that cannot be properly captured by cross-national statistical tests but are nevertheless theoretically interesting and empirically important. For example, issues such as the war on drugs in Bolivia, or Moldova's precarious geopolitical position are important for understanding the trajectories of IMF programs in individual countries. However, the case studies can also identify mechanisms of broader theoretical relevance for understanding the relations between the Fund and developing countries; thus, the ability of certain countries (such as Moldova, Chile, and post-1985 Bolivia) to enhance their political importance by playing the role of showcase reform examples, suggests an interesting deviation from the determinism implied by the statistical results about the uphill battle facing economically marginal countries trying to obtain preferential treatment from the IMF.

Bolivia: The Costs and Benefits of Geopolitical Marginality

At the outset of the 1980s, the Bolivian economy had all the ingredients for economic disaster even when compared to the low regional standards, and during the first half of the decade, the situation continued to decline precipitously. Like many of its neighbors, Bolivia had contracted a sizable foreign debt under the military regime in the context of the boom mentality of the 1970s. Unfortunately, despite being accompanied by commodity-driven solid economic growth until the late 1970s, only a small proportion of these capital inflows resulted in productive capital investments, nor did they lead to significant improvements in the living standards of Bolivia's impoverished population but instead resulted in massive capital flight that by 1980–81 exceeded 10% of GNP (Sachs 1986). Therefore, when capital flows reversed in 1982, the Bolivian economy was singularly ill prepared to weather the external and internal adjustment process required by the exigencies of the debt crisis.

Crisis at the Periphery: Bolivia under Siles

By the time the democratic government of Hernán Siles Zuazo assumed power in late 1982, Bolivia's foreign debt had become a crushing burden on its economy and society. The relative indebtedness was very high (amounting to 114% of the country's annual GNP), thereby placing the country on a par with an unenviable group of highly indebted sub-Saharan African countries hardest hit by the debt crisis. The costs of servicing this debt were exacerbated when the economic slowdown of the late 1970s turned to full-blown recession in 1982–83 (with an annual decline of 4.5% of GDP) and the international price for Bolivia's primary commodities (tin and fuels) declined sharply after 1979 (Klein 1992:271), thereby leading to a sharp decline in exports and foreign currency inflows. Thus, at the beginning of the debt crisis Bolivia's interest payments accounted for a staggering 44.8% of export earnings and 14.2% of GNP, whereas total debt service amounted to 59% of exports, one of the highest debt burdens in the region. The situation improved only after the quasi collapse of the economy in 1985, first due to the temporary suspension of debt payments in conjunction with the aggressive stabilization program of the new Paz government and later as a result of the substantial debt reductions approved by Western donors after 1987. Nevertheless, despite a significant reduction in the level of interest payments (from more than 14% of GNP in 1984 to around 2.8% in 1988–89), overall indebtedness remained high by the end of the decade (92% of GNP in 1989 down from a peak of 171% in 1984), and debt service was still above the regional average in the second half of the 1980s. Meanwhile, the country's foreign reserves, which were mostly below the regional average and declined to critically low levels between mid-1987 and 1988, hardly provided the necessary buffer against short-term capital flow fluctuations.

Considering Bolivia's extremely fragile external position throughout the decade and the Fund's role as an international lender of last resort, Bolivia should have been a prime candidate for IMF programs in the 1980s. Nonetheless, Bolivia did not secure its first IMF standby agreement until June 1986, almost four years after the debut of the debt crisis. While part of this surprising delay was due to the reluctance and inability of Bolivia's leftist government to implement the tough adjustment measures required by IMF conditionality between 1982 and 1985,[1] the relations between Bolivia and the Fund cannot be simply blamed on ideological conflict. Unlike the more confrontational approach of Garcia in Peru and even Alfonsín in Argentina, President Siles, whose track record with IMF program implementation went back to his first stint as a president in 1957, tried to maintain good relations with the West and the IMF. This conciliatory approach is best reflected by the continuation of debt service payments until May 1984 even though these payments exacted a steep price from the crumbling Bolivian economy without being rewarded by access to financing from either private or multilateral lenders. Even after the center-right reformist government of Paz came to power in mid-1985, it took another year for the first IMF program to materialize.

---

[1] The role of partisan politics on economic policies in Bolivia is discussed in more detail in chapter 6.

What explains this remarkably hands-off approach of the IMF in Bolivia, especially in the context of its intense involvement in other highly indebted Latin American countries during the same time period? The statistical results in the previous chapter have suggested that higher levels of financial distress were less likely to result in IMF program initiation in smaller countries, such as Bolivia, since they represented lower threats to regional and international financial stability and were, therefore, lower on the very busy agenda of the Fund. Therefore, the discussion below analyzes the Bolivian experience with IMF conditionality in the 1980s from the perspective of the country's marginal international position in the context of the debt crisis.

Bolivia's high level of relative indebtedness did not create serious political concerns among Western lenders because the overall size of the debt was relatively low by regional and global standards ($3.3bn), and therefore presented no threat to the stability of Western commercial banks. Thus, the exposure of the top nine Western commercial banks to Bolivian debt was only $44m by mid-1987, compared to $15.8bn for Brazil at the same time point (Sachs 1987). The country's marginal international status did not change substantially after the return to democracy in late 1982, even though it somewhat alleviated the country's international isolation compared to the final two years of the military regime, particularly during the violent rule of Garcia Mesa in 1980–81.

In an international context in which debt service moratoriums were not yet widespread and therefore carried high political costs, the Siles government continued to honor its debt service obligations until mid-1984 in an effort to avoid a renewed international pariah status. However, these payments exacted a heavy toll on the Bolivian economy and exacerbated fiscal imbalances and inflationary pressures. Despite an external burden compared by some observers to the war reparations in interwar Germany (Pastor 1992:69), Bolivia was unable to secure an IMF program to reduce the short-term consequences of its government's continuing debt-service payments. While the economic consequences of this hands-off approach were hardly ideal (since they delayed the access to much-needed funds), the less intense political pressure of IMF conditionality gave the Siles government a slightly wider maneuvering space, and may have prevented the further escalation of social tensions and thereby reduced the likelihood of democratic breakdown. Nevertheless, Bolivia's experience with international financial markets in the early years of the debt crisis epitomizes the "all pain no gain" nature of economic adjustment in Latin America in the early 1980s and illustrates the statistical findings about the weak impact on IMF programs of economic crises in systemically marginal countries.

The Paz Government and Its Unexpected Allies:
Jeffrey Sachs, the IMF, and the U.S. Government

Compared to the grim picture of the first part of the decade, after 1985, Bolivia stands out for the unusually cordial tone of its government's relations with international financial institutions, as well as for the relative flexibility of IMF conditionality and the generous terms of the country's debt renegotiation process. Since Latin America during the debt crisis is quite possibly the last place to look for evidence of benevolent Western interventions in developing countries, how can we explain this remarkable turnaround in the country's fortunes? I will argue that this unexpected external boost for the Bolivian reformers can be explained by a fortuitous combination of a number of factors—its marginal importance in the context of the debt crisis, its symbolic role as a poster child for neoliberal reforms and the political priorities of the U.S. war on drugs—which will be discussed in more detail below.

By 1985 Bolivia's relatively low overall debt was of minimal concern to Western financial interests, the more so since the secondary market value of the country's debt had already been reduced to a fraction of its initial value,[2] since repayment looked increasingly unrealistic considering the country's poverty and disastrous economic crisis. Ironically, however, the very marginality that contributed to the failure of the Siles government to secure an IMF agreement prior to 1984 allowed the Paz government more flexibility in the design of its economic program, which was not backed by an IMF program during its first ten crucial months. By avoiding the strict constraints of IMF conditionality, the Paz government was able to delay the resumption of debt-service payments, whose burden could have easily undermined the fragile emerging economic and political stability of the country by providing a rallying point for the losers of the painful adjustment process. The costs of this delay in debt-service resumption were relatively low for both sides; for Bolivia, the sanctions triggered by the moratorium were largely irrelevant, since the country was already excluded from any significant external financing sources after its default in May 1984. Meanwhile, Western lenders (and the IMF) were less concerned with the economic fallout of a temporary moratorium in a small debtor like Bolivia, whereas a similar action may have triggered a stronger reaction in the case of one of the large debtors. Nonetheless, the normalization of relations with the international financial institutions, particularly the IMF, was high on the agenda of the Paz government, since it constituted an important precondition for the resumption of official lend-

---

[2] Thus, by mid-1987, Bolivian debt was trading at 10 cents to the dollar in the secondary market for developing country debt (Sachs and Huizinga 1987).

ing without which the long-term economic recovery of Bolivia seemed highly unlikely.

The answer to Bolivia's international financial dilemma— the tension between the need for IMF approval and the pursuit of economic and political stabilization, which was potentially undermined by standard IMF program requirements such as the reduction of debt arrears and currency devaluations—came in the person of Jeffrey Sachs, the Harvard economist who had advised Banzer during the 1985 presidential campaign, and who became the official economic adviser of the Paz government in January 1986. Sachs not only supported the Bolivian government's decision to delay debt payments and to defend the currency during the inflationary spike following the collapse of tin prices in December 1985, but he became an influential lobbyist for Bolivia in its negotiations with the IMF and conferred a crucial sense of credibility and expertise to the policy decisions of the Paz government. The success of this approach became clear in June 1986, when, after expressing reservations for several months, the IMF agreed to a standby agreement in June 1986 without requiring any changes to the existing framework of the Bolivian government's economic policy program (Conaghan and Malloy 1994:196). Within the context of the formal model, Sachs's role in facilitating the initiation of the IMF agreement can be interpreted as a reduction of institutional uncertainty through his contribution to the formulation of a coherent economic reform program.

Following the initiation of the IMF standby agreement in June 1986, the Bolivian government's commitment to orthodox economic reform was finally rewarded not only through the direct IMF disbursements of SDR 114.9 million in the second half of 1986,[3] but more importantly a rescheduling of Paris Club debt (to official lenders) in June 1986, as well as the initiation of a debt renegotiation process with the commercial banks, which was concluded in 1987 with an agreement whereby Bolivia was allowed to repurchase half its debt in the secondary market at eleven cents to the dollar and to reschedule the rest of the outstanding debt. The remarkable leniency of the IMF and other Western lenders during this period—manifested not only in the surprisingly generous terms of the debt renegotiations[4] but also in the ability of the Bolivian government to obtain new official loans even as it continued to default

[3] Its funding consisted of SDR 32 million through regular standby disbursements, SDR 64 million in compensatory financing for export shortfalls and SDR 18 million through the lower conditionality Structural Adjustment Facility (SAF) initiated in December 1986.

[4] As Pastor (1992:91) points out, developing countries are usually prohibited from entering the secondary market for their own debt obligations because such an option would give them the perverse incentive to restrict their debt service intentionally in order to be able to repurchase their own debt at a lower price.

on its foreign debt service—suggests that Bolivia became the beneficiary of a politically motivated deviation from the usual strict constraints of IMF conditionality.

The relative leniency of IMF conditionality in Bolivia, however, only applied to the external requirements of IMF programs but not to deviations from domestic reform measures. Thus, the IMF withheld funding for much of 1987 in response to the rising budget deficit incurred by the Bolivian government in its effort to fuel economic growth by raising public investment. Aware that the country's macroeconomic stability depended to a large extent on the continuation of amicable relationships with the IMF and foreign creditors, the Paz government reversed its expansionary policies. This reversal may have contributed to its electoral defeat in 1989 but was successful in restoring Bolivia's status as a showcase for neoliberal reforms and was rewarded in July 1988 with the signing of a multiyear Enhanced Structural Adjustment Facility (ESAF) program, whose benefits were supplemented by additional compensatory financing for export shortfalls. Bolivia's successful orthodox reforms in a reasonably democratic context placed it in an ideal position to reap the financial benefits of becoming a showcase example for Western promoters of neoliberal economic policies in a regional context characterized by heterodox deviations from IMF conditionality in the mid-to-late 1980s (e.g., in Argentina, Brazil, and Peru). However, unlike the exceptional status arising from economic or military importance, Bolivia's preferential status was contingent on the strict adherence to the economic tenets of neoliberalism, which drastically restricted the policy maneuvering space of the Paz government.

A similarly mixed blessing underlies the second source of political exceptionalism that influenced Bolivia's interaction with the West, and by extension the IMF: the participation of the Paz government in the U.S.-led war on drugs, meant to reduce the supply of cocaine to Western markets. On the one hand the willingness of the Bolivian government to cooperate with the United States' campaign against coca leaf production in the Andean countries played an important role not only in bringing about U.S. political pressures on the IMF and Western commercial banks for favorable treatment of Bolivia, but it was also an important driver in the rapid increase of Western foreign aid inflows into Bolivia, which rose from $117m in 1984 to $396m in 1987 and became an important source of foreign currency for the Bolivian government. On the other hand, however, the economic costs of the crackdown on coca leaf producers had a serious negative impact on the Bolivian economy, not only because the revenues from illegal coca exports accounted for half the country's total export earnings and for an important portion of deposits in the Bolivian banking system, but also because it exacerbated the poverty of some of the country's least developed rural regions, where the livelihood of more than a quarter million farmers depended on the crop. In addition to these real economic costs, the expectation of export revenue shortfalls associated with the war on drugs fueled speculations about the inevitability of a currency devaluation in the summer of 1986, thereby contributing to the maintenance of high interest rates, which in turn hurt economic recovery (Sachs 1986:33–34).

Overall, the international dynamics of Bolivian reforms in the second part of the 1980s were rather unique by regional standards, in that the country's role as a neoliberal showcase example, combined with its low overall debt and its costly participation in the U.S. war on drugs, resulted in an unusually generous treatment by the IMF and Western creditors. Through its close relationship with Jeffrey Sachs, Bolivia managed to square the circle between gaining international backing for its adjustment efforts and implementing a reform package whose components were tailored to the specific political and economic needs of the country. Thus, in a sense Bolivia represents the ideal-case orthodox adjustment scenario for a highly indebted developing-country during the Latin American debt crisis, and as such the limitations of its success (with respect to growth, redistribution, and democracy) illustrate the narrow confines of the maneuvering space available to Latin American governments during this period.

Adjustment in the Spotlight: Argentina and the Debt Crisis

While Bolivia was learning to cope with the challenges of economic and political marginality, Argentina's troubles were of a different nature. As one of the world's three largest developing-country debtors (behind Brazil and Mexico), with more than $43 billion in foreign debt by the end of 1982, Argentina had a prominent position on the balance sheets of many Western commercial banks and, therefore, played a central role in the political and economic agenda of Western creditors and the Fund's mission in the region. Even though in relative terms the public debt was not excessive by regional standards (accounting for 55% of GNP in 1982), debt service placed a significant and increasingly worrisome burden on public finances, given that interest payments alone amounted to 4.5% of GNP and total debt service used up half the country's export earnings at the outset of the debt crisis and almost 70% by 1983. Even though international reserves were initially relatively solid (around $3 billion or 6.6 months of imports by mid-1982), they only covered the equivalent of one year of debt service payments, hardly a comfortable cushion considering the abrupt halt to foreign capital inflows into the region after Mexico's insolvency announcement in August 1982. As such, Argentina certainly fit the profile of an economically important country in financial distress, which, according to the predictions of the formal model and the findings of the statistical tests, made it an obvious target for IMF conditionality. Indeed, between 1982 and the end of 1989, Argentina entered four IMF standby agreements, one of which was renegotiated and extended in mid-1985 in conjunction with the launching of the Austral Plan. Nevertheless, the relationship between the Fund and Argentina, while never degenerating into open confrontation as in the case of Alan Garcia's Peru, remained uneasy throughout the decade, as reflected in the patchy compliance record of the programs and the occasionally defiant public statements of Argentine officials.

The underlying tone of the relationship between Argentina under Alfonsín and the IMF (as the representative of Western creditors) was set by what large sections of the country's population and civilian elite viewed as the illegitimate nature of Argentina's foreign debt. This sentiment, present to varying degrees in many Latin American countries, was justified by the fact that the bulk of the country's external debt had been accumulated under the brutal and thoroughly discredited military dictatorship (Damill and Frenkel 1996:81), which had "succeeded" to oversee a dramatic increase in public debt (from $8.3 billion in 1976 to $45 billion in 1983)[5] through a combination of costly infrastructure projects and defense spending. This resentment was exacerbated by the Reagan government's ideological support for the military dictatorship prior to the Falklands war[6] and the nationalization of private foreign debt by the outgoing military regime in late 1982, as part of its rapprochement with the West in response to the outbreak of the debt crisis. Moreover, the unusual willingness of the IMF to sign a standby agreement with the lame-duck military government of General Bignone in the context of the country's extreme domestic economic and political instability reinforced the Argentines' distrust of the Western motives in their dealings with developing-country debtors.

Elected after a campaign in which both major parties had emphasized their anti-imperialist foreign policy stance, the new Alfonsín government initially sought a political solution to the debt crisis. Emboldened by the domestic and international legitimacy derived from its democratic credentials, and reassured by the country's relative economic self-sufficiency,[7]

[5] Data from CEPAL 1992 as cited in Damill and Frenkel 1996:100.

[6] Thus, Reagan decried the Carter administration's human rights sanctions as having made "a mess of our relations with the planet's seventh-largest country, Argentina, a nation with which we should be close friends," and praised the military dictatorship for its actions against the terrorist threat (Sklar 1988:61, cited in Vacs 1989:33).

[7] Thus, Alfonsín argued explicitly—and at least to some extent justifiedly—that Argentina with "its own beef, grain, industry and energy resources . . . could go it alone" (cited in Watkins 1985:43).

Argentina emerged as the key promoter of a debtors' cartel, meant to create a unified response of developing countries in their debt negotiations with Western creditors under the banner of the IMF. After several months of intense lobbying from all sides, which culminated in the ironically misnamed "Cartagena Consensus" of June 1984, Argentina only managed to get the endorsement of several smaller countries, whereas Mexico, Brazil, Venezuela, and Colombia favored a more conciliatory approach that eventually resulted in the preferred Western formula of case-by-case negotiations and weakened the bargaining position of the debtors.[8] Unlike the post-1985 Peruvian government, the Argentine government decided to avoid the risky strategy of unilateral defection and, rewarded at least in part by a relatively advantageous initial debt rescheduling, agreed to negotiations with the IMF. Following several months of tense negotiations, punctuated occasionally by intense rhetorical and personal clashes,[9] the Argentine economy minister Bernardo Grinspun eventually signed a letter of intent for an IMF standby agreement in September 1984, which was approved by the IMF Executive Board in late December 1984. However, the Argentine government almost immediately broke some of the program conditions, which, despite an initial funding disbursement in January 1985 and the resignation in February of Grinspun and the equally populist central bank governor Garcia Vasquez in protest against the stringent monetary measures advocated by the IMF,[10] resulted in the breakdown of the program by March 1985 and the end of Argentina's first attempt at orthodox adjustment under the democratic regime.

The eagerness of the Western creditors to continue to engage the Argentine government despite the breakdown of the program and the acceleration of inflation in the second quarter of 1985 was emphasized by the continuation of (albeit fruitless) negotiations during this period between the IMF mission and the new economic team of Juan Sourrouille, Grinspun's successor as economic minister of the Alfonsín government.

[8] While a more detailed analysis of this crucial breakdown of debtor cooperation is beyond the scope of the current discussion, the four "defectors" were motivated by different considerations: Mexico was more dependent than other countries on its close financial and trade ties with the United States (Kahler 1985:379), Brazil was more vulnerable due to its dependence on energy imports (ibid.), whereas Venezuela and Colombia were facing a more manageable debt situation and in fact managed to avoid IMF conditionality until at least 1989.

[9] Aside from the obvious tensions about the relative degree of internal adjustment and external support, the negotiations suffered from increasingly acrimonious relations between the two negotiating teams, which were shouting terms for a while (Stiles 1991:186). Moreover, the Argentine government chose to publicize its defiant stance by flouting standard IMF procedures and submitting a unilateral homemade letter of intent that clearly prioritized domestic growth over debt repayment (ibid.: 185).

[10] Carvounis 1985:39–40, cited in Manzetti and Dell'Aquila 1988:4.

The politically motivated flexibility of the Fund's relationship with Argentina during this period became even more obvious in July 1985, when the IMF staff agreed to accept the heterodox Plan Austral, announced by Alfonsín in a public speech on June 14 without prior consultation with the IMF, as the basis for a renewal and extension of the standby agreement suspended earlier in the year.[11] In doing so, the IMF leadership not only chose to play along with the Argentine government's ostentatious display of economic policy-making independence (whose political importance was particularly salient in the context of the imminent congressional elections), but it also tolerated the program's significant deviations from standard IMF orthodoxy, particularly with respect to the wage- and price-freeze measures instituted by the plan.

The IMF's remarkable tolerance for Argentina's heterodox stabilization approach was reiterated in early/mid-1987, when it extended its seal of approval to the new attempt of the Alfonsín government to cope with the renewed fiscal crisis and inflationary pressures, even though the Australito like its considerably more successful predecessor contained important wage- and price-freeze components. This leniency, promoted by the U.S. government on a number of occasions (such as a program waiver and a $500 million bridge loan negotiated with U.S. support in September 1987), only applied to domestic policies and debt restructuring negotiations but—significantly—not to debt forgiveness, as indicated by U.S. Secretary of the Treasury James Baker's dismissal of an Argentine request for 30% debt reduction in 1988 as "fantasy" (Vacs 1989:43). When the U.S. government finally agreed to significant debt reductions for developing countries as part of the Brady Plan in 1989, the help came too late for the Alfonsín government, which had already completely lost control over the Argentine economy during the first months of that year.

Even a brief comparison of the different experiences of the Argentine and Bolivian governments in their interactions with the IMF during the 1980s provides some interesting insights into the role of Western political and economic considerations in shaping the nature of IMF conditionality during the debt crisis. Thus, whereas the Siles government in Bolivia had failed to secure an IMF agreement during its three-year tenure despite taking a more conciliatory approach toward debt payments and Western conditionality than the Argentine government during the same period, Bolivia's marginality within the broader international context of the debt

[11] While the Argentine government did not consult with the IMF, there were regular consultations with the U.S. administration during this period (personal interview with Juan Sourrouille—April 2006). Thus, it was hardly a coincidence that the IMF approval came shortly after Federal Reserve Chairman Paul Volcker praised the plan and promised direct U.S. support for Argentina's negotiations with the commercial banks and the international financial institutions (Vacs 1989:41).

crisis facilitated a much more generous treatment with respect to debt forgiveness, once the successful orthodox economic reforms of the Paz government after 1985 had elevated the country to the privileged status of a showcase for neoliberal policies. This relative financial generosity, which had the significant advantage of being quite cheap for Western investors (given Bolivia's small overall debt and extremely low likelihood of repayment by 1985), came at the price of strictly enforced domestic conditionality. Meanwhile, Argentina was allowed to "get away" with significant deviations from IMF orthodoxy as long as its policies were broadly consistent with the Western goal of financial stability and timely debt payments; but the price for this relative freedom was the persistence of the high debt service burden, which played an important role in derailing the country's adjustment efforts under Alfonsín. While—as will be discussed in more detail in the following section—it is questionable whether Alfonsín would have been willing or capable of implementing an orthodox reform program along the lines of the Bolivian NEP, Argentina could have hardly hoped for a similarly generous financial treatment given the significantly higher costs of such a concession to Western creditors. These differences confirm that the menu of options available to Latin American governments during the 1980s was shaped in important ways by their relative economic and political importance to the West, thereby creating different sets of incentives to policy makers and ultimately producing different adjustment paths.

Peru: The Art of Mistimed Compliance and Defiance

Peru, like neighboring Bolivia, experienced two radically different phases during its relationship with the IMF in the 1980s: a valiant attempt at compliance under the Belaúnde government until 1985, and an equally brave confrontation attempt under Alan Garcia after 1985. But unlike their luckier neighbors, Peruvian politicians picked the "wrong" timing for both of these approaches to IMF negotiations and ended up with the worst of both worlds for political leaders and citizens alike.

Even though the Belaúnde government certainly had its share of the blame for the failure of its economic reform agenda after 1982,[12] its task was considerably complicated by the unfavorable international economic environment and inflexible initial approach of the IMF to the Latin American debt crisis. Besides Chile, Peru was one of the few committed neoliberal reformers in Latin America prior to 1982, and the Belaúnde govern-

---

[12] See chapter 6 for a more detailed discussion of some these political and economic miscalculations.

ment's solid neoliberal track record between 1980 and 1982 initially resulted in close cooperation with the IMF during the first year of the debt crisis; in fact, the Belaúnde government signed a three-year $650m Extended Fund Facility agreement with the IMF in early June 1982, two months before the official outbreak of the debt crisis. Moreover, despite its heavy debt service burden, which accounted for almost 50% of the country's exports in 1982, the government adhered rather closely to the restrictive terms of the program despite the increasing unpopularity of the austerity measures. However, by mid-1983 the deep recession, combined with increased military expenditures due to the rising threat of the Shining Path insurgency, as well as political pressures in conjunction with the municipal elections in late 1983, contributed to larger-than-expected fiscal-deficit and inflation levels, and eventually resulted in the breakdown of the IMF program by November 1983.

Given the Peruvian government's traditionally close relationship with the IMF, Belaúnde's finance minister, Rodriguez Pastor, attempted to extract concessions with respect to the depth of the austerity measures required as part of the negotiations for the renewal of the IMF agreement in late 1983 and early 1984 (*Wall Street Journal* 1/4/1984). However, despite the country's precarious economic situation and the increasing likelihood of a leftist or populist victory in the rapidly approaching general elections scheduled for July 1985, the IMF maintained a tough bargaining position, which delayed the approval of the program and further complicated Peru's difficult negotiations with the commercial banks. Eventually, following a last-minute intervention from Fund Managing Director de Larosière, the IMF negotiating team agreed in late April 1984 to sign a somewhat "softer" eighteen-month-program to accommodate the electoral concerns of the Belaúnde government.

The course of these negotiations surrounding the 1984 Peruvian IMF program nicely illustrates the predictions of the formal model and the statistical findings of the previous chapter. Thus, as a country of medium size and economic importance,[13] we would expect Peru's experience with IMF program initiation in the early 1980s to occupy the middle ground between Bolivia's futile efforts to secure IMF funding and the much prompter response of the Fund to Argentina's economic woes. In this sense the substantial initiation delays and the initial intransigence of Fund negotiators are balanced by the eventual political intervention that led to the signing of the program. However, as it turned out, this middle ground was hardly a comfortable one for the Peruvian government. During the four-month delay in the approval of the program, the Fund's inflexible

---

[13] For example, Peru's foreign debt in 1983 ($10.7bn) was three times larger than Bolivia's but less than a quarter the size of Argentina's.

approach to Peru's difficult economic and political situation had contributed decisively to the political defeat of the neoliberal reform project in Peru. Under increasing political pressure from his own party and an increasingly impatient population, President Belaúnde fired Rodriguez Pastor for his willingness to accept the stringent austerity measures promoted by the IMF in mid-March 1984. The move was followed by the en masse resignation of the neoliberal technocrats and marked a decisive break in the government's economic policy, which shifted toward a more "reactivationist" stance (*Wall Street Journal*, 3/21/1984). The expansionary policies pursued in mid-1984 led to a ballooning fiscal deficit (6.1% for the year) and resulted in the breakdown of the IMF agreement by mid-September. Moreover, despite its moderate success in reactivating the economy (which grew at 4.8% in 1984), the policy change failed to reverse the political decline of the Belaúnde government and set the stage for the victory of Alan Garcia in the general elections of mid-1985.

A Costly, Mistimed Rebellion: Peru under Alan Garcia

Immediately after his convincing electoral victory in July 1985, the new Peruvian president, Alan Garcia, signaled a decisive departure from the accommodationist relationship with the IMF pursued by the Belaúnde government for most of its tenure. Having thoroughly internalized the political lessons of his predecessor's disappointing experiences with IMF conditionality, Garcia wasted no time in spelling out his confrontational approach to relations with the Fund. Already in his inaugural speech on July 28, 1985, Garcia announced his nonnegotiable opposition to IMF demands, which he regarded as tantamount to giving up the country's political sovereignty (*Wall Street Journal*, 7/29/1985). The populist tone of his rhetoric was matched in policy terms by an official announcement of the government's intention to limit debt service payments to no more than 10% of export earnings in an effort to give Peru the breathing space necessary for economic recovery.

The Fund's reaction to the Peruvian "rebellion" was swift, and in August 1986, the IMF announced that Peru was ineligible for additional IMF loans. Thus relegated to the bottom of the international financial hierarchy alongside a "select" group of IMF delinquents (including Liberia, Vietnam, Guyana, and Sudan), the Peruvian government found itself cut off not only from IMF and World Bank lending but increasingly also from trade credits. This credit shortage was exacerbated by the failure of Garcia's export promotion policies and ultimately contributed decisively to the spectacular collapse of the Peruvian economy starting in 1988. Despite the drastic decline in foreign reserves and international creditworthiness combined with the rapidly increasing inflation during this period, Peru was not able to secure an IMF agreement until after the inauguration of the Fujimori government in 1990. Thus, the international political gamble of the Peruvian government ended in a decisive defeat that illustrated the dangers of open confrontation with the IMF in a period of worldwide neoliberal ascendancy.

While Peru's international isolation was triggered intentionally by the Garcia government, most individual elements of Garcia's political approach were not unique in the context of the often tense relationship between the Fund and Latin American governments in this period. Thus, Garcia's nationalist rhetoric about the skewed priorities of debt repayment were not all that different from some of the statements by members of Alfonsín's government in 1983–84. Similarly, while Garcia's economic program included a number heterodox deviations from IMF policy prescriptions, the same was true of the Argentine Plan Austral, which the IMF tolerated and even supported during the same time period. Furthermore, the Fund also backed the economic program of the Bolivian reformers despite their reliance on fixed exchange rates and their refusal to resume commercial debt payments until late 1986. Moreover, despite his inflammatory rhetoric, Garcia actually adopted a fairly pragmatic approach to debt service in an attempt to preserve crucial sources of private credit for the country.[14]

Even though none of the individual elements that led to Peru's international isolation were uniquely Peruvian, the Garcia government miscalculated in three important ways. First, Garcia misjudged the gravity of the *combined* effect of his strategy's economic, political, ideological, and rhetorical challenges to Western neoliberalism inherent in his frontal attack on the IMF. By comparison, Argentina's confrontational rhetoric in 1983–84 was balanced by a more timely debt service performance, whereas Bolivia's debt moratorium in 1985–86 was accompanied by an ambitious neoliberal domestic reform agenda. Second, perhaps under the spell of his own nationalist rhetoric, Garcia had overestimated his country's importance to Western economic interests and had thus unleashed an uneven conflict from which Peru could only emerge as a loser. Whereas Argentina's potential default would have seriously rattled Western banks, Peru's debt was a much smaller concern, and, therefore—in line with the statistical findings in the previous chapter—triggered a much less flexible reaction from the IMF. Ironically, Peru's higher overall debt and economic importance compared to neighboring Bolivia, may have also contributed to the more serious consequences of its partial debt moratorium, since its

---

[14] In fact, as Pastor (1992:122) points out, Peruvian debt-service payments actually exceeded the 10% ceiling between 1985 and 1987, and the decline in 1988 was due primarily to the incapacity rather than the unwillingness of the Garcia government to pay.

consequences were significantly costlier to Western creditors than for the much smaller Bolivian debt. Finally, Garcia's challenge to the West was undermined not only by the country's modest size but also because it arguably came too late in the debt crisis. Thus, by 1986 the threat of an international debtor's cartel, which had been a major concern for the West in 1983–84, had practically disappeared. At the same time, Western commercial banks had gradually managed to reduce their exposure to Latin American debt, and were therefore in a much less vulnerable position than at the outset of the debt crisis (Aggarwal 1996). These systemic factors further exacerbated the power imbalance between the Peruvian government and Western creditors, and thereby sealed the fate of Garcia's quixotic rebellion against the IMF and the West.

Overall, the relationship between successive Peruvian governments and the IMF during the 1980s illustrates the difficult trade-offs faced by middle-sized countries, whose debt was too small to trigger systemically based preferential treatment (as in Argentina) but too large for massive debt reductions (as in Bolivia). However, Peru's negative experience with both orthodoxy and heterodoxy was also the consequence of their unfortunate timing. Thus, the cooperative stance of the Belaúnde government in the early months of the debt crisis was not rewarded by more flexibility in the Fund's approach to conditionality and ultimately undermined the political feasibility of orthodox economic adjustment in a democratic context. However, the diametrically opposite approach to IMF relations chosen by the Garcia government after 1985 did not produce better outcomes. The severity of the West's punishment of the Garcia government's political "heresy" emphasizes not only the crucial importance of the IMF in the overall international economic context of the debt crisis but also the significant context dependence of developing-country strategies for dealing with the IMF: Even though Garcia's approach combined a number of elements from the more successful Argentine and Bolivian strategies in the mid-1980s, the ultimate economic and political repercussions of his approach were radically different because of its unfavorable timing and its incongruence with Peru's international economic position.

A Strained Alliance—Chile and the IMF in the Mid-1980s

By most standards, Pinochet's Chile in the 1980s was the ideal IMF program candidate. Beside a regionally unique track record of home-grown and ideologically committed economic orthodoxy, Chile also exhibited some of the classic external financial crisis symptoms; thus, in 1982 Chile had not only the second highest interest payment burden in the region (amounting to 10.7% of GNP) but its $17.3 billion overall debt was the fifth highest in Latin America and, therefore, created more significant concerns about a possible default than a smaller debtor like Bolivia. This combination of financial need and size, which was the strongest predictor of IMF program initiation and implementation in the statistical analysis in the preceding chapter, made Chile an obvious candidate for IMF programs. These theoretical predictions were borne out with remarkable consistency if we analyze the broad patterns of the country's initiation and implementation of IMF programs during the 1980s. The first agreement was approved in early January 1983 and over a two-year period provided $500 million in direct loans, which were fully disbursed by the end of the program after a partial renegotiation of program targets in early 1984. Only six months after the expiration of the first program, Chile and the IMF signed a second agreement in August 1985, this time for $750 million over a three-year period, which was in turn extended for an extra year in 1988, also fully implemented. Finally, in early November 1989, just over a month before the country's first democratic elections in two decades, the IMF approved one last $82 million program with the outgoing Pinochet government, which, in a curious departure from standard program procedures, was disbursed immediately in one tranche. Overall, then, since the debut of the debt crisis in August 1982, the Chilean military government had spent less than eighteen months without an IMF-supported program, in what undoubtedly ranks as the closest cooperation between the Fund and any Latin American country during the 1980s.

Nevertheless, a closer look at the interaction between the IMF and the Chilean government reveals a much more complicated picture than suggested by this broad overview. Thus, between 1983 and 1985 Chile underwent a difficult transition from the Chicago-style monetarism of the 1970s to the post-1985 pragmatic neoliberalism, and in the process, the relationship between the Pinochet regime and the IMF went through a rough patch. Even though the Chilean government initially responded to the debt crisis with an IMF-supported classical orthodox adjustment strategy, the economic and political costs of this approach became increasingly obvious to the Pinochet regime during 1983, and Chile suddenly found itself in the unfamiliar position of having to struggle to fulfill the requirements of the IMF agreement it had signed in January 1983. In less than two years, the burden of adjusting to its threateningly high foreign debt had transformed Chile from a poster child of neoliberalism to just another Latin American problem child of the debt crisis.

These problems came to a head in the fall of 1983, when it became clear that Pinochet's political survival hinged on the initiation of economic reactivation measures whose expansionary fiscal implications conflicted with the program targets agreed upon in the IMF standby agreement earlier that year. At the same time, however, the Chilean government could hardly afford to abandon the program, given that its foreign reserves had declined from $3 billion in early 1982 to around $1.3 billion by late 1983, and that the IMF agreement was important not only because of its direct funding but also because the Fund acted as an effective gatekeeper for the country's much-needed debt renegotiations with its commercial creditors. Nevertheless, Chile had two important advantages compared to Peru or Bolivia in its negotiations with the IMF in late 1983, early 1984: First, its larger overall debt raised its economic importance to Western banks and therefore raised the stakes of a possible default. Second, and more important, the ideological and educational value of a successful neoliberal adjustment example was important in the charged political context of Argentina's attempts to assemble a debtors' cartel in early 1984, and Chile was one of the few promising candidates.

As a consequence of the high stakes on both sides, the lengthy negotiations during the winter and spring of 1984 proceeded very discreetly, avoiding the drawn-out rhetorical exchanges and public statements that plagued the Fund's relationship with Argentina and Peru. By mid-February the IMF agreed to grant the Chilean government a waiver that would allow the expansion of the government deficit to almost 5%, which seems relatively generous, considering the Fund's refusal to let Peru get away with a 4% deficit in the same time period. Moreover, following Pinochet's strategic replacement of Finance Minister Carlos Caceres with Luis Escobar, who happened to be the country's former representative at the World Bank and the IMF, in late April the IMF agreed to raise the fiscal deficit target 5.6% for the year. The relative generosity of this target, not only compared to the 4.1% final offer made to Peru that month, but also when judged by Chile's actual deficit in 1984 (4.8%), suggests that Chile did receive preferential treatment in its negotiations with the IMF. The sad irony of the Fund's treatment of Chile and Peru in the spring of 1984 is that the IMF appears to have been more concerned with political feasibility in the case of Pinochet's military dictatorship than with Peru's fledgling democracy.

As will be discussed in more detail in chapter 6, starting in mid-1985, the consolidation of a pragmatic neoliberal political coalition, combined with the country's rapid export-led economic growth in the second half of the 1980s, restored Chile to its "rightful" place as a role model for aspiring neoliberal reformers. However, the severity of the economic and political crisis provoked by the initial orthodox adjustment effort underscores the narrow constraints of politically sustainable neoliberal economic reforms during the 1980s debt crisis even for an "ideal case candidate" such as Chile. Therefore, it should come as no surprise that during the early part of the debt crisis, failed economic adjustment was the rule rather than the exception in Latin America.

Moldova: The Making of an Unlikely IMF "Regular"

In the mid- to late 1990s Moldova became a somewhat unexpected poster child for IMF-style reforms in the non-Baltic former Soviet Union. From December 1993 until May 2000, Moldova was virtually continuously engaged in IMF programs with only a brief two-month hiatus in 1996. The frequent and fairly consistently implemented Moldovan IMF programs are even more remarkable considering the country's unpromising domestic context, characterized by weak institutions and a government dominated by former communists. Therefore, Moldova's close cooperation with the International Monetary Fund represents the perfect example of the crucial importance of external constraints as drivers of the intensive involvement of ex-communist countries with the IMF during the first decade of the transition. In particular, I argue that this unlikely alliance has to be analyzed from the perspective of the country's high financial dependence on multilateral funding, combined with the need for international legitimacy of the fledgling Moldovan state, caught in a tense geopolitical situation between two potential patron states (Romania and Russia). This extraordinary dependence was at least partially balanced by the Fund's need for a "showcase" example of successful IMF conditionality in the former Soviet Union, which contributed to a more forgiving IMF reaction to temporary policy slippage and suggests a broader applicability of the post-1985 Bolivian strategy for overcoming the disadvantages of marginality.

Large Carrots for a Hungry Man

Moldova's post-communist experience can be regarded as a textbook case for situations in which extreme financial need drives desperate governments into the arms of the IMF. Following the breakup of the Soviet Union, the drastic rise in the country's energy costs combined with quasi collapse of its traditional export markets in the former Soviet Union led to high dependence on external funding to cover the country's basic import needs. Like most former Soviet republics, Moldova emerged at independence with virtually no foreign reserves, and the situation improved only slowly and inconsistently over the course of the decade; thus, Moldova's international reserves rose from 1.6 months of imports in late 1993 to around 3 months in 1994–97, before declining again to 1.4 in 1998 due to the fallout of the Russian crisis. Moreover, with the exception of a brief period in 1997, Moldova had essentially no access to international financial markets, which meant that the government's only realistic sources of funding were official donors, particularly Western governments and international financial organizations.[15] In view of Moldova's extremely limited economic and political importance to the West, the only hope for gaining access to Western funding was a close cooperation with the IMF, which was widely regarded as the gatekeeper for official credits in the former communist bloc.

The extent of Moldova's dependence on IMF approval is illustrated by the fact that from 1993 to 1995 official credits from bilateral and multilateral donors accounted for more than 96% of the country's total foreign debt, with about a third of the total funding coming directly from the IMF.[16] The relatively large flows of official funding into Moldova during the mid-1990s were intended not just as a policy incentive for the Moldovan government but as part of a Western strategy to illustrate the benefits of courageous economic reforms in the former Soviet republics.[17] Moreover, the Fund's assessment of Moldovan economic policy played a remarkably clear signaling role in mobilizing/suspending lending by other official donors; thus, the STF and SBA programs in late 1993 were rewarded with additional funding from the World Bank, the EU, and the EBRD, as well as by bilateral assistance pledges from Western governments. Similarly, the IMF's decision to withhold payment on the third tranche of the EFF program in late 1996 also prompted the suspension of a World Bank structural adjustment loan. Thus, the Moldovan case confirms the predictions of the formal model that as long as IMF programs are associated with sufficiently high levels of direct and indirect funding to a sufficiently desperate government, we may get instances of IMF program implementation even under adverse political and institutional conditions.

Choosing Patrons: IMF Conditionality and Moldovan Sovereignty

The second major reason for the Moldovan government's surprisingly close adherence to IMF conditionality goes beyond the economic considerations captured by the formal model and the statistical tests, and has to do with the peculiar nature of Moldova's geopolitical position in the early post-independence period. After gaining its official independence during the chaotic days of the August 1991 coup in Moscow, Moldova had to confront a series of threats not only to its territorial integrity but also to its very existence as a sovereign state. In this context, IMF conditionality,

---

[15] The only non-Western alternatives would have been direct assistance from either the Russian or the Romanian government, each of which was in a dire financial position and hardly able to afford to finance the Moldovan transition.

[16] These figures are based on data from the EIU Country Data statistics, and do not include Moldova's unpaid energy bills to the Russian gas company Gazprom.

[17] See *EIU Country Report*, 2nd quarter, 1994.

while reducing the government's maneuvering space in determining economic policy, played an important role in promoting the international legitimacy of a state whose viability was questionable at the time.

The first and arguably most fundamental threat to Moldovan independence came from the reformist Popular Front of Moldova, which had won the first free elections in 1990 and which actively pursued reunification with Romania. Though many outside observers had anticipated this reunification as an inevitable consequence of the close ethnic and cultural similarities between the two countries, the reunification movement lost momentum starting in early 1992 and has steadily declined ever since. From an internal perspective, popular support for reunification suffered due to mixed memories of Bucharest's interwar rule of the region, fears of ethnic unrest from Moldova's large and vocal ethnic minorities, and to a certain degree as a result of forty years of intense Soviet indoctrination. Moldova's largely Russified elite had good reasons to believe that joining Romania would prove to be a bad career move and deprive them of prestigious posts in the new state (Kolsto, 1996:123). From an external perspective, the separatist crisis in Transdniestr constituted a clear signal that Russia was willing to defend its regional interests through the use of force, and that neither Romania nor the West would be able or willing to intervene. As Moldova has increasingly rejected the possibility of reunification, its leaders have made sustained efforts to popularize the doctrine of Moldovanism, which emphasizes the distinctiveness of Moldova's cultural and historic heritage.[18]

By avoiding reunification with Romania, the Moldovan government ensured the survival of Moldova as a state. But this survival only marked the beginning of a difficult struggle to define the country's position in the international arena in the context of formidable internal and external constraints. The most difficult trial for Moldova was the Transdniestr crisis, which undermined Moldova's territorial integrity and played a decisive role in shaping both Moldova's internal politics and its foreign policy. While ostensibly an internal ethnic conflict, the Transdniestr crisis was the core of the heated debate about Moldova's international status and Russia's role in the region. The importance of the Transdniestr conflict in the wider context of the debate about Moldova's international status and Russia's role in the region was probably best summarized by Moldova's ambassador to the UN, who claimed during a speech in front of the UN General Assembly that Russia was using the crisis as an excuse to justify the continued presence of its armed forces on Moldova's terri-

---

[18] While this unexpectedly successful effort constitutes a fascinating and original approach to the identity crisis facing Moldovan society, its details are beyond the scope of the current discussion. For an interesting analysis of this topic, see Munteanu 1996.

tory. He furthermore accused Russia of ultimately pursuing the goal of "restoring the old imperial structures with the blessing of the international community" (*Moldova Suverana*, 10/14/1993). These claims are supported by General Lebed, the commander of the 14th Russian army, who called Transdniestr "Russia's key to the Balkans" and emphasized that if Russia left this strategic crossroads between the Ukraine, Romania, and the Black Sea, it would lose its influence on the entire region (quoted in Gabanyi, 1996:9). Russia explicitly acknowledged that the importance of its armed presence in the region extended beyond the scope of the Transdniestr conflict and that the timing and order of the troop withdrawal was contingent on Russian-Moldovan relations (Cojocaru 1996:4).

In addition to playing the "Transdniestr card," Russia used Moldova's economic dependence to influence the domestic and foreign policy of the Moldovan government. For example, during the 1996 presidential elections, which pitted the independent-minded acting president Mircea Snegur against the more pro-Russian Petru Lucinschi, the Russian CIS minister, Aman Tuleev, told Pravda that Russia should give no more credits to Moldova if Snegur was reelected president (*Transitions*, 11/16/96). Along similar lines, Moldova's resistance against becoming a buffer state as a consequence of NATO enlargement, was rewarded by Moscow's agreeing to reschedule Moldova's gas debts and to exempt the Moldovan government from the debts contracted by the Trandniestr authorities (Negru 1997:8). Other potentially important economic threats included the introduction of visas for Moldovans looking for work in Russia and the imposition of import tariffs, which would further cripple Moldova's export-dependent economy.

The external pressures from Bucharest and Moscow were also reflected in Moldova's domestic political landscape, with the independence-minded PDAM government facing challenges from the pro-Romanian Popular Front and its successors, as well as from the pro-Russian Socialist Party/Edinstvo bloc. In this context the decision of the Moldovan government to cooperate closely with international organizations represented an astute political maneuver meant to find an alternative patron that could counterbalance the Russian and Romanian claims to influence. The most obvious example in this respect was the close cooperation between the Moldovan government and the CSCE mission in Moldova in trying to solve the Transdniestr crisis. Moldova followed CSCE recommendations on minority policies and language rights, and thereby not only gained the approval of the West, but also weakened the position of Russia and Transdniestr, who found it much harder to blame Moldova for the continuation of the crisis. Moldova's strengthened international position resulting from this rapprochement with the West was illustrated by Moldova's threat to vote against the admission of Russia to the

Council of Europe unless Russia withdrew its troops from Transdniestr (Gabanyi 1996:29).

Seen from this balance-of-power perspective, Moldova's interaction with the IMF went beyond the traditional trade-off between funding and sovereignty inherent in IMF conditionality. Some of the Western support received as a consequence of the "green light" from the IMF was specifically targeted to reduce Moldova's dependence on Russia; thus, the country received support from EBRD to build an oil terminal on the Danube in an effort to reduce its dependence on Russian oil (*Interfax*, 11/29/ 1994). Also, Moldova received a $250m loan from the World Bank to repay Russian oil debts after Russia had temporarily shut off oil supplies in late 1994 (*Journal of Commerce*, 12/8/1994).

Therefore, while IMF conditionality arguably induced the Moldovan government to implement economic policies, which contradicted both its partisan and its electoral interests, and ultimately failed to reverse the country's precipitous economic decline, the funding and "legitimizing" function of IMF cooperation may have actually contributed not only to the survival of the PDAM government but also to the stability of the fledgling Moldovan state. The continuing importance of the IMF in the country's international "equation" was emphasized by the decision of the unreformed communists to "forget" their electoral tirades against Western imperialism and to continue to implement the IMF Poverty Reduction and Growth Facility (PRGF) arrangement initiated by the previous government. Such cooperation is likely to continue for at least as long as the basic economic and political parameters of Moldova's precarious international position remain unchanged.

The Perils of Heresy: Slovakia under Mečiar

When Slovakia obtained its independence on January 1, 1993, the prospects for the new republic were hardly promising. Even though it was not facing security threats comparable to those of Moldova, Slovakia's international position was extremely fragile, with Western observers worrying about "the creation of a state [. . .] with unclear ties to its allies and an uncertain future" (*Washington Times*, 12/15/92). Such worries were exacerbated by the significant pre-independence tensions between the nationalist Slovak government of Vladimir Mečiar and the country's large Hungarian minority, which had also affected diplomatic relations with neighboring Hungary.[19]

---

[19] These tensions were exacerbated by a drawn-out international dispute between the Slovak and the Hungarian government about the building of the Gabcikovo dam on the Danube.

Slovakia's economic situation did not look much more promising either. Even though relatively prosperous and favorably located by Eastern European standards, from a structural standpoint Slovakia's economy was burdened by the preponderance of an antiquated heavy industry with a large military component. This industry relied heavily on energy and raw material imports from the former Soviet Union and produced relatively uncompetitive semifinished products directed primarily at former CMEA markets (Janos 1997:19). To make matters worse, Slovakia had an unusually high concentration of arms manufacturers who saw their traditional markets in the Eastern bloc and the Third World decline following the end of the Cold War. Thus, between 1988 and 1992 the Slovak arms industry shrank by almost 90%, resulting in layoffs of 42,000 out of 52,000 workers employed in the industry, and adding to Slovakia's high unemployment rates (Fisher 1993). Therefore, there could be few doubts about the economic necessity for structural reforms of these Stalinist dinosaurs, an objective agenda that featured high on the list of IMF priorities. Moreover, Slovakia's international reserves were extremely low in the first eighteen months of independence, during which they hovered below the critical value of one month's worth of imports,[20] thereby placing the country at an acute risk of insolvency given that its access to international capital markets was uncertain due to the political instability following independence.

Under such circumstances one would have expected that Slovakia would rush to secure IMF support of its economic policies by subjecting itself to the rigors of an IMF agreement. The logic of this prediction is supported not only by the statistical results from the previous chapter about the strong incentives of low international reserves but also by the fact that the Czech Republic entered an IMF standby agreement in June 1993, despite its incomparably more stable external position and its higher credibility in the West. Nevertheless, in the almost six years between independence and Mečiar's electoral defeat in late 1998, Slovakia experienced only one IMF program, which—tellingly—was initiated by Mečiar's political opponents during the brief six-month power alternation in 1994, and was almost immediately abandoned upon Mečiar's return to power in October 1994. What explains this glaring absence in a region characterized by almost ubiquitous IMF programs? While the domestic political explanations of this puzzle are addressed in more detail in chapter 6, the following discussion focuses on the international implications of the convoluted relationship between the Mečiar government and

---

[20] According to Prime Minister Meciar, reserves fell as low as $25m in the second quarter of 1993 (*EIU Country Report*, 2nd quarter, 1993).

the IMF (and the West more broadly) and reveals the tight ideological constraints on the acceptable economic policies and political rhetoric during the post-communist transition.

The Politics of an Unlikely Standoff: Failed Negotiations in 1993–94

Even though at first Slovakia appeared to conform to expectations, in that negotiations for an IMF standby agreement started almost immediately after independence, the process was abruptly discontinued on February 20, 1993, when the IMF delegation left Bratislava after the Slovak government refused to comply with several key IMF conditions. The official reactions of the Slovak leadership to this conflict are telling: Prime Minister Mečiar argued that the IMF recommendations for a 30% currency devaluation were based on data "of a catastrophic character" from former Czechoslovakian federal sources[21] and lamented that IMF fiscal austerity measures would "affect 50% of all children in the Slovak Republic."[22] The populist-nationalist undertones of the reaction were even clearer in the declarations of the Slovak minister of agriculture, Peter Baco, who claimed that the IMF pressures for agricultural subsidy cuts were aimed to increase food prices in order to allow Western companies to penetrate the Slovak market (*EIU Country Report*, 2nd quarter, 1993).

Even though the Slovak government was careful to avoid a complete breakdown of its relations with the IMF,[23] the relationship between the two negotiating sides continued to be tense until the fall of the Mečiar government in March 1994. Even though Mečiar repeatedly emphasized that the IMF looked at Slovakia with "respect and admiration" (cited in *CTK*, 8/2/1993) and the country managed to secure a $180m credit line from the IMF in June 1993, the two sides continued to disagree about a series of policy conditions. Thus, the June agreement was not a regular standby program, but was part of the lower conditionality structural transformation facility (STF) intended to support transition economies. Therefore, the Slovak government continued its emphasis on selective implementation of IMF policies, such as the 10% currency devaluation in July 1993, which was instituted with a five-month delay and was well

---

[21] Cited in *CTK*, 3/12/1993.

[22] Cited in ibid, 3/1/1993.

[23] Meciar recognized the high stakes of such a break and admitted that some sort of IMF seal of approval was necessary to avoid "the threat of being in dispute with the banking world and in isolation. . . . We could have managed even in the future [without the IMF], but with a considerably slower rate of development" (Slovak Radio 6/18/1993, cited in BBC Summary of World Broadcasts 6/21/1993).

below the 20%–30% level envisioned by the IMF. Instead, the government instituted an unorthodox policy alternative for dealing with trade and balance-of-payments deficits by imposing a 10% surcharge on imports, which became one of the key stumbling blocks in IMF negotiations in subsequent years.

Even though ideologically motivated policy disagreements undoubtedly played an important role in the tense relationship between the Fund and Slovakia during this period, the magnitude of these disagreements was undoubtedly exaggerated by Mečiar's penchant for rhetorical bravado. Thus, when Slovakia eventually caved in to international pressure and devaluated its currency in July 1993, Mečiar could have used the opportunity to emphasize his government's flexibility and readiness to find a compromise with international financial institutions. Instead, he chose to spin the decision as yet another instance of Slovak resistance to IMF demands, and as a national victory: "I was told that no one has ever resisted the IMF for five months. The Swedes tried this, they stood fast for two and a half years, but then they had to apologize. So is this [10% devaluation] a loss or a victory?"[24] The result was a cat-and-mouse relationship with the IMF, which alternated between promises to start negotiating a standby agreement for 1994 to accusations that the World Bank and the IMF were responsible for delaying work on the 1994 budget. Such confrontational tactics intensified after Mečiar's return to power in late 1994, in part because by then the country's foreign reserves had reached more comfortable levels[25] and the country's improving economic performance contributed to better access to international capital markets and thereby reduced the need for direct IMF funding. Therefore, despite some promises to the contrary in mid-1995 and intense pressures from the IMF, the WTO, and the EU, the Slovak government repeatedly postponed the reduction and elimination of the 10% import surcharge instituted in 1993.

Ironically, most of the actual economic policies pursued by the Mečiar government were generally compatible with the main priorities of IMF-style economic reforms; thus, the 23% inflation rate in 1993 was on a par with reform frontrunners such as Hungary and the Czech Republic, while most countries in the region (including many engaged in IMF programs) were still struggling with triple-digit inflation. Similarly, fiscal and

[24] Cited in *CPA*, 12/6/1993.

[25] While foreign reserves increased from $472m at the end of 1993 to around $3.5bn in 1995–96 (with much of this increase occurring during the short tenure of the Moravcik government in 1994), Slovakia's reserves barely exceeded four months of imports even at their peak in late 1995, and then declined to 2.3 months of imports around the 1998 elections. Thus, Slovakia's foreign position was hardly so solid as to take it out of the potential sphere of influence of the IMF.

monetary policies during 1995–96 were in line with IMF conditionality as part of the July 1994 standby agreement, with the budget surplus in 1995 and a very small 1.3% deficit in 1996, while inflation declined even further from 13% in 1994 to 10% in 1995 and an impressive 5.7% in 1996. At the same time, Slovakia privatized and restructured a large part of its economy,[26] and even its main policy disagreements with the IMF— the delayed currency devaluation and the 10% import surcharge—were not particularly severe when compared to the Fund's tolerance for unorthodox stabilization measures in Latin America a decade earlier.

The tense relationship with the IMF had a number of negative repercussions. First, the standoff deprived Slovakia of significant funding opportunities, not only from the IMF but also from other multilateral and bilateral lenders for whom the IMF acted as a gatekeeper. Such funding would have been particularly important during the early postindependence period (1993–94) when Slovakia struggled with low reserves and a precarious economy. Even after this a critical phase, the defiant and occasionally belligerent tone of the Slovak official discourse toward the IMF and the West in general contributed to the significant and costly delays of Slovakia's Western integration, particularly into the EU.[27] Finally, the failure to comply with IMF-style neoliberal policy prescriptions probably played an important role in discouraging foreign direct investment, which was surprisingly low compared to Slovakia's neighbors, especially given the country's solid economic performance in the mid-1990s. This point was emphasized by a World Bank official in early 1995 who warned that "Slovakia cannot get by in its development without foreign investment . . . and Bratislava has to realize that without the removal of legal, economic and trade barriers there will not be any interest in the Slovak market on the part of foreign capital."[28] As a consequence Slovakia found itself in the unenviable position of having to cope with painful economic reforms with minimal international assistance, a situation that exacerbated the short-term costs of economic reforms in the early postindependence period.[29]

As suggested above (and discussed in more detail in chapter 6), Mečiar's insistence on nationalist and confrontational rhetoric undoubt-

[26] The share of the private sector in overall GDP jumped from 30% in 1992 to 55% in 1994 (according to EBRD estimates).

[27] Of course, Slovakia's patchy democratic record and its disputed minority policies toward Hungarians and Romas also played an important role in these decisions (but these factors can also be considered part of the broader populist "package" of Meciarism).

[28] *EIU Country Report*, 1st quarter, 1995.

[29] In 1993 Slovakia suffered the fourth consecutive year of economic contraction (by 3.7%), and unemployment, which averaged more than 14% in 1993–94, was one of the highest in the region.

edly deserves much of the blame for Slovakia's costly international isolation. However, the Slovak experience also illustrates the narrow range of policy options available to post-communist countries during the heyday of the Washington Consensus. When Slovakia finally managed to secure an IMF program in July 1994 during the short tenure of the Moravcik government, it was—despite complaints by a prominent HZDS politician about the softer IMF approach toward the new government—due to the much more accommodating stance of the Slovak reformers, who agreed to the same basic conditions that had been rejected by the Mečiar government earlier in the year.

Summing up, the Slovak case illustrates the high political and economic costs of nationalist-populist deviations from the prescriptions of the Washington consensus in postcommunist Eastern Europe. The Slovak government's repeated resistance to IMF conditionality throughout the mid-1990s is particularly striking, given that at least in the early period (1993–94) the newly created Slovak state needed both the funding and the stamp of the Fund's approval of its economic policies in view of its precarious international position. Thus, Slovakia's experience serves as a reminder that IMF conditionality and the Washington Consensus are not automatically imposed by external pressures even in small, vulnerable countries. At the same time, the consistency with which the IMF punished Slovakia's relatively minor deviations from economic orthodoxy suggests that at least for small countries without the benefits of political favoritism, the range of acceptable economic policies had narrowed considerably by the mid-1990s, at least compared to the "ends-over-means" approach to economic adjustment during the debt crisis in the 1980s.

Conclusion

The interactions between the International Monetary Fund and the four Latin American and two Eastern European countries discussed in this chapter, have confirmed the centrality of financial need in the politics of program initiation and implementation. Thus, concerns about debt servicing in Argentina and low international reserves in Moldova were arguably the main reasons for their repeated involvement in IMF programs despite the fact that their governments were a priori reluctant to engage in IMF-style economic reforms. Among more willing reformers, such as Chile under Pinochet and Peru under Belaúnde, financial considerations not only complemented domestic reform drives but also contributed to the continuation of reforms at critical junctures when the high economic and political costs of adjustment undermined the original domestic commitment to reforms. Still, despite the steep economic costs of avoiding IMF programs in crisis situations, the experiences of Slovakia under Mečiar, Bolivia under Siles, and Peru under Garcia show that even extreme financial need is no guarantee of successful IMF engagements. Even among these outliers, however, financial considerations were not completely irrelevant. Thus, the Siles government in Bolivia repeatedly tried to secure an IMF agreement in response to its crushing debt service burden but failed to do so due to a combination of domestic political paralysis and IMF intransigence. Meanwhile, despite its combative rhetorical stance, the Mečiar government in Slovakia was careful not to trigger a complete breakdown of its tense relationship with the Fund during the early postindependence period when the country was most financially vulnerable due to its extremely low reserves. Slovakia's more consistent rejection of IMF conditionality after 1995 coincided with an improving external position that reduced the country's financial dependence on IMF funding and signaling. The only government to make a decisive break with the IMF under conditions of severe financial duress was that of Alan Garcia in the late 1980s but the high costs of the resulting international isolation served as a stark reminder for developing countries tempted by similar "rebellions."

The cases discussed in this chapter also reveal the different political dynamics and trade-offs of IMF conditionality in countries of different economic and political importance: The Argentine case confirms that large Latin American debtors had fast-track access to IMF funding and were treated more leniently when deviating from economic orthodoxy. However, the generous financial terms secured by Bolivia in the mid to late 1980s and Moldova in the mid-1990s suggest one possible strategy through which small countries can "play the system," namely by fulfilling the role of showcase reformer, which is necessary for the Fund's international credibility and may temporarily elevate even small countries to relative political importance. However, the broader applicability of such strategy for other small developing countries is likely to be limited, since the political value of showcase status is likely to be diminished as soon as more countries follow suit. Finally, if the Peruvian experience of the 1980s is any guide, medium-size countries may have actually received the worst of both worlds, in that even exemplary compliance with IMF conditionality was not rewarded as generously in financial terms as for small countries like Bolivia (since concessions would have been more expensive in absolute terms), but at the same time, any deviations from orthodoxy were punished more severely than for economically more important countries such as Argentina.

While one should be cautious about drawing broad cross-regional generalizations on the basis of six cases, the comparative empirical evidence presented in this chapter suggests a few interesting conclusions about the role of conditionality in the two crises. The experiences of

Moldova, Slovakia under Moravcik, Peru under Belaúnde, and even Chile under Pinochet show that close cooperation with the IMF often carried significant political costs for governments in both regions. With the partial exception of economically more important countries (such as Argentina and to some extent Chile), the Fund appears to have subordinated such political concerns to the consistent enforcement of IMF conditionality. Moreover, the serious repercussions of Slovakia's 10% import surcharge, a measure that had raised few eyebrows in earlier decades,[30] suggests a reduction over time in the Fund's tolerance for policy deviations from economic orthodoxy. Nevertheless, in purely financial terms, IMF cooperation was more attractive for the ex-communist countries in the 1990s, since (as in the case of Moldova) it unlocked significant direct and indirect funding, whereas in Latin America such funds usually left the country almost immediately in the form of debt-service payments. While compliance was no guarantee of economic and political success, outright rebellion against the IMF and the West more broadly was hardly an attractive alternative when considering the steep costs of international isolation triggered by the combative stance of the Mečiar government in Slovakia and especially by the Garcia administration in Peru. Overall, then, financially vulnerable developing countries in both regions had to walk a fine line between domestic priorities and the requirements of IMF conditionality. This trade-off, which in the context of the Latin American debt crisis was exacerbated by the imbalance between the pain of adjustment and the gains of compliance, created difficult political dilemmas for the governments of the two regions in their attempts to address the roots and consequences of the serious economic crisis confronting their countries. These domestic political struggles are the subject of the next two chapters of this book.

---

[30] For example, Uruguay in 1982 and the Nixon administration in 1971 instituted similar measures without triggering similar responses.

−5−

Domestic Political Responses to Economic Crises

THE PRECEDING TWO CHAPTERS HAVE ILLUSTRATED the importance of international political and economic considerations in driving IMF program dynamics. Nonetheless, IMF programs cannot be simply viewed as outside impositions on powerless and compliant Third World governments. As the cases of Bolivia (1982–85), Peru (1985–89), and Slovakia (1993–95) have shown, even extremely vulnerable countries do not automatically subject themselves to IMF conditionality in response to external crises. Moreover, governments occasionally sign and implement IMF agreements even though their international finances hardly require IMF support.[1] To understand these deviations from the traditional logic of program initiation and implementation, chapters 5 and 6 focus on the domestic politics of IMF-style reforms.

As discussed in chapter 2, international financial markets, and the Fund's approach to conditionality set the constraints for what a government *has to do* in order to address its international and domestic economic problems within the context of an IMF program, and such constraints are more likely to be binding, the greater the intensity of the preceding economic crisis. When making their policy choices, however, governments are also guided by what governing parties and politicians *want to do* for partisan reasons. Finally, governments differ in terms of what they *can do* in a given situation, depending on the political influence and policy preferences of the domestic opposition and the reliability of the country's bureaucratic apparatus. Chapters 5 and 6 show that the successful implementation of IMF-style economic reforms requires a difficult and often volatile combination between these three crucial elements: Thus, governments have to strike a delicate balance between their own economic and ideological agenda, the demands of IMF conditionality, and the domestic political and institutional feasibility of neoliberal reform blueprints.

---

[1] See, for example, Vreeland's discussion of Uruguay's (1990) IMF program (2003: 39–51).

Domestic Drivers of Program Initiation

Even though the Fund's primary mission is to address the external imbalances of program countries, domestic economic crises nevertheless figure prominently among the reasons why countries resort to IMF support. In fact, the link between economic crises and reform constitutes one of the classical explanations of neoliberal economic reforms.[2] The underlying reason for this link is that deep crises can help create a societal consensus in favor of reforms, while at the same time weakening the economic and political benefits of previous rent-seeking activities (Williamson 1993). For all the political and scholarly preoccupation with the roots and consequences of economic crises, however, there is surprisingly little agreement on how to conceptualize and assess such crises (Ishihara 2005). For the most part the crisis has been taken as a given—along the lines that you know an economic crisis when you see one—and the debate has focused on explaining its roots or finding the policy solutions for dealing with the crisis.

In line with Ishihara's (2005) argument about the multidimensional nature of economic crises, the present analysis expands the scope of economic crises from the liquidity and debt-service concerns analyzed in chapter 3 to a number of domestic crisis indicators. In particular, I will analyze the implications of three prominent facets of domestic economic imbalances that have been widely used in the prior literature: inflationary crises, recessions, and fiscal deficits—all of which affected many of the Latin American and Eastern European countries discussed in this book.

The inflationary record of Latin American and Caribbean countries during the 1980s was highly heterogeneous: At one extreme—represented primarily by Argentina and Brazil and to some extent by Peru—triple-digit inflation was the norm rather than the exception for most of the decade, and the dismal record was rounded out by hyperinflationary episodes toward the end of the decade. At the low end of the inflation spectrum we find not only Pinochet's Chile, Colombia, and (at least until 1989) Venezuela but also several Central American and Caribbean countries. While the ex-communist countries also experienced high and variable inflation levels, their trajectory nevertheless stands out in several ways. First, with the exception of Hungary and Czechoslovakia, all the ex-communist countries experienced at least one episode of triple-digit inflation after the collapse of communism, and almost two-thirds of them—including not only troubled economies like Georgia and Ukraine, but also advanced reformers like Poland or Estonia—reached hyperinfla-

---

[2] See Stallings and Kaufman 1989, Nelson 1990, Ranis and Mahmood 1992, Rodrik 1994, Haggard and Kaufman 1995, Remmer 1998.

tionary levels (above 500%) at least once in the 1990s. Second, in contrast to Latin America, post-communist inflation appears to have been more of a transitional phenomenon, with only one country (Belarus) stuck above 50% inflation by late 2001.

Economic growth (or more appropriately the lack thereof) also figured prominently on the domestic agenda of the countries of the two regions: In Latin America the debt crisis was appropriately dubbed the "lost decade" as the challenge of debt repayment and the lack of fresh credits seriously depressed economic growth, which averaged less than 1% per annum for the countries in my sample. Even by the low standards of the debt crisis, the output trajectory of ex-communist countries during the 1990s stands out as abysmal with a regional output decline of almost 2.5% per year.[3] However, within each of the regions, there was a great deal of cross-country and cross-temporal variation: In Latin America the almost 20% economic slump in Peru in 1988–89 stands in sharp contrast to the 7% average growth of Chile in the late 1980s, whereas in Eastern Europe the abysmal output declines of countries like Moldova, Ukraine, and Tajikistan (which by the late 1990s had lost more than 60% of their pre-transition output levels) were at least partially balanced by the strong growth performance of Poland, Hungary, and Slovakia, which averaged 5% growth in the late 1990s.

How did these serious domestic economic imbalances affect the program initiation calculus of governments in the two regions? With respect to the most visible crisis aspect—high inflation—the results in tables 5.1a and 5.1b, whose substantive effects are illustrated in figures 5.1a and 5.1b, confirm the theoretical predictions about the importance of domestic economic crises for persuading governments to initiate IMF programs: According to model 1, the effects of inflation were positive and fairly large in both regions, though their statistical significance was somewhat more robust to model specification in Eastern Europe than in Latin America.[4] But whereas the economic and political costs of high inflation acted as important reform catalysts, governments were much less likely to resort to IMF support for dealing with less visible crisis aspects, even if these policies clearly fell within the scope of IMF programs; thus, model 2 suggests that large fiscal deficits not only failed to trigger IMF programs in

---

[3] For both regions the numbers look somewhat better when using median rather than average output: For Latin America the median output performance was a still modest +1.5%, while for Eastern Europe it was +.5%.

[4] Similar but somewhat weaker results were obtained using dichotomous inflation measures (with thresholds of 40% for high inflation and 1,000% for hyperinflation), which suggests that the effects of inflation on program initiation are better conceptualized as continuous rather than step-functions. To deal with the endogeneity of inflationary crises, I also ran a model using an instrumented version of inflation, which confirmed the positive effect of inflation (and actually produced stronger results in Eastern Europe).

TABLE 5.1A
Domestic Drivers of Program Initiation—Latin America (1982–89)

	(1)	(2)	(3)	(4)	(5)	(6)	(7)	(8)	(9)	(10)	(11)
Inflation (lag)	.31* (.19)				.21 (.20)	.31* (.18)	.45* (.21)	-.27 (.42)	.34# (.18)	.36* (.18)	.20 (.23)
GDP change (lag)		-.03 (.05)		-.03 (.05)							
Fiscal balance (lag)		-.02 (.04)		-.10* (.05)							
Reserves (t-1)	-.28** (.10)	-.30** (.11)	-.29** (.10)	-.26* (.10)	-.28** (.10)	-.15 (.17)	-.36** (.11)	-.26* (.10)	-.29** (.11)	-.29** (.10)	-.29** (.11)
Interest/GNP	.88* (.41)	.87* (.44)	.60# (.44)	1.15* (.47)	1.63# (.73)	.86* (.42)	.71# (.46)	1.25* (.49)	-.35 (.77)	1.14** (.40)	.85* (.41)
Gov't ideology	-.29 (.19)		.79 (.61)	.07 (.24)	.43 (.60)	-.09 (.29)		-.35# (.19)	-.24 (.19)	-.14 (.20)	-.33 (.21)
LBP gov't		-.85 (.68)					-3.58# (2.12)				
Quality of bureaucracy	.32# (.25)	.36# (.27)	.41# (.26)	.24 (.27)	.20 (.26)	.28 (.25)	.46* (.25)	-.78 (.75)	-.91 (.72)	.34# (.22)	.34# (.24)
Regime	.03 (.04)	.03 (.04)	.03 (.04)	.02 (.04)	.04 (.04)	.05 (.04)	.01 (.04)	.03 (.04)	.04 (.04)		
Political constraints											1.15 (.91)
Gov't ideology * Inflation			-.27* (.15)								
Gov't ideology * Fiscal balance				.06* (.03)							
Gov't ideology * Interest/GNP					-.41 (.32)						
Gov't ideology * Reserves (t-1)						-.08 (.09)					

Logistic regression coefficients with standard errors in parentheses (#–10%; *–5%; **–1%—one-tailed where appropriate)

TABLE 5.1A (con't)
Domestic Drivers of Program Initiation—Latin America (1982–89)

	(1)	(2)	(3)	(4)	(5)	(6)	(7)	(8)	(9)	(10)	(11)
LBP gov't* Interest/GNP							1.37 (.99)				
Inflation (t-1)*								.31* (.20)			
Quality of bureaucracy											
Interest/GNI*									.67* (.37)		
Quality of bureaucracy											
Seat share of largest gov't party										1.58* (.98)	
Pre-Electoral Period										-.42 (.52)	
Post-Electoral Period											-1.43 (1.35)
Post-Elect. Period*											.35 (.31)
Inflation(t-2)											-.04 (.31)
Total debt	.00 (.29)	.26 (.30)	-.11 (.30)	.05 (.26)	.01 (.29)	.02 (.29)	.12 (.31)	-.21 (.34)	.00 (.27)	-.10 (.26)	.03 (.27)
UN voting (y-1)	.02 (.05)	.01 (.05)	.02 (.05)	.08 (.15)	.03 (.05)	.03 (.05)	.03 (.05)	.02 (.05)	.15 (.14)	.02 (.04)	.02 (.15)
GDP/capita	.08 (.14)	.06 (.14)	.04 (.14)	.08 (.15)	.13 (.14)	.09 (.14)	.03 (.14)	.03 (.14)	.15 (.14)	.08 (.13)	.02 (.15)
IMF Program History	2.43* (1.06)	2.30* (1.07)	2.54* (1.05)	1.82# (1.10)	2.41* (1.06)	2.74* (1.13)	2.41* (1.04)	2.37* (1.07)	1.89# (1.04)	1.08 (1.11)	2.43* (1.05)
Observations	495	495	495	495	495	495	495	495	495	495	490

Logistic regression coefficients with standard errors in parentheses (#—10%; *—5%; **—1%—one-tailed where appropriate)

TABLE 5.1B
Domestic Drivers of Program Initiation—Eastern Europe (1990–2001)

	(1)	(2)	(3)	(4)	(5)	(6)	(7)	(8)	(9)	(10)	(11)
Inflation (lag)	.25* (.14)		.10 (.17)		.23* (.14)	.25* (.14)	.19# (.14)		.26* (.14)	.24* (.14)	-.00 (.19)
Reserves (t-1)	-.58** (.16)	-.62** (.16)	-.59** (.16)	-.60** (.15)	-.59** (.16)	-.58** (.19)	-.61** (.16)	-.60** (.16)	-.41 (.29)	-.56** (.16)	-.58** (.16)
GDP change (lagged)		-.06** (.02)		-.06* (.02)				-.04 (.04)			
Fiscal balance		.04 (.03)									
Interest/GNI	.47 (.43)	.79 (.49)	.41 (.44)	.63 (.45)	.86* (.52)	.47 (.43)	.72 (.45)	.63 (.45)	.46 (.43)	.46 (.43)	.36 (.47)
Anti-reform gov't	-.29 (.36)		-1.58# (.96)	-.27 (.40)	.23 (.53)	-.29 (.52)		-.19 (.37)	-.25 (.37)	-.27 (.36)	-.42 (.40)
Gov't ideology		.05# (.03)					.00 (.04)				
Quality of governance	.58* (.29)	.59* (.32)	.59* (.29)	.77* (.31)	.65* (.30)	.58* (.29)	.58* (.30)	.72* (.32)	.69* (.33)	.57* (.29)	.42# (.26)
Regime	-.04 (.05)	-.08 (.06)	-.03 (.05)	-.08 (.05)	-.04 (.05)	-.04 (.05)	-.05 (.05)	-.08 (.05)	-.04 (.05)	-.04 (.05)	
Political constraints											-.23 (.82)
Anti-reform gov't* Inflation			.28 (.19)								
Anti-reform gov't* GDP chg.				-.01 (.03)							

Logistic regression coefficients with standard errors in parentheses (#–10%; *–5%; **–%1—one-tailed where appropriate)

TABLE 5.1B
Domestic Drivers of Program Initiation—Eastern Europe (1990–2001)

	(1)	(2)	(3)	(4)	(5)	(6)	(7)	(8)	(9)	(10)	(11)
Inflation (lag)	.25*		.10		.23*	.25*	.19#		.26*	.24*	-.00
	(.14)		(.17)		(.14)	(.14)	(.14)		(.14)	(.14)	(.19)
Reserves (t-1)	-.58**	-.62**	-.59**	-.60**	-.59**	-.58**	-.61**	-.60**	-.41	-.56**	-.58**
	(.16)	(.16)	(.16)	(.15)	(.16)	(.19)	(.16)	(.16)	(.29)	(.16)	(.16)
GDP change (lagged)		-.06**		-.06*				-.04			
		(.02)		(.02)				(.04)			
Fiscal balance		.04									
		(.03)									
Interest/GNI	.47	.79	.41	.63	.86*	.47	.72	.63	.46	.46	.36
	(.43)	(.49)	(.44)	(.45)	(.52)	(.43)	(.45)	(.45)	(.43)	(.43)	(.47)
Anti-reform gov't	-.29		-1.58#	-.27	.23	-.29		-.19	-.25	-.27	-.42
	(.36)		(.96)	(.40)	(.53)	(.52)		(.37)	(.37)	(.36)	(.40)
Gov't ideology		.05#					.00				
		(.03)					(.04)				
Quality of governance	.58*	.59*	.59*	.77*	.65*	.58*	.58*	.72*	.69*	.57*	.42#
	(.29)	(.32)	(.29)	(.31)	(.30)	(.29)	(.30)	(.32)	(.33)	(.29)	(.26)
Regime	-.04	-.08	-.03	-.08	-.04	-.04	-.05	-.08	-.04	-.04	
	(.05)	(.06)	(.05)	(.05)	(.05)	(.05)	(.05)	(.05)	(.05)	(.05)	
Political constraints											-.23
											(.82)
Anti-reform gov't* Inflation			.28								
			(.19)								
Anti-reform gov't* GDP chg.				-.01							
				(.03)							

Logistic regression coefficients with standard errors in parentheses (#-10%; *-5%; **-%1—one-tailed where appropriate)

Figure 5.1a: Substantive effects of domestic drivers of initiation—Latin America (1982–89)

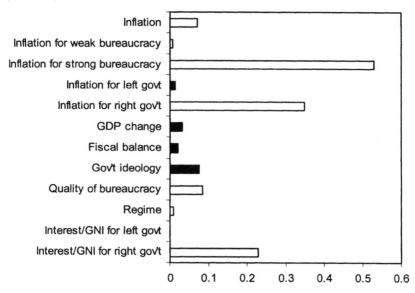

Note: Effects represent change in initiation probability for a change in the variable of interest from the 10th to the 90th percentile. Negative effects are marked as black bars.

both regions but even pointed in the wrong direction in Eastern Europe (albeit not significantly).

As discussed earlier, for the third indicator of domestic economic performance—GDP growth—the theoretical predictions are somewhat more complicated: On one hand, the effects of serious recessions are sufficiently visible to create significant pressures for economic policy change, but on the other hand, the Fund's emphasis on austerity measures and its poor track record of growth promotion (Vreeland 2003) do not necessarily make IMF programs the obvious choice for dealing with recessions. This ambiguity is reflected in the statistical results: Whereas in Eastern Europe countries with poor growth performance were much more likely to resort to IMF support (significant at .01), in Latin America the effects were substantively much smaller and statistically insignificant. These results further reinforce the argument that the different nature of the crises in the two regions led to different perceptions about the role of the IMF; whereas in Eastern Europe the return to growth was predicated on the successful reform push beyond the recession associated with initial partial reforms (Hellman 1998), in Latin America there was much greater skepti-

Figure 5.1b: Substantive effects of domestic drivers of initiation—Eastern Europe (1990–2001)

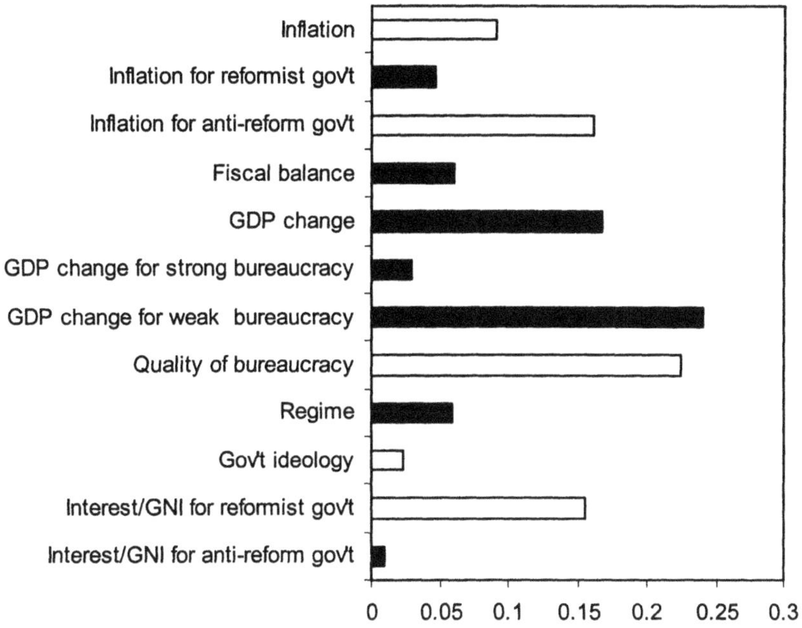

Note: Effects represent change in initiation probability for a change in the variable of interest from the 10th to the 90th percentile. Negative effects are marked as black bars.

cism that IMF policy prescriptions would provide the key to renewed growth (Pastor 1989).

These results suggest that in order for a domestic economic crisis to trigger IMF-style reforms, crisis intensity needs to be reinforced by two additional factors: crisis visibility and the credibility of IMF policy prescriptions. Contrary to Vreeland's claims about the importance of fiscal deficits in driving governments to seek the imposition of IMF conditionality, it appears that governments are much less responsive to such structural problems than to the much more visible repercussions of inflationary crises. Even when crises are visible and politically costly—as in the case of growth—their effects on program initiation hinge on the extent to which IMF-style policies provide credible solutions to the problem at hand. These differences across crisis indicators and regions suggest that we need to go beyond the straightforward crisis-reform link implicitly assumed by much of the statistical literature and pay closer attention to the process through which objective economic crises are filtered through the perceptions and preferences of domestic political actors.

Partisan Policy Responses to Economic Crises

Why does economic crisis result in political action in some settings but not in others? More broadly—what is the process through which certain economic indicators (and the realities they purport to measure) become catalysts of sustained political action to transform, often dramatically, established economic policy patterns, institutions, and social relations? To answer these questions, the analysis moves beyond purely economic crisis indicators to incorporate the insight that—like beauty—economic crisis is often in the eye of the beholder.

As suggested by the formal model, a logical starting point for explaining different responses to economic crises is to look at the partisan preferences of domestic political actors, especially those of top decision makers who play a crucial role in the initiation of neoliberal reforms and IMF programs. As will be discussed in more detail in the following chapter, the reform trajectories of individual Latin American and Eastern European countries (such as Bolivia, Peru, and Slovakia) were significantly shaped by the ideological preferences of their leaders. In this sense, the two regions offer an ideal testing ground for the importance of ideology, since the ideological orientations of the different governments varied along three key dimensions. First, both regions had a broad cross-country spectrum of ideological orientations, ranging from Communists (in Nicaragua and Uzbekistan) to ideologically committed neoliberals (e.g., in Chile in the 1980s and Poland in 1990). Second, both regions offer a number of interesting instances of significant within-country ideological reversals (such as in Bolivia, Peru, Slovakia, and Bulgaria) that facilitate a better understanding of the effects over time of ideological change in a given institutional context. Finally, the cross-regional differences in the nature of the economic crisis and the role of political parties allows for a useful test of the generalizability of the relationship between economic crisis, partisan politics, and reforms in the developing world.

When judged by the standards of the existing literature, models 1 and 2 provide at least some tentative evidence that partisan government orientations affected the politics of program initiation; thus, in Eastern Europe ex-communist/nationalist governments were somewhat less likely to initiate IMF programs (model 1), as were left-leaning governments (when measured by Stone's 21-point ideology scale in model 2) but the results were at best marginally significant. In Latin America, the ideology barrier was somewhat greater (see fig. 5.1a) (but only marginally significant at .1 one-tailed according to model 1), but according to model 2 the effects of having labor-based party governments were negative but not statistically significant.

However, to capture the complexity of partisan responses to economic crises, we need to go beyond these simple additive effects of crisis and partisanship measures and take a closer look at the *interplay* between "objective" economic crisis indicators and the ideological preferences and partisan institutional ties of political leaders who are in power at the time of the crisis. As discussed in chapter 2, these insufficiently studied crisis-partisanship interactions may take a number of different forms depending on how politicians interpret a given crisis. If technocratic crisis reactions predominate, then governments should be more eager to enter IMF agreements in response to economic crises irrespective of their ideological orientations. Under such a scenario, partisan policy differences may exist in low-to-moderate crisis situations but during severe economic crises they give way to *crisis-driven policy convergence*. In other words, ideological deviations from economic orthodoxy are fair-weather "luxuries" that are abandoned in the face of severe economic crises. At the other extreme, ideology matters more in explaining how different governments react to economic crisis than with respect to their noncrisis baseline policies: Right-wing governments seize the crisis as an opportunity to implement IMF-style reforms, which are broadly compatible both with their ideological convictions and with the economic interests of their core constituents. Meanwhile, leftist parties (and their constituencies) are more sensitive to the costs of market reforms, and their ideological disagreements with the IMF may even lead them to interpret the crisis roots and solutions in fundamentally different ways. To the extent that either ideological convictions or partisan ties to likely reform losers are sufficiently strong, such governments will avoid IMF programs even under extreme duress, which leads to *crisis-driven policy divergence* among governments of different political orientations. Finally, if, as implicitly assumed by earlier studies, there is no interaction between crisis intensity and partisanship, we should observe either *nonpartisan technocratic policy responses* (where partisanship is never relevant) or *crisis-independent partisan policy differences* (where partisanship matters uniformly across a wide range of economic conditions).

The earlier comparison of the two crisis settings suggests that we should expect to see crisis convergence or nonpartisan crisis responses in Eastern Europe and crisis divergence in Latin America. Given that the debt crisis was triggered by Mexico's default in August 1982 and because several aggravating circumstances were of an external nature,[5] Latin America witnessed serious debates about the relative weight of domestic

---

[5] Factors included the global recession after 1979, the rise of interest rates, the lower lending willingness of commercial banks, and the deteriorating terms of trade (Eichengreen and Fishlow 1996:22).

versus external responsibility for the debt crisis (Jorge 1985, Pastor 1989). Meanwhile, in Eastern Europe the roots of the economic crisis lay much more clearly in the history of domestic economic mismanagement under communism and therefore did not lend themselves as easily to fundamentally different ideological interpretations. Moreover, the more activist Latin American labor movement with its established formal political ties to major political parties provided a social basis that reinforced the ideological convictions of leftist opponents to IMF policy prescriptions, whereas in Eastern Europe the atomizing legacy of communism combined with the global hegemony of neoliberal economic ideas undermined both ideological and organizational sources of opposition to the IMF.

These predictions are confirmed by the cross-regional differences in the interactions between government orientation and domestic economic crisis indicators. According to model 3 in table 5.1b, Eastern European ex-communist/nationalist governments were noticeably less likely to initiate IMF programs at low inflation levels (significant at .05 one-tailed) but they responded strongly to inflationary crises (significant at .01) while for their reformist counterparts the effect was smaller and failed to reach statistical significance. As a result, as illustrated in figure 5.2b, at high inflation levels, governments of different ideological persuasions were equally likely to initiate IMF-style reforms and in hyperinflationary situations, ex-communists even exceeded the reformers in their reformist zeal (though the difference was not statistically significant). Meanwhile, judging by model 3 in table 5.1a, in Latin America higher inflation greatly increased the likelihood of program initiation for right governments, but the effects disappeared entirely for left governments. As figure 5.2a illustrates, what seems to set leftist and rightist governments apart is not their baseline attitude toward the IMF at low levels of inflation but their different reactions to high inflation, which prompted the Right to initiate IMF-style reforms whereas the Left tried to avoid the high social costs of anti-inflationary measures.

The contrast between *crisis-driven policy convergence* among post-communist governments of different ideological persuasions and the *crisis-driven policy divergence* in Latin America of the 1980s was not limited to inflationary crises but also applied to other aspects of domestic economic crises. Thus, according to model 4, fiscal deficits provoked divergent reactions among Latin American governments of different political orientations, whereas for rightist governments fiscal crises were associated with an increase in IMF program initiation (significant at .05 one-tailed), for leftist governments fiscal crises actually *reduced* the incidence of IMF programs (marginally significant at .1) thereby leading to a sizeable negative effect of ideology in countries facing severe budget deficits (significant at .05). Similarly, recessions in Latin America were associated

Figure 5.2a: Inflation, ideology, and program initiation—Latin America (1982–89)

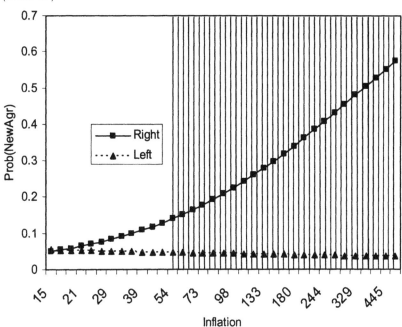

Note: Statistical significance for predictor variable: continuous line (p < .05), dotted line (p > .05). Statistical significance for modifying variable: shaded area (p < .05).

with more IMF programs for the Right and fewer for the Left, and once again this crisis-driven policy divergence resulted in significant ideological effects during extreme crisis situations (but not otherwise).[6] Very similar results were obtained for governments dominated by labor-based parties, which suggests that both ideology and institutional ties to organized labor produced divergent policy reactions to domestic economic crises during the debt crisis. By contrast, model 4 in table 5b suggests that in Eastern Europe, recessionary crises triggered substantively large and statistically significant (at .01) increases in IMF program initiation for both ex-communists and reformers. The effects of ideology were negative but statistically insignificant across the board, and actually decreased slightly in severe crisis situations. Meanwhile, fiscal deficits were similarly weak

---

[6] The *GDP change* results (presented in the electronic appendix) were only marginally significant (at .1 one-tailed) for right governments, but ideology was significant at .05 for moderate-to-severe recessions.

Figure 5.2b: Inflation, ideology, and initiation—Eastern Europe (1990–2001)

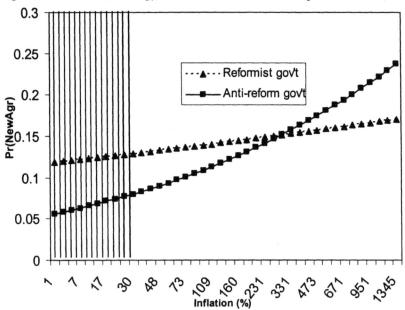

Note: Statistical significance for predictor variable: continuous line (p < .05), dotted line (p > .05). Statistical significance for modifying variable: shaded area (p < .10).

program deterrents for both right and left governments (results omitted), which further highlights the weakness of partisan differences in crisis reactions in ex-communist countries.[7]

Compared to the contrasting interaction patterns between partisanship and domestic economic crises, the partisan dynamics of external crisis reactions are actually rather similar in the two regions. Thus, according to figures 5.3a and 5.3b (based on model 5 in tables 5.1a and 5.1b), in both Latin America and Eastern Europe, higher interest payments caused right and centrist governments to seek out IMF support, but the effect vanished for left governments. As expected, this effect was stronger in both substantive and statistical terms in Latin America, where leftist governments were more likely to blame the West for the severity of the crisis. However, the positive interaction effect between interest payments and LBP governments in model 7 of table 5.1 suggests that Latin American parties with close labor ties were actually more likely to accede to IMF pressures under such crisis circumstances. The contrasting finding for

[7] Very similar results were obtained using Stone's 21-point ideology scale.

Fig 5.3a: Interest payments, ideology, and initiation—Latin America (1982–89)

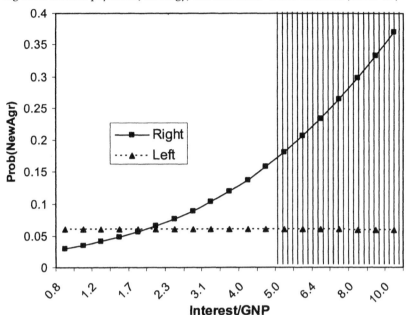

Note: Statistical significance for predictor variable: continuous line (p < .05), dotted line (p > .05). Statistical significance for modifying variable: shaded area (p < .05).

these two alternative measures of partisan orientation suggests that the divergent reactions to debt service crises in Latin America were driven by the ideological convictions of leftist politicians rather their partisan institutional ties.

By contrast, according to model 6, partisan differences did not produce similar policy divergence in countries facing liquidity crises. This effect is hardly surprising in Eastern Europe, where the high salience of liquidity concerns, combined with the relative weakness of ideological convictions meant that both ex-communists and reformers reacted almost identically and very strongly to lower reserves (significant at .01 irrespective of ideology). However, lower international reserves led to policy convergence among governments of different ideological persuasions even in Latin America; thus, in model 6 the effects of lower reserves were more powerful for the left and center-left (significant at .05), and for right-wing governments the effects were no longer statistically significant. Moreover, partisan differences in program initiation only mattered for high reserves but vanished during severe liquidity crises.

Fig 5.3b: Interest payments, ideology, and initiation—Eastern Europe (1990–2001)

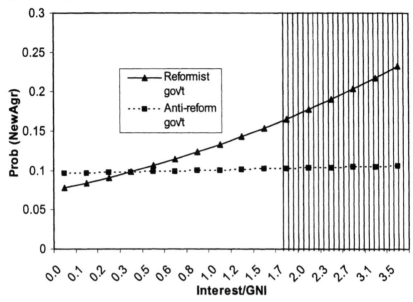

Note: Statistical significance for predictor variable: continuous line (p < .05), dotted line (p > .05). Statistical significance for modifying variable: shaded area (p < .10).

Therefore, it appears that *ideological policy divergence* in response to external economic crises only applied to foreign debt repayments but not to foreign reserves. Given that these results hold in both regions despite the different nature of their crises, it appears that the liquidity crises signaled by low reserves are inherently less susceptible to divergent ideological interpretations, possibly because the threat of insolvency is much more difficult to counter without IMF support than other economic crisis aspects. Meanwhile, as will be illustrated by the Peruvian case study in the next chapter, crushing debt service burdens can be addressed either through orthodox, IMF-backed adjustment measures or through unilateral reductions in debt payments, and the relative propensity of governments to choose between these two options is obviously affected by ideological interpretations about the crisis causes. Seen from this perspective, the ideological policy divergence in response to domestic economic crises in Latin America may be at least part due to the close ties between the debt crisis and the region's domestic economic troubles, as high fiscal deficits were at least partly driven by heavy debt service burdens, inflation was exacerbated by the lack of international credit to finance these deficits in noninflationary ways, and the region-wide recession was also closely linked to the austerity measures associated with debt repayment. By contrast, with the exception of Bulgaria (and to some extent Hungary, Poland, and Russia), Eastern Europe's lower foreign debt service burden could hardly be blamed for the region's domestic economic difficulties. Instead, the roots of fiscal deficits, rising prices, and output declines were much more clearly tied to the structural distortions inherited from communism. Therefore, the propensity of foreign debt to trigger divergent ideological policy responses did not affect the politics of domestic crisis management in Eastern Europe to the extent that it did in Latin America in the 1990s.

Bureaucratic Quality and Program Initiation

Ideological or crisis-driven government policy intentions are not sufficient, however, to ensure the initiation and implementation of IMF-style reforms. Governments also need to be able to translate these policy designs into reality, and one of the crucial factors affecting this process is the effectiveness of bureaucratic institutions. In this respect, Eastern European countries faced particular difficulties (McFaul 1995), since post-communist reforms occurred in the context of extremely underdeveloped markets and political institutions. Especially in the early transition years, most ex-communist countries were plagued by weak legislative and regulatory frameworks, a dysfunctional banking sector, and rudimentary financial markets prone to scandals and speculation. By comparison, despite the importance of the state sector and the distortions created by the large capital inflows of the 1970s, most Latin American countries could at least depend upon the basic legal and institutional framework necessary for the functioning of a market economy. Therefore, we would expect that the variation in the functioning of state institutions to matter more for the success of economic reforms in expertise-scarce Eastern Europe than in Latin America.

Aside from the cross-regional differences, the bureaucratic capacity of governments to get things done also varied to a significant extent within the two regions. In Latin America, judging by the *ICRG bureaucratic quality* scores, Chile, Colombia, Venezuela, and Brazil had significantly better performing bureaucracies than the regional average, whereas impoverished countries like Bolivia, Paraguay, and Haiti ranked at the bottom of the hierarchy, with relatively few significant overtime changes during the 1980s. Meanwhile, among the transition economies, there was a large and temporally persistent gap between the relatively functional bureaucratic institutions in East-Central Europe and the Baltics, and the abysmal state apparatus inherited by most former Soviet republics, particularly in Central Asia. Several Balkan countries—such as Romania, Bulgaria, and Macedonia—started out with fairly modest institutions but improved gradually over the course of the transition, even though they have yet to close the gap that separates them from the transition front-runners.

The statistical patterns of IMF program initiation confirm that bureaucratic quality mattered more in Eastern Europe, where the quality of governance indicator had a substantively large and marginally significant (at .1 one-tailed) positive effect, whereas in Latin America the effect was smaller and failed to reach statistical significance. However, the real test of the importance of bureaucratic capacity is not whether it is associated with more frequent IMF programs but whether it facilitates faster reactions to economic crises. In other words, in line with the formal model predictions, we should observe a positive interaction effect between crisis intensity and bureaucratic quality.

From this perspective, the statistical results from both regions confirm that the quality of bureaucratic institutions mediates the impact of economic crisis on IMF program initiation. As illustrated in figure 5.4a based on model 8 in table 5.1a, the catalytic effects of inflation for program initiation were much stronger for the more capable Latin American governments (significant at .05) but were negligible and statistically insignificant for countries with weak bureaucratic institutions (below the 35th percentile). As a result, the positive impact of bureaucratic quality, which was negligible at low inflation levels, was large and statistically significant (at .05 one-tailed) during moderate-to-severe inflationary crises. A very similar interaction pattern is also reflected in model 9, which suggests that higher interest payment burdens only resulted in more frequent IMF programs in countries with reasonably competent bureaucracies (significant at .05) and that bureaucratic competence mattered most in countries with heavy debt service burdens.

While in Eastern Europe the interaction between governance and inflation was weak (results omitted), figure 5.4b (based on model 8 in table 5.1b) suggests that countries with relatively competent bureaucracies were significantly more likely to resort to IMF programs in response to recessionary crises (significant at .01) whereas the effect was smaller and less significant (.05 one-tailed) in weaker states. Similarly, the negative interaction effect between international reserves and quality of governance in model 9 suggests that countries with better institutions also reacted more decisively to external crises. Conversely, in both models, better bureaucracies mattered most in crisis situations (negative growth, low reserves), where they led to a significantly higher propensity of program initiation (.05 one-tailed), whereas in countries with reassuring growth and reserves, institutional differences mattered less for program initiation.

Figure 5.4a: Inflation, bureaucracy, and initiation—Latin America (1982–89)

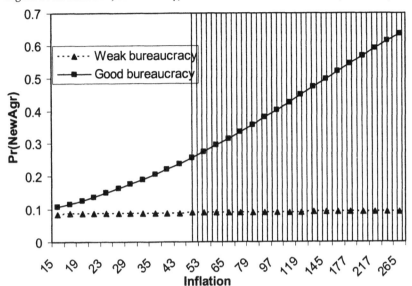

Note: Statistical significance for predictor variable: continuous line (p < .05), dotted line (p > .05). Statistical significance for modifying variable: shaded area (p < .05).

Domestic Political Constraints and Program Initiation

So far, the analysis in this chapter has established that despite their important role in the initiation of IMF-style reforms, economic crises do not automatically and uniformly trigger such reforms but instead are mediated by ideologically influenced crisis perceptions among domestic politicians and by the technical constraints imposed by weak bureaucratic capacities. This section turns to a different type of constraint and focuses on the domestic political process through which the reform pressures inherent in economic crises do or do not produce decisive policy changes. Such a focus is warranted by the fact that the history of IMF programs in the developing world abounds with examples of the intense domestic political struggles provoked by the high-stakes economic adjustment policies required by IMF conditionality. However, in line with the formal model predictions, there is no reason to expect that the prospects of IMF-style reforms are necessarily undermined in situations where the government is not fully insulated from alternative political interests. Instead, the effects of greater political openness should be mediated by the relative policy preferences of the government and the opposition, which means

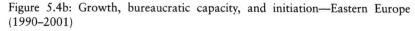

Figure 5.4b: Growth, bureaucratic capacity, and initiation—Eastern Europe (1990–2001)

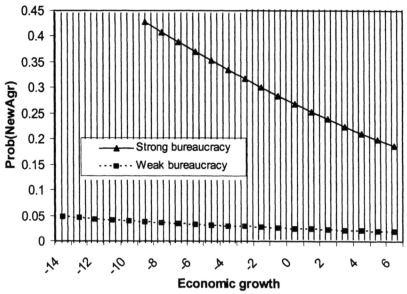

Note: Statistical significance for predictor variable: continuous line (p < .05), dotted line (p > .05). Statistical significance for modifying variable: shaded area (p < .05).

that greater openness may actually promote reforms in situations where the opposition (or the wider public) prefers greater economic reforms than the government. From this perspective, given the greater public opposition to IMF-style economic adjustment policies in Latin America compared to Eastern Europe, we should expect political openness to constitute a greater obstacle to IMF program initiation and implementation during the debt crisis than during the post-communist transition.

While a detailed comparison of political systems in the two regions is beyond the scope of the present discussion, a brief comparison of the two episodes reveals a few important similarities. First, there was a rapid increase of the total share of democracies during the first three years of democratization: Using the score of 16 on the polity regime scale as the democracy cutoff point,[8] the former communist world went from having no democracies in 1989 to having more than half of its ever-expanding number of countries become democracies by the end of 1992 (fifteen of

---

[8] The results are not changed significantly by choosing a slightly higher or lower cutoff point and are therefore not discussed here.

the twenty-six countries in my sample were democratic at that point). Similarly, though slightly less dramatically, whereas in 1982 democracies accounted for only eight of the twenty-two Latin American countries in my sample, by 1985 the tally had risen to thirteen, an almost identical proportion as in the former communist countries by 1992. Following this initial surge of democratization, both regions experienced a democratic plateau for the rest of the decade with the share of democracies virtually unchanged until 1989 in Latin America and 2001 in the transition countries. With respect to other potential measures of political constraints, however, post-communist governments were in a somewhat weaker position than their Latin American counterparts; thus, possibly because of the high volatility inherent in the fledgling post-communist political party systems, the average seat share of the largest governing party in Eastern Europe was noticeably lower than in Latin America (44% versus 66% respectively). Moreover, the more frequent elections in Eastern Europe meant that transition countries were affected more frequently by electoral considerations, which may facilitate greater political input from nongovernmental political actors.

The statistical results in tables 5.1a and 5.1b suggest that at least at the initiation stage, political constraints played a relatively modest role in the IMF programs of both regions. Thus, in Latin America the effects of democracy (models 1–9) and veto points (model 11) were positive but failed to reach statistical significance. Moreover, the tentative conclusion that politically constrained governments were more likely to initiate IMF programs was contradicted by the results in model 10, which reveals an (albeit statistically insignificant) positive effect for the parliamentary seat share of the largest governing party, as well as a modest negative effect for pre-electoral periods. In Eastern Europe the program initiation effects of regime type, veto points, and governing party parliamentary strength were even weaker than in Latin America but model 10 suggests that post-communist governments were actually marginally more likely to initiate IMF programs prior to elections (weakly significant at .1 one-tailed). While their modest statistical significance precludes any strong claims, the contrast in the pre-electoral behavior of Latin America and Eastern European governments confirms the earlier discussion about the steeper political costs of IMF programs during the debt crisis compared to the post-communist transition.

The one noteworthy effect of political constraints on IMF program initiation was the interaction between inflation and postelectoral politics presented in model 11 of tables 5.1a and 5.1b. For both regions inflation was a much stronger driver of program initiation (and only achieved statistical significance at .05) in the immediate postelectoral period but not during other parts of the electoral cycle. In line with earlier discussions about the importance of honeymoon periods (see e.g., Lipton and Sachs 1990, Weyland 1998), this finding suggests that domestic economic crises were best tackled by governments benefiting from a postelectoral legitimacy and power advantage over the opposition. However, it is important to note that this postelectoral program initiation surge did not apply across the board; thus, in Eastern Europe the statistical effect of the postelection dummy was positive and statistically significant only in countries plagued by high inflation[9] but actually turned negative (and barely missed statistical significance) at very low inflation levels. In Latin America the patterns were very similar but statistically weaker, which suggests that in both regions newly elected governments only chose to invest their postelectoral political capital in IMF program initiation if the domestic economic situation was sufficiently critical to warrant such a loss of policy autonomy.

Domestic Drivers of Program Compliance

Despite its bureaucratic demands and its occasionally contentious politics, IMF program initiation constitutes only the first step of the long and difficult process of reform implementation. While the preceding section has shown that economic crises, mediated by partisan politics and bureaucratic capacity, have played a crucial role in spurring the onset of reforms in the two regions, what determines whether this initial reform impetus is sufficiently resilient to ensure implementation, and thereby compliance with program conditions? Based on the formal model predictions, the intensity of the preceding crisis should still matter but not necessarily in a uniform fashion. Instead, the economic crisis incentives should be refracted by the partisan interests of domestic politicians and filtered through the bureaucratic and political institutions of the program country. Given the strong filtering role of the partisanship–economic crisis interaction and at the program initiation stage, we should expect to see weaker ideological effects during implementation, since many of the Fund's most ardent ideological opponents would not have entered a program in the first place. On the other hand, bureaucratic capacity and domestic political constraints should be expected to play a greater role during implementation, as the policy blueprints of IMF programs meet the complicated political reality of crisis-ridden developing countries. The statistical findings, which are discussed in greater detail below, are presented in tables 5.2a and 5.2b, and the substantive effects of the key variables are illustrated in figures 5.5a and 5.5b.

[9] The effect was significant at .1 (two-tailed) for inflation above 250% and at .05 (two-tailed) for inflation above 500% (which corresponds to the 80th percentile).

TABLE 5.2A
Domestic Drivers of Program Compliance—Latin America (1982–89)

	(1)	(2)	(3)	(4)	(5)	(6)	(7)	(8)
Initial inflation	.33		-.20	.38	-.23	.38#	.31	.39#
	(.27)		(.42)	(.29)	(.44)	(.28)	(.30)	(.29)
GDP change (lagged)		-.02						
		(.04)						
Fiscal balance		-.11*						
		(.06)						
Reserves (t-1)	-.20*	-.14	-.19*	-.23#	-.21*	-.22*	-.25*	-.21*
	(.11)	(.12)	(.12)	(.12)	(.11)	(.11)	(.12)	(.11)
Interest/GNP	1.85**	1.68**	2.26**	2.16**	2.33**	.57	2.12**	1.99**
	(.46)	(.48)	(.50)	(.71)	(.52)	(.91)	(.54)	(.48)
Quality of bureaucracy	.48#	.60*	.51#	.40	-.88	-.91	.33	.43#
	(.30)	(.32)	(.33)	(.34)	(.80)	(.83)	(.37)	(.31)
Gov't ideology	-.05	.10	-2.02*	-.05	-.15	-.03		-.28
	(.17)	(.19)	(.97)	(.93)	(.17)	(.18)		(.19)
Regime	-.09*	-.09*	-.12*	-.08*	-.08*	-.06#	-.06	-.07*
	(.04)	(.04)	(.05)	(.04)	(.04)	(.04)	(.05)	(.04)
Initial inflation* Gov't ideology			.53*					
			(.27)					
Interest/GNI * Gov't ideology				-.06				
				(.49)				
Quality of bureaucracy * Initial inflation					.36*			
					(.20)			
Quality of bureaucracy* Interest/GNI						.73*		
						(.42)		
Partisan difference							-.47	
							(.39)	
Regime* Partisan difference							.03	
							(.02)	
Gov't ideology* Pre-Electoral Period								.62#
								(.39)
Pre-Electoral Period								-1.88**
								(.72)
Total debt	-.12	-.07	-.20	-.16	-.36	-.06	-.14	-.20
	(.29)	(.29)	(.31)	(.30)	(.32)	(.31)	(.32)	(.31)
UN voting (y-1)	-.00	.03	-.01	.01	.01	-.00	-.01	-.01
	(.04)	(.05)	(.04)	(.04)	(.04)	(.04)	(.04)	(.04)
Inverse Mills Ratio	3.33**	3.63**	3.79**	3.85**	3.92**	3.94**	4.00**	3.74**
	(.67)	(.71)	(.80)	(.81)	(.82)	(.83)	(.85)	(.80)
Observations	255	255	255	255	255	255	255	255

TABLE 5.2B
Domestic drivers of program compliance—Eastern Europe (1990–2001)

	(1) active	(2) active	(3) active	(4) active	(5) active	(6) active	(7) active	(8) active
Initial inflation	.27		−.02	.23	.96*	.19	.26	.25
	(.20)		(.27)	(.19)	(.38)	(.20)	(.20)	(.19)
GDP change (lagged)		−.05						
		(.03)						
Fiscal balance		.03						
		(.05)						
Reserves (t-1)	−.42*	−.45*	−.41*	−.46*	−.53**	−.63**	−.45*	−.58**
	(.18)	(.19)	(.19)	(.21)	(.19)	(.22)	(.18)	(.19)
Interest/GNI	−.07	−.32	−.33	.04	−1.70*	−7.02**	−.47	−1.31#
	(.64)	(.82)	(.68)	(.00)	(.72)	(2.02)	(.64)	(.70)
Anti-reform gov't	−.14	−.22	−.97	.65	−.06	.02		
	(.47)	(.48)	(1.41)	(.88)	(.51)	(.49)		
Quality of governance	.44	.50#	.58#	.69#	2.30**	−.42	.49#	.78**
	(.37)	(.38)	(.41)	(.51)	(.77)	(.40)	(.33)	(.28)
Regime	.17*	.11	.15	.10	.14*	.24**	.10	.11#*
	(.09)	(.09)	(.13)	(.10)	(.08)	(.07)	(.09)	(.06)
Anti-reform gov't* Initial inflation			.43					
			(.32)					
Anti-reform gov't* Interest/GNI				−.94				
				(.84)				
Quality of governance* Initial inflation					−.31*			
					(.14)			
Quality of governance* Interest/GNI						1.76**		
						(.48)		
Regime* Partisan difference							.06	
							(.07)	
Partisan difference							−1.37	.29
							(1.08)	(.59)
Seat share of largest gov't party* Partisan difference								−1.52
								(1.44)
Seat share of largest gov't party								2.92#
								(1.52)
Total debt	−.48*	−.20	−.42	−.11	−.00	−.50**	−.31#	.19
	(.21)	(.34)	(.35)	(.34)	(.18)	(.18)	(.17)	(.20)
UN voting (y-1)	.04	.02	.02	.02	.06#	.05#	.08*	.08*
	(.03)	(.04)	(.05)	(.02)	(.03)	(.03)	(.04)	(.04)
Inverse Mills Ratio	2.84**	2.89**	2.85**	2.91**	2.86**	2.60**	2.93**	3.16**
	(.60)	(.63)	(.61)	(.59)	(.62)	(.63)	(.63)	(.69)
Observations	404	400	404	404	404	404	404	404

Logistic regression coefficients with standard errors in parentheses (#–10%; *–5%; **–1%—one-tailed where appropriate)

Economic Crises, Ideology, and Program Compliance

The preceding analysis has shown that inflationary crises in both regions, and recessions in Eastern Europe, played an important role in IMF program initiation, thereby complementing the external economic pressures discussed in chapters 3–4. The first two models in tables 5.2a and 5.2b address the question of whether the reform impetus of deeper domestic economic crises is sufficiently durable to contribute to a more consistent implementation of economic adjustment policies in the context of IMF programs. For Latin America in the 1980s, implementation appears to have been facilitated to some extent by the experience of both inflationary crises (marginally significant at .1 one-tailed) and fiscal crises (significant at .05 one-tailed) but not recessions. Meanwhile in Eastern Europe the implementation effects of both inflation and growth pointed in the right direction and were moderately large but in both cases they barely missed statistical significance, whereas fiscal deficits were once again insignificant and incorrectly signed. Overall, these results suggest that the reform impetus of domestic economic crises was somewhat more durable in Latin America but that in both regions such crises were by no means overwhelming drivers of implementation.

As mentioned earlier, given the powerful role of ideology as a filter during IMF program initiation in Latin America, one might expect its influence to be lower during implementation. Indeed, these expectations were borne out with respect to inflationary crises since model 3 in table 5.2a suggests that higher preprogram inflation had a large and statistically significant (at .05) positive impact on implementation for center-left governments but was negligible and statistically insignificant for right and center-right governments. This interaction effect produced a "cross-over" crisis convergence pattern, whereby right governments were more likely to comply at low inflation levels but their centrist and center-left counterparts actually had a better compliance record for programs following high inflation episodes. In Eastern Europe model 3 in table 5.2b reveals a similar cross-over convergence pattern, in that higher pre-program inflation only served as a reform catalyst for ex-communist/nationalist governments, and the effects of the government's partisan orientation depended in crucial ways on the severity of the domestic crisis; at low preprogram inflation levels, nationalist/ex-communist governments behaved as predicted by the formal model in that they had a poorer compliance record than their more reformist counterparts (marginally significant at .1 one-tailed), but at high inflation levels nominally antireform governments actually had a compliance advantage over their more reformist counterparts.[10] These cross-over effects in both regions suggest a Nixon-in-China

[10] However, the statistical significance fell short of traditional significance thresholds (at .2 two-tailed).

Figure 5.5a: Substantive effects of program compliance—Latin America (1982–89)

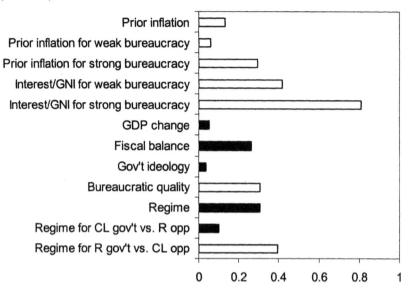

Note: Effects represent change in compliance probability for a change in the variable of interest from the 10th to the 90th percentile. Negative effects are marked as black bars.

scenario, in which reforms in crisis situations were more effectively handled by politicians whose prior partisan inclinations were less favorable toward these reforms.

On the other hand, judging by the large negative interaction effect between interest payments and ideology in model 4 of table 5.2a, ideologically informed interpretation differences about the nature of the debt crisis continued to affect policies even at the implementation stage, in the sense that higher interest payments were associated with more compliance for the right (significant at .05) but not for center-left governments, thereby leading to crisis-driven divergence. Even in Eastern Europe, interest payments produced ideologically based policy divergence but the results in model 4 of table 5.2b were considerably weaker and failed to reach statistical significance. Once again, lower reserve levels were not subject to divergent ideological interpretations in either region judging by the weak interaction between ideology and foreign reserves (results omitted).

Thus it appears that once engaged in IMF programs, right-leaning Latin American governments no longer differed systematically from their

Figure 5.5b: Substantive effects of domestic drivers of program compliance—Eastern Europe (1990–2001)

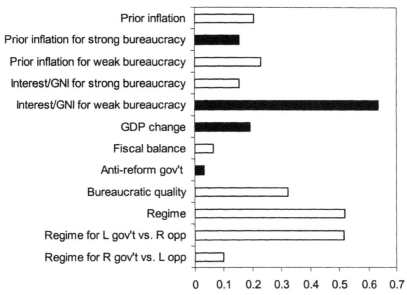

Note: Effects represent change in compliance probability for a change in the variable of interest from the 10th to the 90th percentile. Negative effects are marked as black bars.

leftist counterparts in their propensity to go along with IMF-style economic adjustment, as indicated by the small and statistically insignificant effect of ideology in models 1 and 2, and by the mixed evidence about the crisis-ideology interactions in models 3 and 4. In other words, once having entered an IMF program, Latin American governments appear to have been more willing to discard their ideological baggage at least with respect to domestic economic crisis reactions. Meanwhile, the implementation dynamics in Eastern Europe confirmed the initiation stage trend of ex-communist governments abandoning their reform opposition in the face of significant domestic economic crises.

Bureaucratic Quality and Program Compliance

Whereas the preliminary steps required for the initiation of an IMF program can generally be accomplished by a small team of reasonably competent technocrats, the more complex and far-reaching policy tasks required by program implementation place much greater demands on the state's

Figure 5.6a: Inflation, bureaucracy, and compliance—Latin America (1982–89)

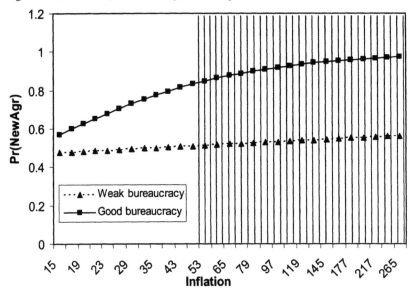

Note: Statistical significance for predictor variable: continuous line (p < .05), dotted line (p > .05). Statistical significance for modifying variable: shaded area (p < .05).

bureaucratic capacity, which should therefore be an even stronger predictor of reforms during the implementation phase. This expectation is confirmed for Latin America, where program countries with better bureaucracies received a noticeable implementation boost. Moreover, as figure 5.6a (based on the interaction effect in model 5) illustrates, the effect of inflationary crises on reform durability in Latin America was significantly mediated by the quality of bureaucratic institutions, in that high inflation elicited decisive reforms in countries with capable bureaucracies but had a negligible impact on the compliance of low-quality bureaucracies (even once they had managed to initiate IMF-style reforms). As predicted by the theoretical model, more capable governments also complied more successfully when faced with external financial crises, judging by the positive interaction effect between interest burden and bureaucratic quality illustrated in figure 5.7a (based on model 6); even though the effects on higher interest payments were positive and statistically significant (at .05) for all but the weakest bureaucracies, the effects were much larger and statistically stronger for countries with more capable bureaucratic institutions.

In Eastern Europe, countries with higher *governance and public administration* scores were also more likely to comply with IMF conditional-

Figure 5.6b: Inflation, bureaucracy, and compliance—Eastern Europe (1990–2001)

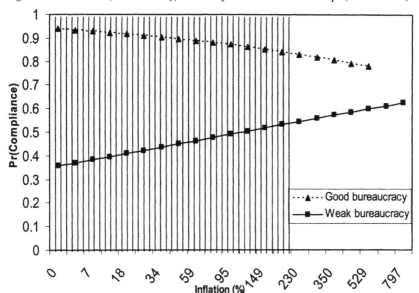

Note: Statistical significance for predictor variable: continuous line (p < .05), dotted line (p > .05). Statistical significance for modifying variable: shaded area (p < .05).

ity, though the statistical significance was slightly weaker than in Latin America (.1 one-tailed in models 1 and 2). While countries with better institutions had better compliance records in both regions, the nature of the interaction between quality of governance and inflation ran in the opposite direction in Eastern Europe compared to Latin America. According to figure 5.6b (based on model 5), the quality of governance had a large and significant (at .01) positive impact on implementation for low pre-program inflation but weak bureaucracies responded more strongly to inflation and as a consequence the good-governance compliance boost vanished in high-inflation environments. With respect to the interaction between bureaucratic capacity and external crises, the results were more mixed: On the one hand figure 5.7b (based on model 6) suggests that (as in Latin America) better bureaucracies were more capable of dealing with the challenges of high interest payments. On the other hand liquidity crises also provided a stronger implementation impetus for weak bureaucracies (results omitted). These findings suggests that sufficiently desperate post-communist governments chose more ambitious reform targets to ensure IMF approval even in the event of policy slippage during implementation. As discussed in the context of the formal model, however, such an

Figure 5.7a: Interest payments, bureaucracy, and compliance—Latin America (1982–89)

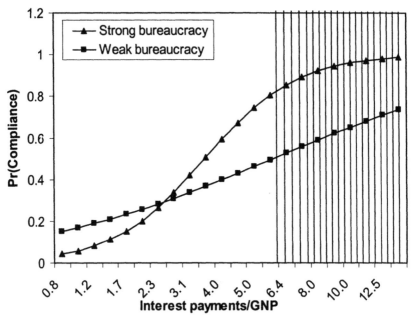

Note: Statistical significance for predictor variable: continuous line (p < .05), dotted line (p > .05). Statistical significance for modifying variable: shaded area (p < .05).

"overshooting" can be economically costly for the program country and politically costly for its government (as illustrated by the Moldovan case study in chapter 6).

Taken together, these findings provide some interesting insights into the comparative dynamics of economic reforms in Eastern Europe and Latin America. The Latin American cases confirm the formal model prediction that bureaucratic capacity should matter most in situations of intense economic crisis, such as high inflation and crushing interest payment burdens. Nevertheless, this relatively successful mobilization among the region's more capable governments appears to have occurred only in response to severe external or domestic crises, which further underlines the unwilling nature of economic reforms throughout much of the region during the debt crisis and explains the stop-go policy cycles in countries with reasonably functional bureaucracies such as Brazil and Argentina. By contrast, during the post-communist transition, bureaucratic capacity made a greater difference in low-crisis environments, which suggests that the

Figure 5.7b: Interest payments, bureaucracy, and compliance—Eastern Europe (1990–2001)

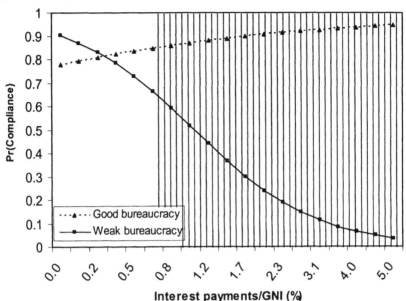

Note: Statistical significance for predictor variable: continuous line ($p < .05$), dotted line ($p > .05$). Statistical significance for modifying variable: shaded area ($p < .05$).

region's more functional states implemented reforms even without immediate economic crisis threats. Meanwhile, countries with weaker institutional capabilities only implemented reforms when facing extreme domestic or international economic pressures. Once they were faced with such immediate economic threats, however, governments in poor-governance countries appear to have been able to make up (at least partially) in political will what they were lacking in institutional capabilities.

Domestic Political Constraints and Program Compliance

How was the difficult process of economic adjustment under IMF auspices affected by domestic political competition in the two regions? While the earlier discussion has suggested that IMF program initiation was only marginally affected by domestic political constraints, there are good reasons to expect that these constraints will play a more important role during implementation. As several of the case studies in the next chapter will show, even governments with strong ideological and financial reform incentives do not necessarily succeed in implementing reforms because IMF-style adjustment policies often breed significant political opposition from groups adversely affected by the redistributive implications of these policies. Therefore, in line with the predictions of the theoretical framework laid out in chapter 2, the successful implementation in IMF programs should hinge not only on economic crisis incentives, partisan political interests, and bureaucratic capacity but also on the relative political power balance between government and opposition. Moreover, in a departure from traditional explanations, the present analysis explicitly hypothesizes that the policy effects of political constraints should be mediated by the relative ideological preferences of the government and the opposition, as well as by the broader political economy environment in which the crisis occurs. More concretely, domestic political constraints should undermine program implementation to a much greater extent when pro-reform governments are facing antireform oppositions than in the reverse partisan scenario. Moreover, politically constrained governments should be expected to have a harder time implementing IMF programs in the polarized political context of the Latin American debt crisis than during the more consensual crisis politics of the post-communist transition.

The statistical patterns of program implementation in tables 5.2a and 5.2b confirm the different political dynamics of crisis management in the two regions. This difference is particularly striking with respect to the role of democracy; judging by the substantively large and statistically significant (at .05) negative effects of Polity regime scores in table 5.2a, IMF program implementation was at odds with democratic politics during the Latin American debt crisis. The widespread unpopularity of IMF-style economic adjustment measures created significant barriers for democratic governments attempting to implement the policy commitments agreed to in their debt negotiations with the Fund and Western lenders. These findings, which are at odds with earlier analysis of IMF programs in Latin America (Remmer 1994), confirm case-based evidence about the greater success of economic orthodoxy in authoritarian regimes like Chile and Mexico (Kaufman 1992), as well as about the tensions between democratic politics and IMF-style reforms in Bolivia, Peru, and Argentina, which will be discussed in the following chapter. Post-communist governments were not confronted with a similarly difficult trade-off between economic reforms and democracy. While democracy had played a marginal role during program initiation, at the implementation stage post-communist democracies appear to have had an advantage over their authoritarian counterparts, as illustrated by the positive effects of Polity

Fig 5.8a: Regime, partisan balance, and compliance—Latin America (1982–89)

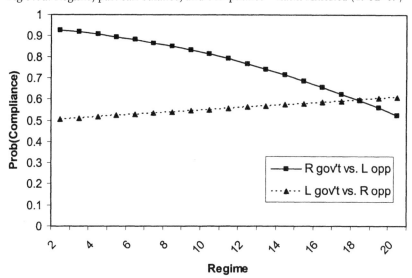

Note: Statistical significance for predictor variable: continuous line (p < .05), dotted line (p > .05).

regime scores in table 5.2b.[11] Therefore, in Eastern Europe, democratic politics did not pose as many obstacles to economic reforms as in Latin America, and it even appears that the legitimacy conferred by democratic governance strengthened the ability of post-communist governments to implement IMF programs.

Despite the cross-regional differences in the overall effect of regime type, the statistical results for both regions confirm the formal model prediction that the effects of institutional constraints on the government's power are mediated by the relative partisan positions of domestic political actors. In Latin America greater democracy did not undermine program implementation in an even fashion; instead, the interaction effect in figure 5.8a (based on model 7 in table 5a) indicates that the negative democracy effect was large and statistically significant (at .05) if right-leaning governments faced leftist oppositions, but was much weaker (and statistically insignificant) when the government was less reformist than the opposition. A similar logic is also reflected by figure 5.8b (based on model 7 in

[11] The statistical significance of the results was relatively modest (.1 one-tailed) and was sensitive to model specifications, largely because of the fairly high correlation between Regime and Quality of governance.

Figure 5.8b: Regime, partisan balance, and compliance—Eastern Europe (1990–2001)

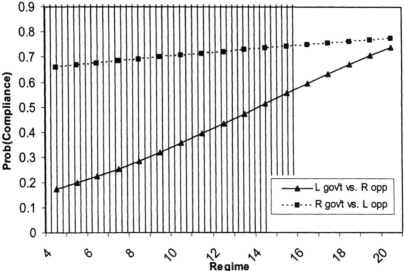

Note: Statistical significance for predictor variable: continuous line (p < .05), dotted line (p > .05). Statistical significance for modifying variable: shaded area (p < .10).

table 5b), which suggests that in Eastern Europe, democracy provided an implementation boost to nationalist/ex-communist governments facing reformist oppositions (statistically significant at .05) but was irrelevant when the government was more reformist than the opposition.[12]

The much more acrimonious politics of IMF programs in Latin America compared to Eastern Europe is also reflected in the electoral political dynamics of program compliance. According to model 8 in table 5.2a Latin American governments were less eager to implement IMF programs prior to elections but this effect was significantly stronger and only achieved statistical significance (at .05) for right and center-right governments. Given that pre-electoral policies reflect government attempts to pander to the economic and political interests of the median voter, these finding further underscore the widespread popular opposition to IMF-style reforms during the Latin American debt crisis. Meanwhile the corre-

[12] The more deleterious consequences of institutional constraints on the power of Latin American governments is also confirmed by the negative and marginally significant (.1 one-tailed) effect of veto points, compared to the positive (but statistically insignificant) corresponding result for Eastern Europe (results omitted).

sponding regression results for Eastern Europe revealed a modest and statistically insignificant pre-electoral implementation boost irrespective of government orientation (results omitted). This (non)finding suggests that the weaker post-communist partisan differentiation with respect to IMF programs is not simply because of the lack of policy responsibility of post-communist political parties (Innes 2002) but also because in Eastern Europe there was much less popular opposition to IMF programs than during the Latin American debt crisis.

Despite the modest effects of the political constraints discussed so far, post-communist IMF program implementation was not simply a technocratic response to economic crises. Thus, model 8 of table 5.2b suggests that implementation in Eastern Europe was significantly more successful when the largest governing party had a larger parliamentary seat share. However, in line with formal model predictions about the interaction effect between partisan balance and political constraints, the effect was the strongest in both substantive and statistical terms (significant at .05) when the governing party was more reformist than the opposition, in which case the governing parties with strong parliamentary support presumably had an easier time pushing IMF-style economic reform packages through the legislature. On the other hand, if the opposition favored greater reforms than the government, larger seat shares for the main governing party had a substantively modest and statistically insignificant effect on compliance, arguably because under such a scenario the opposition would favor IMF-style policies anyway, which obviates the need for large governing majorities. In Latin America the benefit of larger governing party seat shares was also greater for right parties facing leftist oppositions, but the effect was only marginally significant (results omitted). The greater salience of parliamentary strength in Eastern Europe suggests that the challenges to IMF programs were more likely to occur in the parliamentary arena, whereas the importance of regime type combined with the relative weakness of legislative power balance in Latin America points toward a greater role for broader societal challenges to IMF-style reforms during the debt crisis.

Conclusion

The domestic political dynamics of IMF programs during the Latin American debt crisis and post-communist transition that were analyzed in this chapter, have a number of important implications for our understanding of economic reforms in the developing world. In line with the predictions of the theoretical framework developed in chapter 2, these findings emphasize the importance of analyzing economic crises, partisan interests, and domestic institutional and political constraints not as static, additive factors promoting or hindering IMF-style reforms, but in their dynamic (and often nonlinear) interaction with one another.

The analysis confirms the importance of domestic economic crises as reform catalysts, but it also illustrates quite clearly that economic crises are at least to some extent "in the eye of the beholder." Crisis-driven reforms do not occur automatically in reaction to more or less objective economic crisis indicators because key societal interests suddenly agree on the necessity of far-reaching economic reforms. Instead, the nature and timing of such reforms are significantly shaped by the way key political actors interpret the roots of a given crisis and the impact of economic adjustment on their ideal and material interests. The statistical evidence presented in this chapter shows quite clearly that domestic economic crises did not have a uniform effect on the decision to initiate or implement IMF programs but instead were filtered through the partisan preferences of the governing parties. In Latin America left and right parties had similar reform inclinations during periods of relative economic stability (low inflation, solid growth) but experienced policy divergence in reaction to inflationary and recessionary crises, which made right-leaning governments more likely to initiate reforms but had no impact on the left. By contrast, Eastern Europe experienced *crisis-driven partisan policy convergence*: Domestic economic crises acted as stronger reform catalysts for ex-communist/nationalist governments, which were less likely to initiate IMF program in low-crisis environments but were willing to set aside their ideological reservations when faced with inflationary and recessionary crises.

With respect to external economic crises, partisan differences in crisis reactions were similar for the two regions but differed according to the nature of the crisis; thus, higher foreign debt service payments only acted as program initiation catalysts for right-leaning governments and thereby triggered *crisis-driven partisan policy divergence* not only during the Latin American debt crisis but even (to a lesser extent) during the post-communist transition. Meanwhile, the less contentious nature of liquidity crises provoked similar initiation reactions for governments across the political spectrum in both regions, thereby leading to partisan convergence in extreme crisis situations. Despite these similarities, the greater salience of debt service and the closer link between external adjustment and domestic economic imbalances during the debt crisis arguably contributed to the more contentious and ideologically charged politics of domestic economic crisis management in Latin America compared to post-communist Eastern Europe. The ideological differences in international-domestic linkages were amplified by cross-regional variations in domestic political institutions, such as party-system institutionalization and the strength of organized interests (especially labor and business), which played a more active role in Latin America and may explain the greater ideological discipline of Latin American parties compared to their post-communist counterparts. These questions will be addressed in more detail in the case studies in the following chapter, as well as through comparison with the political dynamics of IMF programs in Latin America during the 1990s in the final chapter of the book.

Once reforms were initiated, however, ideological differences ceased to affect governments' policy responses to domestic crises, and variations in implementation success were driven primarily by the severity of the initial crisis and by bureaucratic and political constraints on the policy-making process. However, in both regions the ideological rift persisted with respect to interest payments, which promoted IMF program implementation for right governments but undermined it for the left, thereby underscoring the divisive nature of foreign debt as a source of economic adjustment. On the other hand, liquidity crises continued to exert a powerful and ideologically neutral influence on program implementation in both regions.

These findings suggest that the prospects of IMF-style reforms in reaction to economic crises depend systematically on several crisis attributes. The first factor, suggested by the much greater importance of inflation compared to fiscal deficits, is crisis visibility; even though occasionally governments may initiate IMF programs to address hidden structural crises (Vreeland 2003), the evidence presented in this chapter suggests that more visible crises, such as high inflation or deep recession, have a much greater likelihood of triggering decisive reforms. The second factor is the perceived fit between the type of the crisis and the policy course advocated by the IMF; whereas inflation, where the Fund's track record is generally good, triggered IMF programs in both regions, recessions only mattered in Eastern Europe but not in Latin America, where the Fund's emphasis on austerity measures was seen by many as hurting rather than helping economic growth. The last two factors relate to the interaction between crisis management and ideology in developing countries. Thus, the contrast between the crisis-driven policy divergence in Latin America and the convergence in Eastern Europe suggests that the crisis-reform link depends on the domestic and international context in which a crisis occurs: In periods of genuine ideological contestation at the international and domestic level (such as the 1980s in Latin America), economic crises may be subject to divergent ideological interpretations, whereas in periods of ideological hegemony (such as the 1990s in Eastern Europe), economic crises are more likely to be interpreted uniformly by actors irrespective of their partisan political loyalties. At the same time, the propensity for ideologically divergent crisis interpretation also depends on the specific nature of a given crisis; thus, in both regions, debt service payments received ideologically divergent policy reactions whereas liquidity crises were dealt with in a more technocratic fashion, which suggests that certain types of crises simply lend themselves more easily to contentious political interpretations than other more "objective" crises.

The greater rigidity of partisan fault lines and the lower overall legitimacy of Western objectives and IMF conditionality in Latin America compared to Eastern Europe, also affected other domestic political mechanisms of IMF program initiation and implementation. During the Latin American debt crisis, the widespread perception of IMF programs as external impositions created significant tensions between popular sovereignty and the political imperatives of IMF-style economic adjustment policies. This tension is reflected in the negative relationship between democracy and program compliance in Latin America, which suggests that democratic politics were hard to reconcile with IMF cooperation in the inhospitable international economic environment of the debt crisis. Meanwhile, post-communist compliance with IMF conditionality was actually reinforced by democratic politics, a finding that confirms the more cooperative tone of the relationship between the Fund and many transition economies in the 1990s. The cross-regional popularity differential of IMF interventions was also confirmed by the electoral dynamics of IMF programs in the two regions: The greater reluctance of Latin American right and center-right governments to implement IMF programs prior to elections, combined with the greater likelihood of ex-communist governments to initiate IMF programs during electoral campaigns, confirms that Latin American voters had much more negative views of IMF-style adjustment policies than their East European counterparts.

However, the implications of domestic political constraints on the prospects of IMF program implementation differed not only as a function of the broader international context of the IMF interventions. As predicted by the formal model, in both regions it mattered not only how much voice the opposition had vis-à-vis the government but also whether these outside voices were more or less supportive of IMF-style reforms than the government. Thus, the negative effect of democracy in Latin America affected primarily right-wing governments facing leftist opponents, whereas in Eastern Europe democracy facilitated implementation only when it gave greater voice to a pro-reform opposition facing an ex-communist government. Similarly, the positive impact of larger parliamentary seat share for the largest governing party was much stronger when the beneficiaries had more ambitious reform agendas than their opponents.

This chapter has also confirmed the theoretical predictions about the importance of well-functioning bureaucratic institutions; in both regions, countries with functional bureaucracies were significantly more likely to initiate and implement IMF programs. Moreover, as predicted by the formal model, the positive impact of bureaucratic capacity became particularly apparent during extreme crisis situations, when more capable states were better able to mobilize in order to meet the challenges of IMF-supported adjustment policies. The much weaker (and usually statistically insignificant) effect of economic crisis in countries with weak bureaucratic capacity suggests that in order for economic crises to trigger IMF-style reforms, economic pressures need to be complemented not only by ideological conviction but also by sufficient bureaucratic expertise. This positive interaction between crisis intensity and bureaucratic capacity applied to both domestic and international crises in the two regions, and it affected initiation as well as implementation. The only exception to this pattern occurred during program implementation in Eastern Europe, where the quality of governance mattered less during inflationary crises, as desperate governments appeared to make up in short-term political determination what they lacked in bureaucratic capabilities.

-6-

Domestic Crisis Politics:
Case Study Evidence

THE PRECEDING CHAPTER REVEALED several crucial cross-regional differences in the domestic political dynamics of IMF programs during the Latin American debt crisis and the post-communist transition in Eastern Europe and the former Soviet Union. This chapter revisits the economic reform trajectories of the four Latin American and two Eastern European countries discussed in chapter 4 (Argentina, Bolivia, Chile, Peru, Moldova, and Slovakia) and introduces two additional post-communist cases (Bulgaria and Romania) to illustrate some of the main theoretical predictions and cross-national statistical findings about the domestic politics of economic crises in the context of IMF conditionality. In addition, these brief case studies attempt to capture the domestic political dynamics with greater nuance than allowed by the cross-national statistical indicators used in the previous chapter.

In line with the statistical findings about the crisis-driven ideological divergence of economic policies in Latin America, this chapter traces two of the most dramatic policy reversals of the Latin American debt crisis: Bolivia's remarkable transformation from hyperinflationary paralysis under the leftist Siles government (1982–85) to one of the region's showcase orthodox reformers under the right Paz government in the second half of the decade; and Peru's dramatic rejection of IMF conditionality under President Alan Garcia after 1985 following its earlier costly cooperation with the IMF under the center-right Belaúnde government. A closer look at the political dynamics of these two important economic policy U-turns provides a better understanding of the complicated interaction of ideology and economic crises in the tense political environment of the Latin American debt crisis.

While avoiding Bolivia's and Peru's abrupt policy reversals, the centrist Alfonsín administration in Argentina nevertheless failed to address its country's pressing economic problems. This chapter analyzes the domestic political roots of this failure and focuses on Alfonsín's conflictual relationship with labor and business organizations, as well as on the missed opportunities to leverage postelectoral legitimacy in the context of severe economic crises in order to find a long-term political compromise to the social tensions that fueled inflation throughout the 1980s. Whereas the experiences of Bolivia, Peru, and Argentina illustrate the tension between democratic politics and IMF-style reforms in the context of the pervasive popular resistance to painful austerity measures, this chapter shows that even an ideologically committed, highly authoritarian regime like Pinochet's Chile was not immune to critical political challenges in its attempt to execute an orthodox economic adjustment strategy in the difficult context of the debt crisis. In addition to discussing the implications of the parliamentary power balance between the government and the opposition (in the three democratic cases), the Latin American case studies also analyze the important role of the government's ties to influential organized societal interests, particularly labor unions and business organizations, whose cooperation (or at least acquiescence) played an important role in the success of IMF-style reforms in Latin America.

According to the statistical findings in chapter 5, post-communist IMF programs differed from the predominant pattern of the Latin American debt crisis in that in Eastern Europe, domestic economic crises were more likely to trigger policy convergence among governments of different ideological persuasions. The four Eastern European cases discussed in this chapter illustrate these statistical findings by analyzing the effects of a wide range of ideology-crisis constellations on IMF programs in the postcommunist context; thus, the Slovak case, characterized by relative macroeconomic stability, provides an interesting contrast between the reluctance of the Mečiar government and the eagerness of the Moravcik government to cooperate with the IMF. Meanwhile, the ex-communist governments of Moldova, Bulgaria, and Romania had mixed compliance records, but unlike their Latin American leftist counterparts tended to react to economic crises by seeking closer ties to the IMF. By contrast, the track record of Eastern European pro-reform governments in the four countries suggests a high propensity to seek out IMF conditionality in support of their domestic reform goals, but the modest implementation record of the Moldovan and Romanian reformers suggests that ideological commitment was not sufficient for the success of IMF-style reforms in situations where the government's zeal was undermined by political fragmentation and weak bureaucratic institutions. Finally, while domestic political constraints clearly mattered to the trajectories of IMF programs in the four Eastern European countries, the cases nonetheless suggest that, unlike in Latin America, democratic politics were not inherently incompatible with IMF conditionality, and under certain circumstances more inclusive democratic politics even appeared to facilitate compliance with IMF programs.

From Basket Case to Showcase:
Bolivia's Reform Path in the 1980s

Bolivia's economic reform trajectory during the debt crisis offers an interesting contrast between the economic and political chaos of the first part of the decade (first under a rapid succession of unstable military governments and later under the equally unstable democratic rule of Hernán Siles Zuazo) and the remarkable recovery of macroeconomic stability and governability in the second part of the 1980s, during which Bolivia became a showcase example of successful orthodox reforms under the leadership of Victor Paz Estenssoro. The country's relationship with the IMF closely parallels the dramatic reversal of its economic policy path: Whereas the Siles government had failed to secure an IMF agreement despite several attempts at stabilization packages between 1982 and 1984, the Paz government, despite its initial decision to adopt the stabilization program proposed by Jeffrey Sachs instead of the policy proposals of the IMF, quickly became the darling of the international financial institutions, with the initial standby agreement of 1986–87 being followed by a lower conditionality structural adjustment fund (SAF) program in 1988 in conjunction with active support from the World Bank and bilateral donors. It should be noted, however, that the absence of IMF programs in the context of the severe crisis of 1982–84 was not the result of a confrontational approach toward Fund conditionality (as in Peru under Alan Garcia) but—as will be discussed below—an expression of the political paralysis of the Siles government for most of its three-year tenure.

Since the country's main structural characteristics—its marginal geopolitical position, high indebtedness, weak bureaucracy, extreme poverty, and lack of export diversity—did not change during the 1980s, this sharp intertemporal contrast offers the analytical advantage of allowing us to isolate the domestic political mechanisms that drove this remarkable and unexpected change in economic policy. The Bolivian experience clearly illustrates the theoretical prediction and the statistical findings about the importance of partisan preferences in filtering the effects of external and domestic economic crisis on the likelihood of program initiation. Thus, the center-left UDP government was incapable of overcoming the opposition to IMF-style reforms from the labor unions and from within the governing coalition despite the high economic and political costs of this policy paralysis. By contrast, the center-right MNR-ADN government under Paz Estenssoro used the crisis as a political catalyst for an economic reform program whose orthodoxy was rivaled at the time only by Chile and gradually became a classic success story in the eyes of neoliberal reform proponents.

Economic Crisis and Political Paralysis under Siles (1982–85)

The domestic economic situation in Bolivia at the time of its "democratization by default" in October 1982 was critical. Tax revenues had declined from already low levels (8.3%) in 1980 to 4.2% of GDP in 1982, inflation had reached almost 300% for the year and the economy contracted by 4.4% in the context of an almost complete halt to private investment (2.8% of GDP).[1] To make matters worse from a political point of view, the relative prosperity of the 1970s had not resulted in significant gains in real wages and government services, thereby limiting the scope and political feasibility of classical demand-side austerity measures. The Bolivian economy continued to deteriorate rapidly under the democratic government of Siles Zuazo; thus, by late 1984, early 1985 the Bolivian government had virtually ceased to collect taxes (accounting for less than 1% of GDP) and had lost control over the budget (with the deficit for 1984 reaching 22.9%). In the absence of external financing options, this fiscal imbalance was financed almost exclusively by domestic money creation and resulted in one of the most spectacular episodes of hyperinflation in the postwar period with a yearly inflation rate well above 10,000% between late 1984 and mid-1985. Even though, as discussed in chapter 4, this catastrophic domestic economic crisis was complemented by an equally critical external debt service burden, the Siles government failed to mount a policy response capable of tackling the crisis and securing IMF support for its economic adjustment efforts. How can we explain this remarkable failure to respond to a crisis, whose staggering economic costs affected most of Bolivian society and, therefore, exacted a heavy political price for the government? To answer this question, the following section takes a closer look at Bolivia party politics and its implications for economic reforms.

THE LEGACY OF THE UNFINISHED BOLIVIAN REVOLUTION

The social and political roots of the conflicts over economic policy making during the 1980s cannot be properly understood without reference to the legacies of the Bolivian revolution of 1952 and the succession of civilian and military regimes that ruled (or at least attempted to rule) the country in the three decades prior to the debt crisis. This historical background is important both because several of the key political personalities of the 1980s (such as Hernán Siles Zuazo and Victor Paz Estenssoro) played a major role since the 1952 revolution or at least during the various authoritarian regimes of the 1960s and 1970s (e.g., the ex–military dictator Hugo

---

[1] Data based on Pastor 1992:70–71, 79.

Banzer), and because the key conflict lines of Bolivian society remained remarkably consistent from the mid-1950s to 1985.

Despite the sometimes important differences in the ideological platforms and democratic commitment of successive twentieth-century Bolivian governments, political patronage remained a constant and often the most important element in the power struggle between different factions and interest groups. This pattern goes back at least as far as the late nineteenth- and early twentieth-century rivalry between the traditional Conservative and Liberal parties, which were primarily personalistic cliques competing for the spoils of power rather than coherent ideological platforms. While this thinly veiled caudillismo was a widespread political phenomenon in Latin America at the time (and has shown remarkable persistence in countries like Colombia, Uruguay, and Paraguay), Bolivia's dependence on primary exports (first silver, later tin, and then oil/gas) combined with the weakness of the domestic manufacturing sector, created strong incentives for the Bolivian middle class and elite to rely on state patronage as a significant source of income.[2] Since the structural roots of this widespread middle-class economic dependence on the state did not change significantly in the second half of the twentieth century, the central importance of patronage to party politics remained unchanged even after the popular revolution of 1952. The high stakes of the conflicts over the distribution of patronage are illustrated by the fact that the 1964 coup led by General Barrientos against the first Paz Estenssoro's government was supported by important factions within the ruling Movimiento Nacionalista Revolucionario (MNR) after Paz had broken the underlying patronage-sharing bargain of the 1961 Constitution by inserting a clause allowing for his reelection.

The second salient characteristic differentiating the Bolivian political scene from most of its neighbors was also an outgrowth of the revolutionary struggle of 1952: the strength and the semi-independent position of the labor unions, the Central Obrera Boliviana (COB). Unlike the Mexican PRI and the Argentine PJ, the populist Bolivian MNR did not succeed in co-opting and subordinating the popular sectors mobilized by the revolution, in particular the militant labor unions concentrated in the country's strategic mining sector. The tensions between the state capitalist development project of the MNR and the often intransigent wage demands of the unions surfaced after a brief honeymoon period in the context of the fiscal austerity dictated by Bolivia's first IMF agreement in 1956 (Gamarra and Malloy 1995:403). To make matters worse, the MNR was

---

[2] The Bolivian saying that "La industria mayor de este pais es la politica" (This country's biggest business is politics) is indicative in this respect (Malloy 1970, cited in Gamarra and Malloy 1995:401).

equally incapable of controlling the armed forces, which had been strengthened with U.S. support to control popular revolts but ended up adding to the cycle of political instability and bad governance during its almost eighteen years in power starting in 1964.

Thus, the dominant pattern of political competition in pre-1985 Bolivia was one of gridlock between a fractionalized, patronage-dependent middle class and elite on one hand, and a labor movement strong enough to block most attempts at painful economic reforms but too weak to gain power and rule by itself. Despite repeated violent attempts to crush the labor movement during the 1970s, successive military regimes proved incapable of replicating Pinochet's successful repression of the powerful Chilean union movement. This resilience of organized labor, combined with a gradual loss of political support from the middle class, eventually weakened Hugo Banzer's military regime to the point where it agreed to democratic elections in 1978. As three rounds of inconclusive elections in three consecutive years (1978–80) made abundantly clear, democratization in Bolivia did not occur as a result of pressures from a strong, coherent democratic opposition but rather because of the obvious inability of a weak military government to manage the country's increasingly critical economic situation.

THE RETURN OF DEMOCRACY AND THE ROAD TO HYPERINFLATION

Following the shameful final *salida* of the military after an increasingly chaotic and violent succession of short-lived governments during the transition period 1978–82, in October 1982 Bolivia returned to democracy under the presidency of Hernán Siles Zuazo, who had received the largest vote share in the presidential elections of 1980 but was prevented from assuming power by the military coup of General Garcia Mesa. The return to democracy did not, however, coincide with a return to governability, since Siles could only count on the support of a plurality of congressional votes (36%) and faced a strong opposition from both the center-right MNR under the leadership of Paz Estenssoro (one of the veterans of the 1952 revolution) and the right-wing Acción Democrática y Nacionalista (ADN), which served as the electoral vehicle for one of the more unlikely democratic candidates, former longtime dictator Hugo Banzer Suarez. Moreover, the governing Unidad Democrática y Popular (UDP) was plagued by internal splits between center-left parties such as Movimiento Nacionalista Revolucionario de Izquierda (MNRI)[3] and the Movimiento

---

[3] The MNRI was formed in the early 1970s by Siles Zuazo and several other members of the leftist faction of the original MNR and became one of the major political forces during the three chaotic elections of the democratic transition period (1978–80).

de Izquierda Revolucionaria (MIR),[4] and the more radical Marxist Partido Comunista Boliviano (PCB). In a sense, at least from the point of view of the center-right and right opposition, this political situation could be dubbed "ungovernability by design," given that they opposed new elections in 1982 for fear that they might result in a strong mandate for the left, which had already achieved significant gains in 1980 compared to 1979 and benefited from its more resolute opposition to the discredited military regime.

The government's uneasy middle ground between a militant and mobilized left and an entrenched right with strong ties to the country's military and economic elite was also reflected at the societal level. Despite its initially strong support from organized labor, the Siles government obtained at best the conditional acquiescence but never the full support of the labor movement, after turning down the COB's claims for co-governance at both the political and the public enterprise level during the first months of the administration (Malloy and Gamarra 1987:115). At the same time, the government was on even shakier ground in its relations with the business sector, represented for the first time in a more unitary fashion by the Confederation of Private Entrepreneurs, which distrusted the leftist-populist electoral discourse of the UDP and grew increasingly frustrated with the government's inability to control the economy.

This political gridlock, which had undermined the emergence of a coherent developmental strategy during the economic boom of the 1960s and 1970s, had even more troubling economic consequences in the context of an economic slowdown that started in 1978 and was exacerbated by the reversal of capital flows after 1981. The inflationary crisis, which started amid the political chaos of the final months of the military regime in 1982 and culminated in the hyperinflation of early 1985, was precipitated by the unfortunate interaction of two factors. The first—a large and growing primary fiscal deficit—was rooted in the inability of successive Bolivian governments to impose the cost of economic adjustment on either the business sector (tax revenues declined rapidly from 8.3% in 1980 to 4.2% in 1982 until they bottomed out at 1.6% in 1984)[5] or the popular sector, given that the already low social expenditures were difficult to reduce any further and that unions successfully resisted additional wage cuts in 1982–83 and managed to obtain a clearly unsustainable doubling of real wages in mid-1984. Moreover, the frequent indexation of wages added an important inertial component to inflation, even though the magnitude of this effect remains a debated subject among analysts

---

[4] The MIR's history also goes back to the early 1970s, when it had formed around a group of young leftist intellectuals, including the future president Jaime Paz Zamora.

[5] Data based on Pastor 1992:79.

(Morales 1987, Pastor 1991). The second factor, which explains the relative timing of the increase in inflationary pressures starting in 1982, is connected to the evolution of capital flows during this period. Whereas the wide availability of foreign credits had facilitated the noninflationary financing of the budget deficit until the late 1970s, by the turn of the decade the increasingly large burden of servicing this foreign debt became an important driver of the ballooning fiscal deficit, which grew from 7.5% in 1981 to 14.2% in 1982. The inflationary effect of the rising debt service expenditures was exacerbated by the abrupt drying up of foreign credit lines following the official debut of the debt crisis in the months preceding the inauguration of the Siles administration, because it forced the government to finance this deficit through inflationary domestic monetary emissions.

In the context of the severely constrained access to domestic and international sources of credit and the rapidly mounting inflationary crisis, the Siles government should have been an obvious candidate for an IMF program in the 1982–85 period. While the more radical left parties of the governing coalition (particularly the PCB) were opposed to IMF conditionality on ideological grounds, the same cannot be said about President Siles Zuazo, whose track record with the IMF program implementation went back to his first stint as president in 1957. The concern of the Bolivian government with maintaining good relations with the West and the IMF is best reflected by the continuation of debt service payments until May 1984 even though these payments exacted a steep price from the crumbling Bolivian economy without being rewarded access to financing from either private lenders or the IMF and the World Bank.

As a consequence, the failure of the Siles government to secure an IMF agreement during its three years in office can be explained neither by the lack of financial incentives (given Bolivia's dire financial situation) nor by an ideologically motivated confrontational stance along the lines of Peru under Alan Garcia. In fact, after a first unsuccessful attempt at heterodox stabilization in late 1982, the Siles government made a series of attempts to introduce economic packages designed with the intention of gaining IMF support, but these technocratically designed *paquetes* invariably failed after being first watered down by debates within the governing coalition, later sabotaged by an increasingly assertive congressional opposition, and finally hindered in their implementation by frequent and sometimes violent labor protests (Malloy and Gamarra 1987:115).

The conflicts triggered by these timid reform efforts reached a peak in April 1984, when the COB called a general strike in response to the government's new stabilization package following an IMF delegation visit to La Paz earlier that month. After the general strike, lacking significant support in both Congress and the broader society, the Siles government essentially renounced all efforts to control the country's rapidly deteriorating economic situation. After stopping debt service payments in May 1984 and making important wage concessions to the unions during the summer, the window of opportunity for addressing Bolivia's crisis within the parameters of IMF conditionality had permanently closed for the Siles Zuazo administration. For the remainder of Siles's tenure, which was cut short after he agreed to early elections in the face of a constitutional coup mounted by the opposition with wide civil and military support, the Bolivian government watched helplessly as the economy drifted toward hyperinflation and the country became virtually ungovernable. Thus, the economic reform efforts of Bolivia's first democratically elected government in two decades were thwarted by a combination of internal ideological conflicts, a strong parliamentary opposition, and an unresolved legacy of class conflict that resulted in a zero-sum logic in the interactions of organized labor and business. These political difficulties were undoubtedly exacerbated by the sheer magnitude of the economic adjustment task confronting the Bolivian government in an extraordinarily inauspicious international economic environment, but, as we will see in the following section, such obstacles could be overcome with the right political strategy.

The Path to Economic and Political Stability: The Paz Government (1985–89)

Rather than retelling the fascinating story of the "Bolivian miracle" in the second half of the 1980s, this section will attempt to identify the political mechanisms that help explain the divergent outcomes in terms of economic reforms and IMF relations between the governments of the two former revolutionary comrades, Hernán Siles Zuazo and Victor Paz Estenssoro. The analysis illustrates a number of key statistical findings from the previous chapter, particularly about the interaction between ideology and economic crisis in triggering reforms, and the tension between democratic politics and IMF programs during the debt crisis.

At the outset, the newly elected Paz government hardly seemed to have much better economic or political prospects than its predecessor. The economy was in its fourth year of recession, inflation was raging at a monthly rate of 66% in July 1985 (the month of the election), unemployment was around 18%, and the country had defaulted on its foreign debt and had no access to new loans from either private or official creditors. Politically, the situation was equally unpromising, with the only real achievement of the Siles administration—the preservation of the country's nascent democracy—threatened by the weak commitment of major political actors to formal democracy. Thus, during the 1985 electoral campaign, the COB had openly tried to provoke a coup to preempt the inevitable victory of the right at the polls, and democracy arguably only survived because the recent memory of its catastrophic governments between 1978 and 1982 made the military reluctant to intervene openly in the political process (Malloy and Gamarra 1987:115). Despite the decisive defeat of the left, which had split into several factions and whose combined vote share barely exceeded 20%, the 1985 elections failed to produce a decisive majority in Congress, where the center-right MNR of Victor Paz Estenssoro and the right-wing ADN of the former military dictator Hugo Banzer were virtually tied with about a third of parliamentary seats. To make matters worse, Paz was elected president after a congressional vote, given that in the first round of the presidential elections he had not only failed to achieve an absolute majority that had actually been a close second with a mere 26.4% of the popular vote. Moreover, Paz hardly fit the profile of a dynamic young politician who would revolutionize Bolivian politics, since, as with his predecessor Siles, he was one of the old caudillos of the 1952 revolution and had played an important role in creating the foundations of Bolivian state capitalism during his first two presidential terms between 1952–56 and 1960–64.

Against all these odds, Paz presided over one of the region's most ambitious and successful stabilization programs of the 1980s. The basic ingredients of his economic policy have been discussed in great detail elsewhere (Sachs 1987, Pastor 1992) and will only be summarized briefly here. The New Economic Policy (NEP), launched by decree on August 29, 1985, included (1) a unified exchange rate without capital or exchange controls; (2) improved fiscal discipline through a combination of a public-sector wage freeze and employment cuts, a public sector price liberalization (especially energy prices), and spending cuts in public investment; (3) trade liberalization, which effectively limited the ability of local producers to raise prices; (4) tax reform based on a regressive value-added tax structure; and (5) a conscious effort to improve relations and credibility with official creditors, including the IMF, in order to obtain new credits and renegotiate existing loans. It should be noted, however, that this rapprochement with the IMF did not translate into the wholesale adoption of the Fund's adjustment recipe during the first year of reforms. Most importantly, Bolivia did not resume its debt service payments during the first months of reforms, and, when the peso came under pressure following a temporary inflation spike in December 1985–January 1986, the Bolivian government ignored the Fund's advice to devalue the currency and instead followed Jeffrey Sachs's strategy of defending the peso by selling off foreign reserves in the (ultimately justified) hope that a stable exchange rate would reduce inflationary pressures and thereby restore financial market confidence in Bolivia (Pastor 1992:88). Despite its modest effect on growth for the duration of the Paz government and the uneven distribution of adjustment costs to the detriment of labor (as reflected by the initial drop and slow recovery of real wages and the persistence of unemployment levels in the 20% range), the NEP's economic results were remarkable, particularly with respect to inflation and fiscal discipline.

In addition to its successful fight against inflation, the Paz government achieved a fundamental transformation of Bolivian political dynamics based on an unexpected political consensus (at least at the elite level) around a neoliberal economic policy that proved remarkably resilient during the subsequent decade. How can we explain this remarkable turnaround and what are its theoretical implications for our understanding of the politics of economic reforms and IMF program initiation and implementation? Below I will argue that this success was based on a combination of Paz 's skillful political alliances and repression in a domestic environment unsettled by the trauma of hyperinflation.

One of the classic explanations for the initiation of economic reforms (and IMF programs) is the catalytic effect of economic crisis, which can help overcome resistance to reforms by influential social actors or interest groups. In the Bolivian case the depth of the crisis—particularly with respect to inflation levels—clearly played an important role in convincing significant segments of the Bolivian elite and population that the status quo economic policies and their political foundations were exceedingly costly to maintain. In this context, the event of hyperinflation, despite its high short-term economic costs and political risks, can be regarded as an important (and possibly necessary) intermediate step for overcoming long-term fiscal imbalances. However, inflation in Bolivia had been extremely high on several occasions in the three years preceding the enactment of the NEP—reaching annual rates 757% in the third quarter of 1982, 826% in the fourth quarter of 1983 and 3,735% in the second quarter of 1984—but none of these inflationary episodes had resulted in a political consensus for a decisive stabilization program under the Siles government.

By contrast, Victor Paz Estenssoro proved remarkably adept at using the traumatic social and economic consequences of the crisis to create political support for and to undermine opposition to his ambitious economic reform plans. In a landmark speech immediately following his election, Paz claimed that the country was dying and the economy was in a coma, whereas the U.S.-educated head of Paz's economic team, Gonzalo Sanchez de Lozada, concluded that "the state is practically destroyed," and therefore, "the first political goal consists of reestablishing the authority of the state over society."[6] Aware that the effectiveness of such crisis rhetoric declines rapidly after a brief postelection honeymoon period, the Paz government moved quickly to take advantage of the brief window of opportunity provided by the gravity of the economic crisis and the legitimacy of its recent electoral success. As will be discussed in more detail below, the domestic political strategy aimed at restoring the country's governability included a patronage-based parliamentary alliance with Banzer's ADN, a tough stance toward organized labor, and the creation of a pro-business economic environment while at the same time minimizing the influence of particularistic business demands on economic policy. Thus, the Bolivian case provides further evidence for the earlier statistical findings that the effects of domestic economic crisis on the initiation and implementation of economic reforms (and IMF programs) are mediated by the partisan political preferences of the government and that similar degrees of crisis can lead to divergent policy responses for right and left governments.

A closer look at the political developments in the immediate aftermath of the launching by decree of the New Economic Policy on August 29, 1985, reveals the serious nature of the political challenges faced by the proponents of reforms, as well as the difficult economic and moral trade-offs inherent in political strategies aimed at ensuring the sustainability of these reforms. Less than a week after the official launching of the reforms, the Paz government already faced its first challenge from the COB, which continued its confrontational tactics from the previous government and launched a national strike that triggered a series of hunger strikes, roadblocks, and building occupations throughout the country. Recalling the paralyzing effects of labor unrest on its predecessor's reform attempts, the Paz government moved decisively against the COB by declaring a state of siege on September 19, 1985, and arresting more than two hundred labor leaders, many of whom were sent to internment camps in remote parts of the country until the COB agreed to suspend the strike and negotiate with the government two weeks later (Conaghan and Malloy 1994:149). While such repressive measures (repeated on a smaller scale during the miners' march on La Paz in August 1986) represented significant deviations from standard democratic practices,[7] they did not seriously undermine political support for the Paz government, partly because the unions' popular backing was undermined by the marginal role of the industrial proletariat in the Bolivian economy and the fact that

[6] Sanchez de Lozada 1985:6, cited in Conaghan and Malloy 1994:144.

[7] These tactics provoked unease for the more democratically minded members of the Paz cabinet, one of whom later admitted that the government had "behaved like authoritarian pigs" (cited in Conaghan and Malloy 1994:149).

many Bolivians held the unions at least partially responsible for the country's economic and political crisis. Moreover, the government gradually managed to erode union power by significantly reducing employment in the union stronghold of the state-owned tin mines, which had become increasingly unprofitable following the collapse of tin prices in late 1985 (Klein 1992:276). At the same time, however, the Bolivian government minimized protests over the layoffs through severance payments and the creation in 1987 of a Fondo Social de Emergencia (FSE), designed to provide temporary public-sector jobs for lower-class workers.

The importance of the selective use of discretionary resources to ensure the political feasibility of economic reforms was even more striking in the case of the Pacto por la Democracia, the parliamentary alliance between Paz Estenssoro's ruling center-right MNR and the largest opposition party, the right-wing ADN of the ex-dictator Hugo Banzer. Initiated by Paz at the height of the government's confrontation with organized labor and signed on October 16, 1985, the unlikely alliance with the ADN not only ensured parliamentary backing for the state of siege but ensured a working majority of congressional votes that facilitated the passage of crucial reform legislation through Congress and allowed Paz to avoid the two-front political battle (in Congress and society) that had brought the Siles government to its knees. In exchange for its political support, Banzer's ADN was granted an important share of state patronage in the form of public employment and control over a number of state corporations (Gamarra and Malloy 1995:414). While this pact, driven largely by the two parties' respective leaders (at times against the wishes of important factions within their own parties), undermined the government's ability to reduce public-sector employment and reduced Congress to the symbolic role of rubber-stamping executive initiatives, it nevertheless contributed decisively to the restoration of governability in Bolivia, and to the creation of an elite consensus in favor of neoliberal economic reforms.

The third important domestic political aspect of the Paz administration's reform strategy was its relationship with the business sector. On one hand, business had benefited from the restoration of political order following the 1985 elections, especially given that the costs of macroeconomic stabilization and fiscal discipline had fallen disproportionately on the shoulders of labor. On the other hand, domestic private business lobbied against the reduction of tariffs and private-sector credits, which were part of the NEP economic package, but their demands were largely ignored by the technocrats in charge of the Paz government's economic policy. The government's relative autonomy from business demands was crucial not only in controlling inflation (by limiting the local producers' ability to raise prices) but also in reducing the social tensions inherent in its tough policies against organized labor and the social costs of fiscal austerity measures.

Idiosyncrasy or Blueprint:
Some Tentative Conclusions Based on the Bolivian Experience

As the preceding analysis has illustrated, the sharp break in 1985 in Bolivia's domestic economic reform trajectory and its relationship with the IMF and Western lenders can be traced to the profound political transformation initiated by the Paz government upon coming to power at the peak of a profound economic and governability crisis. While the traumatic experience of hyperinflation was certainly conducive to breaking the social and political stalemate that had paralyzed economic policy making in the preceding years, it by no means guaranteed the sharp turnaround the country experienced beginning in mid-1985. The decisive component was the emergence of a stable pro-reform coalition between the ruling center-right MNR and the largest opposition party, the rightwing ADN. The coalition, largely a product of the acute political instincts of the two parties' leaders, Victor Paz Estenssoro and Hugo Banzer, was cemented by elaborate patronage and power-sharing agreements and ensured the political stability necessary for the initiation and implementation of a coherent economic reform program. In this respect, the Paz government differed sharply from the Siles administration, which was paralyzed not only by infighting but also by a hostile and powerful parliamentary opposition. Thus, the Bolivian case confirms the statistical findings about the importance of stable pro-reform coalitions at the parliamentary level for the successful implementation of IMF-style reforms, and it highlights the important role of individual leaders in bringing about such coalitions.

At the same time, however, Bolivia's political trajectory emphasizes the importance of looking beyond parliament in analyzing the sources of political support and opposition to economic reforms. In particular, the resolute resistance of a powerful organized labor sector played a more important role in the failure of successive stabilization attempts under the Siles government than the ideological opposition within the center-left governing coalition. In this context, one of the crucial manifestations of the partisan differences between the two successive Bolivian governments was the way they dealt with the challenge of union opposition to economic reforms: whereas the Siles government repeatedly gave in to union pressures (even though it received only qualified political support from organized labor), the Paz administration opted for a mix of repressive measures and material inducements that succeeded in significantly reducing the political influence of labor unions and thereby paved the way for the implementation of its ambitious reform agenda. These different approaches also illustrate the difficult trade-offs between governability and democratic norms in the context of the painful economic adjustment required by the debt crisis of the 1980s.

Bolivia's trajectory after 1985 compares favorably to most of its peers—not only in terms of inflation,[8] but also in terms of political stability—a conclusion that is all the more remarkable given the country's extreme poverty, history of class conflict, and state weakness. Seen from this perspective, Bolivia can be regarded as an example how a group of political leaders, motivated by little more than the desire for political survival succeeded in creating a political coalition that not only achieved the long-elusive macroeconomic stabilization but created the foundations for the consolidation of its political and economic reforms over the next two decades. Bolivia under Paz nevertheless remains one of the few examples from the 1980s of highly indebted developing countries that managed to square to circle between Western pressures, domestic demands, and tight economic constraints in the context of a relatively democratic political system.

At the same time, however, the peculiar mix of political pacts, repressive labor practices, and patronage politics reveals the difficult trade-offs between democracy and economic adjustment inherent in an economic environment whose parameters were set by the primacy of Western concerns with international financial stability during an international debt crisis. These inherent tensions were further emphasized by the electoral defeat of the MNR in the 1989 elections; thus, despite the notable economic and political achievements of the Paz government, the slow pace of economic recovery[9] put a damper on initial popular support for economic reforms. Even though successive democratically elected Bolivian governments continued the broad parameters of Paz's neoliberal economic policies, the country's fragile economy[10] and widespread poverty ensured that economic policy making in Bolivia remained a game of delicate

[8] With a brief exception in early 1986, inflation in Bolivia after the initial stabilization in late 1985 was kept at annual levels below 25% in the second half of the decade, a resounding success not only by historical standards but also compared to the performance of its Latin American peers (most notably Argentina and Brazil) who continued to battle chronically high levels of inflation until the early 1990s.

[9] Despite the macroeconomic stability, the country's real economy recovered only slowly starting in 1987, with economic growth between 2.6% and 3% in 1987–89, unemployment levels of about 20% throughout the late 1980s, and real wages, still lower in 1989 than at the outset of the debt crisis.

[10] The continuing decline of the tin industry and the country's growing dependence on two potentially conflicting sources of foreign currency—foreign aid on one hand and the export earnings from the illegal sale of coca leaves on the other—meant that the Bolivian economy continued to lack a stable basis of sustainable economic development.

political brinkmanship long after the 1985 crisis had abated. The political upheaval of recent years suggests that despite ushering in almost two decades of relative economic and political stability, these reforms ultimately failed to reverse Bolivia's deep-seated legacies of poverty, inequality, and social polarization.

Failed Orthodoxy and Heterodoxy: Peru under Belaúnde and Garcia

In July 1985, while the newly elected Bolivian government was embarking on the road to economic orthodoxy, in neighboring Peru, the president-elect, Alan Garcia, initiated a dramatic reversal of the Belaúnde government's earlier path of neoliberal economic management under close IMF supervision. As in Bolivia, this sharp policy reversal occurred in the unstable political environment of an impoverished fledgling democracy and was the result of fundamentally different ideological interpretations of how to tackle the severe economic imbalances of the Latin American debt crisis. However, unlike Bolivia's relative success after 1985, Peru's two democratic governments of the 1980s failed in their attempts to tackle the country's severe economic crisis, and when Alberto Fujimori won the second round of presidential elections in early 1990, the very existence of democratic elections was quite possibly the only real achievement of a decade of democratic rule in Peru.

What explains Peru's remarkable economic debacle under its two democratically elected governments of the 1980s? Structural legacies cannot provide a satisfactory answer, given that in most respects Peru's economic and political background at the start of the debt crisis was quite typical of the rest of the region: In 1982 foreign debt accounted for 45% of GDP (slightly below the regional average for that year); inflation ran at 65%, which was higher than in most Latin American countries but not unmanageable, particularly since the fiscal deficit of 3.2% was well below most of its peers; and the economy was reasonably diversified, especially by comparison to Bolivia. Politically, despite the prevalence of personalism and patronage politics, at the time of the 1980 elections, the Peruvian party system showed considerable promise of consolidation (Cotler 1995:335) and the far-left guerrilla movements (such as Sendero Luminoso and Tupac Amaru) did not yet pose a significant challenge to the country's governability. If structural legacies cannot account for the Peruvian debacle, the obvious alternative would be to look at the policies of the country's two governments during this period.

Orthodoxy Punished:
The Failure of Economic Adjustment under Belaúnde

From 1980 to 1985, under the presidency of Fernando Belaúnde, the Peruvian government pursued one of the region's most ideologically committed neoliberal reform strategies of the period. The genesis of this strategy, intended to adopt the basic economic tenets of the Chilean model in Peru's democratic context, is unique in Latin America of the early 1980s in the sense that it was adopted by a democratically elected government prior to the debut of the debt crisis and in the absence of immediate pressures from the IMF. In part, this unexpected democratic neoliberalism can be interpreted as a political reaction against another "original" Peruvian political phenomenon—the leftist military regime of general Velasco—whose economic failures not only prepared the way for the transition to democracy but also discredited the statist ISI model promoted by Velasco. Moreover, the positive economic results of an IMF-supported orthodox stabilization program under the transitional government of General Morales Bermudez in 1978–79, combined with the widely publicized success of the Chilean free-market strategy in the late 1970s, convinced important sectors of the Peruvian elite to throw their support behind a small group of Western-trained technocrats who became the core of Belaúnde's economic team (Pastor 1992:110–11).

Initially, the political prospects for the Belaúnde government and its economic reform agenda looked rather promising. Belaúnde had won the 1980 presidential elections with a comfortable 45%–27% margin over the second-ranked candidate, and his party, the center-right Acción Popular (AP), had secured an absolute majority of 54.4% in the Lower House of Parliament. Belaúnde's power in Parliament was further strengthened by the alliance with the rightist Partido Popular Cristiano (PPC), as well as by the infighting in the (misnamed) leftist Izquierda Unida (IU), and the willingness of the AP's traditional rival and largest parliamentary opposition party—the center-left APRA—to take on the role of "loyal opposition" while overcoming significant internal strife after the death of its founding leader, Haya de la Torre (Cotler 1995:340). At the societal level, the AP government also benefited from a favorable situation, given that it could count on business support for its neoliberal economic agenda and because the political power of labor unions had been weakened by their confrontations with the military regime during the Morales Bermudez governing period.

During the Belaúnde government's first two years in power, the country's solid growth rates of 4.5% in 1980 and 1981 seemed to confirm the optimistic expectations of the neoliberal reformers and initially strengthened their political power. However, these early economic successes, driven to a large extent by healthy capital inflows and a temporary rise in the country's commodity export prices, may have ultimately contributed to the political defeat of the neoliberals, who witnessed their political support evaporate overnight as the economy took a turn for the worse in mid-1982 with the debut of the debt crisis. While it is unclear whether any kind of democratic neoliberal coalition could have survived the depth of Peru's 1983 economic crisis[11]—especially because the initial reforms were launched in a relatively low-crisis environment and therefore lacked the "redemptive" quality of the post-1985 Bolivian reforms—the Belaúnde government undoubtedly undermined its initial political capital through its exclusionary governing style. Buying into the neoliberal assumptions about the benefits of insulated technocratic decision making, the Belaúnde government ruled primarily by executive decree, without even the pretense of soliciting the input of parliament or business and labor organizations. As a consequence, when the deterioration of the country's external position and a string of natural disasters undermined the effectiveness of the monetarist model after mid-1982 and deflated the expertise-based legitimacy of the technocrats, the Belaúnde government suddenly found itself cut off from political support not only at the societal level but even within the governing AP. The increasing political weakness of the Peruvian government starting in mid-1983 eventually created important tensions within the core economic team and resulted in increasingly incoherent economic policies and ultimately in the abandonment of orthodox adjustment, as reflected in the government's repeated failure to comply with IMF conditionality after late 1983.

In a sense, the failure of orthodoxy under Belaúnde, combined with the setbacks suffered by neoliberal reform efforts in Chile and Mexico during the same period, illustrates the important limitations of the IMF economic adjustment recipe in the first part of the debt crisis. The significant trade-offs between the IMF's debt repayment agenda and the domestic economic growth objectives of Latin American countries created a political environment that made the task of successful economic adjustment in a democratic context exceedingly difficult. Whereas Chile's military government and Mexico's one-party dominant regime weathered the crisis through a combination of deviations from orthodoxy, Western support, and exclusionary politics, the Belaúnde government essentially collapsed under the weight of the crisis. While it is difficult to know whether Peru, if it had continued its pursuit of economic orthodoxy, would have experienced a similar economic recovery as Chile in the second part of

---

[11] After stagnating in 1982, the Bolivian economy plunged by almost 13% in 1983 while inflation reached 125% in the same year despite the government's desperate stabilization efforts.

the 1980s, the circumstances of Belaúnde's political defeat confirm the inherent tension between democracy and consistent neoliberal reforms. From this perspective, it is particularly telling that the final blow to the Belaúnde's government came when most of the ruling party withdrew its support for the president's sinking neoliberal ship in anticipation of the voters' harsh judgment of the government's economic record in the 1985 elections. Thus, the Peruvian experience confirms the statistical findings about the greater reluctance of right-of-center governments to pursue IMF-style reforms prior to democratic elections.

Heterodoxy and International Isolation: Peru under Garcia (1985–90)

Having won the July 1985 elections by riding a wave of popular discontent with his predecessor's IMF-style economic policies, Peru's newly elected president, Alan Garcia, almost immediately set out to tackle the country's economic problems, which included a heavy debt service burden and triple-digit inflation in 1985. However, in line with the statistical findings in chapter 5, this economic crisis did not trigger the IMF-backed reforms one may have expected from a newly elected government facing significant economic challenges. Instead, in line with his party's center-left political platform and his populist electoral promises, Garcia reversed his predecessor's neoliberal domestic agenda as well as the country's international economic strategy. In addition to a widely publicized break with the IMF and the decision to limit debt service payments to no more than 10% of export earnings, the Garcia government instituted a heterodox economic policy program based on a combination of fixed exchange rates and price controls to reduce inertial inflation, as well as a series of growth stimulating measures, including lower interest rates, reduced taxes, increased subsidies, and higher wages (Pastor 1992:122–23). The short-term results of this strategy were remarkably positive: Relieved of the heavy burden of the payments, the Peruvian economy grew by an impressive 9.5% in 1986 and 7.8% in 1987, while inflation fell from almost 160% in 1985 to 63% in 1986.[12] Therefore, Garcia's populism resonated not only with the economic frustrations and resentments of large segments of the Peruvian population against the neoliberal agenda of the previous government and the IMF, but its early economic achievements reinforced the credibility of Garcia's interpretation of the country's initial economic crisis as stemming from the inopportune application of IMF-style policies.

[12] Data from Pastor 1992:116.

Despite these early successes, the Peruvian government's risky strategy started to unravel by mid-1987, as inflation started to pick up again (rising to 114% for the year) and the costs of the country's international economic isolation started to affect economic growth. The following two years witnessed an economic crisis that looked bleak even by the low regional standards at the end of Latin America's lost decade: Inflation grew steadily and reached crippling levels from mid-1988 until early 1990,[13] and the economy was affected by a deep two-year recession, leading to declines in real wages and living standards, which wiped out the gains of the temporary recovery between 1985 and 1987.[14] While Chilean and Bolivian orthodoxy, and the Argentine "middle-of-the-road" approach were not without their costs and drawbacks, Peru's dramatic failure in the late 1980s arguably did more to discredit heterodox adjustment policies in Latin America than the combined theoretical arguments of neoliberals in the region and elsewhere. While some have argued that Peru's failure does not necessarily prove that a "well conceived and well-implemented heterodox program cannot work" (Paus 1991:427), it nevertheless illustrates the magnitude of the difficulties encountered by such programs in the increasingly orthodox international economic environment of the emerging Washington Consensus.

Given these staggering economic costs and their inevitable repercussions on Garcia's political support among the poor, the traditional crisis-reform paradigm would predict a reformist turn in the policy approach of the Garcia government as the failure of heterodox adjustment was becoming increasingly obvious. Instead, for the remainder of its increasingly chaotic term in office, the Garcia government chose to "muddle through" with a series of halfhearted heterodox policy packages, which failed to arrest the country's economic freefall. In this sense, Peru's post-1985 trajectory confirms the statistical findings in the previous chapter about the crucial interaction between economic crisis and the government's partisan orientation in driving the initiation and implementation of IMF-style reforms. Of course, by late 1987, the status-quo bias in the economic policies of the Peruvian government was largely overdetermined: First, having been the most vocal proponent of heterodoxy during its first two years in office, the Garcia government could have hardly afforded to abandon its

[13] Starting in mid-1988, inflation never fell below 20% per month (equivalent to an annual rate of almost 1000%) and reached alarming levels (as high as 114% in September 1988) on several occasions prior to the 1990 elections (data from Pastor 1992:128–29).

[14] The economy declined by 8.8% in 1988 and 10.4% in 1989, thereby contributing to the 3.1% average annual decline in per capita GDP during the 1980s. The real minimum wage in 1989 was less than a quarter of 1980 levels and had even declined by more than half since 1985, despite an initial improvement in the first two years of the Garcia administration (data from Pastor 1992 and ECLAC 1990).

ideological position, on which much of its initial legitimacy and popularity were based. Second, the Garcia government was ill equipped politically to implement the painful adjustment measures inherent in IMF-style reforms, given that much of APRA's rank-and-file would have feared the negative repercussions of austerity and possible labor unrest, whereas the business sector deeply distrusted Garcia and could therefore hardly form the backbone of an APRA-led reform coalition.[15] Finally, even in the unlikely event that the domestic political will to initiate neoliberal reforms had existed, Peru under Garcia would have faced a costly uphill battle to reverse the damage of the acrimonious confrontation with the Fund and Western lenders after 1985. This strong status quo bias on both the domestic and the international front helps explain the statistical finding in chapter 5 that higher inflation levels only promote IMF program initiation in the aftermath of elections, when governments have not yet burned bridges with a variety of potential domestic and international allies.

The Uncomfortable Middle Ground:
Argentina under Alfonsín

Argentina's economic reform trajectory during the lost decade of the 1980s, closely paralleled by its relationship with International Monetary Fund, represents a microcosm that contains an impressive array of the many economic experiments and political struggles experienced by Latin American countries in their attempt to come to terms with the debt crisis in the delicate political context of democratic transitions. Between 1982 and 1989 Argentina experienced in rapid succession (1) the breakdown of its military regime following the disastrous defeat in the Falklands war and increasing economic paralysis (1982–83); (2) a brief flirtation with Keynesian experiments and a short-lived attempt to create a debtor's cartel to counter Western adjustment pressures (late 1983 to mid-1984); (3) an unsuccessful attempt at IMF-style orthodox liberalization and a gradual slide toward hyperinflation (late 1984 to mid-1985); (4) an unorthodox stabilization program with IMF support (mid-1985 to early 1986), whose remarkable early success prompted premature policy relaxation and a return to inflation that proved increasingly unresponsive to successive heterodox stabilization attempts (early 1986 to mid-1987); (5) a renewed turn to orthodoxy and a failed attempt at structural reforms in the context of growing domestic opposition and reluctant

---

[15] After some initial attempts at cooperation with local capitalists, Garcia's relationship with the business sector deteriorated sharply following his heavy-handed attempt to nationalize domestic banks in July 1987 (Pastor and Wise 1991:23).

Western support (mid-1987 to mid-1988); and finally (6) one last stabili- zation attempt—the Primavera plan initiated August 1988—whose failure in February 1989 resulted in the decisive electoral defeat of Al- fonsín's Radical Party amid political chaos and hyperinflation. Thus, while one can hardly accuse the Argentine government of not having tried a variety of economic strategies to deal with the country's predicament, by the end of the decade its careful game of political brinkmanship be- tween the competing claims of domestic and international interests had reaped very modest economic achievements and succeeded in alienating many of the government's erstwhile supporters. While the Alfonsín gov- ernment succeeded in what it viewed as its most important task—provid- ing sufficient breathing space for Argentina's fragile democracy in the context of a deep economic crisis—the ultimate failure of its economic policy reinforces the conclusions drawn from the Bolivian and Peruvian cases about the narrow maneuvering space of democratic governments between the political demands of labor and business in an inhospitable international economic environment.

Economic Crisis, Political Parties, and Organized Interests

To an even greater extent than in its international political initiatives, the Alfonsín government made a concerted effort to find a middle-ground compromise solution between the conflicting claims of domestic social and political actors in devising its domestic political approach to the im- plementation of economic reforms. As mentioned above in the context of the country's costly external adjustment and the zero-sum political con- flict mentality that dominated Argentina during this period, this quintes- sentially democratic approach to economic policy making ended with complete economic and extensive political failure by the end of Alfonsín's six-year tenure. When placed in comparative context, the failure of Argen- tine economic policy during this period illustrates a number of crucial mechanisms that can further our theoretical understanding of the political economy of successful economic reforms under democracy. Structured to a large extent as an (at least implicit) comparison to the successful eco- nomic reforms in Bolivia after 1985, this subsection emphasizes the cru- cial elements that undermined the emergence of a durable political coali- tion in support of reforms and hence the implementation of a coherent economic reform policy in Argentina during the 1980s. The timing, na- ture, and initial perception of the economic and political crisis at the out- set of the debt crisis prevented the emergence of a stable political coalition at both the congressional and societal level during the early period of exceptional politics. This pattern of "fair-weather" coalitions between an increasingly isolated government and powerful independent business and

organized labor interests was reinforced by the initial success of heterodox stabilization and thereby undermined the government's ability to impose the considerable costs of adjustment on any particular group. From
this perspective, the inflationary spiral Argentina experienced in 1989,
much like Bolivia's hyperinflation four years earlier, was symptomatic of
the extreme difficulty of finding a democratic solution to the long-standing social conflicts of the highly polarized Latin American societies during
the debt crisis.

THE FLEETING DEMOCRATIC CONSENSUS: MISPLAYING THE CRISIS CARD

The economic situation inherited by the Alfonsín government from its
military predecessors displayed crisis symptoms that were very similar to
the economic legacy of the collapsing military regime in Bolivia a year
earlier: high inflation levels of almost 350% in 1983; a contracting economy, whose modest recovery in 1983 hardly balanced out the recession
of the preceding four years; a large and growing budget deficit (approaching 8% in 1983 up from 5% in 1982); and an unsustainable
foreign debt situation that raised serious questions about the prospects
for long-term economic recovery. Even though the 1983 Argentine crisis
fell short of the dramatic economic and political ungovernability that
characterized the hyperinflationary episodes of Bolivia in 1985 or Peru in
1988–89, its deep historical roots at both the domestic and international
levels arguably required a profound transformation of the country's political economy trajectory.[16] From this perspective, the democratic transition
of 1983 could have provided a unique opportunity to initiate such a transformation, not only because the power of the Argentine military was at
an all-time low following its military defeat in the Falklands and its disastrous governance record between 1976 and 1983, but also because of
the relative disarticulation of labor and business organizations during the
repressive military rule (Acuna 1992:7–9).

Despite its unquestionable democratic legitimacy following its clear
1983 electoral victory, the Alfonsín administration failed to take advantage of the initial opportunity to use Argentina's political and economic
crisis as a rallying point for creating a powerful and stable reform coalition to support the government's economic policy agenda. Part of the

---

[16] Thus, the failed stabilization effort under Martinez de Hoz after 1978 was only the
most recent of a long succession of military and civilian governments that had proven incapable of resolving the zero-sum economic conflict between organized labor and various
competing sectoral business interests. Moreover, at the international level, the state capitalist development model of the preceding two decades had done little to reverse the country's
dependence on traditional exports and in a sense exacerbated Argentina's foreign dependence through the accumulation of a sizable foreign debt, particularly starting in the
mid-1970s.

reason for this failure was the Alfonsín government's lack of a clear ideological position on economic matters. On one hand the Radical Party leadership distrusted orthodox economic prescriptions, largely because they were associated in the minds of many Argentines with the discredited military regime and the equally distrusted IMF pressures. On the other hand the vaguely populist themes that had dominated the electoral campaign hardly provided an alternative ideological blueprint for domestic economic policy making, and, as a consequence the Alfonsín government reinforced the unfounded popular optimism that democracy would almost automatically solve the country's economic crisis. Therefore, Alfonsín committed the classical mistake—which was to be repeated over and over by equally well-meaning democratic reformers in Eastern Europe—of equating democracy with economic prosperity when he claimed that "with democracy you eat, you get educated, and you get cured" (cited in Canitrot 1994:81). This conflation of democracy and economic well-being had the double disadvantage of denying the short-term importance of political solidarity and economic sacrifices by key social actors, and triggering the longer-term delegitimation of democracy by tying it directly to Argentina's uncertain economic prospects.

The government's second opportunity to use economic crisis as a catalyst for changing the political power balance in its favor came in the spring of 1985, due to the rising inflationary pressures resulting from the powerful sectoral demands and the interruption of IMF support. Faced with the alarming specter of hyperinflation, Alfonsín gave a memorable speech on April 26 in front of 200,000 supporters that marked an important reversal in the government's early optimistic rhetoric by acknowledging the severity of the economic crisis and the necessity of economic sacrifices prior to any recovery; and he even claimed that the country was in the midst of a "war economy." This dramatic crisis rhetoric was followed six weeks later by the announcement of the Plan Austral, which despite its important heterodox elements, was considered by some observers as "more IMF than the IMF" because of its ambitious fiscal and monetary targets. As a result, the IMF resumed the disbursement of credits on the standby program suspended earlier in the year, and Argentine adjustment seemed to be back on track.

Emboldened by the remarkably fast anti-inflationary success of the Austral and the Radical victory in the September 1985 parliamentary elections, Alfonsín called for a new consensus in support of his government's economic reform program in his famous "Parque Norte" speech in November 1985 (Smith 1990:12). Ironically, however, the surprisingly painless success of the stabilization package arguably undermined the long-term prospects for economic reforms for at least two reasons. First, it led to a retrospective "deflation" of the severity of the crisis and thereby contributed to the self-defeating success of heterodox stabilization due to the rapid resumption of societal pressures for inflationary economic stimulus measures (Manzetti and Dell'Aquila 1988:2). Second, it reinforced the government's penchant for relying on insulated executive initiatives as the basis for economic policy instead of forging a broader political coalition for reforms, particularly in the context of the heightened importance of political coordination in the difficult task of the structural reforms that constituted the crucial second step of the Austral plan.

THE (UN)MAKING OF A FAIR-WEATHER COALITION

Alfonsín and his Radical Party (UCR) came to power following the October 1983 elections, after a surprising victory over the Peronists (PJ) who suffered their first defeat in a freely contested democratic election. Given that the UCR obtained only a razor-thin majority in the House of Representatives (with 129 of 254 seats) and actually trailed behind the PJ in the Senate (with 18 of 46 seats), Alfonsín hardly commanded the parliamentary support required for potentially painful economic reforms, especially because the Argentine electoral system schedules lower-house parliamentary elections every two years. At least in retrospect the obvious solution to the problem would have been the initiation of a formal "national unity" pact at the congressional level between the UCR and the PJ, which could have delivered reliable political support and shared responsibility for the government's economic policy in return for some form of power-sharing agreement. Such a co-optation of the Peronist leadership would have been important not only due to the political legitimacy derived from congressional support but also because it could have facilitated the government's difficult negotiations with organized labor, a close ally of the Peronists. Furthermore, the period immediately following the 1983 elections provided a real window of opportunity for such a grand alliance, given that the two parties had come a long way in reconciling their better historical rivalry due to their shared suffering under the military regime, and that—unlike in 1989—the two parties differed only minimally in their ideological platforms (McGuire 1995:222–23).

However, for a number of reasons, the newly democratic Argentina did not witness the emergence of a political pact at the party level along the lines of the Bolivian Pacto por la Democracia of 1985. First, many Radicals erroneously interpreted their electoral victory and the PJ's subsequent internal conflicts as a sign of the decisive decline of Peronism and, therefore, underestimated its considerable residual political power. This sense of confidence reduced the Radicals' willingness to seek political compromise with the Peronists, who in turn proceeded to rebuild their party unity in opposition to the Alfonsín government, thereby further complicating any attempts at political cooperation (Torre 1993:76–77).

Second, the quasi-complete loss of legitimacy by the military reduced the short-term probability of a coup, and thus diminished the importance of a broad civilian alliance against a common authoritarian threat. Third, the government's focus on the external dimension of the crisis, combined with the aforementioned optimism about the domestic economic prospects, relegated domestic coalition building to the margins of the political agenda during the first months of the Alfonsín government. Therefore, Alfonsín missed the opportunity to forge a political coalition from a position of strength in late 1983, and then again after the initial success of the Austral plan and the renewed UCR victory in the 1985 parliamentary elections. Instead, the first major concession to the Peronists occurred from a position of weakness in mid-1987 with the appointment of Carlos Alderete, one of the leaders of the antireform wing of the Peronist labor movement, as minister of labor. This concession failed to produce the political benefits expected by the Radical leadership, given that Alderete's presence in the cabinet merely provided the opposition with a "Trojan horse" in the government, as evidenced by his vocal opposition to Sourrouille on monetary policy and his support for labor in the debates over the collective bargaining laws (Smith 1990:21). Therefore, it hardly came as a surprise that following the 1987 elections, the new Peronist-dominated Congress actively tried to sabotage most of the government's economic policy initiatives, especially with respect to the structural reform efforts at the core of the IMF-supported orthodox stabilization program in late 1987, early 1988. The resulting policy paralysis was an important reason for the collapse of the IMF program and contributed to the rising inflation, which increasingly affected the Argentine economy after mid-1988 and eventually degenerated into hyperinflation in the second half of 1989. These parliamentary roadblocks to Argentine reforms illustrate the statistical findings in chapter 5 about the importance of comfortable parliamentary majorities for governments trying to initiate IMF-style reforms in the tense political context of the Latin American debt crisis.

As in the Bolivian case, however, any account of the politics underlying Argentina's reform path in the 1980s has to focus on the partisan preferences and relative political power not only of political parties but also of key social actors, particularly the interests of labor unions and the business organizations of key economic sectors. While this brief analysis can hardly do justice to this complex and important aspect of Argentine economic reforms,[17] I will nevertheless point out the crucial factors shaping the temporary achievements and ultimate failure of Alfonsín's economic policy efforts.

---

[17] For more detailed analytical accounts of these relations, see Carlos Acuna 1992, Marcelo Luis Acuna 1995, William Smith 1990.

From the outset, the Alfonsín government faced a number of handicaps in its political relationship with organized interests. Unlike the Peronists, the Radicals appealed to voters as individual citizens rather than as members of corporate groups, which deprived them of the corporate structures of political support available to their opponents. This unease with Argentina's organized corporate interests was reflected by the official rhetoric coming from the Radical party leadership at various key political junctures, starting with the 1983 electoral campaign, continuing during the inflationary crisis in the spring of 1985, and culminating during the government's late turn toward orthodoxy, when Sourrouille echoed the standard neoliberal complaint about the resistance of powerful sectoral interests to "the transformations demanded by Argentine society."[18]

The political consequences of this mutual distrust were exacerbated by the relative strength of labor and business groups during the 1980s. Since Argentina's industrial sector was fairly large and diversified by Latin American standards (especially compared to Bolivia and Peru), industrial workers represented a more significant (though declining) proportion of the population, which translated into greater popular support for the labor movement and would have significantly raised the political costs of coercive actions by the government against labor unrest (along the lines pursued by the Paz government in Bolivia). Moreover, despite its aggressive antilabor policies, the Argentine military government had been significantly less effective than its Chilean counterpart in dismantling the organizational structures of organized labor. Argentina's various business organizations (representing the often conflicting interests of different sectors) had also weathered the military repression reasonably well, and looked upon democracy as a political opportunity to pursue its economic interests.

Aware of the close political ties between the labor unions and the opposition Peronists, and anticipating the rise of union demands in a democratic context, the Radicals had started their confrontational approach against organized labor during the electoral campaign. However, unlike the Bolivian MNR, the Alfonsín government limited its attacks on union power to strictly democratic procedures throughout its tenure, despite the unions' active—and frequently obstructive—opposition to most of the government's economic initiatives, as indicated by the remarkable frequency and extensiveness of strikes and labor protests between 1983 and 1989. The first—and arguably most important—government attempt to curb the power of the Peronist unions occurred in February 1984, when the so-called Mucci Law, intended to democratize internal union elections and thereby reduce the political power of old-style Peronist union leaders,

[18] Sourrouille 1989:80–86, cited in Smith 1990:18.

failed in the Senate after an extremely close (24–22) vote. This narrow defeat not only deprived the government of gaining more influence in the politics of Argentina's labor unions but it also enforced an atmosphere of political distrust that permeated all subsequent negotiations between the two sides. During the following years, despite a number of occasional cooperation attempts, the bargaining positions of the two sides hardened and drifted apart even farther as the government moved away from its early populism under Grinspun to an increasingly orthodox approach to economic adjustment by the end of the decade. As discussed earlier, relations barely improved even after the Alfonsín government's conciliatory move to designate a prominent union leader, Carlos Alderete, as labor minister in 1987, given that the unions refused to moderate their economic demands to the increasingly isolated administration during this period.

Compared to the Peronist loyalties of the labor movement, the business sector emerged from the dictatorship with uncertain political loyalties, considering its increasingly conflictual relationship with the military government, its traditional distrust of the Peronists, and the absence of a credible pro-business party on the Argentine political spectrum in 1983. However, even though the government's relations with business were generally less conflictual than with organized labor, the business sector organizations did not emerge as a key political support basis for the Radical government. In part, the reason for this outcome was the government's initial failure to involve corporate interests in the design of economic policy, which contributed to an unexpected antigovernment alliance between key labor and business interests in the months leading up to the launching of the Austral Plan. This so-called production front brought together the General Confederation of Labor (CGT) and leading business organizations (including the representatives of manufacturing interests and agroexporters) and resulted in higher wages, whose costs were then passed on to the producers in the form of higher prices due to the semiclosed nature of the Argentine economy.

Following the success of the Austral Plan, business confidence in the government increased, which allowed the Alfonsín administration to dissolve the "production front" and replace it with the government-overseen Economic and Social Conference (CES). The CES, however, proved to be little more than lip service to the notion of a social pact between government, labor, and business because it provided corporate interests with no real input into policymaking, and completely excluded the important agricultural and banking sectors from the process (Smith 1990:12–13). Moreover, when in July 1986, following a thirty-three-day strike by the metal workers, the government pressured the Metallurgical Industry Association (ADIMRA) to accede to the wage demands of the unions, the compromise not only fueled inflation by encouraging similar deals in other industries but it also dealt a severe blow to the business sector's confidence in the government (Acuna 1991:17). This downward trend continued during 1987–88 in line with the government's increasing inability to control fiscal and inflationary pressures. As a consequence, despite Alfonsín's announcement of an "alliance between production and democracy"[19] in mid-1988, business support for the government's increasingly neoliberal economic policies was at best mixed, and vanished almost completely as the economy started its inevitable drift toward hyperinflation by late 1988.

Conclusion: Liberal Democracy
and Economic Adjustment in the 1980s—Pick One?

The Argentine case illustrates the significant trade-offs between the democratic agenda pursued by the Alfonsín government between 1983 and 1989 and the difficult economic-adjustment tasks facing Argentina during this period. The Alfonsín government tried to steer a careful middle course between the various conflicting domestic and international demands, a strategy that yielded some temporary gains but ended in hyperinflation and complete political defeat. Unwilling to resort to the labor repression strategies employed by the Chilean and to a lesser extent the Bolivian government, and incapable of co-opting crucial business and labor organizations under the banner of its economic reforms, the Argentine government was unable to find a political solution for distributing the economic burden of adjustment. As in Bolivia prior to 1985, the economic manifestation of this political deadlock was the recurring problem of high inflation, which by 1989 had degenerated to hyperinflationary levels.

Keeping in mind these important economic and political constraints, the preceding analysis nevertheless suggests that the Alfonsín government shares at least part of the blame for these unfortunate results. Thus, the government failed to take advantage on two occasions (in late 1983 and in mid to late 1985) of the unique political opportunity provided by the combination of a fairly severe economic crisis and the political legitimacy of recent electoral victories to forge political pacts at the parliamentary and the societal level in support of the economic reform agenda. Instead, Alfonsín relied primarily on a small team of technocrats in the design of economic reforms and, as a consequence, was only able to muster political support when it was least necessary, namely during the successful first stage of the Austral Plan between the summer of 1985 and the spring of 1986. Once the immediate crisis had abated, organized interests renewed

[19] La Nacion (August 13, 1988:1), cited in Acuna 1991:25.

their redistributive pressures and showed little interest in supporting the government's structural reform agenda, which was needed to complement the initial heterodox stabilization program. Realizing its increasing isolation, the Alfonsín government belatedly tried to forge an alliance first with the Peronist unions and later with the business organizations but its concessions were rightly interpreted as a sign of weakness and, therefore, failed to produce the expected results. Ironically, the political lessons of Alfonsín's failure seem to have been thoroughly internalized by his political successor—the Peronist Carlos Menem—who in the early 1990s managed to assemble precisely the neoliberal labor-business coalition that had eluded Alfonsín in the 1980s.

The Crisis and Transformation of the Chilean Model

Compared to the tense and reversal-prone IMF relations of most Latin American debtors, Chile's close and consistent involvement with the Fund during the debt crisis of the 1980s appears as little more than a theoretically overdetermined case. After all, Chile had had a solid track record of orthodox economic policies for several years prior to the debut of the debt crisis. After almost three decades of sustained scrutiny from academic and policy circles, the broad parameters of the Chilean model are rather well established: a highly centralized military regime under the leadership of General Augusto Pinochet, which, through the suppression of leftist parties and labor unions and the selective co-optation of business interests, insulated a coherent team of Chicago-educated neoliberal technocrats from the political pressures of special interests and as a result created a model of neoliberal social and economic transformation, hailed by the neoliberals and decried by many critics for its consequent policy application of neoclassical economic principles. Given that by mid-1982 Chile also suffered from one of the heaviest debt burdens in the region—with debt service payments using up to more than 70% of export revenues and interest payments alone accounting for 10% of GNP—the Pinochet regime had the partisan and financial motives, as well as the political and administrative means that made it the ideal candidate for IMF conditionality.

These theoretical predictions were borne out with remarkable consistency judging by the repeated patterns of timely program initiation and solid implementation of IMF programs during the 1980s, which were described in chapter 4. Beneath the surface of this neat high-level correlation, however, one finds a much more complicated and contradictory set of political processes at the domestic level. Despite its initial strength and ultimate political survival until the end of the decade, between 1983 and

1985 the Pinochet government experienced the most significant political crisis of its seventeen-year rule. Despite its undeniable status as a darling of international finance during the 1970s, Chile was not spared the politically difficult trade-off between honoring its external debt obligations and promoting domestic economic recovery. The political solutions to this tension entailed a combination of political repression and policy concessions, which entailed significant pragmatic deviations from the tenets of the strict economic orthodoxy advocated by both the Chilean government and the IMF at the outset of the debt crisis.

The Rise of Neoliberal Pragmatism: Redefining the Chilean Model

Whereas as late as mid-1981 Milton Freedman had sung the praises of the unfolding neoliberal Chilean boom, barely eighteen months later the economic miracle had come to an abrupt end. The Chicago Boys' insistence on a monetarist response to the external shock of the debt crisis had disastrous effects on the economy, which contracted by an unprecedented 14.5% in 1982, while inflation doubled compared to 1981 and reached 20%. Moreover, private consumption decreased by 16%, and unemployment reached the catastrophic level of 30% by the end of 1982.[20] To add ideological insult to economic injury, the Chilean government was forced to preempt the imminent failure of several large- and medium-size banks by nationalizing more than a third of the country's banking system, which increased both the size of the state sector and the government's foreign debt. Just as ironically, considering the Chicago Boys' emphatic rejection of the populist public spending projects in other parts of Latin America during the 1970s, the rapid expansion of private-sector consumption and private-sector foreign debt after 1976 created very similar balance-of-payment difficulties for Chile when capital flows reversed in mid-1982.

As predicted by the formal model and confirmed by the statistical findings, the initial reaction of Chile's technocratic government to the eruption of the crisis in 1982 was driven by its ideological convictions about the appropriate economic policy response to financial crises. Since the Chilean government had no democratic elections to worry about, it initially ignored the growing pressures from business organizations and popular sector groups for a softening of the austerity measures agreed to with the IMF in January 1983. Gradually, however, Pinochet became concerned by the increasingly energetic demands of the broad center-left umbrella organization Alianza Democrática (AD), which organized monthly large-scale national protests and demanded a rapid transition to democratic rule, reactivating economic measures and a tougher negotiat-

[20] Data from Borzutsky 1987:78 and Silva 1996:180.

ing stance toward the IMF (Silva 1992:86). The situation became positively threatening to the survival of the Pinochet regime, when in August
1983 the country's top business organizations, united under the umbrella
of the Confederation of Production and Commerce (CPC) started to signal the possibility of an alliance with the AD, which would have
amounted to a radical loss of political support from one of the pillars of
the Pinochet government since the 1973 coup. This surprising estrange-
ment between the military regime and its erstwhile loyal supporters in the
business sector emphasizes the tensions between the IMF's emphasis on
austerity and debt repayment, and the political viability of domestic neoliberal coalitions, in the context in which Latin American governments
were forced to choose between the conflicting demands of foreign banks
and domestic producers.

Pinochet's reaction to this unprecedented political challenge to the
survival of the military regime was based on a two-pronged approach.
First, he refused to enter into dialogue with the AD and began to use
massive military repression against the pro-democracy protesters, which
in August 1983 resulted in the deployment of eighteen thousand troops
in Santiago and left at least thirty dead, and continued with varying degrees of intensity until early 1985 (Borzutzky 1987:83). At the same time,
however, Pinochet pursued a number of economic measures meant to de-
fuse some of the economic discontent of the population by promoting
some social protection and public work projects. Second, Pinochet moved
quickly to regain the confidence of the business sector through a combination of policy changes designed to reactivate economic growth, and a comprehensive cabinet change, which drastically reduced the policy influence
of the Chicago Boys and paved the way for the "pragmatic neoliberalism"
political pact between the military government and the CPC during the
second half of the 1980s. One of the most prominent victims of this re-
shuffle was the finance minister Carlos Caceres, who was fired in mid-
April 1984 in the midst of the country's efforts to clinch a more flexible
deal in its renegotiation of the 1983 standby agreement with the IMF.
Pinochet's dismissal of Caceres, whose commitment to austerity had made
him equally unpopular with labor and business, closely parallels the
forced resignation of Belaúnde's neoliberal finance minister Rodriguez-
Pastor during the Peruvian IMF renegotiation process in the previous
month. If, in addition, we recount the resignation in February 1985 of
Bernardo Grinspun in the heat of the conflict over the country's failing
IMF program, the remarkable connection between the pressures of IMF
conditionality and domestic political instability in Latin America becomes
a pattern that is difficult to ignore. On the other hand, the radically different responses of the three governments—political paralysis in Peru, pragmatic neoliberalism in Chile, and heterodox adjustment in Argentina—

emphasize that external pressures were refracted in very different ways by the domestic political constellations of the program countries.

Slovakia—Conditionality versus Populism

From its unpromising birth into nationhood in January 1993 until the parliamentary elections in late 1998, Slovakia, under its nationalist-populist prime minister Vladimir Mečiar, represents one of the most intriguing cases in the political economy of post-communist reforms in Eastern Europe. Unlike its East-Central European neighbors, Slovakia's attitude toward Western integration and conditionality was lukewarm, controversial and often contradictory. The country's rocky relationship with the IMF during Mečiar's rule, which was discussed in some detail in chapter 4, was emblematic of the peculiar reform approach of the Mečiar government, which combined a fairly prudent fiscal and monetary policy with a mixture of nationalist-populist rhetoric and policies. In line with the statistical findings in the previous chapter, the contrast between Mečiar's defiance of IMF policy prescriptions and the country's eager embrace of the same prescriptions during the brief interlude of the reformist Moravčík government in mid-1994 illustrates that partisan differences also mattered in the post-communist transition, as long as the domestic economic crisis was not too severe.

The Domestic Political Roots of Mečiar's Anti-IMF Stance

As discussed in chapter 4, Slovakia under Mečiar repeatedly resisted the demands of IMF conditionality despite its very fragile initial external position. While chapter 4 explored the international political dynamics and consequences of this conflict, the present discussion focuses on the domestic political dimension of Slovakia's peculiar approach to economic reforms under the leadership of Vladimir Mečiar. In particular, it is important to understand why Mečiar decided to forego the potentially important benefits of funding and outside validation associated with successful IMF involvement despite the fact that—as mentioned in chapter 4—the actual policy disagreements between the Fund and the Mečiar government were hardly insurmountable.

One possible answer suggested by the statistical findings is that the Slovak government may not have had the bureaucratic capacity and expertise necessary to implement the demanding structural reforms required by IMF conditionality. Indeed, Slovakia had to tackle its structural economic distortions inherited from communism in the chaotic institutional environment of the early postindependence period, when the daunting task of setting up state institutions and formulating economic policy was complicated by the serious shortage of qualified specialists.[21] Nonetheless, despite a large fiscal deficit of 6.8% in 1993, monetary policy was surprisingly successful, resulting in an inflation rate of 23% for the year, which was remarkably low by regional standards. While Mečiar's claims about IMF's appreciation for the exceptional effectiveness of the Slovak government (*Slovak Radio*, 641993) were likely exaggerated, the better-than-expected economic results during Slovakia's first year of independence suggest a fairly rapid improvement in the institutional capacity of the fledgling state. Moreover, even though lagging behind the Czech Republic and Hungary in terms of its quality of governance, Slovakia was nevertheless well ahead of countries with much more consistent IMF track records, such as Moldova and Azerbaijan. Therefore, the Mečiar government's failure to initiate and implement IMF programs can hardly be blamed on institutional weakness. Instead, Mečiar's "rebellion" has to be analyzed in the context of the implications of IMF conditionality for the domestic political power balance in Slovakia.

While the tension between program conditions and national self-determination is an integral part of IMF conditionality, for the Mečiar government this dilemma was further complicated by the role of Western economic and political influence on the domestic political power balance of Slovakia. Even though Mečiar's Movement for a Democratic Slovakia (HZDS) was an outgrowth of the anticommunist Public against Violence (VPN), Mečiar's prominent role in the breakup of Czechoslovakia, combined with his nationalist rhetoric against Slovakia's Hungarian minority, his intolerance of internal dissent, and his populist tendency to blame the hardship of the economic transition on the West, set Mečiar at odds with the Western establishment even prior to the country's independence. As a consequence, Mečiar's policies were frequently subjected to outspoken criticism in Western media and diplomatic circles, and the domestic opposition invoked its closer ties to the West in its increasingly bitter political struggle against Mečiar.

Against this domestic political background, Mečiar's decision about the optimal strategy vis-à-vis the IMF entailed a significant trade-off. On one hand, a close cooperation with the IMF may have allowed Mečiar to improve his image in the West and to challenge the opposition's claims of being the only real hope for the country's Western integration efforts. On the other hand, acquiescence to IMF demands would have meant playing on the reformist opposition's policy home turf, while at the same time weakening Mečiar's political support among reform losers, who would have probably defected to other more outspokenly antireform parties.

---

[21] The problem was particularly acute in terms of financial expertise, given that most of the senior staff in the financial institutions of the former Czechoslovakia had been Czechs (*Montreal Gazette* 3/26/1993).

Moreover, bowing to IMF pressures would have undermined Mečiar's populist image as the "father of the people," on which much of his electoral appeal rested. Finally, Mečiar was probably aware that even in the event of a close relationship with the IMF, his government still faced an uphill battle in securing Western approval, given the country's other outstanding problem areas, such as minority rights and corruption. Therefore, Mečiar opted for a more confrontational approach to IMF negotiations, a strategy that came at an economic cost but allowed him to play a much more familiar and electorally successful domestic role as a political maverick defending Slovakia's interests against various outside threats. The resulting siege mentality had the added advantage of allowing Mečiar to paint his opponents as unpatriotic, and of justifying his semi-authoritarian governing style.

While some of Mečiar's public statements may be dismissed as inconsequential populist rhetoric,[22] the actions of the Slovak government in late 1993 and early 1994 were largely consistent with this rhetoric. Even though Mečiar's ruling HZDS suffered a number of political defections and lost its political majority in mid-1993, the fragmented pro-reform opposition proved incapable of mounting a serious political challenge, which may have forced Mečiar to adopt more reformist policies. The government's nationalist-populist stance became even more strident when Mečiar entered an alliance with the extreme nationalist Slovak National Party (SNS) in October 1993. Therefore, the Slovak government dragged its feet in its IMF negotiations, resisting a number of unpopular conditions such as the increase in value added taxes (VAT) and the regulation of salaries.

Overall, Slovakia's failure to initiate an IMF standby agreement in the early post-independence period is consistent with the statistical findings that at low inflation levels nationalist/populist and ex-communist governments were less likely to initiate IMF programs. Considering Slovakia's low inflation in 1993–94, Mečiar's ideologically motivated defiance of the IMF is consistent with the notion that in the postcommunist context, anti-reform governments were likely to pursue their ideological leanings as long as they managed to avoid severe domestic crises. Since post-independence Slovakia never experienced triple-digit inflation, let alone hyperinflation, we can only speculate about whether Mečiar would have relented to IMF pressures if his "original" reform recipe had produced a more severe and visible domestic economic crisis.

---

[22] For example, Mečiar downplayed the Fund's influence on Slovak economic policy making by claiming that the IFIs were expected "to fill just a consultancy role and make recommendations, which the government often does not observe, as the situation forces us to do something else" (cited in CTK, 11/24/1993).

What we do know, however, based on the discussion in chapter 4, is that Mečiar's ideologically based disagreements with the Fund precluded an IMF agreement at a time when Slovakia's fragile external reserves would have predicted a more conciliatory approach by the Slovak government.

IMF Cooperation during the 1994 Neoliberal Intermezzo

The importance of partisan politics in driving Slovakia's IMF relations is reinforced by the radical change of tone following the fall of the Mečiar government after a vote of no-confidence in March 1994. Immediately upon assuming office, the caretaker coalition government of Prime Minister Jozef Moravčik announced the resumption of negotiations with the IMF to obtain the second tranche of the June 1993 STF program and to sign a new standby agreement. Despite complaints by a prominent HZDS politician about the softer IMF approach toward the new government, the new standby agreement signed in July 1994 by the Moravčik government included the same basic conditions, which had been rejected by the Mečiar government earlier in the year. Sergej Kozlik, one of Mečiar's deputies, described this process in amusingly rustic terms, comparing the IMF agreement to a cowpat in a field: "One person stops before it, the other treads in it. Whose boots are going to stink now? The Moravčik government's!"[23]

Somewhat surprisingly, the inexperienced and highly fragmented coalition government managed to comply with IMF conditionality in the months preceding the SeptemberOctober 1994 elections, and was rewarded by high praise and significant loan disbursements by the IMF and the World Bank. Nevertheless, Kozlik's prediction was ultimately accurate, since the Slovak reformers paid the political costs of the austerity measures implemented as part of the IMF program by losing the elections in late 1994. While this electoral outcome was obviously driven not only by the politics of IMF conditionality but by the superior organizational capacity of Mečiar's HZDS and the fragmentation of the reformist camp, the situation nevertheless illustrates the difficult trade-offs between domestic political imperatives and external pressures in the context of IMF programs.

Back to Confrontation—Mečiar's Return to Power

Following his return to power, Mečiar formed a coalition with the right-wing Slovak National Party (SNS) and the extreme-left Association of Slovak Workers (ZRS). Given that the former protested against "national impoverishment by international capital," while the latter professed to be

[23] Cited in ibid., 6/20/1994.

"basically against the EU, NATO and the IMF" (cited in the *Economist*, 11/12/1994), this coalition exacerbated Mečiar's populist tendencies. Moreover, Mečiar's authoritarian governing style, which included attempts to control the mass media and the harassment of political opponents,[24] limited the influence of the reformist opposition. The problem was exacerbated by the deep personal rivalries between Mečiar and many opposition leaders (Peter Weiss, Milan Kňažko, Ján Čarnogurský), which precluded the formation of a more moderate governing coalition, as well as by the political infighting between the various opposition parties, who failed to pose a serious political challenge until the 1998 elections.

The country's prudent fiscal and monetary policies during 1995–96 led to a further decline in inflation (to single digits), which, combined with the equally impressive economic growth (exceeding 6% per annum from 1995 to 1997), confirms the ability of the Mečiar government to manage the economy. Therefore, the failure to comply with IMF conditionality after the 1994 elections cannot be blamed on institutional weakness but rather on the unwillingness to comply with "politically inconvenient" IMF conditions in the context of a fairly benign economic environment. Thus, the Slovak government's repeated resistance to the reduction and elimination of the 10% import surcharge instituted in 1993 was in line with the nationalist and protectionist stance promoted by the Slovak finance minister Sergei Kozlik, who also resisted the sale of state assets to foreigners, based on his conviction that Slovakia "should prosper on the basis of its own resources."[25] Moreover, while privatization continued despite initial warnings about a complete moratorium and a possible reversal of privatization deals initiated by the Moravčík government, the privatization strategy favored direct sales over voucher privatization and attracted intense criticism about preferential treatments for Mečiar's political allies. Nevertheless, despite the somewhat bizarre situation in which the privatization minister Peter Bisak (a member of the extreme-left ZRS) opposed privatization of any kind, Slovakia emerged as one of the countries with the highest private-sector shares (83% in 1998 according to EBRD estimates). Other politically motivated disagreements with the IMF during this period included welfare spending (raising the retirement age and reducing family benefits by 40%) and energy price controls.

---

[24] Possibly the most prominent example of these tactics was Mečiar's long-standing conflict with President Michal Kovac, who played an important role in the nonconfidence vote against the Mečiar government in March 1994. Thus, in August 1995 the Slovak Intelligence Service (SIS) allegedly kidnapped Kovac's son and handed him over to Austrian police, who were investigating him on criminal charges. Other tactics included the publication by the SIS of forged documents according to which President Kovac supposedly stole and illegally exported large sums of money (*ERWI*, April 1997).

[25] Cited in *EIU Country Report*, 1st quarter, 1995.

Implications and Conclusions

Slovakia's surprisingly solid economic performance before 1998 suggests that the failure to comply with IMF conditionality cannot be traced to the pervasive institutional weakness that hindered economic reforms elsewhere in the region. Instead, the country's strained relationship with the IMF should be seen primarily as the result of the incompatibility between the strict prescriptions of IMF conditionality and the nationalist-populist agenda of Slovakia's leader, Vladimir Mečiar, in the context of the country's polarized domestic political scene. The importance of ideology in the Slovak case is further reinforced by the dramatic reversal of the country's relationship with the IMF during the brief tenure of the reformist government of Jozef Moravčík. Thus, Slovakia's experience serves as a reminder that in the absence of a severe domestic economic crisis IMF conditionality cannot simply be imposed even on small, vulnerable countries if it conflicts with the interests and/or convictions of domestic political actors.

Moldova—The Politics of an Unlikely Cooperation

Whereas Slovakia under Mečiar illustrates the importance of partisan convictions and domestic political considerations as filters of IMF conditionality, Moldova's post-communist experience illustrates the powerful impact of severe domestic and external economic crises, which resulted in a surprisingly consistent engagement with the IMF, despite an unfavorable domestic political situation and a weak institutional framework. Despite the dominance of former communists in both the governing and the main opposition party, and the high social and economic costs of reforms, the relationship between the Fund and the Moldovan government during the mid-1990s was remarkably close and cooperative (especially compared to the non-Baltic former Soviet republics).

The Background: Economic Free Fall and Political Turmoil

At the time of its independence declaration from the Soviet Union in August 1991, Moldova's economy displayed all the ingredients for disaster: a large, unreformed agricultural sector; an outdated, energy-intensive industry; and an almost complete dependence on external energy. Since trade accounted for more than 50% of Moldova's GDP before the collapse of the Soviet Union, and the vast majority of this trade was directed toward other Soviet republics (Crowther 1996:128), the collapse of these markets in 1991–92 was fatal for large sectors of the Moldovan industry. The effects of this quasi disappearance of traditional markets for Moldo-

van products were exacerbated by the de facto secession of the Transdniestr region in Eastern Moldova, where 40% of Moldova's industry
and more than 80% of the country's energy-generation capacity was located. The extreme dependence on external energy sources was not substantially reduced after independence (Bercu 1997:5) and generated high
economic costs, given that starting in 1992 Moldova ceased to benefit
from massively subsidized Russian energy prices and thus experienced a
40-fold rise in gas and petrol prices and a 100-fold increase in coal prices
(*World Bank* 1994:5–6).

The economic consequences of these structural difficulties were drastic even by post-communist standards. Thus, by the end of 2000, Moldovan real GDP (in constant prices) was at 34% of 1990 levels, making
Moldova the poorest country in Europe with a GDP per capita of around
$300 per year. Moreover—unlike other countries in the region, which
experienced sharp initial economic contractions—the Moldovan economy only started to show clear signs of recovery in 2001. The human
costs of this economic crisis were equally drastic: Real wages declined to
about a quarter of their 1990 levels by the end of the decade, the access
to health care and education was severely reduced particularly in rural
areas, and the consumption of basic foods (meat, milk, eggs) declined by
50% by 1996, to levels that were less than half of those in Belarus.[26]

While the structural weakness of the Moldovan economy and the
high social costs of economic reforms hardly boded well for the prospects
of compliance with IMF conditionality, the situation looked equally unpromising from an institutional perspective. Even though the Moldovan
Central Bank has played an important and consistent role in promoting
monetary stability (particularly after it achieved a higher degree of independence in 1995), other parts of the state apparatus have been notoriously weak. Thus, tax evasion has been consistently high due to the large
size of the unofficial economy, the predominance of barter trade, and the
inability to enforce tax penalties on companies with significant tax arrears. Moreover, given the government's failure to provide even basic services such as law enforcement, health care, and education in many rural
areas, the reach of state authority was drastically diminished throughout
the country, and particularly in regions with ethnic autonomy claims
(Transdniestr and Gagauzia). Another important obstacle to the design
and implementation of coherent reforms was Moldova's lack of experts
with relevant exposure to Western political and economic models. These
problems were exacerbated by the massive post-1990 brain drain, as
600,000 of Moldova's 4.2 million citizens went abroad in search of better-

---

[26] For an in-depth analysis of the crippling social costs of Moldova's transition, see Orlova and Ronnas 1999.

paying jobs (*Economist*, 7/15/2000). Moreover, at least from 1990 to 1992, Moldova had very limited access to Western economic advice, and was largely left to deal with its staggering economic and political problems on its own (Socor 1994, Orlova and Ronnas 1999). Arguably, this early isolation was due to the West's concern for stabilizing the geo-political situation in the disintegrating Soviet Union by preventing a possible unification between Moldova and Romania, and by encouraging Moldova first to stay in the Soviet Union and later to join the Commonwealth of Independent States.[27]

Finally, Moldova's post-communist transition was significantly complicated by the ethnic conflict in Transdniestr, where a group of hard-line Communists under the leadership of Igor Smirnov set up a quasi-independent breakaway republic with direct and indirect support from Moscow.[28] While the still-unresolved status of Transdniestr has played a crucial role in shaping Moldova's domestic politics and foreign policy during the 1990s,[29] it also negatively affected the country's economy in several ways: first, through the direct costs of the military confrontations in 1992; second, through the Moldovan government's inability to control and tax a large part of the country's industrial base; third, via the loss in potential foreign investments in the context of high political instability; and finally—and most ironically—through the accumulation of debts by the Transdniestr authorities, for which the Moldovan government was held responsible.[30]

The Politics of an Unlikely Cooperation

Moldova's economic policy during the early post-independence period was roughly in line with the dire predictions of its difficult structural legacy. Burdened by the disruptive effects of the Transdniestr conflict and the intense parliamentary debates about a possible unification with Ro-

---

[27] According to Alexandru Mosanu, the head of the Moldovan parliament, "we were pushed into CIS by several large Western powers. They have counseled us in this direction and even reproached us because we, as democrats, do not want to join the CIS" (quoted in Gabanyi 1996:28).

[28] Moscow did not just arm the separatist rebels, but units of the Russian 14th Army actually joined the Dniestr forces in their open battles with the Moldovan forces (Crowther 1996:345).

[29] For example, during the 1996 presidential elections, one of the key campaign promises of the former Communist Party secretary Petru Lucinschi was that his close connections to the Russian would help him solve the Transdniestr problem (*RFE/RL*, 12/30/1996).

[30] In a remarkable display of cynicism, the Russian gas company Gazprom claimed that Moldova was fully responsible for the $300m debt owed by the Transdniestr authorities, even though Russia does not recognize Transdniestr as a sovereign state *Central European*, 9/1998.

mania, the Moldovan government pursued a largely ad hoc economic policy. However, starting with the structural transformation facility (STF) program in mid-1993 and a standby agreement in December 1993, Moldova embarked on one of the most ambitious economic reform programs in the region with the support of the IMF and other international financial institutions. Moldova's economic policy was under quasi-permanent IMF supervision for the entire decade: Within a week of the expiration of its first standby agreement, Moldova signed a second agreement in March 1995, which was followed in March 1996 by a three-year Extended Fund Facility (EFF) program (extended later until May 2000) and finally by another three-year Poverty Reduction and Growth Facility (PRGF) program signed in December 2000.

While far from perfect, the implementation record of successive Moldovan governments has been remarkably consistent, particularly compared to other countries of the region (Russia, the Ukraine, Belarus, Romania). Thus, the first stand-by agreement was fully implemented, and even though the IMF disbursed only three of the five planned tranches of the 1995 stand-by program, there was no conflict between the Fund and the government, as indicated by the quick agreement on the terms for the 1996 EFF agreement and the continuation of funding by the World Bank and the EBRD. Similarly, while the IMF postponed the disbursement of funding at several points during the 1996–2000 EFF program, these tactical delays were primarily targeted at specific conditions (e.g., land reform and the privatization of the wine and tobacco industry), while the Fund was careful to commend the Moldovan government for its progress with respect to the broader reform process. Moreover, the program never went completely off track, as indicated by the resumption of lending after such delays in both 1997 and 1999.

Moldova's status as a model of harmonious IMF cooperation among the non-Baltic former Soviet republics is particularly striking, given that at least until 1998 its domestic political scene was dominated by parties and politicians with close ties to the Communist regime. Thus, the ruling Democratic Agrarian Party (PDAM) appealed primarily to a reform-shy rural electorate and relied on a network of collective farm chairmen, agronomists, rural mayors, and district-level executive officials (Socor 1994:8). Moreover, the country's leading politicians—President Mircea Snegur, Prime Minister Andrei Sangheli and the Parliament Speaker Petru Lucinschi—were all former high-ranking communist officials, who, although relatively reformist, never officially broke with the Communist Party (ibid. 9). The prospects for reforms were further complicated by the prominent role of hard-line communists in Parliament, with the Socialist Party–Edinstvo claiming a quarter of the seats in the 1994 elections and the re-legalized Moldovan Communist Party winning almost 40% of the seats in the post-1998 parliament. The extreme left not only rejected the "colonialism" inherent in Moldova's market reforms and accused the government of allowing the IMF to rule the country, but even rejected Gorbachev-style reform communism in favor of the "golden age" of the Soviet period (Munteanu 1997). Since many of the extreme left's anti-reform ideas resonated with an impoverished and disillusioned Moldovan electorate, how can we explain the perseverance of the Moldovan government in pursuing IMF-style economic reforms, which seemed to contradict the ruling party's partisan and electoral interests?

The answer to this question actually conforms rather closely to the statistical findings about the penchant of ex-communist parties to abandon their reform reluctance in the face of extreme economic crisis. Thus, in the immediate post-independence period, Moldova's economic policy was largely in line with its leaders' statist convictions[31] and its extremely underdeveloped state institutions. However, after two years of dramatic economic decline, low international reserves, and rising inflation (which exceeded 1000% by late 1992), Moldova's sharp policy turn toward IMF-style reforms confirms that sufficiently desperate ex-communist governments can overcome their ideological reluctance to neoliberal reforms and bridge even sizable governance gaps in order to preempt a complete economic breakdown. Similarly, the over-time decline in Moldova's compliance record illustrates the importance of severe domestic economic crisis as an impetus for IMF-style reforms, particularly in the case of ex-communist governments; thus, the close adherence to the targets of the first standby agreement of 1993 occurred in the aftermath of the raging inflation of late 1992, early 1993. Meanwhile, the more extended implementation lapse starting in late 1997 occurred in the context of single-digit inflation and a much more comfortable foreign reserve position, which suggests that as soon as the most immediate economic threats subsided, partisan concerns and bureaucratic capacity limitations once again played a more prominent role.

The economic and political repercussions of this unexpectedly close IMF cooperation by the reformed Moldovan ex-communists were decidedly mixed. On the economic front, the successes of bringing inflation under control and improving foreign reserves were counterbalanced by the poor growth performance and the rapid growth of foreign debt. Judged by the outcomes of the 1998 parliamentary elections, the political implications were even more intriguing; thus, on one hand, the ruling PDAM suffered a resounding electoral defeat, with many of its voters defecting to the relegalized Communist Party (PCRM), which gained almost 40% of the parliamentary seats on an outspokenly antireform and

---

[31] According to Moldova's President Mircea Snegur, cited in EIU, 2nd quarter, 1993.

anti-Western electoral platform. On the other hand, the 1998 Moldovan elections did not replicate the dynamics of the 1985 Peruvian elections by catapulting anti-Western populists into power as a backlash against IMF-style austerity measures. Instead, Moldovan voters placed their trust in a broad reformist coalition, the Democratic Convention of Moldova (CDM), which had campaigned on a platform of accelerated economic reforms and Western integration. This remarkable outcome further confirms the greater patience of Eastern European voters for reform-related economic hardships, and explains the positive relationship between democracy and program implementation revealed by the statistical results chapter 5.

The story of Moldova's unlikely neoliberal reforms in the 1990s, however, does not have a happy ending characterized by a virtuous cycle of economic and political liberalism. The CDM's efforts to accelerate economic reforms under IMF guidance were at best partially successful, as reflected in the government's patchy compliance record with the EFF program it had inherited from its predecessor. The main political reason for this failure to live up to its electoral promises was the crippling internal conflict between the different members of the governing coalition. Formed in opposition to the growing popularity of the hard-line communists in the run-up to the 1998 elections, once in power the CDM spent too much time and energy on political infighting to be able to devise and implement a coherent economic reform program. As such, the succession of CDM governments between 1998 and 2001 provides a perfect illustration of the statistical findings about nefarious consequences of not having a political party with a strong parliamentary mandate in charge during periods of intense neoliberal reforms. This political stagnation was exacerbated by the absence of an immediate inflationary or external payments crisis, which could have rallied the supporters of more ambitious reforms; such an interpretation is supported by the fact that the most successful compliance episode of this period occurred in 1999, when inflation rose from single digits to over 50% during the course of the year, while foreign reserves fell once again below two months of imports. Finally, Moldova's weak bureaucratic capacity became even more of a liability in the absence of an immediate crisis, especially in the context in which further reform progress had to include much more institutionally demanding structural reforms. This recognition arguably triggered the shift in late December 2000 to a lower-conditionality PRGF program designed for developing countries for which standard IMF programs are too demanding.

After almost eight years of painful and inconclusive economic reforms under IMF supervision, in the early elections of February 2001 the Moldovan voters finally handed a decisive electoral victory to the hard-line PCRM, which won 70% of seats on a 50% vote share.[32] Despite their electoral promises to reverse the country's market-oriented economic policies, the communists did not initiate a dramatic redirection of Moldova's domestic or international trajectory along the lines of the Garcia government in Peru. In fact, the PCRM government of Vasile Tarlev initially retained a number of technocrats from the outgoing reformist government of Dumitru Braghiş, and continued to comply to a sufficient degree with the conditions of the PRGF government to ensure a positive Fund evaluation of the country's monetary and fiscal policies and a disbursement of funding in July 2002. Even though the PCRM government subsequently failed to secure further disbursements or to renew the program after it expired in 2003, it nevertheless pursued prudent fiscal and economic policies, and starting in 2005, it attempted a renewed rapprochement to the West and the international financial institutions, which ultimately led to a new IMF PRGF program in May 2006. Overall, even though it signaled the limits of popular patience with painful economic reforms, the return to power of the unreformed Moldovan communists nevertheless confirmed that in the post-communist context the economic policy reverberations of electoral changes are likely to be relatively modest, at least for economically vulnerable countries like Moldova.

Bulgaria and Romania—The Fragile Political Balance of IMF-Style Reforms

Whereas the cases of Slovakia and Moldova were situated at opposite ends of the IMF interaction spectrum and illustrate how specific factors (nationalism/populism in Slovakia and extreme economic vulnerability in Moldova) may "overpower" the effects of other political and economic considerations, Romania and Bulgaria can be considered more mainstream candidates for IMF programs. The reason for devoting this section to a comparison of the IMF programs of the two countries is that, after a remarkably similar political and economic trajectory prior to 1996, Bulgaria became the showcase example of IMF conditionality, whereas Romania experienced four years of inconclusive reforms and a checkered IMF track record. I argue that this unexpected disjunction can be explained by the deeper preceding crisis in Bulgaria and the higher political cohesion of the Bulgarian reformers, as well as by a certain degree of path

---

[32] As in the case of the Romanian center-right a few months earlier, Moldova's reformist incumbents managed to further damage their precarious electoral standing by failing to unite forces and thus wasting almost 17% of votes due to the inability of various parties to cross the electoral threshold.

dependence in the evolution of reforms in the two countries. Therefore, I emphasize the fragility of the political balance underlying IMF-style reform efforts and the importance of context-specific approaches to IMF program design.

Common Legacies (and Some Differences)

Among the transition countries, Romania and Bulgaria are probably more similar to each other in terms of economic and political legacies than to any other country in the region. They share a somewhat marginal geographic position on the southeastern fringe of Europe, a long history of imperial domination (first under the Ottomans and later under the Soviet Union), and a border with ex-Yugoslavia, which imposed significant economic and political costs at various points during the 1990s. Predominantly agrarian before World War II, both countries experienced a rapid industrialization process under communism and inherited industrial sectors that were inefficient and energy intensive even by Eastern European standards. These structural problems were exacerbated by the fact that, unlike Poland and Hungary, the two countries were ruled by hardline Stalinists (Ceauşescu and Zhivkov) who resisted the economic reforms and the political opening initiated under Gorbachev in the Soviet Union (Janos 2000). Therefore, Romania and Bulgaria embarked on the difficult path of democratization and marketization with less developed civil societies and political parties, fewer Western-trained specialists and less hope of Western assistance, poorer populations, and more distorted economies. Not surprisingly, post-communist reforms in Bulgaria and Romania turned out to be more contorted than in their Central European neighbors: Whereas Hungary, Poland and the Czech Republic had successfully "graduated" from the IMF by the mid-1990s, Romania and Bulgaria became quasi-permanent IMF "pupils" with mixed and often unpredictable "grades" for most of the 1990s.

At the same time, however, Bulgaria's and Romania's legacies and post-communist prospects were not nearly as bleak as those of Moldova and other former Soviet republics. Being among the few independent states whose borders did not change after 1989, Bulgaria and Romania were spared the additional burden of creating state institutions from scratch, while at the same time pursuing deep-reaching economic and political reforms. Therefore, the quality of their administrative institutions, while significantly below Central European levels, was nevertheless noticeably better than in the non-Baltic former Soviet republics.

The most important legacy difference between the two countries was the evolution of their foreign debt during the 1980s. Even though the two countries had comparable indebtedness levels in the early 1980s, Romania under Ceauşescu pursued an aggressive debt repayment strategy for most of the final decade of communist rule and emerged essentially debt free at the start of the transition: In late 1989 the country's total external debt stood at only $1.1bn (or about 2.5% of real GDP) and was more than outweighed by the country's solid foreign and gold reserves, totaling $2.7bn. By contrast, in late 1989 Bulgaria had a crushing $10.1bn foreign debt (net of reserves) in an economy with an annual real GDP of just above $15bn. As a consequence, Bulgaria's debt service accounted for 63% of the country's export earnings in 1989 and put significant pressures on government finances throughout the 1990s. On the other hand, Romania's comparatively advantageous external position came at a substantial economic and political cost, given the draconian austerity measures instituted as part of the debt repayment efforts of the 1980s. Ceauşescu's shock therapy not only ruined the economy (which contracted by almost 11% in 1988–1989), but the drastic reduction in consumption and social services during that period created an understandable aversion in large portions of the Romanian population toward economic policies requiring further sacrifices (Daianu 1997).

The Politics of Partial Reforms in the Early Transition Period

Prior to the watershed elections of late 1996 in Romania and early 1997 in Bulgaria, the two countries' economic and political trajectories were remarkably similar. Following the collapse of their respective hard-line communist regimes, both Romania and Bulgaria witnessed the return to power of only marginally reformed communist successor parties—the National Salvation Front (FSN) in Romania and the Bulgarian Socialist Party (BSP) in Bulgaria—following free but not entirely fair elections in 1990. As a consequence, no real reform efforts were made during the first year of post-communism, but the rapidly rising economic imbalances eventually led to the collapse of the BSP government in Bulgaria in November 1990 and to the strengthening of the reformers (under the leadership of Prime Minister Petre Roman) within the ruling FSN in Romania. Both countries turned to the IMF in early 1991 and made a first attempt at liberalization and stabilization for the remainder of the year. Even though both reform programs made some significant progress and were rewarded by several IMF disbursements, stabilization was ultimately unsuccessful, largely due to high levels of political instability. In Bulgaria, the interim government of Dimitar Popov struggled with its lack of a clear political mandate and was eventually replaced following the parliamentary elections of October 1991, in which the pro-reform Union of Democratic Forces (SDS) emerged victorious but without an absolute parliamentary majority. In Romania, in September 1991, bands of miners, protesting the government's reformist economic policies, rioted through Bucharest and even occupied the parliament in an eventually successful attempt to overthrow the government of Petre Roman. Even though Roman's successor, Theodor Stolojan, was a politically unaffiliated, reform-minded technocrat, the riots had longer-term reverberations on the political prospects of Romanian economic reforms, since they eventually precipitated a split in the ruling FSN between a more reformist camp around former Prime Minister Roman and a more hard-line leftist group loyal to President Ion Iliescu.

Despite a number of country-specific variations, the same pattern of stop-go reforms, punctuated by IMF pressures, popular resistance, and political instability continued throughout the early transition period in both countries. Thus, during 1992 the newly instated SDS government of Filip Dimitrov pursued an ambitious economic reform strategy in conjunction with a stand-by agreement with the IMF signed in April, and with the longer-term goal of deepening structural reforms by entering an Extended Fund Facility later in the year. However, the unpopular austerity measures contributed to the dissolution of the fragile alliance between the ruling SDS and the predominantly Turkish Movement for Rights and Freedom (DPS), on whose tacit support the survival of the Dimitrov government depended. As a consequence, the Dimitrov government resigned, leading to a protracted political crisis and the suspension of IMF support in October 1992. The new government, headed by the independent Lyuben Berov, with the tacit support of the BSP and the DPS, as well as a breakaway faction of the SDS, tried to balance the conflicting imperatives of Bulgaria's increasingly pressing debt burden, whose resolution required IMF support and, hence, an acceleration of economic reforms, and the debilitating political constraints of a government without a clear power base in either the parliament or society. Even though the Berov government, pressed by increasingly urgent debt-rescheduling negotiations with the London Club, initiated a new IMF agreement in April 1994 and attempted to implement an austere budget for the year, the rising political costs of the austerity measures yet again undermined the reform program, leading to the fall of the Berov government in October 1994 and the suspension of IMF credits shortly thereafter. The ensuing parliamentary elections in December 1994 produced a narrow majority for the leftist BSP, which captured 125 of the 240 seats in the parliament and was able to form a government under a young reform-Communist, Zhan Videnov. However, after a brief period of relative political stability in 1994 and the first half of 1995, Bulgaria's increasingly weak external position and economic performance during 1996 precipitated a renewed political crisis at the end of 1996, leading to the resignation of the Videnov government in February 1997, following several weeks of severe economic crisis and massive antigovernment demonstrations.

During the same time period, political instability was slightly lower in Romania, but the underlying conflict between reformers and reform opponents in the context of economic crisis and external conditionality yielded a very similar stop-go pattern of economic reforms. Thus, in the spring of 1992 the caretaker government of Theodor Stolojan negotiated a new standby agreement and managed to comply with IMF conditionality long enough to obtain three tranches of the standby loan between June and November 1992. However, inflation for the year still ran at more than 200%, partially because the Romanian economy reacted poorly to the demand restraint measures and contracted by almost 10% for the year, creating stagflationary pressures. Also, the political pressures of the electoral campaign for the October 1992 general elections interfered with the reform program of the Stolojan government, and the victory of the leftist Party of Social Democracy (PDSR) resulted in a renewed slowdown of the reform momentum and in the suspension of IMF support. The political environment of economic reforms was further undermined by the failure of the victorious PDSR to forge an alliance with the pro-reform opposition clustered around a heterogeneous center-right coalition, the Democratic Convention (CDR). As a consequence, the PDSR formed a minority government led by a nominally independent technocrat, Nicolae Văcăroiu, with the tacit support of four small extremist parties: the nationalist, Transylvania-based Party of National Unity (PUNR); the ultranationalist/xenophobic Greater Romania Party (PRM); the barely reformed communist-leaning Socialist Work Party (PSM); and the somewhat more moderate Democratic Agrarian Party (PDAR). While the Văcăroiu government managed to hold on to power for the four years of its mandate, it did so by pursuing an uneven and often inconsistent reform policy, characterized by alternating episodes of orthodox reforms and populist measures meant to buy political support from its anti-reform parliamentary allies and electorate (Pop-Eleches 1999). Predictably, the Romanian government's relationship with the IMF was equally mixed during this period; after almost a year of avoiding IMF conditionality in the aftermath of the 1992 elections, the Văcăroiu government eventually responded to the rising inflation, which exceeded 300% by late 1993, and, in line with the statistical findings in chapter 5, initiated and implemented a relatively successful stabilization under IMF guidance in mid-1994. Ironically—but once again in line with the regionwide statistical patterns—this rapid success undermined the longer-term macroeconomic stability prospects, since they gave the PDSR government the opportunity to pursue a Mečiar-style eclectic approach to reforms and IMF cooperation in 1995–96 in the context of rapid-growth, moderately successful fiscal and monetary policies and populistnationalist tendencies resulting from the alliance with the red-brown satellite parties and the electoral challenges in the months prior to the 1996 elections.

The Prelude to Political Change: Partial Reforms and Crisis in 1995–96

Despite the stop-go approach to reforms during their tenure, the leftist governments of Romania and Bulgaria scored some initial successes in terms of controlling inflation and promoting economic growth, particularly during late 1994 and 1995. Thus, under the Văcăroiu government Romania recorded four years of continuous economic growth between 1993 and 1996, including a 7% rise in GDP in 1995 and 4% increases in 1994 and 1996. Moreover, inflation slowed in mid-1994 and averaged less than 40% during 1995 and 1996, despite an electorally driven acceleration of inflation at the end of 1996. Even the less successful Videnov government in Bulgaria recorded positive growth of 2.8% in 1995, in conjunction with a reduction of inflation to just above 60% in the same year. While hardly spectacular in absolute terms, these achievements were remarkable considering the two governments' poor reform records, and led to a slight puzzle among foreign observers, given that Romania and Bulgaria were the only two transition economies to have experienced renewed growth prior to full stabilization (Fisher et al. 1996, Gerloff 2000).

BULGARIA IN FREE FALL

However, the sustainability of these "half-way reform miracles" turned out to be limited, particularly in the Bulgarian case. Given its rather comfortable foreign reserve position for much of 1995, the Videnov government behaved in line with the theoretical expectations of an anti-reform government facing only moderate financial pressures and failed to comply with the conditions of the 1994 standby agreement, which led to the suspension of the IMF program. For most of 1995, the Videnov government, while not rejecting IMF negotiations altogether, resisted IMF pressures for an acceleration of structural reforms, particularly with respect to loss-making SOEs and the struggling banking sector. Instead the Bulgarian government tried to live up to its contradictory campaign promises of simultaneously reducing inflation and stimulating employment. It did so, with some initial success, by pursuing an expansionary credit policy and counteracting inflationary pressures through price controls. Predictably, the high quasi-fiscal deficits due to the extension of easy credits to loss-making SOEs further weakened Bulgaria's fragile banking sector, as illustrated by the high ratio of nonperforming assets on the commercial banks' balance sheets and the failure of the Vitosha Bank for Agricultural Credit in early 1996, followed by two other banks later in the year.

The domestic economic problems were exacerbated by Bulgaria's increasingly vulnerable external position due to the rapid decline of foreign reserves from $1.5bn in August 1995 to below $700m in April 1996 and the large, projected debt service amounting to $1.25bn in 1996 and $1.6bn in 1997 (*EIU Country Report*, 2nd quarter, 1996). Despite Bulgaria's positive trade and current account balance in the previous year, it became increasingly clear that the country would not make it through the following months without the support of the IMF and the World Bank. In line with the statistical findings in chapter 5, the immediate danger of default persuaded the BSP government to sign a standby agreement in July 1996, which included austere fiscal and monetary policies, drastic energy price increases, and a commitment to deepening structural reforms (including enterprise closures leading to the loss of at least 40,000 jobs, as well as a program to recapitalize the struggling commercial banks). However, facing opposition from labor unions and from within the ruling BSP, and hampered by the inherent difficulties of rapid structural reforms in a weak institutional environment, the Videnov government soon fell behind in its commitments to industrial and financial sector restructuring, which prompted the IMF to stop the disbursement of funding after August 1996.

The developments during the following six months precipitated an economic and political crisis of major proportions, which led Bulgaria to the brink of chaos. With reserves continuing to decline in the absence of multilateral funding, the Bulgarian National Bank was increasingly limited in its ability to intervene in foreign exchange markets. The resulting rapid devaluation of the Bulgarian lev further fueled inflation, which reached an annual rate of more than 250% by the end of the year, and degenerated into hyperinflation in the first two months of 1997. At the same time, in its attempts to control inflation, the government raised interest rates drastically in late 1996, which contributed to the further weakening of the banking sector[33] and to a deep recession, with the economy contracting by more than 10%. In November 1996 the IMF started to insist that the only solution to Bulgaria's economic woes was the introduction of a Currency Board, which would have pegged the Bulgarian currency to a foreign currency (the German D-mark or the U.S. Dollar) under the supervision of an independent Currency Board replacing the Bulgar-

---

[33] In addition to the five banks (including a major state bank) involved in bankruptcy proceedings after June 1996, nine other banks were placed under close government supervision in September, and the Bulgarian minister for economic development, Rumen Gechev, admitted in late October that only fourteen of the country's forty-four banks could be considered stable (cited in EIU Country Report, 4th quarter, 1996).

ian Central Bank as the country's supreme monetary authority. Though the appropriateness of such a solution for countries with chronic financial instability was debated even within the IMF and was certainly at odds with the BSP's policy preferences, Prime Minister Videnov appeared willing to accept it to secure IMF support and avoid a debt default and complete economic chaos.

Videnov's sudden willingness to accommodate drastic IMF policy conditions illustrates the importance of IMF influence and the relative weakness of ideological convictions in situations of extreme financial crisis during the post-communist transition. However, as things turned out, Bulgaria did not emerge as a second Moldova, with former communists in the unlikely role of orthodox neoliberal reformers under the close guidance of the IMF. Part of the explanation may have been the IMF's reluctance to trust the BSP government with the implementation of the Currency Board, given the BSP's mixed implementation track record. The extent to which the IMF has tried to actively affect Bulgarian domestic politics is difficult to assess. However, several facts suggest at least an indirect influence of the IMF stance on the domestic power balance in Bulgaria. Thus, the head of the Bulgarian opposition, Ivan Kostov, met with high-ranking IMF officials in Washington shortly before the signing of the July 1996 standby agreement and declared that the West did not see the Bulgarian government as a suitable negotiation partner (cited in *Sofia Kontinent*, 731996). Seen from this perspective, the IMF's tough stance with respect to both structural reforms and the currency board, seems to confirm that by late 1996 the Fund was not willing to give the embattled Videnov government much breathing space.

However, even in the context of a more flexible IMF conditionality stance, it is unclear whether the Videnov government (or any other BSP-led government) could have exercised sufficient political authority to bring the country's economic free fall under control. Thus, following the sound defeat of the BSP candidate, Ivan Marazov, in the presidential elections of November 1996, Videnov's position within his own party became increasingly vulnerable, and he resigned at the Party Congress on December 19, after weeks of internal conflicts between different factions within the BSP. Following Videnov's resignation, the BSP tried to form a new government under the former interior minister Nikolai Dobrev, which included more than half of the ministers of the outgoing Videnov government. This decision prompted not only vehement protests from the opposition but also several weeks of violent street protests throughout the country. In the face of a virtually ungovernable country and an imminent economic disaster (with monthly inflation above 40% in January), the BSP finally agreed to the creation of a nonpartisan interim government under the leadership of Stefan Sofianski, the mayor of Sofia. The parliamentary elections in April 1997 reflected the dramatic decline of the BSP, which obtained less than a quarter of the votes and parliamentary seats, whereas the center-right coalition between the SDS and two minor coalition partners received 52.3% of the vote, and thus obtained 137 of the 240 parliamentary seats. Since the BSP did not recover from this blow until 2005—their vote share dropped to 17% in the 2001 elections—the crisis of 1996–97 seems to have marked the end of Bulgaria's experiment with "selective" stop-go reforms and emphasizes the narrow maneuvering room for such policies in an economy with Bulgaria's debt burden and external vulnerability. As I will argue below, the severity of the 1996–97 crisis emphasized (in the eyes of both the elite and the electorate) the utter failure of the BSP's approach to solving Bulgaria's economic problems, thereby paving the way for the thorough reforms of the following four years.

ROMANIA'S INCONCLUSIVE CRISIS

Unlike the catastrophic economic performance of the Bulgarian economy in the last year of the Videnov government, Romania's evolution prior to the 1996 elections is much harder to evaluate. For much of the 1994–96 period Romania performed remarkably well in terms of its growth performance (with cumulative growth of 15.7% for the three years), and with relative macroeconomic stability starting in mid-1994, even though inflation rose above 50% in late 1996, largely due to the expansionary policy pursued by the PDSR government prior to the October 1996 elections. Given the drastic change in economic policy following the PDSR's loss of the 1996 elections, it is difficult to know whether Romania was headed down the same road of growth reversal and financial turmoil as its southern neighbor. Rather than engaging in such counterfactuals, I will analyze Romania's structural problems in the broader context of the country's relationship with the IMF and international financial markets prior to 1996.

Following the successful stabilization of mid-1994 and a fairly comfortable external reserve position at the end of 1994 (with international reserves in excess of $3bn, corresponding to 3.1 months of imports), the PDSR government faced relatively low external pressures for most of 1995, especially since the country managed to gain access to international capital markets by securing a loan from Citibank in March 1995. This relatively low financial dependence on the IMF, combined with the Fund's tough negotiating stance on structural reforms and fiscal discipline and the PDSR's efforts to pacify its nationalist coalition partners contributed to a relatively strained relationship between the Romanian government and the IMF during 1995. When the IMF postponed the disbursement of an outstanding structural transformation facility tranche in March 1995 due to the slow progress with structural reforms, the Romanian minister for economic reform, Mircea Coşea complained that the IMF and the World Bank had insufficient understanding of the Romanian situation and that their imposition of unnecessarily harsh measures risked pushing the Eastern European countries back to communism (*EIU Country Report*, 2nd quarter, 1995). However, toward the end of the year, the rapidly rising current account deficit put serious pressures on the Romanian currency and led to a reduction in the country's foreign reserves (to 2.6bn or 2.8 months of imports). This greater external vulnerability prompted a temporary rapprochement with the IMF and resulted in the extension of the 1994 standby agreement and the disbursement of a funding tranche in December 1995.

The parallels between the Romanian and the Bulgarian governments' relationships with the IMF during 1995–96 go beyond the pattern of initial resistance to conditionality due to relatively strong external positions and economic performance, followed by rapprochement with the Fund in the face of external and internal economic imbalances. The evolution of the PDSR's interaction with the Fund in 1996 mirrors several important elements of its Bulgarian counterpart's efforts to balance external needs and political constraints in the context of IMF conditionality. Even though Romania's smaller foreign debt and its better access to private capital markets made it somewhat less dependent on IMF approval, the Romanian government nevertheless had few hopes of financing its large current account deficit without securing IMF approval, given that more than half of Romania's debt was owed to multilateral institutions (including the IMF) and access to private capital was sufficiently fragile to suffer significantly in the case of an open conflict with the IMF. Therefore, as in Bulgaria, the IMF used its high leverage over the Romanian government to impose tough conditions for the December 1995 standby agreement, including a 2.2% budget deficit, a reduction in bank credits and wage increases, substantial financial sector reforms, and the elimination of foreign exchange restrictions.

As in Bulgaria, the Văcăroiu government initially tried to fulfill the requirements of the IMF program and scored some early successes by reducing inflation to a monthly average of 1.6% for the first three months of 1996. This relative financial discipline, resulting at least in part from the breakdown of the governing coalition of the PDSR with its nationalist communist satellite parties, was soon undermined by the governing party's political considerations in the context of the approaching general elections. In an increasingly desperate effort to pacify the Romanian electorate, the Văcăroiu government tried to maintain the subsidies to troubled state-owned enterprises in both industry and agriculture, and tried to boost living standards by allowing nominal wages to grow at a higher rate than inflation. To control the inflationary pressures of these expansionary fiscal policies, the Romanian authorities delayed the elimination of foreign exchange restrictions and accelerated the buildup of quasi-fiscal deficits by ordering state banks to give generous credits to SOEs. Predictably, these policies drew harsh criticisms from the IMF on a number of occasions and eventually led to the suspension of the stand-by agreement in July 1996.[34] This breakdown actually conforms to the regionwide statistical patterns discussed in chapter 5 in the sense that Romania's fairly mild economic crisis provided the leftist PDSR government with sufficient breathing space to pursue its partisan political agenda in the context of the upcoming general elections of November 1996.

The ambiguity of the PDSR's economic legacy had important repercussions for the prospects of subsequent economic reforms in Romania. On one hand, there is little question that the policies pursued in the pre-election months would have been unsustainable in the long run, given the country's declining foreign reserves and the need for IMF approval to continue accessing private capital markets (from which Romania had borrowed more than $1.5bn in 1996). Moreover, the delay of banking reform[35] and the widespread use of preferential credits to subsidize loss-making sectors, led to massive nonperforming loans in the portfolios of many state banks.[36] On the other hand, given its lower foreign debt it is unlikely that Romania would have experienced a crisis of Bulgarian dimensions. More importantly—the full repercussions of the PDSR's partial reforms were not reflected as clearly in inflationary and growth terms by the time the 1996 elections transferred the responsibility of governing and cleaning up the mess to the center-right opposition.

Explaining the Post-1997 Disjunction

Following their accession to power in late 1996, early 1997, the pro-reform coalitions of Romania and Bulgaria initiated immediate and ambitious economic reform programs in close coordination with the IMF.

---

[34] The costs of this suspension were mitigated by the World Bank's unexpected decision to continue disbursing substantial funding to Romania despite the IMF sanctions, as well as by Romania's successful international bond issues of over $1bn in 1996. This outcome illustrates the importance of effective signaling mechanisms in ensuring compliance with IMF programs.

[35] By the end of 1996 privatization in the banking system had basically not started, as illustrated by the fact that Romania's state banks still accounted for 78% of total banking-sector assets.

[36] Most of the bad loans in Romania's banking sector were due to two banks, Bancorex and Banca Agricolă, which together accumulated by early 1997 a total of US $2.25 billion of bad loans—an equivalent of about 6% of GDP.

However, whereas the Bulgarian government successfully implemented its 1997 standby agreement and became the IMF "poster child" for successful adjustment by initiating and carrying through a three-year Extended Fund Facility program between 1998 and 2001, Romania's reform trajectory during the same period was marked by a series of costly and ineffective partial reform efforts that resulted in an equally ambivalent relationship with the IMF. Following the failure of the initial standby agreement in the fall of 1997, the Romanian government failed to secure a new agreement until mid-1999, when the country faced severe balance-of-payments difficulties. However, even under strong external pressures, the government's implementation record was unimpressive, resulting in the disbursement of only two more IMF tranches in August 1999 and June 2000 prior to the government's decisive defeat in the elections of November 2000. What accounts for this remarkable disjunction, given that the two countries' trajectories had been so similar until 1996, and given that the two countries resembled each other in terms of both economic structure and the political objectives of their respective governments? Below, I will argue that the disjunction can be explained by a set of political and institutional constraints that were reinforced by the nature of IMF conditionality and can be largely traced back to the variations in the extent of the economic and political crisis preceding the initiation of reforms.

THE INITIAL REFORM WAVE: COPING WITH SHOCK TO GET TO THERAPY

For most of 1997 both the Bulgarian and the Romanian governments attempted to work through the vast reform backlog left behind by their socialist predecessors, and they did so by replicating the shock-therapy approach the Balcerowicz government had implemented in Poland in 1990. Thus, the Ciorbea government in Romania, in close cooperation with the IMF, launched a reform program, whose sweep was more radical than any of the previous shock therapy initiatives tried elsewhere in the region (*EIU Country Report*, 1st quarter, 1997) and included the standard policy package of monetary and fiscal austerity, trade, exchange rate, and price liberalization, combined with ambitious privatization and restructuring measures. As mentined, the Bulgarian program also included the setup of a Currency Board, whose details were finalized in June 1997, thereby creating a powerful commitment mechanism for Bulgarian policy makers. As expected, the short-term effects of these programs were drastic, with sharp declines in output (of about 7% in 1997 for both countries), lower real wages and consumption levels, and rising poverty and unemployment. However, by midyear both countries had achieved their stabilization goal, with monthly inflation falling below 4% in July 1997.

Starting in the fall of 1997, however, the reform trajectories of the two countries started to diverge, with Bulgaria staying comfortably within the parameters of its standby program, while Romania started to slip. Since the difference during the first year cannot be attributed to greater popular resistance to painful reforms,[37] I argue that the failure of the Romanian reforms in late 1997, early 1998 can be explained by the gap between an overly ambitious IMF-inspired reform agenda and the limited institutional capacity and political cohesion of the Romanian government. To start, there is little doubt that the designers of the Romanian reform program in early 1997 underestimated the negative response of the Romanian economy; instead of an expected midyear recovery, the economy continued to plummet in the second part of the year for a total decline of almost 7%, almost three times higher than initially forecast.[38] By contrast, the Bulgarian economic contraction was concentrated in the first few months of 1997 (largely before the SDS government took office in April), and by midyear, Bulgaria had returned to growth, which was to continue (admittedly at moderate rates) for the next three years.

The consequences of this growth differential were important for both economic and political reasons. From an economic point of view, the unexpected depth of the Romanian recession led to significant stagflationary effects, which undermined the government's efforts to control inflation, thereby creating problems with IMF target fulfillment.[39] Politically, the rapid return to growth of the Bulgarian economy helped convince both politicians and the public that reforms were working, and contributed to a virtuous cycle of political commitment to reforms and good economic performance, which was reinforced by the significant capital inflows associated with the Fund's stamp of approval.[40] By contrast, Romania entered a vicious cycle, in which poor growth fueled opposition to economic reforms and led to incoherent economic policies and low levels of external financing.[41] In other words, there was a crucial juncture sometime in late

[37] According to the Soros Public Opinion Barometer in March 1998 the Romanian government was still viewed positively by more than half the population.

[38] In defense of the IMF it should be said that other external observers were equally overoptimistic about Romanian economic prospects: Thus, in May 1997 the reputable EIU Country Report predicted that a recession could be avoided due to healthy growth in the second part of 1997.

[39] Varujan Vosganian, a Romanian economist, argues that the excessive focus on demand-side determinants of inflation ignored the serious supply-side effects of the adjustment process, which meant that even though money supply declined in real terms, inflation continued to grow due to the even faster decline of output (1999:145–46).

[40] Thus, from 1997 to 2000, Bulgaria received over $1.36bn from the IMF, compared to only $350m for Romania. Moreover, FDI in Bulgaria increased by almost 400% in 1997, and by 2000 it was almost nine times higher than in 1996 (*EIU Country Data*).

[41] With the exception of a large (and excessive) initial capital inflow in 1997, Romania suffered net capital outflows between 1998 and 2000, partially due the negative effects of the Russian crisis in 1998 and the Kosovo crisis in 1999.

1997, when the Bulgarian government managed to consolidate its reform gains by starting negotiations for the 1998 EFF program and slowly moving from shock to therapy, whereas the Romanian government slipped into political infighting and lost the momentum necessary to fulfill the demanding conditions of the IMF reform program. While it is unclear whether adhering religiously to IMF prescriptions would have led to similarly successful outcomes in Romania,[42] the country's post-1997 reform strategy (or lack thereof) arguably achieved the worst of both worlds, with high social and economic costs and low benefits (at least in terms of IMF recognition and funding).

The Fragile Equilibrium of Reform:
Political and Institutional Factors

Given that the prospects for successful economic reforms in Romania declined steadily starting in mid-1998 due to the increasing popular distrust in the CDR-led coalition government and the rising popularity of the PDSR and other anti-reform parties, the present discussion will focus primarily on the "honeymoon" period, during which the reformist government appeared to have a strong reform mandate following its victory in the 1996 elections. In addition to the already discussed overly ambitious reform targets of the 1997 economic program, I argue that the Romanian government's reform efforts were hampered by two structural factors: a weak and unstable governing coalition and weak institutional capabilities.

The first factor, the weak and fragmented governing coalition, has been frequently invoked in the Romanian media as the prime reason for the country's economic woes, largely because the constant political infighting between the coalition partners became an everyday aspect of Romanian public life. Ironically, the roots for this political paralysis go back to the fact that life under the PDSR had not been nearly as bad as under the BSP in Bulgaria. Since prior to the 1996 elections there were few obvious signs of an imminent economic crisis, the victorious Democratic Convention, a broad center-right coalition, only obtained 30% of the vote, and had to form a coalition with the center-left Democratic Party (PD) led by former Prime Minister Petre Roman and the ethnic Hungarian Democratic Union in Romania (UDMR). The relative ideological heterogeneity of this coalition was exacerbated by the lack of a strong leadership in the CDR, which had not recovered after the death of Corneliu Coposu, the leader of the National Peasants' Party (PNTCD), in late 1995. Mean-

---

[42] After all, the IMF medicine seems to have worked better in Bulgaria than in Romania even before the Romanian reform program derailed in late 1997.

while, in Bulgaria, the victorious SDS not only commanded an absolute majority in the parliament (even without the support of its minor coalition partners) but the party had become a great deal more cohesive in the months preceding the 1997 elections, aided by the BSP's catastrophic governance and the good organizational capabilities of the SDS leader, Ivan Kostov.

When the economic and political costs of the radical reforms became apparent in mid-1997, the heterogeneity and fragmentation of the Romanian government started to become an obstacle for the implementation of the IMF program, as the two minority coalition partners threatened to withdraw their support for the Ciorbea government. While some of these conflicts had no direct connection with the IMF program,[43] others were driven by the PD's concern about the rising social costs of economic reforms, and thereby contributed to the more cautious approach to restructuring in late 1997. However, despite growing IMF criticisms about the slowdown of structural reforms in October 1997, the fatal blow to Romanian reforms was the intense and protracted governmental crisis that started with the PD's withdrawal from the Ciorbea government in late December and did not subside until Ciorbea's resignation and his replacement with Radu Vasile in April 1998. During the three months of political paralysis, economic reforms were stalled, leading to the suspension of funding under the 1997 IMF standby agreement. Since the incoming Vasile government was unable to negotiate a new agreement until mid-1999, the governmental crisis of late 1997 can effectively be considered the death knell of rapid reforms in Romania. By contrast, the Bulgarian government, admittedly facing more favorable economic conditions, was able to keep a united front through the first three years of reforms, which helps explain its remarkable consistency in IMF program implementation.

Turning to the second structural factor—weak institutional capabilities—the Romanian case provides rather convincing evidence that part of the problem was that the government did not know how to go about implementing reforms in an effective matter. With the exception of a few PD leaders (who had participated in the 1990–92 FSN government), most members of the post-1996 cabinets had very limited policy-making experience. Therefore, it is hardly surprising that the CDR government had a difficult time handling the complex challenges of economic reforms, particularly with respect to privatization and restructuring.[44] In this re-

[43] Thus, the PD and the CDR disagreed over the size of land restitution, the UDMR was primarily concerned with the fulfillment of its ethnic rights claims, and many of the disputes were of a purely personal nature, such as the conflict between Prime Minister Victor Ciorbea and the PD minister of transport, Traian Basescu.

[44] In fact, Stan (2001) argues that the quality of governance in Romania has declined substantially in the 1997–2000 period compared to the previous government (1993–1996).

spect, it is telling that in November 1997 the minister of reform, Ulm Spineanu, resigned following IMF criticisms that reforms had been slowed by the lack of interdepartmental coordination within his ministry (*EIU Country Report*, 4th quarter 1997). The consequences of these weak administrative institutional capabilities were that restructuring proceeded at a slower pace than expected and undermined stabilization, thereby drawing repeated criticisms from the IMF and the World Bank. Even when restructuring occurred, the lack of government expertise undermined the benefits of reforms; thus, in mid-1997, the government offered miners prohibitively costly severance packages to induce them into leaving. While this approach avoided short-term labor unrest, it not only placed a high burden on the budget but it also failed to solve the long-term employment problem in the affected regions, since it was not accompanied by adequate programs to help the miners find alternative employment and income sources. Moreover, the government's effectiveness was also undermined by the failure of successive CDR governments to combat corruption, despite the prominent role of anticorruption measures in its electoral campaign and a number of early successes.[45]

While institutional weakness contributed to the Romanian debacle, how can we explain the Bulgarian "miracle"? After all, at least at the outset of reforms, there was little evidence that Bulgarian institutions were functioning significantly better than their Romanian counterparts, especially after the chaos of the crisis in late 1996.[46] Nevertheless, the Bulgarian government largely managed to avoid the policy blunders that had undermined the credibility of the Romanian government. There are three tentative explanations for this outcome: First, the Bulgarian SDS could draw on its (albeit limited) governing experience in 1991–92, during which the new prime minister, Ivan Kostov, had served as a finance minister. Second, the Bulgarian government proved more effective in combating corruption, which improved the functioning of the state apparatus (Ganev 2000). Finally, despite its comfortable parliamentary majority, the government promoted a more inclusionary style of economic policy making that minimized the conflicts with both the parliamentary opposition and the labor unions, thereby facilitating the implementation of politically sensitive economic reforms. By contrast, lacking the

[45] Whereas in December 1997, opinion polls indicated that 59% of Romanians approved of the government's performance in reducing corruption, the figure fell to 29% by June 1998 and finally to 4% in November 2000.

[46] Thus, the two countries' scores on the *Nations in Transit* "quality of governance and public administration" measure were almost identical during 1996 and 1997, though the Bulgarian score improved in later years, whereas Romania stagnated along this measure as well.

party discipline of the SDS, the Romanian reformers resorted to governmental decrees for many key reform measures, which further undermined the legitimacy of economic reforms, as well as the likelihood of their successful implementation. The greater success of Bulgaria's more inclusive policy-making process confirms the positive correlation between democracy and program implementation revealed by the regionwide statistical patterns in chapter 5.

Implications and Conclusions

This comparison of the Bulgarian and Romanian reform trajectories and IMF interactions before and after 1997 illustrates a number of political and institutional mechanisms that shape the dynamics of IMF programs. Prior to losing power in late 1996, early 1997, the socialist governments of Romania and Bulgaria pursued very similar strategies of stop-go reforms, oscillating between their largely antireform preferences and constituencies, and their recognition that they needed international support to address their countries' significant economic problems. The narrow maneuvering room left by IMF conditionality eventually contributed to the electoral defeat of the two parties, but whereas in the case of the BSP, IMF pressures led to a last-minute (and ultimately failed) attempt to implement drastic reforms, the financially less dependent Romanian ex-communists instead chose a more extreme nationalist-populist policy alternative that reduced their political losses.

In contrast to their earlier parallel developments, the reform trajectories of the two countries diverged significantly starting in late 1997. This divergence can be traced to the relative timing and visibility of the economic crises in the two countries: Whereas in Bulgaria the inflationary and recessionary consequences of the BSP's partial reforms were painfully clear to both political elites and ordinary citizens, in Romania the visible economic costs of delayed structural reforms largely occurred after the newly elected reformers had launched their ambitious IMF-backed economic adjustment program. The much clearer economic crisis responsibility contributed to the clearer electoral victory of pro-reform parties in Bulgaria compared to Romania. The unexpected depth of the Romanian recession, combined with the government's political vulnerability and lack of experience, ultimately undermined the ability of the Romanian authorities to pursue IMF-style reforms. Meanwhile, the Bulgarian government, despite dealing with similar structural difficulties, took advantage of its higher political coherence and successfully implemented IMF-style reforms for the duration of its tenure. Therefore, Bulgaria experienced a virtuous cycle of good economic performance, political stability, and foreign assistance mutually reinforcing one another. Thus, the comparison of the two cases underscores the delicate political and institutional balance inherent in the implementation of IMF programs.

Conclusions

Along with the statistical findings in chapter 5, the case studies confirm the importance of many classical explanations of economic reforms, including intense financial need, ideological commitments to neoliberalism, powerful and unified governments, and capable bureaucracies. However, even the necessarily brief profiles of the eight Latin American and Eastern European countries discussed in this chapter demonstrate that none of these factors represents either necessary or sufficient conditions for successful IMF programs. Instead the comparison of the different national trajectories reveals the complex interactions between economic crises, ideological preferences, domestic power relations, and institutional constraints shaping the trajectory of IMF program initiation and implementation in the two regions. Beneath this complexity, however, it is possible to discern several key themes that can help us gain a clearer understanding of the domestic political dynamics of economic reforms in Latin America and Eastern Europe.

First, the case studies confirm the fundamental cross-regional differences in how governments of different ideological persuasions reacted to varying degrees of economic crisis. In Latin America severe inflationary and/or balance-of-payments crises triggered ambitious orthodox economic reform efforts from right and center-right governments in Chile, Bolivia (under Paz), and Peru (under Garcia). Similar crises resulted in more inconsistent policy responses under the centrist Alfonsín government in Argentina, whereas among the region's leftist governments, extreme hyperinflationary crises resulted in either policy paralysis (Bolivia under Siles) or outright defiance (Peru under Garcia), which actually further reduced the prospects of IMF cooperation. By contrast, the experiences of Slovakia under Mečiar and, at certain junctures of the socialist governments, of Romania and Bulgaria confirm that, unlike in Latin America, in Eastern Europe the anti-reform ideological preferences of nationalist/populist and ex-communist governing parties mattered only in relatively stable domestic economic environments in which governments could afford the luxury of pursuing their partisan agendas at the expense of better relations with the Fund. However, as soon as inflationary pressures or balance-of-payments difficulties intensified, Eastern European governments appeared to be much more willing than their Latin American counterparts to cast aside their ideological aversion to IMF-style reforms, as illustrated by the reform efforts of former communists in Moldova (1993–97), Romania (1993–94), and even Bulgaria (1996).

Second, the comparison of the relationship between democratic politics and IMF programs in the countries of the two regions complements the statistical findings about the greater compatibility of IMF conditionality with democracy during the post-communist transition than during the Latin American debt crisis. The trajectories of the three democratic Latin American countries discussed in this chapter (Argentina, Bolivia, and Peru), suggest that successful long-term economic stabilization in a democratic context could only be achieved when a newly elected government coming to power following a period of traumatic economic crisis was able to take advantage of its political honeymoon legitimacy to break the traditional war-of-attrition between business and labor, which has fueled Latin American political and economic instability for several decades. The experiences of Peru under Garcia, Bolivia under Siles, and Argentina under Alfonsín suggest that once a government missed the initial opportunity to undertake neoliberal economic reforms to tackle the domestic economic crisis, its ability to respond to later inflationary crises was greatly reduced even when the costs of inaction were very high in both political and economic terms. Moreover, the steep price exacted by IMF-style austerity measures created significant trade-offs between respect for civil and political rights on one hand, and program implementation on the other; this tension led to some significant deviations from democracy under the Paz government in Bolivia, while undermining the compliance efforts of Alfonsín in Argentina, Siles in Bolivia, and Belaúnde in Peru. By comparison, in Eastern Europe democratic politics were less at odds with neoliberal economic reforms, at least in part because the more reluctant economic reformers (such as the HZDS in Slovakia, the PDSR in Romania, and the PCRM in Moldova) were also less committed to democratic norms than their pro-reform political opponents. Unlike in Latin America, where elections usually undermined economic reforms,[47] Eastern European voters were more likely to recognize the necessity of neoliberal adjustment policies and, therefore, showed greater patience for the considerable economic costs inherent in such reforms. In this respect it is telling after several years of stop-go reform efforts with significant IMF involvement, voters in Romania (1996), Bulgaria (1997), and Moldova (1998) decided to vote their respective reformed ex-communist govern-

---

[47] This could happen either because governments would abandon costly reforms prior to elections (e.g., the Belaunde government in Peru) or because electoral outcomes would shift the political balance in favor of parties opposed to IMF reforms (e.g., Peru in 1985, Argentina in 1987). The one notable exception is the 1985 election in Bolivia, where the abysmal results of the governance by the leftist *UDP* coalition set the stage for a democratic mandate for faster economic reforms.

ments out of office in favor of broad anti-communist coalitions that had campaigned on platforms of accelerating economic reforms.[48] The greater popular legitimacy of market-based economic policies, combined with the more marginal role of the weakly organized Eastern European labor and business sectors, had two important implications for the relationship between democratic politics and IMF-style reforms: First, the weaker societal resistance to reforms meant that post-communist democratic governments appear to have been less dependent on the postelectoral window of opportunity in their efforts to address economic crises, as illustrated by the successful midterm reform initiatives in Moldova (1993) and Romania (1994). Second, the weakness of interest groups placed a much lower emphasis on government insulation for successful IMF program implementation in the post-communist context than during the debt crisis in Latin America. In fact, the comparison of Bulgaria's and Romania's post-1996 reforms suggests that the more inclusive and consultation-based governing strategy of the Bulgarian SDS facilitated IMF program compliance to a much greater extent than the top-down executive decree-based approach of the Romanian CDR.

Finally, the case studies emphasize that even a combination of significant economic crisis and ideologically pro-reform governments may not be sufficient to guarantee the successful design and implementation of IMF-backed economic reforms. A first important stumbling block for would-be reformers was the penchant for political infighting in government coalitions that could undermine the coherence and credibility of economic reform efforts. Thus, the often paralyzing conflict between the parties in the governing coalition further undermined the cautious reform efforts of the Siles government in Bolivia in 1982–85 while its political successor, under the leadership of Victor Paz Estenssoro, largely managed to maintain government unity through the use of an elaborate patronage-sharing system. In Eastern Europe, in line with the statistical findings, the experience of Moldova (1998–2001) and Romania (1997–2000) confirms that weak and fragmented governments had a much harder time implementing IMF programs under pro-reform coalition governments, whereas the more cohesive Bulgarian reformers had a much better compliance record.[49] Another potentially serious obstacle—especially in the for-

---

[48] Even though all three governments eventually lost subsequent elections, the main reasons for this electoral rejection were not excessively ambitious economic reforms but, rather, prominent corruption scandals (in Bulgaria) and the inability to implement reforms due to infighting and incompetence (in Romania and Moldova).

[49] The highly fragmented Slovak reformers managed to initiate and comply with an IMF standby agreement but since they were swept out of power less than half a year into the program, it is impossible to tell whether they would have been able to avoid the paralyzing internal conflicts of their Romanian and Moldovan counterparts.

mer communist countries—was the weakness of state institutions and the lack of qualified bureaucratic personnel, which hampered reform efforts in Eastern Europe, particularly in situations such as Moldova (after 1998) and Romania (after 1996) where anti-communist governments had little prior governing experience. In Latin America, state capacity limitations arguably undermined macroeconomic stability by limiting tax revenues (especially in poor countries such as Bolivia), but at the top leadership level the human capital deficit was generally a lot less problematic than in Eastern Europe.

Overall, the analysis of the domestic politics of IMF program initiation and implementation in the eight Latin American and Eastern European countries suggests important variations in the domestic political constellations that are most conducive to reforms. In Latin America during the 1980s, the most reform-conducive domestic political constellation combined severe domestic and external economic crises, a government with a pro-market ideology, and weak opposition whose anti-reform objections could be either suppressed by autoritarian regimes (as in Chile) or dismissed as illegitimate following decisive electoral defeats in democratic elections (as in Bolivia in 1985–86). In Eastern Europe during the post-communist transition, domestic economic crises and external financial need also played an important catalytic role for IMF-style reforms, but ideological differences mattered much less for crisis-driven reforms, and successful implementation hinged primarily on cohesive governments and capable bureaucracies rather than on the political power to shut out the parliamentary and societal opposition.

−7−

The Great Reconciliation?— Latin America and the IMF in the 1990s

IN DECEMBER 1998 THE ARGENTINE PRESIDENT, Carlos Menem, addressed the joint meeting of the International Monetary Fund and the World Bank in the wake of the East Asian financial crisis, during which the Fund's policy prescriptions had attracted sharp and widespread criticism from a wide range of observers. Menem recounted Argentina's remarkable turnaround following the hyperinflationary chaos of the 1989–91 period, and ascribed this success to his government having "worked side by side with the IMF, the World Bank, and the IDB to achieve macroeconomic stability, deepen structural reforms, and adopt policies aimed at improving the economic fortunes of the poorest members of society."[1] Coming from the leader of the populist, labor-based Peronist party a year before a crucial presidential and parliamentary contest, this neoliberal proclamation in the very cradle of the Washington Consensus would have been inconceivable barely a decade earlier. And Menem was not alone in this posture of an unexpected Latin American neoliberal: The list of committed market reformers also included Brazilian president Enrique Cardoso, one of the intellectual founders of the Latin American dependency school, and Alberto Fujimori, the Peruvian populist president, whose initial electoral campaign in 1990 had stressed the avoidance of painful austerity measures. However, only a few years later, the political pendulum in Latin America started to swing back to the left following a series of decisive victories for presidential candidates ranging from moderate social democrats, such as Chile's Bachelet, Uruguay's Vazquez, and (somewhat unexpectedly) Brazil's Lula, to more combative leftists such as Argentina's Kirchner, and particularly Bolivia's Morales and Venezuela's Chavez (Castaneda 2006).

While this chapter is not intended as a detailed analytical account of these two remarkable ideological swings, its focus on the politics of Latin American IMF programs from 1990 to 2001 complements the earlier

---

[1] Speech transcript in *IMF Press Release* No.5, October 6–8, 1998.

analysis of the Latin American debt crisis and the post-communist transition and thus creates a broader framework for understanding the interaction between economic crises, Western conditionality, and partisan politics in shaping the economic policy choices of developing countries. The analysis in the preceding four chapters has revealed a series of important differences in the political dynamics of IMF programs and policy responses to economic crises in Eastern Europe and Latin America; during the debt crisis of the 1980s, Latin American governments had reacted to domestic and international crises in ideologically divergent ways, and neoliberal adjustment policies were generally hard to reconcile with democratic politics, whereas during the post-communist transition, economic crises had triggered policy convergence among governments of different ideological orientations, and economic reforms were compatible with and even facilitated by democratic politics.

However, as discussed in chapter 1, the two IMF-program episodes differed along a number of different dimensions that could have contributed to the divergent political dynamics revealed by the comparison. First, the much more hostile international economic environment of the debt crisis and the widespread perception of the IMF as the debt collector for Western commercial banks created an adversarial relationship between the Fund and Latin American debtors that contrasted with the more constructive IMF role as a reform and international integration advisor during the postcommunist transition. As a corollary, the severe domestic economic crisis of the early transition period was widely regarded as a legacy of communist-era economic mismanagement, which arguably facilitated the nonpartisan response to the crisis and the greater popular support for painful adjustment measures in Eastern European countries. By contrast, in Latin America the debt crisis exacerbated the latent domestic economic imbalances of the traditional ISI models, thereby triggering widespread popular opposition to neoliberal reforms and paving the way for the ideologically divergent interpretations of the roots and solutions to the stagflationary crises experienced by many countries in the region during the early 1980s.

But the two regions also differed with respect to their domestic social and political landscape, in the sense that Latin America in the 1980s had much-better-organized interest groups (especially labor and business organizations) than its Eastern European counterparts, whose social and organizational capital had been decimated by decades of totalitarian communist rule. As a consequence, Latin American political parties, which had largely survived the much shorter authoritarian spells in their respective countries, had stronger institutional ties to organized interests, and were therefore more constrained in their ability to shift their policy positions to accommodate IMF demands, even if the economic costs of noncompliance were significant. Eastern European parties, on the other hand, largely "floated" on top of disarticulated and atomized societies and, therefore, had greater leeway in pursuing policies demanded by international financial institutions including the IMF. Seen from this perspective, the compatibility of painful economic reforms with democracy in the post-communist transition is not the result of synergies between economic and political liberalism but rather a consequence of the inability of post-communist citizens to hold their governments accountable for their policies between successive elections.[2] By the same token, the tension between democracy and IMF-style reforms during the Latin American debt crisis can be interpreted as a function of the much greater organizational capacity of Latin American reform opponents, which often left governments with the difficult choice of either allowing these groups to derail (or at least slow down) economic reforms or to use repressive measures to push through their reform agenda.

Thus, the cross-regional divergence in political responses during the two crisis episodes can be attributed to two different (but not necessarily mutually exclusive) mechanisms: The first stresses the link between the international environment, the resulting role of IMF interventions, and the domestic political perceptions about the nature of the crisis and the appropriate policy responses. The second explanation instead emphasizes differences in the domestic articulation and aggregation of economic interests, and their consequences for the partisan politics of economic reforms. This chapter's analysis of Latin American IMF programs after 1990 offers the ideal testing ground for evaluating the relative explanatory power of these two approaches. Thus, Latin American countries in the 1990s, like their post-communist counterparts, benefited from the more favorable international economic and political environment following the resolution of the debt crisis and the end of the Cold War. At the same time, Latin American governments of the early 1990s inherited the polarized social and political landscape of the previous decade, even though this landscape started to evolve rather dramatically in response to the deep structural transformations of the last two decades.[3] Therefore, to the extent that the international environment explanation is correct, we should expect the political dynamics of Latin American IMF programs in the 1990s to resemble those of the transition economies during the same period, that is, to produce crisis-driven ideological convergence and to display a harmonious coexistence between neoliberal economic re-

---

[2] For a discussion of electoral accountability without policy accountability in Eastern Europe, see Innes 2002.

[3] For an interesting discussion of how this transformed social and political landscape affects the democratic prospects of the region, see Kurtz 2004.

forms and democratic politics. If, however, the earlier divergence was due primarily to deep-seated institutional differences in the articulation of domestic economic interests, then the changed international environment should not alter the traditional patterns of ideological polarization and hard-to-reconcile tensions between democracy and economic reforms that had characterized Latin America in earlier decades.

To anticipate the answer provided by the analysis in this chapter, the political dynamics of the post-1990 Latin American IMF programs were more similar to those of Eastern Europe during the same time period, in that economic crisis reduced the policy differences among governments of different ideological persuasions, and democratic politics were no longer incompatible with neoliberal economic reforms. These findings emphasize the importance of the more favorable international economic and political environment of the 1990s, which provided greater rewards for countries complying with the neoliberal policy prescriptions of the IMF (and the Washington Consensus more broadly) and, therefore, led to greater support for economic reforms—or at least less spirited opposition—at both the elite and the popular level. However, two important caveats are in order: First, the structural reforms of the 1990s undermined the collective action capabilities of the Latin American popular sector (especially with respect to organized labor) and, therefore, reduced the ability of reform opponents to mount effective political challenges to neoliberal economic policies (Kurtz, 2004). Second, even in the favorable international context of the 1990s, Latin America did not experience an Eastern European–style mutually reinforcing relationship between economic and political liberalism, and once the boom of the 1990s gave way to the gloom of the immediate post-2001 era, Latin America once more returned to greater ideological polarization and a much more ambivalent attitude toward/ IMF programs, and Western economic and political conditionality more broadly. Therefore, on balance, the post-1990 Latin American track record with IMF programs suggests that—in line with the theoretical approach advanced in this book—the politics of IMF-style reforms has to be understood as an interaction between the nature of the international environment, which was considerably more favorable during the "roaring 1990s" than during the periods immediately preceding and following them, and the much more deeply rooted cross-regional differences in the organization of societal interests and popular attitudes toward Western conditionality. Seen from this perspective, the relatively consensual politics of economic reforms in Latin America during the 1990s were brought about by a combination of an international credit boom, a changed IMF approach to conditionality, and a partial reduction in the organizational capacity of reform opponents. However, once the international environment, punctuated by the 9/11 attacks and the Argentine crisis, changed for the worse, the previously subdued resistance to the IMF-promoted neoliberal reforms of the 1990s once again found a political outlet and contributed to the subsequent increase in antimarket and anti-American rhetoric and policies in large parts of Latin America.

In the remainder of this chapter, I first briefly outline the broad economic and political background of Latin American IMF programs in the 1990s. Next, I present statistical evidence about the broad economic and political drivers of IMF program initiation and implementation during this period, and compare these dynamics to the earlier findings from the Latin American debt crisis and the post-communist transition. The following section briefly revisits the four countries discussed in chapters 4 and 6 (Argentina, Bolivia, Peru, and Chile) to trace the political trajectories of their economic reforms in the 1990s and beyond. The final part discusses the theoretical implications of these findings and of the recent left turn experienced by much of Latin America.

A Region Transformed—Latin America after 1990

Back in Business: Latin American Economic Trends in the "Roaring Nineties"

Latin America emerged from the lost decade of the debt crisis with a decidedly mixed economic situation. The various economic adjustment efforts—whether orthodox or heterodox—had ultimately resulted in steep social and economic losses, as reflected in the decline in per capita income and real wages, and the rise in unemployment and poverty for most Latin American countries and for the region overall. To add insult to injury, even the indicators for the main objectives of the painful adjustment process of the 1980s were rather disappointing; thus, the region's external debt still accounted for 45.8% of gross national income at the end of 1989, which was significantly higher than 36.2% in late 1981 prior to the debut of the debt crisis. Meanwhile, international reserves had declined from 4.4 months of imports in 1985 to less than 3 months in 1989, while the share of multilateral debt had more than doubled compared to 1981 as a consequence of the limited access to private capital markets during the 1980s. Nor had anti-inflationary efforts been much more successful, considering that the relative successes of Bolivia, Mexico, and Costa Rica were overshadowed by the dramatic hyperinflationary episodes raging in Argentina, Brazil, Peru, and Nicaragua.

On the other hand, amid all the gloom, there were also a few signs of hope, coming largely from the outside. Thus, the Brady Plan of March 1989, along with a series of Paris Club debt reschedulings in the late 1980s and early 1990s led to a gradual but significant decline in overall

Figure 7.1 Indebtedness and interest burden—Latin America (1981–2004)

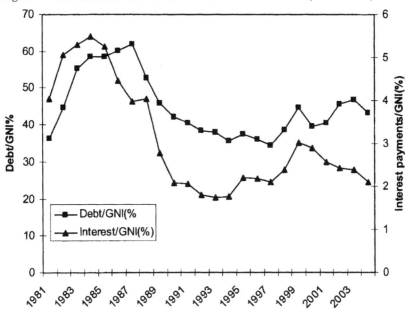

indebtedness, which, as illustrated in figure 7.1, declined from 62% of gross national income in 1987 to 35% in 1994. Even more importantly, the debt renegotiations, combined with declining U.S. real interest rates after 1989, led to a significant reduction in the interest payment burden from 5.5% in 1984 to 1.7% in 1993. At the same time, the financial recovery of the Western commercial banks and the newfound appetite of international financial markets for emerging-markets bonds contributed to a massive inflow of new outside funding into the region. As illustrated in figure 7.2, the remarkable foreign lending boom of the 1990s marked a drastic departure from the lean years of the 1980s, during which voluntary lending to most of Latin America had been virtually nonexistent.

The domestic economic reverberations of this international turnaround were equally impressive. Relieved of much of the debt burden, which had choked growth and fueled fiscal deficits and inflation in the 1980s, Latin American economies started to recover vigorously starting in 1991, and except for a dip in 1995 (following the Mexican Tequila Crisis), regional economic growth averaged a healthy 4.1% between 1991 and 1998. Moreover, during this time, governments in the region managed to reduce the endemically high inflation that had been a trademark of Latin American political economy for several decades; thus, by late 1992 the governments of Argentina, Peru, and Nicaragua had successfully reigned in the hyperinflationary crises they had inherited at the start of

Figure 7.2: Total long-term debt trends—Latin America (1981–2004)

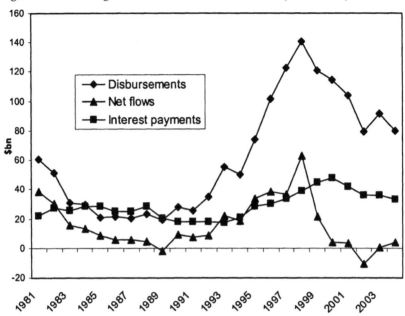

Source: Global Development Finance

the decade, leaving Brazil as the last inflationary problem child in the region. After Brazil's successful stabilization in mid-1995, inflationary crises virtually disappeared from the Latin American economic and political agenda, with most countries achieving and maintaining single-digit or low double-digit inflation by the mid- to late 1990s.[4]

Thus, while the domestic economic stagnation of the 1980s had been triggered and exacerbated by an extremely unfavorable international economic environment, the region's substantial recovery in the early and mid-1990s also had important external roots. This clear link between the international lending boom and domestic economic recovery had important repercussions for the domestic and international political economy of neoliberal reforms and IMF programs in Latin America during the 1990s. First, Latin American political and economic elites quickly realized that in order to take advantage of the international credit boom, they had to pursue economic policies in line with the increasingly hegemonic prescriptions of neoliberalism. Compared to the commercial bank

[4] The only partial exceptions to this trend were Ecuador (where inflation briefly exceeded 100% in the second part of 2000) and Venezuela (which experienced inflation in the 100%–110% range in late 1996).

lending of recycled oil profits in the 1970s, the foreign direct investment and portfolio investment of the 1990s was much more likely to respond to positive or negative signals about the economic and political climate in a given country. Therefore, unlike in the 1970s, the IMF was not relegated to just dealing with the basket cases left outside the regional lending boom but played an important signaling role for international investors looking for guidance about the credibility of Latin America reform efforts. Whereas during the debt crisis compliance with IMF conditionality had largely meant fiscal austerity and higher debt service payments (in return for fairly limited concessions from the creditors), in the 1990s IMF cooperation had the potential to unlock significant outside funding, which set the stage for the more harmonious relationship between the Fund and Latin American governments that Menem mentioned in his 1998 Washington address.

The return to growth and the remarkably successful fight against inflation also played an important role in swaying popular sentiment toward neoliberal reforms. Even though Latin American publics were still wary of many individual components of the neoliberal reform agenda promoted by the IMF, reform-minded governments could at least point to some tangible economic benefits of such reforms. Even though the uneven distribution of these gains meant that large segments of society experienced minimal improvements in living standards, the situation nevertheless compared favorably to the economic turmoil of the 1980s, as illustrated by the genuine popular support for Fujimori and Menem in the early to mid-1990s despite the contrast between their populist campaign promises and the reality of their neoliberal reform policies (Stokes 2001). As a consequence, Latin American voters no longer viewed IMF-style reforms as inevitably harmful foreign impositions, which meant that politicians no longer faced as stark a trade-off between satisfying the policy requirements of Western conditionality and abiding by the rules of democratic politics.

The Only Game in Town: Democratic Stability in the 1990s

As the debt crisis drew to an end in 1989, Latin America's political landscape presented a mixed picture. On the positive side, despite the staggering economic costs of the debt crisis, the region's fledgling democracies emerged from the 1980s shaken but largely intact. Moreover, the end of the Cold War contributed to a more pro-democratic international climate, as the United States began to withdraw support from its authoritarian allies in the region, a shift that contributed to the end in 1989 of two of the most resilient Latin American dictatorships—Pinochet's in Chile and Stroessner's in Paraguay—and led to the ouster of Manuel Noriega in

Panama. On the other hand, Latin American democracies had experienced significant difficulties in coping with the political challenges of economic adjustment, raising significant concerns about the long-term viability of democracy in countries such as Argentina and Peru, which managed democratic turnovers of power in 1989–90 but remained mired in significant economic and political turmoil. Nonetheless, by early 1990, almost three-quarters of the twenty-one Latin American and Caribbean countries included in the present analysis could be considered democratic,[5] most of them with at least five years of democratic experience. In this respect, the Latin American experience of the 1990s differed significantly from that of Eastern Europe, where the ex-communist countries were just taking their first tentative steps toward democratization and marketization.

After decades of rapidly alternating episodes of democratic and authoritarian experiments, the 1990s finally ushered in a period of unprecedented democratic stability for most Latin American and Caribbean countries. The democratic transitions of late 1989, early 1990 in Chile, Panama, Nicaragua, and (somewhat more gradually) Paraguay were followed in the mid-1990s by civilian takeovers in Guatemala and Haiti, and by the gradual liberalization of Mexico's one-party-dominated system. Of course, the process was not a uniform, irreversible march toward democracy; thus, Peru experienced a temporary but significant democratic setback following Fujimori's 1992 *autogolpe*, civil and political liberties continued to be tenuous in several countries (including Honduras, Guatemala, and the Dominican Republic), popular riots with military participation triggered questionable government changes in Ecuador and Haiti, and two of the region's oldest democracies (Colombia and Venezuela) experienced a gradual erosion of democracy. Nonetheless, except for Castro's Cuba, free and relatively fair elections became the norm for most of the countries of the region throughout the 1990s, in line with an international environment dominated by Western-democracy promotion efforts and fewer geopolitically motivated exceptions for "friendly dictators."

This remarkable resilience of electoral democracy and its surprisingly harmonious coexistence with market-oriented reforms for much of the 1990s raises the interesting question of why Latin America was largely able to avoid the most extreme political expressions of the deeply ingrained social and class tensions bred by the region's endemic poverty and inequality: riots and coups. In addition to the beneficial effects of the economic boom discussed in the previous section, this unexpected tranquility of Latin American politics may have also been supported by

---

[5] The standard used for this classification is a score of at least 6 on the −10 to +10 Polity regime scale.

the relatively recent memories of the high economic and political costs of the military dictatorships of the 1970s and the massive strikes and riots of the 1980s. Just as importantly, however, the privatization and labor market reforms of the late 1980s and early 1990s triggered a profound transformation of the Latin American social and political fabric by weakening the labor-union movement and contributing to the growth of the informal sector throughout the region (Centeno and Portes 2006). As a consequence, the popular sector had a harder time overcoming collective action challenges to pursue its economic agenda by putting direct political pressure on parties and elected officials. On the positive side, the lower degree of popular mobilization in the 1990s reduced the potential for violent social conflict and political instability compared to earlier decades. The trade-off, however, was that many Latin American democracies in the 1990s resembled O'Donnell's (1994) model of delegative democracies in which citizens only influence policy making during relatively brief preelectoral periods but delegate decision-making power to political elites for the rest of the electoral cycle.

Government accountability toward its citizens was further reduced by the external policy constraints imposed by the much higher capital mobility following the financial deregulation and liberalization of the last two decades. While even democratic governments only had to worry about voters once every few years in order to get reelected, they could be punished quite swiftly by highly mobile international investors, who could relocate their capital more easily than the average Latin American citizen could move to another country. Therefore—and this was one of the key points of the antiglobalization left—it is not surprising that despite their redistributive electoral promises, even leftist and populist governments usually pursued rather prudent, market-friendly economic policies once in power. The net result of these developments was a shallower democracy that provided fewer redistributive benefits to the poor but provoked fewer concerns among the rich and, therefore, contributed to the survival of democracy by removing the classic justification for antidemocratic coups.[6]

Finally, the catastrophic failure of the region's heterodox economic-policy experiments in Argentina, Brazil, and especially Peru in the late 1980s, juxtaposed with the relative success of neoliberal reforms in Chile and Bolivia provided a regional reinforcement of the global ideological ascendancy of neoliberal economic ideas following the end of the Cold War and the demise of communism in Eastern Europe. In the emerging Washington Consensus (Williamson 1990) there was much less political

---

[6] For interesting discussions of this mechanism, see Boix 2003 and Acemoglu and Robinson 2005.

room for alternative ideological interpretations of economic crises and significant deviations from economic orthodoxy. Therefore, in the statistical analysis presented in the next section, we should expect to see much less tension between democracy and IMF programs during the 1990s, as well as fewer ideologically driven policy reversals than in earlier decades.

The Politics of IMF Programs in the 1990s

By the end of the 1980s the future of IMF involvement in Latin America was hanging in the balance. Despite having managed to prevent a disastrous international financial meltdown, the Fund's thankless job as a middleman between distressed borrower countries and equally distressed Western commercial banks drew criticisms from all quarters. Even relatively sympathetic observers tended to question the continued relevance of the Fund in an international financial environment, which had largely outgrown the IMF's original mission. Thus, an editorial in the *Economist* (1988) painted a rather bleak picture of the Fund's future relevance: "There may be no way out for the IMF. As co-operation on exchange-rate policy continues to evolve, the Fund will be tossed occasional bones—some statistics to collect, some indicators to keep an eye on, and so forth. But if the past few years are any guide, the agreements that matter will be settled privately between the finance ministers of the big economies."

Back for More: IMF Program Initiation in the 1990s

Even apart from the broader questions about its systemic relevance, the continued IMF presence in Latin America during the 1990s was highly uncertain considering that its policy interventions in the region during the 1980s had been largely reviled as external impositions on countries with few outside options.[7] In the much more favorable international financial context of the 1990s, during which the credit ratings and market access of most Latin American countries rebounded considerably,[8] one would have expected the IMF to return to its 1970s role of providing emergency financing to the small number of basket cases that were unable to access private lending to cover their financing need. Instead, the IMF

---

[7] This sentiment is echoed in the *Economist*'s 1988 assessment that following its highly politicized role during the debt crisis; "[I]t may be too late for the IMF to retreat to its neutral role as a short-term provider of finance."

[8] See figure 3.2 in chapter 3 for an illustration of the rapid and steady improvement of the region's sovereign credit ratings after 1990 based on the Institutional Investor Survey average for the twenty-one countries in the present sample.

continued to be actively involved in Latin America throughout the 1990s; thus, the twenty-one Latin American and Caribbean countries in my sample initiated forty-eight new high-conditionality IMF programs between 1990 and 2001. Even though this tally represents a lower concentration of programs than during the previous decade (or compared to transition countries during the same time period), it nevertheless suggests the fairly prominent role of the Fund in the region's political economy. Indeed, several countries, including Argentina, El Salvador, Peru, and Uruguay, were almost permanent IMF clients during this period, and almost all countries in the region had at least some exposure to IMF conditionality after 1990.[9]

While the frequency and the broad distribution of programs did not change dramatically after the end of the debt crisis, the drivers of IMF-program initiation during the 1990s in Latin America differed substantially from the dynamics of the debt crisis and the post-communist transition. As discussed in chapters 3 through 6, inflationary crises played a central role in the domestic economic calculus of IMF involvement during both episodes, whereas external concerns were dominated by the debt crisis in Latin America during the 1980s and by liquidity concerns in the post-communist countries. By contrast, the Latin American experience of the 1990s lacked a unifying crisis "theme"; thus, the burden of interest payments declined substantially from its peak in the late 1980s, inflation also ceased to be a critical concern after 1992 for most countries in the region, and international reserves, which even in the 1980s had been significantly higher than in Eastern Europe, continued to improve as a consequence of the easier access to hard-currency loans for most countries in the region.

The statistical results in table 7.1, whose main substantive effects are illustrated in figure 7.3, confirm the lower overall salience of traditional financial need and economic crisis indicators in driving IMF program initiation in the 1990s. First, in marked contrast to the debt crisis and the post-communist transition, governments dealing with high inflation were actually less likely to initiate IMF programs, as illustrated by the negative effect of lagged inflation in table 7.1.[10] These findings confirm the much lower profile of inflation in the political economy of post-1990 Latin America, and suggest that governments generally tried to get their house

[9] Thus, eighteen of the twenty-one countries in the sample initiated new IMF programs between 1990 and 2001. Of the remaining three. Chile successfully finished its earlier standby agreement by late 1990 (but then stayed away for the rest of the decade), Bolivia had two lower-conditionality PRGF programs in the mid-1990s, and Paraguay waited until 2003 to initiate its first IMF program.

[10] The results were not affected by excluding hyperinflationary cases, and were consistent across different time periods.

TABLE 7.1
Drivers of Program Initiation—Latin America (1990–2001)

	(1)	(2)	(3)	(4)	(5)	(6)	(7)	(8)	(9)	(10)
Inflation (lag)	−.29	−.53#	−.06	−.28	−.29	−.18	−.25	.35	.17	−.31
	(.25)	(.28)	(.18)	(.25)	(.24)	(.20)	(.26)	(.41)	(.25)	(.25)
GDP change	−.07									
	(.05)									
Fiscal balance	.01								.22*	
	(.04)								(.10)	
Reserves	−.02	−.07	.03	−.06	−.16	.26*	−.10	−.06	.05	−.04
	(.08)	(.10)	(.06)	(.08)	(.20)	(.12)	(.09)	(.08)	(.07)	(.09)
Interest/GNI	.48	.12	.11	−.20	.34	.06	−.42#	.81	−.10	.43
	(.63)	(.92)	(.51)	(1.33)	(.68)	(.53)	(.85)	(.68)	(.69)	(.66)
Total debt	.43#	.92*		.25	.40	.37*	.77*	.56*	.28#	.50#
	(.30)	(.38)		(.73)	(.44)	(.20)	(.41)	(.29)	(.22)	(.31)
Bureaucratic Quality	.18	.61	.06	.21	.21	−.13	.42	.04	−.09	.19
	(.37)	(.50)	(.29)	(.36)	(.36)	(.28)	(.52)	(.35)	(.35)	(.34)
Regime	−.03	−.04	−.03	−.02	−.02	−.02	−.06	−.00	−.04	
	(.08)	(.11)	(.07)	(.08)	(.08)	(.07)	(.10)	(.09)	(.08)	
Gov't Orientation	−.11	.04	−.23	−.12	−.11	.57#	−2.67**	.89	−.68*	−.18
	(.23)	(.29)	(.19)	(.23)	(.22)	(.34)	(.88)	(.74)	(.32)	(.23)
Rescheduled debt/GNI		.84**								
		(.27)								
IIS Credit Rating		−.07#								
		(.05)								
UN voting				−.01						
				(.01)						
US imports				−.00						
				(.17)						
Interest/GNI* Total debt					.25					
					(.53)					
Reserves* Total debt						.03				
						(.06)				
Reserves* Gov't Orientation							−.18*			
							(.07)			
Interest/GNI* Gov't Orientation								1.75**		
								(.57)		
Inflation* Gov't Orientation									−.31#	
									(.20)	
Fiscal balance* Gov't Orientation										−.15*
										(.08)
Political constraints										−2.27#
										(1.31)
Pre-Electoral Period										.16
										(.44)
IMF Program History	−1.19	−.45	−.17	−1.33	−1.18	−.47	−2.48	−1.54	−2.06#	−1.17
	(1.16)	(1.24)	(.86)	(1.18)	(1.20)	(.86)	(1.66)	(1.12)	(1.06)	(1.09)
GDP/capita	.19	.51*	.18#	.19	.17	.21*	.33#	.24	.29*	.28#
	(.13)	(.21)	(.09)	(.15)	(.14)	(.10)	(.19)	(.19)	(.12)	(.15)
Observations	733	711	733	733	733	733	733	733	668	733

Logistic regression coefficients with standard errors in parentheses (# −10%; * −5%; ** −1%—one-tailed where appropriate)

Figure 7.3 Substantive effects of drivers of program initiation—Latin America (1990–2001)

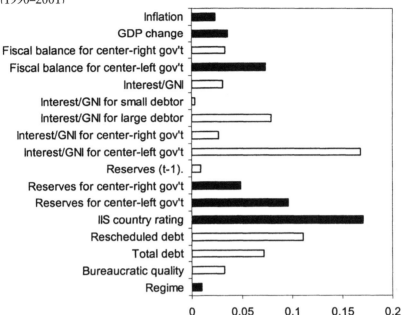

Note: Effects represent change in initiation probability for a change in the variable of interest from the 10th to the 90th percentile. Negative effects are marked as black bars.

in order before entering IMF agreements. But this vacuum was not filled by other domestic economic problems: According to model 1, countries experiencing recessions were somewhat more likely to turn to the IMF (but the effect fell just short of being statistically significant), while the less visible affliction of fiscal deficits once again had a very modest effect. Nor were the traditional external crisis indicators any better in predicting IMF programs: The lower prominence of interest payments on the balance sheets of Latin American governments was reflected in the substantively and statistically modest effect *Interest/GNI* in table 7.1. Finally, the weak effects of *foreign reserves* during the 1990s in Latin America stands in marked contrast to the Fund's prominent lender-of-last-resort role during the post-communist transition and the Latin American debt crisis.

The findings so far confirm that by the 1990s Latin America had largely left the economic woes of the debt crisis behind. Nonetheless, the aftershocks of the crisis left their imprint on IMF programs, especially in the early 1990s; according to model 2, new IMF agreements coincided with more generous reschedulings of foreign debt (significant at .01). Since debt reschedulings were crucial for allowing Latin American coun-

Figure 7.4: Debt size, interest payments, and initiation—Latin America (1990–2001)

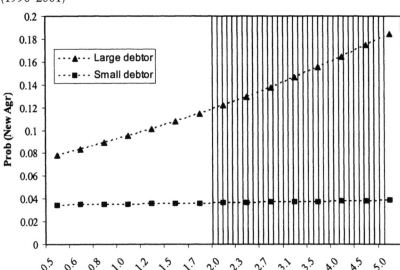

Note: Statistical significance for predictor variable: continuous line (p < .05), dotted line (p > .05). Statistical significance for modifying variable: shaded area (p < .05).

tries the necessary breathing space for domestic economic recovery and an orderly return to international financial markets, the Fund's facilitating role in this process gave it important leverage over many debtors, especially during the early 1990s. Nevertheless, the substantively large negative effect of the Institutional Investor Survey (IIS) country risk rating in model 2 (marginally significant at .1) suggests that this leverage declined rapidly once countries improved their access to alternative credit sources. This pattern stands in clear contrast to the program initiation patterns in Eastern Europe during the same time period, where IMF programs tended to be more frequent for countries in the middle range of risk ratings. On one hand this contrast could simply reflect the greater experience of Latin American borrowers with international financial markets. On the other hand, since this track record was hardly stellar for many Latin American countries, the rapid drop-off in program-participation rates could also reflect the region's much more troubled relationship with the IMF discussed in prior chapters.

Large Latin American debtors were more likely to be involved with the IMF, as reflected by the positive (but inconsistently significant) effect of debt size in table 7.1. As illustrated most vividly by the Argentine case, the Fund was more likely to get involved in countries whose economic stability had wider regional and international repercussions. Unlike in the 1980s, however, the greater program incidence among large debtors was no longer limited to extreme crisis situations, as required by the standards of systemic stability. While figure 7.4, based on model 4, suggests that the effects of debt size were larger at high-interest payment levels, the interaction effect was fairly modest and debt size was positive across the board and at least marginally significant even for moderate interest payment burdens. Moreover, the interaction between reserves and debt size in model 5 pointed in the opposite direction, suggesting that large debtors had easier access to IMF lending when faced with comfortable foreign-reserve levels (marginally significant at .1 one-tailed), while the effect largely disappeared during liquidity crises. To some extent, the Fund's shift from reactive crisis management in the 1980s to a more balanced combination of crisis management (e.g., in Mexico 1994, Brazil 1999, Argentina 2001) and proactive policy involvement in the 1990s can be interpreted as a symptom of the economic normalization experienced by Latin America during this period. On the other hand, this pattern also suggests a more problematic side of the Fund's involvement in Latin America, namely that through its frequent involvement with the region's largest debtors in the context of a much weaker leverage in the 1990s, the Fund may have unwittingly provided a false sense of security to both borrowers and lenders, despite the growing evidence of deteriorating domestic and international conditions. While this consistent large-country bias is a deviation from both technocratic uniformity and purely systemic exceptionalism, according to model 3, neither U.S. geopolitical allies nor large U.S. trading partners were rewarded with more frequent IMF programs in Latin America during the 1990s.

The Latin American IMF programs of the 1990s also reveal a fundamentally different picture of partisan policy responses to external economic challenges. Unlike the divergent ideological responses to the debt crisis, external financial pressures triggered policy convergence among governments of different ideological orientations: As illustrated in figures 7.5 and 7.6 (based on models 6 and 7 in table 7.1), when facing comfortable external financial positions—such as higher reserves and low interest payments—left governments were more likely to avoid the IMF (significant at .05) but reacted much more strongly to financial duress than their right-leaning counterparts, and, therefore, had higher initiation rates in situations of extreme financial difficulties.[11] Partisan reactions to domestic

---

[11] However, the cross-over effect in model 6 fell short of achieving statistical significance, while in model 7 it was only significant at .05 for the highest interest-payment burdens (above the 99th percentile). However, results were stronger for labor-based parties, which

Figure 7.5: Reserves, ideology, and initiation—Latin America (1990–2001)

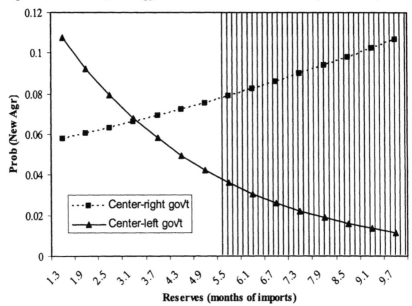

Note: Statistical significance for predictor variable: continuous line (p < .05), dotted line (p > .05). Statistical significance for modifying variable: shaded area (p < .05).

economic crises were mixed: On the one hand model 8 reveals a negative interaction effect between inflation and ideology that is reminiscent of the crisis-driven ideological divergence of the 1980s, in the sense that higher inflation was associated with more frequent IMF programs for right governments but was an impediment to program initiation for left governments, and as a result left governments were less likely to initiate at high inflation levels. On the other hand, these effects were only weakly significant,[12] were very sensitive to model specification,[13] and did not hold for

---

were significantly more likely to enter IMF programs than their nonlabor counterparts when facing serious external crises (results omitted).

[12] Government orientation was significant at .05 one-tailed for very high inflation (above the 90th percentile), but inflation was not significant for any type of government.

[13] The interaction effect disappeared (and even changed sign) once the pre-coup Fujimori administration in Peru is excluded from the analysis. While Fujimori's government prior to the 1992 elections is coded as center-left due to his "anti-shock" electoral-campaign message in the 1990 elections (see below), the country's delay in entering an IMF agreement was not due to ideological opposition but to the slow normalization of the country's relationship with the IMF after Garcia's break with the Fund in 1986.

Figure 7.6: Interest payments, ideology, and initiation—Latin America (1990–2001)

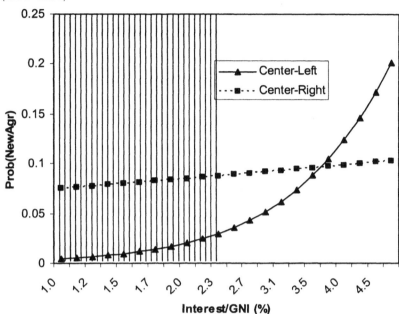

Note: Statistical significance for predictor variable: continuous line (p < .05), dotted line (p > .05). Statistical significance for modifying variable: shaded area (p < .05).

alternative indicators of government orientation.[14] Moreover, the negative interaction effect between fiscal balance and government ideology in figure 7.7 (based on model 9) indicates that fiscal deficits acted as program catalysts for the left (significant at .05) but not for the center-right and the right, thereby leading to crisis-driven ideological convergence (and even cross-over) in countries experiencing serious fiscal crises.[15] Overall, the ideological patterns of crisis response in Latin America during the 1990s are much more similar to the Eastern European findings than to the ideologically charged environment of the debt crisis.

Domestic political and institutional constraints were also less prominent than during the debt crisis. Thus, the effect of better bureaucratic institutions was positive but statistically insignificant across different

[14] Thus, there was an (albeit weak) positive interaction between inflation and labor-based-party governments.

[15] Similar but statistically weaker crisis-driven convergence also occurred with respect to recessionary crises (results omitted).

Figure 7.7 Fiscal balance, ideology, and initiation—Latin America (1990–2001)

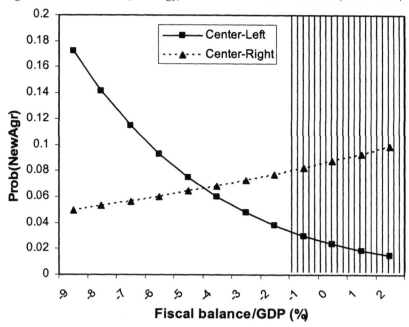

Note: Statistical significance for predictor variable: continuous line (p < .05), dotted line (p > .05). Statistical significance for modifying variable: shaded area (p < .05).

models, suggesting that expertise was less crucial in the context of the more favorable economic conditions of the 1990s. The weak positive effect of the *pre-electoral period* in model 10 reflects the fact that IMF programs were less of a political liability in Latin America after the end of the debt crisis but the effect was substantively and statistically much weaker than in Eastern Europe, which suggests that the pre-electoral initiation boost was a uniquely post-communist phenomenon. Among the other potential indicators of political constraints on government policy making, regime type was also rather weak across different specifications, but model 10 provides at least tentative evidence that governments constrained by multiple domestic veto players were somewhat less likely to enter IMF programs (marginally significant at .1 two-tailed).

Overall, the dynamics of Latin American IMF program initiation in the 1990s marked an important departure from the earlier interactions between the Fund and Latin American debtors. IMF program initiation was no longer driven by concerns about classical domestic or international economic-crisis indicators, such as inflation, reserves, or interest payments, though Fund support was still instrumental for dealing with debt reschedulings and weak capital market access. Since IMF conditionality during the lending boom of the 1990s was generally associated with the benefits of greater access to international financial markets rather than the pain of debt repayment, external financial crises triggered policy convergence among governments of different ideological persuasions, as only leftist/labor-based parties used these crises as an IMF program initiation impetus. In low-crisis situations, however, ideological differences persisted beneath the veneer of the neoliberal consensus of the 1990s, but its manifestations were largely muted by the strong international economic incentives for complying with the dominant pro-market policy paradigm of the first post–Cold War decade.

Drivers of Program Compliance in the 1990s

The compliance record of post-1990 IMF programs in Latin America and the Caribbean was slightly better than during the Latin American debt crisis and the post-communist transition, with program countries eligible to draw on the committed funds for almost three-quarters of the time in which agreements were in place. While this performance was not dramatically higher than in the other two episodes, it nevertheless confirms the more voluntary nature of IMF programs compared to the impositions of the 1980s and the lower degree of institutional uncertainty compared to the transition countries. However, the relative performance of different countries once again varied significantly, ranging from the modest performance of Haiti and Venezuela, to the more consistent compliance records of Peru and Argentina.

The statistical findings about economic and political drivers of program compliance are presented in table 7.2, and the key substantive effects are illustrated in figure 7.8. These tests confirm the initiation-stage findings about the particular nature of the political economy of reforms in Latin America during the 1990s. Thus, inflationary crises did not provide a compliance impetus for governments engaged in IMF programs; in fact, higher levels of inflation tended to undermine implementation during the 1990s, as indicated by the consistently negative (and statistically significant) effects of pre-program inflation across the different statistical models in table 7.2. Model 1 indicates that once again, growth performance was the only domestic economic crisis aspect that contributed to closer IMF cooperation (marginally significant at .1 one-tailed) while the effects of fiscal balance were negligible. Higher interest payment burdens, which had played a positive role during initiation (at least for leftist governments), did not help compliance efforts in the 1990s and may have even undermined them, judging by the negative effects of *Interest/GNI*

TABLE 7.2
Drivers of Program Compliance—Latin America (1990–2001)

	(1)	(2)	(3)	(4)	(5)	(6)	(7)	(8)
Pre-program inflation	−.67**	−.81**	−.68**	−.63**	−.80**	−.51*	−.55**	−.59*
	(.24)	(.27)	(.25)	(.24)	(.29)	(.22)	(.20)	(.23)
GDP change	−.08#				−.02			
	(.05)				(.10)			
Fiscal balance	.01							
	(.05)							
Reserves	−.14#	−.07	−.26*	−.29	−.18#	.12	−.15#	−.05
	(.09)	(.10)	(.11)	(.24)	(.13)	(.17)	(.09)	(.11)
Interest/GNI	−1.01	−1.04	−3.74*	−1.12	−1.34#	−.69	−.64	−.41
	(.76)	(.77)	(1.76)	(.74)	(.80)	(.71)	(.62)	(.68)
Total debt	.77*	.62*	−.29	.51	.89*	.48#	.66*	.46#
	(.31)	(.33)	(.81)	(.41)	(.39)	(.34)	(.31)	(.34)
Regime	.05	−.01	.10	.13	.07	.03	.10	
	(.11)	(.13)	(.12)	(.11)	(.11)	(.11)	(.11)	
Bureaucratic Quality	−.62#	−.27	−.51	−.71*	−.59	−.64#	−.67*	−.41
	(.37)	(.39)	(.40)	(.35)	(.39)	(.37)	(.34)	(.38)
Gov't Orientation	.25	.34	.26	.27	.39	.83*		.27
	(.23)	(.24)	(.24)	(.23)	(.30)	(.39)		(.24)
Rescheduled debt/GNI		.79**						
		(.29)						
IIS Credit Rating		−.10*						
		(.05)						
Interest/GNI* Total debt			1.03#					
			(.63)					
Reserves* Total debt				.05				
				(.06)				
Gov't Orientation* GDP chg.					−.04			
					(.05)			
Gov't Orientation* Reserves						−.13#		
						(.08)		
LBP gov't							.80	
							(.74)	
Pre-Electoral Period								−.65#
								(.45)
Political constraints								−3.54*
								(1.78)
GDP/capita	−.03	.39#	−.12	−.14	−.10	.09	−.07	.21
	(.16)	(.23)	(.15)	(.16)	(.19)	(.19)	(.14)	(.19)
Inverse Mills ratio	3.44**	3.50**	3.42**	3.33**	3.48**	3.43**	3.44**	3.37**
	(1.01)	(.98)	(1.00)	(.96)	(1.05)	(.99)	(.94)	(.94)
Observations	379	379	379	379	379	379	379	378

Logistic regression coefficients with standard errors in parentheses (# −10%; * −5%; ** −1%—one-tailed where appropriate)

Figure 7.8 Substantive effects of drivers of program compliance—Latin America (1990–2001)

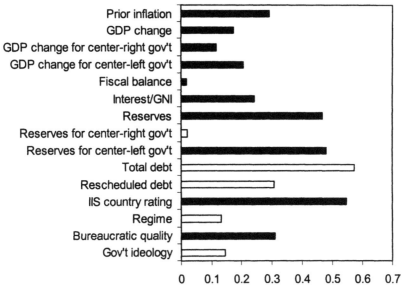

Note: Effects represent change in compliance probability for a change in the variable of interest from the 10th to the 90th percentile. Negative effects are marked as black bars.

across different model specifications. These results suggest that the potential reform impetus of greater financial need was canceled out by its negative side effects on fiscal balance and the timely repayment of debt obligations. The substantively large negative effect of *international reserves* in table 7.2 indicates that liquidity concerns played a much stronger role during implementation than during initiation, and thus resembles more closely the program implementation dynamics of the debt crisis and the post-communist transition.[16]

With respect to the Fund's role as a mediator between developing countries and international financial markets, the implementation-stage findings closely mirror the program initiation patterns. According to model 2, the prospects of rescheduling significant amounts of debt contributed to much more conscientious implementation by Latin American governments (significant at .01 one-tailed). However, the highly significant negative effect of IIS risk ratings indicates that the compliance commitment declined for countries with more comfortable access to interna-

---

[16] However, the results were only marginally and inconsistently significant in statistical terms and should be interpreted with some caution.

tional financial markets and reflects the weaker leverage of the Fund over all but the neediest Latin American program candidates during the global financial boom of the 1990s.

The Fund's systemic role is also reflected in its preferential IMF treatment of large debtors, as suggested by the substantively large and statistically significant implementation effect of *Total debt* in table 7.2. However, the interaction between systemic importance and external crisis intensity once again deviates from the strict expectations of systemic exceptionalism. Thus, even though the positive interaction effect between debt size and interest payments in model 3 was in line with the systemic exceptionalism hypothesis, large debtors had better compliance records (significant at .05) for all but the lowest levels of interest payments, which suggests that preferential treatment was not limited to extreme crisis situations. Moreover, the interaction effect in model 4 points in the "wrong" direction in that it suggests that the compliance advantage of large debtors was actually greater at comfortable reserve levels.[17] While such treatment may have contributed to the more cooperative relationship between the Fund and the region's largest debtors (Argentina, Brazil, and Mexico) in the 1990s, it also drew criticisms (especially in the Argentine case) for allowing them to postpone necessary adjustment measures, which ended up exacerbating later crises.[18]

The partisan policy responses to economic crises at the program implementation stage further confirm that in the 1990s Latin America had discarded the ideologically based policy divergence that had characterized the 1980s. For example, according to figure 7.9 (based on model 5) left-leaning governments reacted to recessionary crises by closer adherence to IMF program conditions (significant at .05 one-tailed) whereas for their center-right counterparts the effect was substantively and statistically weaker. With respect to external crises, figure 7.10 (based on model 6) indicates that left-leaning governments had a worse implementation record when their countries had high levels of international reserves. However, leftist governments were much more sensitive to deteriorating external financial situations and, as a consequence, actually had stronger implementation records than their rightist counterparts in situations of extremely low reserves (significant at .05 two-tailed). Overall, these policy patterns confirm the significant departure from the "classical" ideological blueprint of the 1980s; rather than reacting to crises by becoming more entrenched against IMF reform pressures, in the 1990s left-leaning Latin American governments were more likely to respond by embracing IMF-

---

[17] During liquidity crises small debtors narrowed the compliance gap, but debt size was positive and statistically significant for all but the lowest reserve levels.

[18] See, for example, Feldstein 2002.

Figure 7.9: Growth, ideology, and compliance—Latin America (1990–2001)

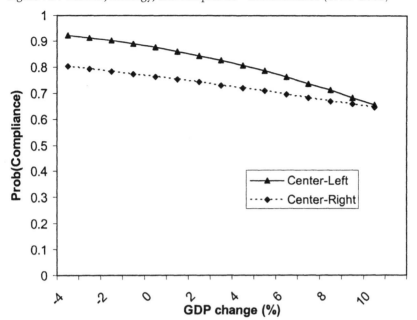

Note: Statistical significance for predictor variable: continuous line (p < .05), dotted line (p > .05). Statistical significance for modifying variable: shaded area (p < .05).

style policies, and in doing so they often outdid their right-leaning counterparts, in a manner reminiscent of the unlikely crisis-driven reformist zeal of former communists in Eastern Europe. In fact, the predominant pattern was that of a "leftist" implementation advantage for Latin American IMF programs in the 1990s, as the effects of both ideological orientation (in models 1–4) and labor-based party governments (in model 6) were consistently positive (though they fell just short of achieving statistical significance).

The results in table 7.2 also reflect another important departure from the acrimonious politics of IMF programs during the debt crisis; whereas in the 1980s, democratic regimes had experienced a significant implementation disadvantage compared to their authoritarian counterparts, this handicap disappeared in the 1990s. In fact, the generally positive (though statistically insignificant) effect of *Regime* in table 7.2 suggests that more democratic regimes may have actually had a slight edge in their implementation efforts, which confirms the greater compatibility of democracy and neoliberal economic reforms in the more favorable international context of the 1990s. However, even in the 1990s the democratic boost to eco-

Figure 7.10: Reserves and ideology in program compliance—Latin America (1990–2001)

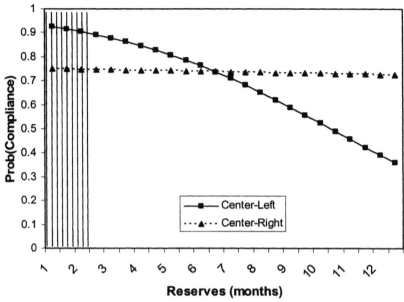

Note: Statistical significance for predictor variable: continuous line (p < .05), dotted line (p > .05). Statistical significance for modifying variable: shaded area (p < .05).

nomic reforms was not nearly as consistent in Latin America as in Eastern Europe. Moreover, model 6 suggests that implementation was adversely affected by electoral campaigns (though the effect was at best marginally significant), and governments facing multiple veto players had a statistically significant disadvantage (.05 two-tailed) when trying to implement IMF programs.

This section's brief analysis of Latin American IMF programs in the 1990s has revealed a political economy landscape whose dynamics were closer to those of the post-communist transition than to the Latin American experience during the debt crisis of the 1980s; thus, external financial pressures reduced and even reversed traditional ideological policy differences between the left and the right, and democracy was no longer incompatible with the neoliberal reform agenda promoted by the IMF. Seen from this perspective, the crucial driver of this transformation appears to have been the dramatic change from the inhospitable international economic environment of the 1980s to the much more favorable climate of the 1990s. Given the Fund's intermediary role between developing country governments and international financial markets, this international economic transformation set a very different basic tone for the interactions between the Fund and its potential clients; thus, as a debt collector with more sticks than carrots at its disposal, the IMF's interventions during the 1980s triggered heated ideological debates and widespread popular resistance, thereby shaping the divisive and confrontational nature of economic reforms during the debt crisis. By contrast, the significant economic benefits of the international financial and economic boom of the 1990s allowed the Fund to play a much more constructive role as a facilitator of international economic integration, which muted the ideological undertones of domestic policy debates and reduced the tensions between democratic politics and neoliberal reforms.

The End of the Neoliberal Consensus?

The findings of the statistical analysis in the preceding section explain why until recently scholars of Latin American political economy focused much of their attention on the roots and implications of the remarkable neoliberal consensus,[19] and of the remarkable coexistence of neoliberal economic policies and democratic politics in a region traditionally known for the tension between the two.[20] However, by the end of the 1990s the neoliberal consensus started to come under increasing pressure, and recent years have witnessed a regionwide reverse political wave: Hugo Chavez's presidential victory in Venezuela in late 1998 was followed by a series of electoral victories by leftist and populist/nationalist candidates, including Lula in Brazil (2002), Lucio Gutiérrez (2002) and Rafael Correa (2006) in Ecuador, Nestor Kirchner in Argentina (2003), Tabaré Vázquez in Uruguay (2004), Evo Morales in Bolivia (2005), René Preval in Haiti (2006), and Alan Garcia (2006) in Peru. While the policy implications of the Latin American left turn have been mixed—ranging from open confrontation with the Western economic and political establishment in the case of Chavez and Morales to centrist pragmatism in the case of Lula and Bachelet[21]—it nevertheless signals a significant shift in the public mood toward economic neoliberalism and raises important questions about the nature of the earlier neoliberal consensus and the reasons for its rather sudden demise.

In hindsight it is clear that beneath the surface of macroeconomic stability, growth, and international investor confidence, Latin America

---

[19] See, e.g., Armijo and Faucher 2002.

[20] See Weyland 1998, Stokes 2001, Kurtz 2004.

[21] For analyses of the different types of emerging Latin American leftist politicians, see, e.g., Castaneda 2006, Cleary 2006.

had not fully succeeded in squaring the circle of achieving a stable equilibrium characterized by sustainable development, neoliberal economic policies, and democratic governance. While an exhaustive discussion of what went wrong—and whether it could have been avoided—is well beyond the scope of the present chapter, it is nevertheless useful to identify some of the key elements that contributed to the gradual dissolution of Latin America's "neoliberal consensus" of the 1990s. The most obvious element was rooted in the changing Latin American fortunes in international financial markets: As reflected in figure 7.2, long-term loan disbursements to Latin America declined significantly after 1998 in response to growing investor uncertainty following the East Asian financial crisis of 1997 and the Russian default of 1998, which were reinforced in the Latin American context by the Brazilian crisis of 1999 and the Argentine default of 2001. Even though access to foreign funding has not dried up to nearly the same extent as during the debt crisis of the 1980s, the comparative trends of net flows and interest payments on long-term debt in figure 7.2 provide a telling story; thus, during the heyday of the credit boom (1993–98) net flows on foreign debt[22] for the region exceeded interest payments, which meant that Latin America experienced a net inflow of funds even once we account for the cost of borrowing. However, by 1999, interest payments, which had been rising steadily since the mid-1990s, started to outstrip the net flow of long-term loans resulting in a return to the pattern of the 1980s with Latin America experiencing a net outflow of hard currency as a result of its interaction with international financial markets. At the same time, regional GDP and consumption growth significantly slowed down after 1999, reaching levels that more closely resemble the stagnant 1980s than the economic boom of the 1990s.[23] In other words, despite some significant variations in the nature and sources of international lending, the credit boom of the 1990s, followed by the gloom of recent years, bears some striking resemblance to the previous international lending cycle in which the commercial bank lending of the 1970s fueled impressive but ultimately unsustainable economic growth, only to be followed by the painful reckoning of the debt crisis in the 1980s.

At this point, it is too early to judge whether Latin America is heading for a decade of renewed economic stagnation or whether the economic recovery of 2004–2007 will prove to be sustainable. What is clear, however, is that the changing international circumstances have increasingly

---

[22] Net flows represent the difference between new loan disbursements and principal repayments on long-term total debt (WDI 2006).

[23] Thus, the average regional growth for Latin America was 1.25% for 1982–90, 3.67% for 1991–98, and 1.95% for 1999–2004. For household final consumption expenditure, the corresponding growth averages were 1.4%, 3.8%, and 1.3%, respectively (data based on WDI 2006).

led to a return to the logic of a zero-sum relationship between domestic economic and political priorities on one hand and the interests of international investors and international financial institutions on the other. Thus, the negotiations surrounding the Argentine default of 2001 marked a return to earlier disputes about the appropriate way to apportion the inevitable economic losses produced by the default. The decisions by the Argentine and Brazilian governments to pay off their IMF obligations ahead of schedule in a nod toward domestic critics of IMF-style policies,[24] further emphasize the significantly cooler relationship between the Fund and Latin American debtors compared to the heyday of cooperation in 1998.[25] Opposition to IMF-promoted structural reforms also played an important role in Evo Morales's electoral appeal, and so far, the Bolivian government has failed to sign a follow-up agreement to the EFF program that Morales inherited from his predecessors but that expired in March 2006.

However, the significant mood change toward neoliberal economic policies in Latin America in recent years cannot be solely attributed to the weaker financial incentives related to the cyclical nature of international lending. Two additional factors undermined the hegemony of neoliberal economic ideas starting in the late 1990s. The heated debates sparked by the Fund's handling of the East Asian financial crisis meant that the IMF was no longer under fire only from the antiglobalization left but from within the Washington establishment, as prominent figures such as World Bank chief economist, Joseph Stiglitz, joined the chorus of IMF critics with unexpected vigor.[26] The fact that the Washington Consensus was no longer a consensus even in Washington lowered the costs of deviating from the conventional wisdom of neoliberal economics.[27] The spate of leftist victories throughout the region has reduced the specter of international and regional isolation to which leftist regimes such as Castro's Cuba and Chavez's Venezuela had been condemned until very recently.

At the same time, as illustrated in greater detail by the case evidence from Bolivia, Argentina, and Peru in the following section, neoliberal economic policies became increasingly unpopular on the domestic front. The earlier statistical results about the electoral politics of IMF programs in the 1990s suggest that even in their heyday, IMF-style economic policies were not exactly popular among Latin American voters and were, there-

---

[24] See *The Economist* 12/20/2005.

[25] For example, in November 1998, IMF singled out Brazilian president Cardoso and Argentine president Menem among "the best of modern political leaders," who "do not cower when crisis looms" (cited in *Deutsche Presse-Agentur* 11/10/1998).

[26] See, e.g., Stiglitz 2000.

[27] The visible tensions between the United States and Western Europe during the run-up to the Iraq war exacerbated this trend by exposing additional fault lines within the previously more monolithic "Western democracies."

fore, downplayed during electoral campaigns. By the late 1990s the widespread and highly publicized corruption allegations against many of the most prominent promoters of neoliberal reforms—including Menem in Argentina and Fujimori in Peru—further undermined the legitimacy and popularity of neoliberal reform efforts. Performance-based legitimacy also declined as the initial relief about the victory over inflation gradually gave way to a sense of disappointment over the slow pace of tangible improvements in the lives of ordinary citizens. This economic discontent was amplified by the post-1998 economic slowdown, which, combined with the region's high and rising inequality, provided ample ammunition for domestic critics who charged that the reforms of the 1990s had primarily benefited the economic and political elites, while the poor had to bear their costs in the form of price liberalizations, government spending cuts, and increased job insecurity.

Neoliberal Reforms and Their Aftermath: Country Evidence

This final section briefly revisits the four Latin American country cases discussed in chapters 4 and 6. This discussion makes no claim to provide a detailed analytical account of the political economy trajectories of Argentina, Bolivia, Peru, and Chile after 1990—rather, it is intended as a postscript to the earlier case studies and as an illustration of the theoretical points raised by this chapter. The first three cases represent interesting variations on the broader theme of the rise and fall of popular support for neoliberalism across a range of different political constellations: neoliberal populism in Menem's Argentina, elite pacts in post-1985 Bolivia, and a mixture of populism and authoritarianism in Peru under Fujimori. Somewhat ironically (given its experience under the Pinochet dictatorship), Chile managed to steer a much steadier middleground under a succession of center-left Concertación governments and provides one of the few instances where market-oriented economic policies have been consistently compatible with democratic politics.

Argentina's Unlikely Reforms

When Carlos Menem was elected president in 1989, Argentina hardly seemed a promising candidate for becoming one of the showcase examples of neoliberalism for the following decade. The country was mired in political paralysis and hyperinflation after almost six years of inconclusive reform efforts by the centrist Alfonsín government, and Menem's populist electoral campaign combined with the Peronists' parliamentary opposition to Alfonsín's last-ditch adjustment efforts, hardly promised a drastic turnaround in the country's political and economic trajectory. Once in power, however, Menem almost immediately signaled his reform intentions by entering an IMF agreement in late 1989 and, despite some setbacks during the first two years in power, oversaw the implementation of the Convertibility Plan in mid-1991, which finally succeeded in stabilizing the Argentine economy.

Even though these reforms were at odds with Menem's electoral promises (Stokes 2001) and the traditional power base of the Peronist Party, Menem was able to implement his agenda through a mixture of skillful political deals and favorable domestic and international circumstances. Even though some of the more popular policies were instituted through presidential decrees, Menem benefited from the Peronist majority in Congress and the weakness of the opposition following the debacle of the last two years of Alfonsín's rule. With respect to the extraparliamentary opposition, Menem was able to leverage his party's traditional ties to the union movement to broker a number of political deals that assured the acquiescence of the union leadership (Etchemendy 2001) and, therefore, avoided the labor protests that had undermined similar efforts by the Alfonsín administration. Thus, the Argentine case provides a useful illustration of the political process underlying the reform advantage of labor-based parties in Latin America during the 1990s. Since the successful control of hyperinflation by late 1991 was complemented by strong economic growth in the context of a favorable international environment, Menem was reelected by a decisive margin in 1995, which confirmed not only his personal popularity but also indicated the broad popular endorsement of his government's economic policy agenda in the early 1990s.

Despite the strong political mandate of the 1995 electoral victory, Menem's second presidential term already signaled the declining political fortunes of neoliberalism in Argentina. Even though the economy recovered relatively quickly from the recession induced by the Mexican Tequila Crisis, the more volatile international economic environment took its toll on the economy, which never returned to the impressive growth levels of the early 1990s.[28] Moreover, as the memories of inflation and economic stagnation during the "lost decade" of the 1980s started to recede into the past, voters started to focus more on the downside of reforms, such as the stagnant real wages and the significant rise in unemployment subsequent to the early 1990s.[29] Nonetheless, the Peronist electoral losses in the parliamentary election of 1997 and the presidential contest of 1999

[28] After shrinking by 2.8% in 1995, growth averaged almost 6% from 1996 to 1998 but was followed by another 3.4% decline in 1999.

[29] Thus real wage increases average less than 1% from 1997 to 1999, while unemployment had fallen from its peak of 18.8% in 1995 but was still above 14% in 1999.

cannot be interpreted as an outright popular rejection of neoliberal policies because the victorious centrist Alianza had not advocated a drastic change in the country's economic policies. Instead, much of the opposition targeted the widespread corruption in the Menem administration, which had been denounced publicly by Domingo Cavallo the architect of the Argentine Convertibility Plan, prior to his resignation from his ministerial post in 1996. In the end, some of the very political deals, which had facilitated the implementation of reforms in the early 1990s, ended up undermining the political appeal of "Menemism"—and in the long run of neoliberalism—in Argentina.

Argentina's decisive break with neoliberalism did not fully occur until the financial collapse of 2001, and as such had important international roots. As mentioned at the outset of the chapter, Menem's time in office marked an unprecedented rapprochement with the IMF and resulted in Argentina becoming a somewhat unexpected poster child of successful neoliberalism in Latin America until the end of the 1990s. However, the Currency Board, which had been the centerpiece of the Convertibility Plan of 1991 and had played an important role in restoring international investor confidence in Argentina, became an increasing economic and political liability by the late 1990s when the appreciation of the dollar undermined the competitiveness of Argentine exports and contributed to an alarming growth in the current account deficit. This imbalance was exacerbated by the Brazilian devaluation of 1999, and by the declining flows of fresh foreign investment after 1998. Despite a series of increasingly desperate IMF-backed attempts by the Argentine government to reassure foreign investors and save the Currency Board, Argentina eventually defaulted on its foreign debt in December 2001 following weeks of violent protests and the early resignation of President De la Rua.

The immediate economic fallout from the crisis was profound: The economy shrank by more than 15% in 2001–2002, as did real wages and private consumption levels, unemployment levels rose to almost 20%, a large portion of domestic savings were wiped out, and half the Argentine population was living below the poverty level. Even though the vigorous economic recovery since 2003 has brought GDP, wage and consumption levels back above pre-crisis levels, the crisis had significant long-term repercussions for the country's domestic power balance, as well as its relationship to the Fund and international financial markets. The crisis aftermath marked a return of the more traditional leftist wing of the Peronist Party under the interim presidency of Eduardo Duhalde and, following the 2003 elections, under the leadership of Néstor Kirchner. Kirchner largely lived up to the leftist political agenda he had laid out during the 2003 presidential campaign by assuming a rather tough bargaining stance during the debt renegotiation process with the country's foreign creditors between 2003 and 2005. Once this strategic objective was achieved, Kirchner followed Lula's example and paid back all of Argentina's outstanding financial obligations to the Fund ahead of schedule, in a symbolic move meant to mark the country's independence from IMF conditionality. On the domestic front, Kirchner clearly distanced himself from Menem's neoliberal policies and resisted Fund pressures for faster structural reforms.

Thus, the end of Argentina's neoliberal reform experiment had a number of significant commonalities with its birth more than a decade earlier: First, it occurred in the midst of a profound domestic economic crisis that convinced large parts of the population that the existing political economy approach had failed and needed to be replaced. Second, the domestic crisis was triggered at least in part by the country's inability to honor its foreign debt obligations and in the context of serious pressures from the IMF and international financial markets. Finally, both the rise and demise of neoliberalism originated in the country's most powerful political machine—the Peronist Party—which was able to harness its appeal among the poor and its organized labor ties to enact policy turnarounds which had eluded its UCR predecessors.

However, the two episodes also differed in important ways, which explains the opposite direction of the two policy reorientations; thus, in 1989–90 international financial markets were emerging from the debt crisis, and cooperation with the Fund's neoliberal policy prescriptions promised (and delivered) substantial financial rewards in terms of foreign funding inflows, which helps explain Argentina's much better compliance record with IMF conditionality in the 1990s. Moreover, whereas the primary domestic economic concern in 1989—the crippling and persistent inflation—could plausibly be addressed through orthodox stabilization measures (as illustrated by Bolivia's experience in 1985–86), the main domestic concerns after 2001 were the high unemployment levels and the weak economic growth of recent years, for which IMF-style austerity measures seemed an unlikely solution (Vreeland 2003). Finally, while Menem had successfully hijacked the Peronist Party in support of his neoliberal reforms, by 2001 the traditional party base among organized labor and the country's poor had largely rallied behind the leftist wing of the party represented by Duhalde and Kirchner and was once again ready to take to the streets to voice its concerns (Etchemendy and Collier 2007). Therefore, throughout its extended neoliberal adventure in the 1990s, the Argentine society continued to harbor important latent elements that would ultimately reverse Menem's ambitious marketization drive, including a strong mobilizational culture, a deep-seated distrust of the Western agenda in the region, and a political party whose traditional popular-sector roots were not completely severed during the 1990s.

Bolivia—The Limits of Democratic Neoliberalism
in a Poor Country

As discussed in chapter 6, after 1985 Bolivia under the leadership of Victor Paz Estenssoro had emerged as one of the few instances of successful orthodox economic stabilization under a reasonably democratic regime. Even though the social costs of the austerity measures and the country's slow growth undermined the high initial popularity of Paz's government, the two parties of the ruling coalition (the center-right MNR and the right ADN) occupied the first two positions in 1989 parliamentary and presidential elections with over 45% of the vote, compared to only 7.2% for the candidate of the leftist Izquierda Unida. These results confirm that despite the drawbacks of the neoliberal economic policies of the late 1980s, Bolivians were willing to extend their support for the representatives of the pro-market status quo. However, as a result of the collapse of the ruling pact between the MNR and ADN in early 1989, Banzer's ADN backed the third-place finisher, Jaime Paz Zamora (from the center-left Movimiento de la Izquierda Revolucionaria) in the parliamentary runoff vote and handed him the presidency. The somewhat odd resulting *Acuerdo Patriótico* alliance between the two erstwhile enemies from the 1970s confirmed the pragmatic, deal-based governing approach of the Bolivian political elite and ensured the continuity of pro-market economic policies until the 1993 elections. Even though the government's tenure was riddled by allegations of corruption and ties to drug traffickers, the country's solid economic performance during this time period, combined with the continued disunity of leftist parties and the declining mobilizational capacity of organized labor, led to a renewed electoral domination by the mainstream political parties (MNR, ADN, and MIR) in the 1993 elections and a fairly strong political mandate for the presidential winner, the outspokenly neoliberal former finance minister from the 1985–89 period, Gonzalo Sánchez de Lozada.[30] Despite the widespread popular opposition to some of Sánchez de Lozada's ambitious structural reforms, the 1997 elections once again merely amounted to a shuffle between the traditional parties and resulted in a new ADN-MIR coalition government. Even though Hugo Banzer's presidential campaign had promised to reverse some of the unpopular reforms of the previous government, and, once elected, he included two smaller populist parties in the governing coalition, the election did little to signal a significant challenge to the neoliberal status quo of the previous twelve years. The first more significant

---

[30] Even though Sánchez de Lozada's first-round vote share was only 33.8%, this support was significantly higher than that received by the winners of the previous two presidential contests and caused second-placed Banzer to step down in the parliamentary runoff.

electoral challenge came in 2002, when Evo Morales, leader of the left-wing Movimiento al Socialismo (MAS), finished second in the presidential poll, but the second-round runoff in the parliament went to Sánchez de Lozada by a 2–1 margin.

Thus, between 1985 and 2002, Bolivian voters reliably returned politicians associated with neoliberal economic policies through democratic elections. Even though the political parties associated with this political mainstream nominally represented different ideological orientations (ranging from the center-left MIR to the right-wing ADN) and in some cases even had bitter, long-standing ideological rivalries,[31] their economic policies revealed little variation and stayed within the broad confines of the broader neoliberal consensus of the 1990s, despite the fact that the intensity of neoliberal reform efforts was somewhat greater during the MNR administrations of 1985–89 and especially 1993–97. This neoliberal policy continuity in a poor, democratic country with a long history of coups, riots, and policy reversals can be traced to a number of favorable circumstances: First, the country's close cooperation with the IMF throughout the 1990s[32] yielded significant financial benefits not only from direct IMF funding but also from the World Bank and IADB, and—in line with the statistical findings—also helped the country secure a large amount of debt-service relief from official external creditors under two successive rounds of the Heavily Indebted Poor Countries (HIPC) Initiative.[33] Second, while hardly spectacular given the country's low starting point, Bolivia experienced fairly steady output, consumption, and wage growth in the context of low inflation for much of the 1990s,[34] an outcome that compared favorably to the disastrous economic performance under the leftist Siles government in 1982–85. Third, in line with the statistical findings about the ideological convergence of the 1990s, the political pacts between the three main parties of the mainstream political elite (MIR, ADN, and MNR) contributed to considerable political stability and avoided the polarization and infighting that had paralyzed successive pre-1985 governments. Finally, despite a series of local riots and protests, for most of the 1990s, the fragmented left and the increasingly marginalized union movement lacked the organizational capacity to mount a serious challenge to the neoliberal establishment.

[31] For example, the leftist MIR was heavily persecuted during the military dictatorship of future ADN leader, Hugo Banzer, in the 1970s.

[32] Even though the country did not enter another standby agreement until 2003, it was quasi-permanently involved in a series of lower conditionality PRGF programs.

[33] This debt relief amounted to US $760m in 1998 and US $1.2 bn in 2001 (IMF Press Release no. 01/29).

[34] Thus, average GDP growth from 1990 to 1998 was 4.4%, while private consumption grew by 3.7% per annum during this time period.

The demise of the Bolivian neoliberal miracle was surprisingly swift considering its remarkable resilience for almost two decades after 1985. Even though popular protests against particular economic reform measures had occurred repeatedly in the late 1980s and through most of the 1990s, successive Bolivian governments had managed to minimize their political fallout, even if at times that meant resorting to excessively forceful interventions.[35] However, these protests against neoliberal policies began to intensify starting in 2000, fueled by the government's unpopular war on coca producers and the controversial scheme to use a Chilean pipeline to export Bolivian natural gas. By 2003 these protests gained sufficient momentum to lead to political paralysis and the resignation of President Sánchez de Lozada, following months of massive protests that were violently repressed by security forces and resulted in dozens of deaths. Strikes and protests continued throughout the following two years amid growing popular opposition to neoliberalism, and eventually led to early elections that were won with a clear majority by Evo Morales on an outspokenly antineoliberal and anti-Western electoral platform.

While it is too early to assess the full economic and political consequences of Morales's victory, it clearly marks the end of almost two decades of Bolivia's peculiar brand of democratic neoliberalism. Some of the roots of this ultimate failure echo the Argentine case; thus, while the use of state resources had played an important role in ensuring the survival of (sometimes unlikely) pro-reform coalitions, the widespread corruption involving key figures from all the major parties[36] eventually undermined the legitimacy of not only the implicated politicians but of the entire neoliberal reform enterprise because it fueled popular perceptions that economic reforms had added to the wealth of the political elite at the expense of the country's impoverished masses. As in Argentina, popular support for neoliberalism declined as the memories of successful solution to hyperinflation receded into the past and were replaced by concerns about economic stagnation and poverty. However, the role of international factors in the demise of neoliberalism differed significantly from the Argentine case; thus, Bolivia, which even during the lending boom of the mid-1990s had relied primarily on bilateral and multilateral loans, was less affected by the reversals in international lending patterns after

[35] For example, in late 1989, President Jaime Paz Zamora declared a state of siege in response to a massive strike of the teachers union, which resulted in two thousand arrests and the internal deportation of two hundred of those arrested.

[36] For example, in 1996, during the first Sánchez de Lozada presidency, eight MNR deputies were forced to resign and ten others were temporarily suspended due to a corruption scandal over fabricated expenses. Meanwhile, Paz Zamora, the MIR leader and Bolivian president (1989–93), had his U.S. visa revoked in 1996 due to his questionable ties to narcotraffic circles.

1999 and did not suffer from an external shock of the magnitude of the 2001 Argentine crisis. However, Bolivian popular discontent was fueled by the cooperation of successive Bolivian governments with the U.S.-led war on drugs, and triggered the rise of the coca-growers' union under the leadership of Evo Morales. Moreover, the controversial role of Western multinationals in the Bolivian economy (especially during the Cochabamba water scandal and the exploitation of the country's recently discovered vast natural gas reserves) provided a focal point for a variety of different opponents of neoliberalism. This focal point was particularly important since, unlike in Argentina, the Bolivian opposition to neoliberalism did not find an outlet through any of the traditional political parties but rather grew out of a variety of loosely connected interest groups and social movements, including the traditional labor unions, indigenous groups, and coca growers. Since these groups represented the many Bolivians who felt that they had been excluded from the neoliberal consensus of the 1990s, the Bolivian case illustrates the limitations of democratic neoliberalism in poor and unequal countries. On the other hand, it is equally unclear whether the heterogeneous coalition, which propelled Morales to the presidency in 2005, will survive the demise of its common enemy and manage to articulate and implement a coherent developmental alternative for Bolivia.

Neoliberal Populism: Peru under Fujimori

The economic and political evolution of Peru under the leadership of Alberto Fujimori represents an interesting deviation from the broad general pattern of democratic neoliberalism that dominated the Latin American political economy in the 1990s. On one hand, in the early 1990s Fujimori oversaw a remarkable economic policy turnaround that reversed the economic free fall of the last three years of the Garcia administration and brought the country back into the favors of international financial markets and the IMF. In fact, since 1993 Peru has been involved quasi permanently in a series of largely implemented IMF programs that added the international seal of approval to the country's ambitious neoliberal policies after 1990. However, countering the regionwide democratization trend of the last two decades, Peru experienced a lengthy period of democratic retrenchment after Fujimori's 1992 constitutional coup, and despite the legitimating effect of his 1995 electoral victory, Fujimori's ten-year rule was marred by a series of significant deviations from democracy until his controversial reelection in 2000 and his resignation less than a year later.

At first glance, therefore, the Peruvian experience of the 1990s appears like a throwback to the authoritarian economic reformers of the

1980s. However, a closer look at the succession of political events surrounding Fujimori's authoritarian adventure suggests a more complicated picture. Leading up to his surprising 1990 electoral victory on a vague platform of "work, technology, honesty," Fujimori was arguably seen by most voters as a compromise solution between Garcia's costly anti-Western heterodoxy and the unabashedly pro-market message of his main rival, Mario Vargas Llosa. However, once in office, Fujimori joined Menem as one of the quintessential examples of a new breed of Latin American neoliberal populists.[37] Faced with Alan Garcia's disastrous economic legacy, which combined persistent hyperinflation, a deep recession, and quasi-complete international economic isolation, Fujimori instituted a drastic program of economic reforms—popularly referred to as Fujishock—to tackle the debilitating crisis. The initial results of these reforms were remarkably positive in the sense that within a year of assuming power, Fujimori had succeeded in checking hyperinflation, restoring economic growth (at an admittedly modest rate of 2.2% in 1991), and reducing unemployment (from 8.3% in 1990 to 5.9% in late 1991). However, it should be noted that this initial adjustment occurred in the absence of an IMF program, given that the large arrears inherited from the Garcia administration made Peru ineligible for fresh IMF funds until early 1993. In this respect, Peru fit well with the broader regional trend suggested by the statistical tests, whereby in the 1990s countries generally tackled their worst domestic economic problems before initiating IMF programs.

As the intensity of the economic crisis began to subside, however, Fujimori found himself increasingly at odds with the parliament, which was largely controlled by the traditional political parties and opposed Fujimori's austerity measures for the 1992 budget. Lacking Menem's congressional support and control over an effective political machine, Fujimori instead resorted to an army-backed *autogolpe* in April 1992, during which he dissolved the congress and the judiciary with the stated aim of rooting out corruption. Thus, on one hand, Fujimori's coup fits the earlier pattern of Latin American regimes overstepping the boundaries of democratic politics in order to impose market reforms. On the other hand, despite being clearly antidemocratic from a procedural point of view, Fujimori's *autogolpe* actually had overwhelming popular support due to the promising economic results of the initial economic reforms and the appeal of his claim that the measures were necessary to overcome the entrenched interests of the country's traditional political elite. Thus, unlike the typical pattern of authoritarian repression of popular resistance to austerity measures, Fujimori's transgression was of a more plebiscitary nature given his genuine popular support among ordinary Peruvians eager for a solution to the country's prolonged economic and political malaise. This popular-

[37] See, e.g., Roberts 1995, Weyland 1999.

ity was confirmed during the (admittedly flawed) parliamentary elections of November 1992,[38] and once more by Fujimori's overwhelming victory in the presidential and parliamentary elections of 1995.[39]

The international reaction to Fujimori's *autogolpe* is indicative of the significant international political changes since the 1980s. The coup provoked strong reactions not only from Latin American governments and the Organization of American States, but also from the U.S. and Western European governments, which suspended foreign aid to the Peruvian government. Even the IMF, despite commending Fujimori for his austerity budget, threatened to delay the normalization of Peru's relationship with the international financial community until the country resumed its democratic path. This remarkably consistent international reaction to the coup marked a clear departure from the 1980s, when Western donors condoned the Fund's close ties to Latin American authoritarian regimes such as Pinochet's Chile. Faced with the prospect of extremely costly economic sanctions, Fujimori did not backtrack on his actions but compromised by meeting with the opposition parties and calling earlier parliamentary elections (in November 1992) than originally envisioned. The Peruvian case shows that compliance with only the economic aspects of Western liberalism no longer provided the same benefits as during the more "pragmatic" Western approach to foreign policy in the 1980s, which helps explain why, in the 1990s, IMF-style reforms were more likely to be accompanied by at least formally democratic governance.

While this prompt international reaction arguably reduced the coup's negative repercussions for Peruvian democracy, ulterior developments illustrate some of the limitations of the new Western approach to promoting economic and political liberalism in the developing world. Thus, despite the problematic nature of the 1992 parliamentary elections and the persistence of important deviations from standard democratic practice throughout the 1990s,[40] Peru's relationship with the international community was largely normalized by late 1992, facilitating the resumption of bilateral aid and international financial reintegration. Arguably, the crucial drivers behind this swift normalization—U.S. concerns about the Shining Path insurgency and Peruvian cooperation with U.S. drug eradication efforts—ultimately overshadowed concerns about democratic practices as long as Fujimori was willing to maintain at least a semblance

---

[38] Fujimori's Cambio 90 party secured an absolute majority of seats based on a 38% vote share in an election, which was largely considered free and fair by international observers but which had been boycotted by the major opposition parties in protest over the greatly increased constitutional powers of the presidency vis-à-vis parliament.

[39] Fujimori won 64.4% of votes compared to 21.8% for his closest rival, Javier Pérez de Cuéllar, while his party secured 67 of the 120 parliamentary seats.

[40] On the −10 to 10 Polity regime scale, Peru scored between −3 and 1, well below the usual cutoff point of 6 for democracies.

of democratic rule. The extensive human rights violations that accompanied the government's anti-insurgency campaign, further undermined the quality of Peruvian democracy but had limited repercussions on Fujimori's domestic and international legitimacy due to the campaign's unexpected success in getting the rebellion under control after more than a decade of widespread violence (Stokes 2001). Therefore, the drivers and the political feasibility of Fujimori's semiauthoritarian leadership style were rooted in Peru's geopolitical exceptionalism rather than in the tension between his aggressive neoliberal reforms and democratic politics. This interpretation is further justified by the fact that once the insurgency threat faded by the late 1990s, both domestic and international public opinion showed much less patience toward Fujimori's deviations from democracy, and eventually contributed to his downfall.

Fujimori's political star began its descent almost immediately following his electoral triumph in 1995. However, unlike in neighboring Bolivia, the main reason for Fujimori's declining popularity was not his continued pursuit of neoliberal reforms in close cooperation with the IMF. Even though output and private consumption growth slowed down considerably starting in 1998,[41] while real wages declined steadily after their pre-electoral spike in 1994, Peru did not experience significant popular mobilization against neoliberal policies, despite the prominent role played by foreign companies in the privatization process and the extraction of natural resources.[42] Instead, the political opposition focused increasingly on the corruption allegations against Fujimori and his entourage,[43] as well as on the government's occasionally heavy-handed attempts to control the media, repress the opposition, and manipulate the judiciary. Therefore, the main challenge during Fujimori's controversial third bid for the presidency came from Alejandro Toledo, a U.S.-educated economist focusing on Fujimori's corruption and patronage legacy rather than on reversing economic neoliberalism. Even though Fujimori won the controversial 2000 elections amid fraud allegations and widespread protests, his third term was cut short in the fall of 2000 when a final high-profile corruption scandal[44] led to his resignation and exile to Japan.

---

[41] Thus, GDP growth averaged only 1% between 1998 and 2000, compared to 7.1% per year from 1993 to 1997, while for private-consumption changes, the corresponding averages were 0.7% and 6%, respectively.

[42] The one notable exception was a one-day general strike in April 1999 against low wages, the government's privatization program, and Fujimori's attempt to run for president for a third time.

[43] Fujimori's image suffered significantly as a result of repeated corruption allegations from his estranged wife following a highly publicized divorce in 1985.

[44] The scandal involved a tape of Vladimiro Montesinos, one of Fujimori's closest associates and head of the security services, bribing an opposition congressman, Alberto Kouri, in order to ensure a congressional majority for the president.

Even though economic grievances played only a secondary role in Fujimori's declining popularity during the late 1990s, domestic opposition to neoliberalism steadily increased after his resignation. The first clear signal of this change in public mood came during the 2001 presidential elections, in which Fujimori's main challenger from 2000, Alejandro Toledo, barely defeated the former president, Alan Garcia, despite the latter's abysmal governing record from 1985 to 1990. Despite a relatively healthy economic recovery after 2002, Toledo's administration was plagued by a series of high-level corruption scandals, and by growing popular opposition to the government's neoliberal economic policies under IMF guidance.[45] This discontent was reflected in the outcome of the 2006 election, whose runoff pitted Alan Garcia against Ollanta Humala, whose outspoken anti-neoliberal rhetoric and past history as a coup organizer echoed the background of Venezuelan president Hugo Chavez. In the end Garcia's narrow victory, combined with his remarkable conversion as a centrist social democrat, has meant that economic policies in Peru have stayed remarkably close to their earlier neoliberal trajectory, including a new two-year precautionary stand-by agreement with the IMF, signed in January 2007. However, Humala, whose party controls the largest share of parliamentary seats, remains an important political challenger to the country's tenuous neoliberal continuity.

Despite their obvious differences in democratic governance, the neoliberal reform trajectories of Peru and Argentina reveal some interesting parallels. In both cases reforms were initiated in the midst of severe inflationary crises by recently elected presidents, who, once in power, quickly reversed their vague populist electoral promises of gradual reforms and took advantage of their political capital and of the temporary disarray of traditional reform opponents to impose drastic market reforms with IMF backing. In both cases, the considerable short-term economic success of these adjustment policies translated into genuine popular support for the two leaders, Menem and Fujimori, who won convincing electoral victories in the mid-1990s. However, as memories of the traumatic crises of 1989–90 started to fade, the two leaders became victims of their own governing styles as corruption scandals (for both Menem and Fujimori) and growing concerns about Fujimori's authoritarian tendencies contributed to their eventual political demise. Thus, Menem and Fujimori compromised not only their own political careers but also the popular appeal of neoliberalism, which was indelibly linked to images of the two leaders and, therefore, lost much of its moral legitimacy.

[45] Under Toledo's presidency, Peru was one of the few remaining Latin American countries to be engaged in quasi-permanent precautionary IMF programs.

Pinochet's Unexpected Legacy:
Democratic Neoliberalism in Chile after 1990

Following the remarkable stability of its neoliberal, authoritarian, political-economy model under Pinochet, Chile's trajectory after 1990 once again stands out for its continuity in a region marked by volatile politics and increasingly volatile economic policies. Since the return to democracy in December 1989, successive governments of the center-left Concertación coalition pursued consistently pro-market economic policies in a democratic context without triggering the types of societal protests and electoral challenges that ultimately undermined neoliberalism in Argentina, Bolivia, and increasingly Peru. The drivers of Chilean exceptionalism, which will be briefly discussed in this section, help identify the circumstances under which the neoliberal consensus of the 1990s could survive the international economic and political changes of the post-2001 era. In particular, the resilience of liberal economic policies in Chile was facilitated by the country's better track record in fighting poverty and corruption, the ideological moderation and consistency of the mainstream political parties, as well as the greater societal reluctance (and capacity) to engage in widespread protests given the chaotic experience of the Allende regime and the subsequent repression under Pinochet.

Somewhat ironically, many of the drivers of Chile's stable, democratic neoliberalism are a legacy of Pinochet's military dictatorship from the 1970s and 1980s. Thus, unlike the Bolivian reformers in 1985 and their Argentine and Peruvian counterparts in 1989–90, the comfortably low inflation inherited by the victorious Concertación alliance in Chile did not require the kind of drastic adjustment policies that eventually ended hyperinflation in its much more chaotic neighboring countries. Instead, one may have expected the new government to reverse some of the features of the "Chilean economic model" instituted during the military dictatorship, given that much of Concertación's electoral support came from the popular sector, which had suffered disproportionately from the high social costs of the austerity measures of the early to mid-1980s. Moreover, while excluding the hard-line communists, the governing coalition nonetheless largely consisted of left-of-center parties,[46] which by the partisan logic of the 1980s should have redirected the country's economic policies toward greater state intervention and government spending to compensate for the decade and a half of sustained neoliberal reforms.

---

[46] Thus, in late 1989, the Partido Socialista (PS) was still officially committed to Marxism (a position that it only renounced 1996), and even the centrist Partido Demócrata Cristiano (PDC) only dropped its traditional advocacy of "communitarian socialism" from its party program in late 1991 (*EIU Country Profile*, 1996).

Instead, over the last decade and a half, successive Concertación governments have pursued a remarkably consistent neoliberal economic course, characterized by prudent fiscal and monetary policies, continued structural reforms, and international financial liberalization and economic integration. Moreover, even though Chile did not initiate any IMF agreements following the successful completion in November 1990 of the "legacy" standby agreement initiated in the final weeks of the outgoing Pinochet government, Chilean economic policy has repeatedly met with IMF approval, which confirms that the absence of official IMF involvement was a sign of Chile having "graduated" from a group of countries needing IMF conditionality to reassure foreign investors and ensure economic discipline. Just as remarkably (considering the experience of its neighbors), this economic orthodoxy has not triggered the rise of significant anti-neoliberal challenges at either the electoral or the societal level; indeed, since 1989, Concertación has achieved the remarkable performance of five consecutive electoral victories in a region known for its fickle political allegiances, and in each of these elections the main challenge has actually come from the right of the political spectrum, that is, from parties advocating even greater reliance on markets.

The explanation for this seeming paradox, which further confirms the statistical findings about the much lower salience of ideology and the greater compatibility between democratic politics and economic neoliberalism in the 1990s, relies on a combination of broader regional trends and country-specific factors (which nevertheless have important theoretical implications). First, after the painful recession of 1982–83, the Chilean economy had started to recover gradually and, by late 1989, was in the third year of an economic boom, with average GDP growth of 8.8% from 1987 to 1989, rising consumption levels, and steadily declining unemployment.[47] Under such circumstances it would have been risky to attempt to fix an economic policy course that by early 1990 was clearly successful, especially because the healthy economic growth promised to attenuate some of the key concerns of the left, such as poverty and redistributive conflicts. This performance-based legitimacy of neoliberalism has arguably continued to be one of the crucial factors for its political stability throughout the post-1990 period; thus, the Chilean economy grew at an impressive rate for most of the 1990s, and its export-led growth was much less affected by the regional economic downturn in recent years than for most of its neighbors.[48] Perhaps more importantly for the political appeal

[47] Thus, employment declined from a staggering 19.6% in 1982 to 5.3% in 1989 (*EIU Country Data*).

[48] From 1990 to 1998, the average growth rate was 7.5% per year, and after a one-year recession triggered by the Brazilian crisis of 1999, growth resumed once more at a respectable average rate of 4.3% from 2000 to 2005.

of neoliberalism, the Chilean government's commitment to fight poverty has not been only rhetorical but has resulted in a significant reduction of poverty and extreme poverty levels since 1990, whereas elsewhere in the region poverty levels have actually increased even during the economic boom of the 1990s (Korzeniewicz and Smith 2000, Portes and Hoffman 2003, Hoffman and Centeno 2003). Therefore, despite the persistence of high levels of inequality, Chilean neoliberalism has been much less vulnerable to the common charge that the benefits of neoliberal growth have largely eluded the poorest members of society, which may explain the lack of significant left-populist electoral challenges and (until very recently) the virtual absence of riots.

The second reason for the unexpected continuity of neoliberal economic policies under the center-left Concertación echoes the earlier discussion about the powerful international incentives to adopt pro-market policies in the early 1990s. While Chile emerged as one of the region's most creditworthy countries,[49] and as such was less dependent on IMF lending, the country's economic stability in the early 1990s depended on securing more favorable loan terms to reduce the high-interest payment burden, which at more than 6% of GDP in 1989–90 was among the highest in the region. Finally, in line with the statistical findings, Chile's compliance with its 1990 IMF program may have been driven at least in part by the fact that the rescheduling of $4.2bn of its foreign debt in 1990 could have been significantly complicated if the new government had initiated a drastic reversal of neoliberal economic policies.

The third—and decidedly more problematic—reason for the policy restraint of Chile's leftist government and the virtual absence of organized societal resistance to neoliberalism is an even more direct political legacy of the Pinochet dictatorship. In the most immediate sense, having exited power through a negotiated transition and with considerable societal support, the military continued to be a towering presence during the early years of Chile's nascent democracy and could therefore impose rather tight constraints on acceptable economic policies due to the implicit threat of renewed military intervention. At least in the early 1990s this credible threat probably also acted as a disincentive for strikes and societal protests against neoliberal reforms. Even beyond these immediate constraints, the systematic and brutal repression of labor unions and left-wing political organizations during the sixteen years of the dictatorship significantly undermined the organizational capacity of the most likely reform opponents. In this respect, the Chilean experience more closely

---

[49] In fact, Chile had the highest IIS credit rating score in the region in early 1990, and it defended and even extended its lead for the rest of the decade.

Figure 7.11: Corruption in Latin America (1996–2005)

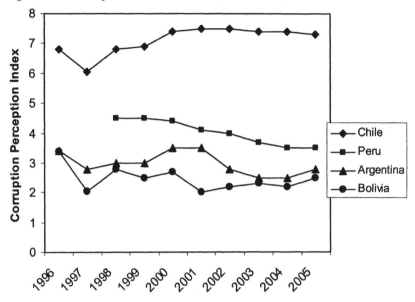

Source: Transparency International (higher scores indicate lower corruption)

resembles the political situation in the post-communist countries, where the longer and "deeper" authoritarian experience resulted in a weaker articulation of societal interests (Bunce 1998) and, therefore, reduced active popular resistance to neoliberal economic policies.

Finally, successive Chilean governments have managed to eschew corruption to a much greater extent than most other Latin American countries and have, therefore, avoided the crippling corruption scandals that have undermined the credibility of neoliberal reformers in Argentina, Bolivia, and Peru. Judging by the overtime evolution in the *Transparency International* Corruption Perception Index for the four countries, illustrated in figure 7.11, corruption levels in Chile have not only been uncharacteristically low by regional standards but have been slightly improving since the mid-1990s. By contrast, the corruption increased steadily in Peru and fluctuated at catastrophic levels in Argentina and Bolivia. Given that Uruguay, the country with the second-best corruption track record in Latin America, has also experienced a high degree of political stability and neoliberal policy continuity in a democratic context in the 1990s, it appears that the importance of corruption in the eventual demise of Latin American neoliberalism may be generalizable beyond the four cases discussed in this chapter.[50] At the same time, however, it is important to recall that in both Argentina and Bolivia the tenuous political coalitions in favor of neoliberal reforms were held together through strategic use of discretionary resources. Since the line between such political deals and outright corruption is often very blurry, these findings suggest a rather paradoxical conclusion, namely that in countries with mobilized anti-reform groups, the very tactics necessary to build reform coalitions usually end up undermining the long-term legitimacy and visibility of neoliberal reforms.

Conclusion

This chapter has analyzed the economic and political drivers of Latin American IMF programs after 1990. The statistical findings and the case evidence from Argentina, Bolivia, Chile, and Peru reveal that, in the 1990s, IMF-style reforms were no longer at odds with democratic politics and did not elicit the ideologically charged policy reactions that had been typical during the debt crisis of the 1980s. Instead, as in the post-communist transition, ideological differences only mattered at low levels of financial need but vanished (and were even reversed) in the face of serious external economic crises. The two strongest economic drivers of IMF programs in the 1980s—inflation and interest payments—no longer mattered in the 1990s as high inflation virtually disappeared after 1992 and debt-service burdens declined in the context of the more favorable international economic environment. Nonetheless, the IMF still played an important role in countries with low international reserves and in facilitating the debt-rescheduling agreements of the early 1990s that paved the way for the reentry of Latin American debtors into international financial markets.

The similarities between the political dynamics of Eastern European and Latin American IMF programs of the 1990s and the contrasts to the more antagonistic interactions of the 1980s confirm the importance of the changing international economic and geopolitical environment that allowed the IMF to play a much less controversial role during the economic boom of the 1990s than during the debt crisis. The greater international benefits of adopting IMF-style policies, combined with the domestic successes of neoliberal reformers in controlling hyperinflation and delivering economic growth, paved the way for a period of unprecedented democratic neoliberalism in Latin America, as illustrated by the Argentine, Bolivian, and Chilean cases discussed in this chapter. Even where

---

[50] Unfortunately, systematic corruption data is only available since the mid-1990s and therefore does not lend itself to statistical testing in the current context.

democratic politics suffered significant temporary setbacks—as in Peru after 1992—democracy was not undermined by neoliberal reforms, and international pressures (including from the IMF) were less likely to ignore democratic concerns in favor of pro-market economic policies.

In recent years, however, this neoliberal consensus has unraveled throughout much of Latin America, giving way to a wave of leftist electoral victories and social movements opposed to the neoliberal policies of the 1990s. Judging by its timing and the comparative evidence from Argentina, Bolivia, and Peru, this chapter has argued that this reversal was driven by the changing dynamics of international financial markets that have been a lot less favorable toward Latin America in recent years and have had negative repercussions on domestic economic performance in Argentina and elsewhere. However, the analysis also reveals significant differences between the resilience of democratic neoliberalism in Chile, its ultimate collapse in Argentina and Bolivia, and its uncertain status in Peru. These contrasts suggest that the broader international changes were filtered through the particular political and economic circumstances of individual countries: In particular, the ability of Chilean reformers to control corruption and reduce poverty has played an important role in ensuring the continued legitimacy and political feasibility of neoliberalism in Chile, whereas in Argentina, Bolivia, and Peru, widespread corruption and increasing poverty have undermined the credibility of neoliberal reformers and have fueled the eventual backlash against neoliberalism. These findings suggest that the widespread compatibility between democracy and the IMF-style reforms in Latin America during the 1990s was in many cases the product of a favorable international environment, but where neoliberal reformers failed to address the crucial developmental problems of their countries, the fair-weather reform alliances dissolved in the face of the domestic and international economic slowdown after 1999.

– 8 –

Theoretical Conclusions and Policy Implications

THIS BOOK HAS ANALYZED THE POLITICAL DYNAMICS of IMF programs in the developing world. Given their location at the intersection of multiple domestic and global interests, IMF programs are shaped by actors as diverse as the U.S. State Department, technocrats within the IMF and the finance ministries of developing countries, government and opposition political parties, labor and business organizations, and guerrilla movements. Therefore, it is hardly surprising that despite the relative uniformity of the Fund's theoretical approach to conditionality, the actual trajectories of IMF programs are as diverse as the political and economic environments in which they unfold.

Toward a More Comprehensive Theory
of Neoliberal Reforms

While acknowledging and capturing the complex drivers of IMF-style reforms, the structured cross-regional and cross-temporal comparative analysis developed in this book allows us to go one step farther and to propose a more integrated theoretical explanation of the political dynamics of IMF programs and neoliberal economic reforms. The book's central comparison—between IMF programs during the Latin American debt crisis and the post-communist transition—reveals a wide range of differences in the political economy of IMF program initiation and implementation, which will be summarized in more detail below. However, the defining difference between the two crisis episodes lies here: In Latin America during the 1980s, IMF interventions triggered significant domestic and international political contention that resulted in divergent ideological policy responses to economic crises and pitted neoliberal reform priorities against the region's nascent democratic politics. In contrast, democracy in Eastern Europe was compatible with and even conducive to IMF-style economic reforms, and economic crises in this region triggered policy convergence between governments of different ideological persuasions.

The contrast between these two crucial episodes of IMF interventions in the developing world has important theoretical implications for the domestic and international political economy of neoliberal reforms. As illustrated by the analysis in chapters 3 and 4, the tone and the broad parameters of the interaction between the IMF and the governments of the two regions were largely determined by the international financial and political environment in which the two crises unfolded. Western concerns for international financial stability and the survival of the troubled Western commercial banks resulted in an IMF agenda that heavily emphasized a combination of debt servicing and domestic austerity measures for Latin American debtors in the 1980s. The bitter medicine prescribed by the IMF, combined with the weak palliative prospects of private lending as a reward for compliance, resulted in widespread popular opposition to the neoliberal reform agenda of the IMF, thereby creating significant trade-offs between compliance with IMF conditionality and democratic politics. Moreover, given that the debt crisis occurred in the bipolar international environment of the last decade of the Cold War,[1] the Fund's policy prescriptions and the nature of the region's economic crisis triggered divergent ideological reactions, as the right largely agreed with the IMF diagnosis and initiated orthodox economic reforms in response to economic crises, while populist and left-leaning governments either avoided reforms or attempted heterodox policy alternatives.

Meanwhile, Western priorities for the post-communist transition primarily targeted the integration of Eastern European countries into the world economy while avoiding political unrest and a possible return to communism. Since debt played only a marginal role in Eastern Europe, the IMF played a much less controversial role as a neoliberal reform adviser to countries dealing with the complicated economic legacy of communism and trying to gain access to the international financial boom of the 1990s. Therefore, reform-oriented governments could point to the significant economic gains associated with IMF compliance, while blaming many of the costs on communist-era distortions, a strategy that led to weaker popular resistance against market reforms and a more harmonious relationship between democracy and neoliberalism. Moreover, in the absence of a real ideological alternative to the liberal Washington Consensus, the policy choices of governments of different ideological persuasions converged in the face of economic crisis, as even former communists went along with the Fund's policy prescriptions when facing significant economic difficulties. The crucial importance of the international economic

[1] At least until the late 1980s, the existence of the communist bloc offered both an ideological reference point for left-wing parties and potential economic support to counter (at least partially) the U.S. economic and political dominance of the region.

and political environment is further confirmed by the analysis in chapter 7, which indicates that in the context of the financial boom of the 1990s, and the ideological exhaustion of alternatives to Western liberalism (Edwards 1995), the politics of Latin American IMF programs were more similar to the post-communist experience than to the region's own recent track record during the debt crisis. The unexpectedly peaceful coexistence of democratic politics and neoliberal reforms and the equally remarkable ideological flexibility in a region with a history of deeply rooted class conflict and ideological polarization reinforces the book's argument about the crucial importance of the international reward structure in driving the political dynamics of IMF programs and of neoliberal reforms more broadly.

The importance of international economic policy incentives is further emphasized by the recent left turn in Latin American politics: As discussed briefly in chapter 7, the net funding outflows from Latin America after 1999, combined with the growing internal fissures in the Washington Consensus, have weakened the incentives for Latin American governments to comply with IMF policy prescriptions, and have contributed to a significant cooling down of the earlier close cooperation with the Fund by the Argentine and Brazilian governments. This new international reality also had important repercussions for the domestic politics of economic reforms, as recent years have witnessed a renewed rise of popular opposition to neoliberalism and a series of leftist and populist political parties and leaders whose economic-policy stance marks a much more significant departure from neoliberalism than had been the norm after the end of the debt crisis.

Despite the obvious importance of systemic incentives, several aspects of the present analysis suggest that the domestic politics of economic reforms cannot be simply reduced to a mechanical transmission of global economic and ideological pressures to the national level. Instead, these international pressures and incentives are filtered through the domestic constellations of economic and political interests as well as through domestic institutional and cultural legacies that differed significantly across regions, as well as between countries within the two regions. Thus, even during the heyday of the 1990s, several countries from both Latin America and Eastern Europe[2] resisted the neoliberal policy advice of the IMF and other international financial institutions. Similarly, the recent turn away from neoliberalism has not affected all Latin American coun-

---

[2] Examples include Cuba and more recently Venezuela and Bolivia in Latin America, as well as Belarus, Uzbekistan, Turkmenistan, and until recently Yugoslavia among the post-communist countries.

tries equally.[3] Finally, a closer look at the individual cases suggests that even in countries with superficially similar economic reform trajectories—such as Argentina and Peru in the 1990s—the politics behind the rise and fall of the neoliberal consensus was driven by very different constellations of domestic and international factors.

Just as importantly, Eastern Europe has not experienced a similar left turn in recent years,[4] which raises some interesting questions about the roots of the renewed resurgence of political resistance to IMF-style reforms in Latin America. One reason is arguably the persistence in Latin America of popular distrust of the IMF throughout the boom of the 1990s, which is underscored by the fact that the IMF program implementation record of Latin American governments was worse prior to elections. Moreover, the continued economic and political incentives of European integration for many transition countries have arguably reduced the impact of the recent changes in international financial markets. The other crucial reason for this disjuncture was the persistence of important cross-regional differences in the domestic articulation of economic and political interests; even though the decline of labor unions and the rise of the informal sector have weakened the strong traditional organizational bases for social mobilization, the popular sector in Latin America nevertheless retained a stronger organizational capacity and protest culture than the highly disarticulated economic interests of post-communist citizens. As a consequence, the rising popular discontent with neoliberal policies since the late 1990s has given rise to a wave of anti-neoliberal protests in much of Latin America, accompanied by a revival of organized labor (Collier and Etchemendy 2007) and the rise of leftist parties that appear more responsive to these policy demands than most of the nominally leftist communist successor parties in Eastern Europe.

Thus, the broad compatibility of neoliberal economic policies and democratic politics in the 1990s were not the beginning of a liberal Fukuyama-style "end of history" but rather a rational response of elites and populations in the two regions to the powerful economic incentives of a global financial boom and the unprecedented international dominance of Western economic and political liberalism. By contrast, in periods with weaker and/or contradictory international incentives, such as the debt crisis of the 1980s and to a lesser extent the post-9/11 era, the politics of

[3] As discussed in chapter 7, the recently reelected center-left Concertación coalition in Chile is likely to continue its steady pro-market policies of the last seventeen years. Similarly, recent electoral results in Mexico and Costa Rica signal a continuation of these countries' earlier economic policies.

[4] Thus, the victories of communists in Moldova and of reformed ex-communists in Bulgaria have been more than balanced by the victories of pro-Western reformers in Romania, Ukraine, and Georgia, as well as by the clear victory of the pro-market right in Poland.

IMF programs were more likely to reflect the domestic tensions between the redistributive demands of democracy and the uneven gains of neoliberal economic policies. However, the extent to which these tensions had significant political and policy reverberations was mediated to a great extent by the organizational capacity of societal actors, which has generally been significantly higher in Latin America than in post-totalitarian Eastern Europe.

Dealing with Complexity: Methodological Implications

Considering the complex and continuously evolving nature of the domestic and international drivers of IMF programs, the quest for universal explanations of the political dynamics of program initiation and implementation is likely to be elusive (and ultimately misguided). While attractive in their brevity for both theoretical and practical reasons, monocausal explanations of IMF program dynamics—as of most other complex political phenomena—run the inevitable risk of doing violence to reality as soon as their theoretical predictions are exported beyond the original set of cases. Obviously, monocausal claims can be justified when trying to explain empirical outcomes in a single case or a small set of similar cases; thus, for example, Slovakia's rocky relationship with the IMF in the mid-1990s can be explained rather convincingly by the rhetorical and ideological tensions between Mečiar's nationalist-populist discourse and the narrow constraints of IMF and Western conditionality during the heyday of the Washington Consensus. The importance of partisan politics in the Slovak case is emphasized not just by the suggestive rhetorical war between the two sides but also by the fact that during the six-month interregnum in 1994, the first political initiative of the reformist Moravcik government was to initiate and implement an IMF program that was then promptly derailed upon Mečiar's return to power later that year despite negligible changes in the economic and institutional parameters affecting IMF programs.

On the other hand, the theoretical "mileage" we get from monocausal explanations depends to a large extent on the validity of the implicit ceteris paribus assumption underlying such claims, and unfortunately—at least for social scientists—all other things are rarely equal, especially when we compare cases across time and space. Consider the cases of Peru and Argentina, whose governments both employed confrontational rhetoric and policies toward the IMF in the mid-1980s but with radically different consequences. As discussed in chapter 4, the dramatic change in Peru's relationship with the IMF and Western creditors after 1985 can be largely explained as the inevitable result of Alan Garcia's confrontational rhetoric against the international financial establishment, and particularly the

IMF. The problem with this explanation is that Argentina's rhetoric during the 1984–85 period was hardly more accommodating but did not result in a similarly sharp deterioration of its relationship with the IMF. One possible explanation for these different outcomes is that Argentina's size and the timing of its confrontational tactics resulted in different payoffs for Western lenders whose interests were seriously threatened by a possible Argentine default, especially in the context of the precarious financial position of Western banks prior to 1985. Meanwhile, Peru's default was much less threatening not only because of the smaller overall size of its debt but also because by mid-1986 the worst of the debt crisis was over at least from the point of view of the commercial banks. At that point the importance of the demonstration effect of the Peruvian case outweighed the direct financial losses and resulted in a more uncompromising attitude by the IMF and the West. This comparison between Argentina and Peru does not, however, imply that ideological confrontations were irrelevant in the context of the debt crisis, but that their effect on a country's relationship with the IMF was mediated by the country's systemic importance and by the timing of these conflicts.

At the other extreme of the methodological spectrum, one can argue that since no two IMF programs are exactly alike, any attempt to go beyond "thick descriptions" of individual program instances is likely to do injustice to the rich social and political context in which these programs unfold. While detailed case studies are obviously important for both generating and testing theoretical claims, as well as for substantiating the mechanisms underlying the broad correlations across cases, in this book I have proceeded from the methodological belief that deductive theorizing and broad cross-country and cross-regional comparisons are important complements for case-specific empirical knowledge in driving our understanding of social science phenomena. Therefore, I have proposed a theoretical framework that is at once sufficiently comprehensive to capture the key drivers of IMF programs, flexible enough to accommodate causal variation across cases and case clusters, and tractable enough to produce reasonably specific and testable empirical hypotheses.

The theoretical model developed in chapter 2 (and formalized in the appendix) captures the variety of political and economic considerations that influence the decisions of the program country government and the IMF. The government tries to balance its *partisan policy preferences* with the *financial considerations* inherent in IMF programs subject to the *political constraint* of having to placate domestic opposition to economic reforms. The IMF also attempts to pursue a number of potentially conflicting objectives: First, as a financial institution that cares about being repaid, the Fund has an incentive to lend only to countries pursuing policies conducive to the timely repayment of loans. Second, given its role as an international lender of last resort the IMF is expected to be more willing to lend to countries facing serious crises, particularly if the size of the country in crisis poses a credible threat to international financial stability. And, finally, the Fund may deviate from the technocratic principles above in order to accommodate the strategic geopolitical goal of its largest contributors (primarily the United States and its Western European allies).

Testing the Model: Cross-Country Statistical Tests and Case Comparisons

In the interest of ensuring causal homogeneity, the statistical tests in chapters 3, 5 and 7 were executed separately for the two regions and time periods. As discussed in more detail in the introduction, this decision was justified by the important changes in the international economic environment, the differences in IMF conditionality, the variation in the nature of the economic adjustment task facing developing countries and the differences in the domestic political setting in which IMF programs unfolded. The variation in some of the crucial parameters affecting IMF program dynamics in the two regions questions the assumption of causal homogeneity that would have to be fulfilled in order to justify "lumping together" the cases of the two regions into one statistical model. Put differently, rather than assuming uniform IMF intervention patterns in the developing world over two decades, the current analysis has addressed the more specific question of how the political dynamics of IMF programs in Latin America during the 1980s have differed from the interventions in the former communist countries (and Latin America) during the 1990s. Of course, such an approach does not preclude the possibility that some factors may have played very similar roles across regions and time periods. Indeed, the tests for two regions confirmed not only the overall importance of external financial need in driving program initiation and compliance but also the interesting interaction between crisis intensity and a country's economic importance, which suggests the persistence in the Fund's differential treatment of countries whose economic difficulties could destabilize the global economy.

On the other hand, for some of the other drivers of IMF programs, the statistical results differed significantly across the two IMF program clusters; whereas in Latin America, during the 1980s, domestic economic crises (such as recession or inflation) persuaded only rightist governments (but not their leftist counterparts) of the necessity of IMF program initiation, in the former Soviet bloc inflationary and recessionary crises made all governments more likely to enter IMF agreements, and the effect was stronger for ex-communist and nationalist/populist governing parties.

These findings suggest a different political logic of crisis-driven economic reforms in the two episodes, and thereby illustrate the methodological advantage of systematic cross-regional and cross-temporal comparisons for addressing international and domestic political economy questions.

While the cross-national statistical tests for the three episodes of IMF programs provided substantial empirical support for the changing nature of the interaction between international and domestic politics in the two regions and time periods, the case studies of the trajectory of four Latin American and four Eastern European countries in chapters 4, 6, and 7 complemented these broad cross-national trends in several different ways. First, the cases painted a more detailed and nuanced picture of the causal mechanisms underlying the correlational patterns established by the statistical tests. For example, the divergent trajectories of post-1997 economic reforms in Romania and Bulgaria reveal an interesting path-dependent causal mechanism whereby the deeper initial economic crisis in Bulgaria contributed to a more decisive electoral victory of neoliberal reformers and ultimately ensured the greater political viability of IMF-style reforms in Bulgaria compared to Romania.

Second, the case studies have helped identify important aspects of the political economy of IMF programs, which do not lend themselves to being analyzed statistically, either because the phenomena are not easy quantifiable or because sufficient data is not available for cross-country regressions. One prominent example in this respect was the important role of the relationship between Latin American governments and labor and business organizations during the 1980s. Thus, the tense relationship with the labor unions and the mutual distrust that prevailed in the relationships with the business sector played a key role in the failure of reform efforts by the Siles and Alfonsín governments, whereas Paz's ability to marginalize the unions and co-opt business support significantly eased the implementation of reforms. Another instance where the case comparisons provided new theoretical insights, which an exclusive reliance on statistical testing would have been missed, was the role of corruption and poverty in the eventual decline of the neoliberal consensus in Latin America in the 1990s. Thus, while the coverage of poverty and corruption data is insufficient to allow for systematic statistical tests, Chile's superior performance in combating corruption and poverty during the 1990s compared to the significant shortcomings of neighboring neoliberal governments in Argentina, Bolivia, and Peru helps account for the greater legitimacy and continuity of neoliberal economic policies in Chile even after the end of the international lending boom of the 1990s.

Finally, the case studies revealed a number of factors that greatly affected the trajectories of IMF programs and neoliberal reforms in individual or small groups of countries but whose significance at the broader regional level would have been negligible and therefore hard to detect statistically. Examples in this respect include the effects of the war on drugs, which have alternatively facilitated and complicated the relations of successive Bolivian and Peruvian governments with the United States (and, implicitly, with international financial institutions) and Moldova's need to secure Western political support in its attempts to counter Russian threats to its independence and territorial integrity. Besides underscoring the multiplicity of IMF program drivers, such country-specific factors may at times reveal crucial facets of IMF conditionality in the developing world, such as the potential for smaller countries such as Bolivia after 1985 and Moldova in the mid-1990s (as well as to some extent Chile in the 1980s and Bulgaria in the late 1990s) to secure preferential IMF treatment by fulfilling the important political role of neoliberal reform showcases.

Interpreting the Empirical Evidence: Comparative Assessments and Policy Implications

Rather than providing an extensive review of the book's empirical findings, in this final section I emphasize several key themes that have emerged from the preceding analysis. In doing so, I discuss the theoretical contributions of the book to a number of academic debates in domestic and international political economy, as well as the policy implications of these findings for the design of more politically feasible IMF programs in the future.

Financial Need, Dependence, and Adjustment: Developing Country Strategies on the International Stage

One of the most consistent empirical regularities emerging from this book is the importance of external financial need as a driver of IMF program initiation and implementation. Despite regional and temporal variations in the predominant nature of financial dependence—in Latin America, debt service burden was crucial, whereas in Eastern Europe low levels of international reserves played a more important role—there can be little doubt that most governments in the two regions entered IMF programs in response to external financial constraints. However, these effects were significantly weaker in Latin America during the 1990s, where countries entered IMF programs less in response to immediate financial crises than to facilitate access to international financial markets.

Though countries occasionally avoided IMF programs even in situations of extreme financial need, the Peruvian case after 1985 demonstrates the extremely high economic costs of such resistance, given the Fund's importance not only as source of scarce direct funding but also as a gatekeeper for many other potential credit sources, including the World Bank and bilateral and private-sector lending. Since few developing countries were (or are) economically or politically important enough to pose a significant unilateral threat to Western interests, and because collective action problems and Western pressures have undermined developing countries' efforts to form a credible interest coalition, individual governments have generally suffered from an important power imbalance in their negotiations with the IMF. Therefore, the domestic social concerns and political priorities of program countries have generally been of secondary importance in the design of IMF programs compared to the systemic economic and political concerns of the Fund's largest members and the theoretical tenets of the economic orthodoxy prevailing within the IMF at a given point in time.

Nevertheless, the empirical evidence in this book suggests that even among developing countries, the relationship of individual countries with the IMF can vary significantly for several reasons. First, in line with earlier findings (Thacker 1999, Barro and Lee 2002, Oatley and Yackee 2004, Dreher and Jensen 2006), I found empirical evidence that Western geopolitical allies and important trading partners received preferential treatment from the IMF. However, such narrowly motivated deviations from technocratic lending practices were largely limited to IMF interventions in Eastern Europe, where Western concerns with the region's geopolitical and economic reorientation sometimes overshadowed technocratic and systemic priorities. However, the more modest and statistically inconclusive evidence of narrow preferential treatment in Latin America (in both the 1980s and the 1990s) suggests that the misuse of IMF lending by its largest shareholders is not as systematic and widespread as earlier studies have suggested.

The importance of the broader regional and international context is also apparent with respect to the second reason why certain developing countries may receive preferential treatment during IMF program negotiations. As discussed in chapter 2, unlike earlier works, this book has differentiated between the narrow "realist" deviations from technocratic lending discussed above and the preferential treatment reserved for countries whose systemic importance may affect international economic stability. When such "too-big-to-fail" countries experience severe economic crises, preferential treatment by the IMF may actually be justifiable on the basis of the Fund's institutional mission to promote international financial stability and the orderly expansion of global trade. The salience of such systemic considerations depends not only on the interaction between a given country's economic size and crisis severity but also on the relative regional and global economic health at a certain point in time. In line with these expectations, the evidence for systemically based preferential treatment was by far the most consistent during the Latin American debt crisis, where Western concerns about a widespread default by developing country debtors were reflected in preferential treatment of large debtors with respect to IMF program initiation, loan size, and compliance records. Moreover, in line with systemic stability predictions, such preferential treatment during the debt crisis was limited to extreme crisis situations, such as crushing debt-service burdens and low foreign-reserve levels. By contrast during the financial boom of the 1990s the lower prominence of systemic threats was reflected in the different IMF program dynamics: In the context of the complicated post-communist transition in Eastern Europe, where the crises of individual countries could credibly threaten regional (but probably not global) economic stability, systemic concerns appear to have affected program initiation but not loan size and compliance patterns. Meanwhile in Latin America during the 1990s, the region's much more stable economic situation is reflected in the much weaker evidence of systemic preferential treatment during both initiation and implementation.

These statistical patterns are confirmed by the case evidence presented in chapter 4: Western concerns about a possible Argentine debt default explain the Fund's willingness to "put up" with Argentina's defiant stance in 1984 and early 1985, and then to support an economic stabilization plan whose heterodox emphasis on price and wage controls deviated in important ways from IMF orthodoxy. Meanwhile, Peru's more marginal international economic role resulted in a more inflexible IMF negotiating position, despite the cooperative attitude of the Belaúnde government, and eventually contributed to the country's complete international isolation after Alan Garcia adopted a more confrontational stance toward the IMF and Western banks. The comparison between Argentina and Bolivia, however, reveals a different facet of the relative costs and benefits of size in the context of the Latin American debt crisis: Whereas Argentina "paid" for its relative domestic economic-policy freedom by receiving relatively few concessions in terms of debt forgiveness (due to the higher cost of such measures for Western creditors), the Bolivian reformers were able to use their strict domestic adherence to economic orthodoxy and the small overall size of the country's foreign debt to obtain the most generous debt renegotiation in the region. Even more remarkably, Bolivia was allowed to get away with a complete moratorium on its foreign debt service during the early and crucial period of its reforms, whereas Peru had to pay a steep price for its decision to limit the debt-service payments to 10% of exports during the same period.

The Fund's preferential treatment of Bolivia during this period emphasizes not only the importance of rhetorical nuances in the charged political context of the debt crisis but also reveals a possible strategy for marginal countries to receive preferential treatment in their relations with the IMF. Due to the high political costs of IMF compliance for many governments, the Fund occasionally needs to be able to point to obvious success stories in order to counter criticisms and to illustrate the benefits of compliance. Elements of this "showcase phenomenon" are also reflected in the concessions Chile received during the 1980s, in the generous terms of Poland's debt renegotiation in conjunction with its IMF-supported shock therapy in 1990, in Moldova's temporary preferential status as a model post-Soviet reformer, and in Bulgaria's treatment during its successful reform turnaround after 1997. With the partial exception of Chile, in all of these cases preferential treatment did not mean a relaxation of IMF conditionality (since such an action would have diluted the "educational value" of the example). However, the showcase reformers received more generous financial incentives both through direct IMF funding and through successful coordination with other private and official lenders. While such examples provide neither a generalizable blueprint (considering the diminishing marginal utility of such showcase examples) nor a recipe for domestic political success (given that none of the governments in the showcase countries actually gained reelection), they nevertheless suggest a way in which marginal developing countries can "play the system" and make the best of their otherwise limited policy options.

Aside from the significant implications of a country's economic and political importance, the relative payoffs of different country strategies for dealing with the IMF also depended on their relative timing. Thus, whereas the Peruvian and Chilean experiences of the early 1980s illustrate the steep economic and political costs of adherence to IMF orthodoxy, the Bolivian post-1985 experience reveals the significantly higher rewards of domestic economic orthodoxy during the second half of the 1980s as Western priorities shifted from saving the commercial banks to promoting neoliberal reforms in the developing world. Similarly, the much higher international price exacted by Garcia's confrontational rhetoric toward the West and the IMF from 1986 to 1989 compared to the negligible repercussions of Argentina's resistance from 1983 to 1985 were arguably due not only to size differences but also to the fact that prior to 1985 the real possibility of a debtors cartel could have seriously undermined Western commercial banks, whereas after 1985 such a scenario became highly unlikely. Finally, the steep economic costs of Mečiar's populist rhetoric in the mid-1990s, despite the country's prudent fiscal and monetary policies, suggest that IMF and Western tolerance for deviations from neoliberalism had further declined after the 1980s at least as far as economic and politically marginal countries were concerned.

Domestic Economic Crisis and Political Responses

Despite the undeniable importance of systemic factors in driving the nature of IMF conditionality in the two regions, the crises experienced by most IMF program candidates had important and often predominantly domestic roots. Particularly for the transition economies, there can be little doubt that the underlying domestic economic imbalances would have required comprehensive social and economic reform programs even in the absence of liquidity concerns and IMF policy pressures. At the outset of the two main crises discussed in this book, the traditional economic models in the two regions—ISI-based state capitalism in Latin America and centralized command economies in the Soviet bloc—showed important symptoms of exhaustion.[5] However, these economic problems did not create an overnight neoliberal reform consensus, especially in the context in which influential economic and political actors had a vested interest in the preservation of the status quo. Moreover, many of the economic reforms promoted by the IMF—particularly expenditure cuts, price and trade liberalization, and industrial restructuring—entailed important short-term costs for large segments of the population in exchange for uncertain future benefits. In view of these important political obstacles, how can we explain the sweeping reforms implemented in many countries of the two regions during the time periods discussed in this book?

One potential explanation—Western imposition via IMF conditionality—is useful in explaining the similarity of many reform blueprints but it misses many important cross-country and cross-temporal variations in both the initiation and implementation of IMF-style reforms in the two regions. A more promising explanatory alternative—advanced by a number of studies on the comparative political economy of reforms (Haggard and Kaufman 1995, Remmer 1998)—is the importance of the depth of the initial economic crisis, which can help reduce resistance to reforms and thereby facilitate reform initiation. Indeed, the statistical tests presented in chapter 5 confirm that—especially among the transition economies, where domestic considerations trumped international pressures—inflationary crises and recessions were associated with higher likelihoods

---

[5] In Latin America these symptoms included a dramatic slowdown in economic growth by the late 1970s, as well as rising inflationary pressures, as the large fiscal deficits could not be financed through external borrowing after the debut of the debt crisis. In Eastern Europe and the Soviet Union, growth had also slowed down significantly during the 1980s, and economic problems were compounded by shortages, repressed inflation, and declining living standards (Kornai 1992, Janos 2000).

of IMF program initiation and implementation even controlling for other potential domestic or international political and economic factors.

However, both the statistical results and the case-study evidence presented in this book suggest some important qualifications of the crisis hypothesis. From a political point of view—and not unlike the international crisis dynamics discussed earlier—domestic crises were at least to a certain extent "in the eye of the beholder." Due to the complex and often controversial nature of the determinants of economic crisis, the causes and even the severity of a given crisis were open to different interpretations. A reform consensus does not emerge through some functionalist miracle from the rubble of the economic crisis. Instead the catalytic effects of economic crisis are mediated by the ideological inclinations and partisan ties of key political players.

The specific patterns of partisan political mediation reflect both the international incentives and the domestic structural and institutional characteristics in which a given economic crisis unfolds. During the Latin American debt crisis, which took place in the ideologically polarized context of the final Cold War decade and pitted the interests of creditors and debtors against each other in a zero-sum fashion, domestic economic crises triggered IMF-backed adjustment efforts from right governments but not from their leftist counterparts and resulted in crisis-driven *partisan policy divergence*. By contrast, the international financial boom of the 1990s and the ideological unipolarity of the Washington Consensus produced very different partisan responses to domestic economic crises. On one hand the statistical findings and the experience of Romania and Bulgaria in the mid-1990s suggest that in low-crisis situations ex-communists were less likely to promote IMF-style reforms than their center-right counterparts, thereby confirming Frye's (2002) argument about postcommunist policy polarization. On the other hand, in the face of severe domestic crises, leftist governments abandoned their reluctance toward IMF-style economic policies, and therefore economic crises triggered *partisan policy convergence* in Eastern Europe during the 1990s. During the 1990s, partisan dynamics changed even in Latin America, as illustrated by the crisis-driven policy U-turns of Menem and Fujimori and by the statistical evidence of partisan policy convergence in the face of recessionary and liquidity crises. While the latent cross-regional differences in the strength of organized labor and societal mobilization played a modest role during the "roaring 1990s," the recent left turn of Latin America compared to the neoliberal continuity in Eastern Europe suggests that dormant social and political cleavages can be reactivated once international economic and political incentives are no longer as unequivocally conducive to neoliberalism.

The case studies reveal some of the political mechanisms underlying the complicated path from economic crisis to successful reform initiation and implementation. First, the economic crisis has to be sufficiently intense and affect a broad enough range of people that the continuation of the status quo policies would be considered undesirable by the majority of relevant political actors. In this respect, extreme stagflationary episodes—such as the ones experienced by Bolivia in 1985, Argentina in 1989, and to a lesser extent Bulgaria in 1997, have the most far-reaching social consequences and are therefore ideally suited as starting points for the dramatic reorientation of a given country's political economy trajectory. The least favorable crisis scenario is probably the one characterized—as in Romania in early 1997 and to a certain extent in Bolivia in 1982 and Argentina in 1983—by important structural weaknesses (near bankrupt banking systems, looming fiscal deficits), whose full effect on the real economy has not yet "hit" at the time when the political opportunity for initiating reforms—usually an electoral victory—presents itself. Under such circumstances, would-be reformers have a much more difficult time making a convincing argument that the bitter medicine of neoliberal reforms is the only plausible cure for the country's economic illness. Instead, as happened in Romania, reformers get blamed for the cumulative woes of the inherited economic crisis and the painful neoliberal "treatment." These patterns are confirmed by the statistical findings that inflationary and recessionary crises are more conducive to the initiation of IMF-style reforms than fiscal deficits, whose lower visibility makes them unlikely rallying points for reform coalitions.

Beyond the intensity of the preceding economic crisis, a crucial element for the emergence of a crisis-born reform consensus is the willingness and ability of a political leader or party to galvanize public support in favor of reforms through the skillful use of crisis rhetoric in the period immediately preceding and following the announcement of economic reforms. As several of the case studies indicate, such an action has a number of prerequisites: First, as Alfonsín's overoptimism in late 1983 suggests, the political leaders have to recognize the severity of the crisis. Second, unlike Garcia in post-1985 Peru and (to a lesser extent) the Moldovan communists in 2001, political leaders have to diagnose the crisis as driven by domestic economic and political problems rather than Western imperialism, and they have to consider IMF-style economic policies as an appropriate remedy for their economic problems. This point is further reinforced by the statistical findings that recessions were more likely to trigger IMF programs in Eastern Europe and Latin America during the 1990s than in Latin America during the 1980s, which reflects the greater tension between IMF policy prescriptions and growth during the debt crisis than during the boom of the 1990s. Finally, judging by the failed reform efforts of the Bolivian government in late 1984, the Alfonsín administration in 1988, and the Bulgarian socialists in late 1996, political leaders need sufficient domestic and international credibility to be able to take advantage of crisis situations in launching IMF-style reforms.

While the skillful exploitation of crisis rhetoric usually sufficed to secure political support for the initial launch of economic reforms—particularly in the political honeymoon period of newly elected democratic governments—the crucial task of ensuring the long-term political viability of reform programs turned out to be considerably more complicated. After all, Belaúnde in 1980, Alfonsín in late 1985, the Romanian reformers in 1997, and their Moldovan counterparts in 1998 all had (what at that time appeared to be) a solid political mandate for economic reforms, only to watch this "consensus" evaporate in subsequent years as the memories of the initial crisis faded in comparison to the more immediate social costs of economic reforms.

Judging by the experience of the more resilient reformers discussed in this book—Chile, Bulgaria, and (for almost two decades) Bolivia—the key ingredient facilitating the continuation of reforms beyond the initial honeymoon period was the creation of durable political coalitions in support of the government's economic policies and concerted actions to shift the long-term balance of political power in society in favor of neoliberal reformers. Whereas the "Chilean model" of the 1980s—based on insulated technocratic decision-making in conjunction with repressive measures against leftist parties and labor unions and combined with the co-optation of the domestic business sector—has traditionally received the most attention in the literature, the experiences of post-1985 Bolivia, post-1997 Bulgaria, and post-1990 Chile suggest a number of interesting—and more palatable—functional political equivalents in a more democratic setting. Having failed to secure a parliamentary majority in the 1985 connections, the Paz government initiated a patronage-based political pact with the largest parliamentary opposition party, thereby avoiding serious legislative challenges to the government's economic reform agenda. At the societal level the Bolivian government combined the use of moderate repression and selective incentives in a successful bid to reduce the political power of the militant labor movement, while at the same time gaining business support without subordinating economic policy to special-interest pressures.[6] The Bulgarian government managed to avoid repression altogether, partly because it faced a much less militant labor

---

[6] As discussed in chapter 7, however, the post-1985 Bolivian neoliberal "model" started to show signs of exhaustion amid rising anti-market protests in the late 1990s and came to an official end following the decisive electoral victory of Evo Morales in the December 2005 presidential contest.

movement and popular sector and partly because of its ability to use its parliamentary strength and the weakness of its largely compromised political opponents to create quasi-consultative procedures that greatly improved the legitimacy of economic reforms. Moreover, Bulgaria's adoption of a Currency Board under the "national unity" government prior to the 1997 elections, effectively allowed the Bulgarian government to counter redistributive pressures by pointing to the prohibitive costs of abandoning the Currency Board. Finally, the continuity of liberal economic policies in democratic Chile after 1990 was the result of a mix of solid economic performance, clean government, and greater concern for reform losers by successive center-left governments. Combined with the relative organizational weakness of reform opponents, this centrist approach created a political environment in which market-oriented economic policies were democratically feasible in the long term, even in the absence of severe economic crisis or external pressures.

Democracy and IMF-Style Economic Reforms

This book also contributes to what can in many respects be considered the most important political economy debate of the last two decades: the relationship between democracy and neoliberal economic reforms in the developing world. Rather than proposing a straightforward "iron law" relationship between the two, this book has shown that the compatibility of democratic politics and neoliberal economics depends on context-specific international and domestic political considerations. The three clusters of IMF programs discussed in this book reveal three different correlational patterns between democracy and program compliance. During the Latin American debt crisis, the high social costs of IMF-promoted austerity programs, combined with active resistance from highly mobilized labor unions and populations, created important tensions between governments' respect for democratic principles and their ability to implement IMF-style reforms. In some instances—such as that of Peru under Belaúnde and Argentina under Alfonsín—external economic adjustment was eventually subordinated to the preservation of democracy, whereas in other situations, such as Bolivia under Paz, democratically elected governments resorted to repressive measures in their reform implementation efforts. By comparison, for Eastern Europe in the 1990s, both the statistical results and the prolonged compliance with IMF conditionality by democratic governments in Moldova and Bulgaria suggest that democratic governments actually had an advantage over their authoritarian counterparts in implementing IMF-supported economic reforms. Finally, in Latin America during the 1990s, the initiation and implementation of IMF-style reforms was largely unrelated to regime type, but the widespread coexistence of economic and political liberalism suggests a significant reversal of the serious tensions between the two during the 1980s.

These different base-line effects of democracy can be traced to the different nature of IMF programs in the two regions: Whereas Latin American IMF programs in the 1980s were largely perceived as Western-imposed attempts to save the troubled Western commercial banks, in the post-communist transition, the IMF played more of a supporting and legitimizing role for domestic reform initiatives. The important interregional differences in the relative weight of domestic and external determinants of program initiation may explain why, even though IMF-style reforms were hardly popular among Eastern Europeans, IMF programs nevertheless met with considerably less open hostility than in Latin America during the debt crisis, where strikes and riots were a frequent response to IMF-imposed austerity measures.

The remarkable coexistence of democratic politics and neoliberal economic reforms in both Eastern Europe and Latin America during the 1990s, does not, however, necessarily imply that economic and political liberalism were mutually reinforcing: Neither the Bulgarian nor the Moldovan reformers were subsequently reelected, whereas in Romania, IMF-supported reforms failed at least in part due to the inability of a weak democratic government to overcome political opposition at the parliamentary and societal level. Similarly, many economic reform measures were enacted through methods that circumvented the democratic political process, such as emergency ordinances and decrees in Romania and Russia, or backstage political deals in Argentina and Bolivia.

Instead, the analysis suggests that the greater compatibility of neoliberalism and democracy in the 1990s compared to the 1980s may be due to a several factors. First, IMF programs during the 1990s arguably entailed less dramatic social costs due to the reduced emphasis on unpopular fiscal expenditure cuts, partly in response to criticisms about the Fund's socially insensitive handling of the Latin American debt crisis and partly because debt-service payments imposed smaller burdens on government budgets. Second, compliance with Western conditionality (including IMF interventions) entailed greater benefits during the economic boom of the 1990s than during the Latin American debt crisis, when the emphasis on debt repayments led to a zero-sum relationship between debtor and lender interests in the region. Moreover, the more consistent Western emphasis on democracy as a precondition to economic integration benefits in the 1990s (especially but not exclusively in the context of European integration) meant that governments had stronger incentives to pursue economic and political liberalism simultaneously. Finally, the weakness of labor unions and the political apathy of the general public reduced the scope of active popular resistance to painful reform measures and thereby mostly spared Eastern European democratic governments the dilemma faced by their Latin American counterparts of having to choose between the continuation of economic reforms and the preservation of basic democratic rights. While this trend may have contributed to a shallower version of democracy in the 1990s in both Latin America (Kurtz 2004, Weyland 2002) and Eastern Europe (Innes 2002), it nonetheless facilitated the coexistence of electoral democracy and neoliberal economics even in poor countries such as Moldova and Bolivia.

Policy Implications

Rather than uncovering a foolproof reform recipe for developing countries, the analysis has illustrated the delicate political balance underlying the initiation and implementation of IMF-style reforms. The case studies from the two regions confirm that—with a few notable exceptions—most developing country governments eventually respond to the combination of international pressures and external and domestic economic crises by initiating economic reforms in the context of IMF programs. However, the weak compliance record of many programs continues to be a serious problem in many developing countries. Therefore, this final section draws upon the analysis in this book to identify a number of policy implications for a more effective political approach to IMF conditionality. Such an approach may contribute to the design of more politically feasible IMF programs and therefore reduce the incidence of program breakdowns, partial reforms, and policy reversals that have plagued many developing countries in the last two decades.

Given the Fund's delicate political position as a mediator between developing countries on one hand and international financial markets and advanced industrial democracies on the other, the legitimacy and effectiveness of IMF interventions hinges to a large extent on the credibility of the Fund's claim of technocratic impartiality. In situations where the IMF is widely regarded as privileging Western economic interests over those of developing countries—as happened most prominently during the Latin American debt crisis—IMF programs are likely to trigger popular resistance, partisan polarization, and ultimately halfhearted implementation. The loss of legitimacy is likely to be even greater when IMF lending reflects narrow, politically motivated favoritism toward Western allies in the two regions, as such actions arguably undermine the effectiveness of conditionality, not only (as Stone 2002 demonstrates) in the privileged countries but also elsewhere in the developing world, by reinforcing the stereotypical view of the IMF as a tool for Western political and economic interests. Therefore, it would be important to curb the practice of using "soft conditionality" IMF loans as a way to reward strategic Western allies. Such a practice is not only an inefficient use of scarce IMF resources but significantly complicates the Fund's delicate political mission in the developing world, especially given the fundamental legitimacy deficit inherent in the under-representation of developing-country interests in IMF governance structures (Birdsall 2005).

An alternative venue for improving the effectiveness of IMF programs is to increase the financial rewards of compliance. Since the Fund's direct lending is unlikely to increase sufficiently in the foreseeable future to provide benefits commensurate with the policy adjustments mandated by IMF conditionality, the effectiveness of Fund interventions hinges on its ability to mobilize additional funding from third-party lenders. As illustrated by the Moldovan case, one way to achieve this is through close coordination in the lending decisions of various bilateral and multilateral official lenders, which can greatly enhance the financial incentives for compliance. Alternatively, the Fund's approval of a country's economic policies could unlock significant private funding; but for such multiplier effects to function properly, the program country must be at least reasonably attractive to foreign investors and the Fund's signals must be sufficiently credible. The IMF's credibility and effectiveness in this respect largely depend on the willingness of large IMF shareholder countries to abstain from using the Fund for narrow economic and geopolitical purposes.

Rather than focusing exclusively on "fixing the IMF," analysts and policy makers intent on improving the dynamics and consequences of IMF programs should pay closer attention to the domestic politics of IMF-style reforms. As the analysis in this book has demonstrated, the success of most IMF programs ultimately hinges on the domestic constellations of economic and political interests, power relations, and institutional arrangements. To the extent that neoliberal reforms in a democratic context succeeded in any but the most developed countries of the two regions, the examples discussed in this book—post-1985 Bolivia, post-1990 Peru and Argentina, and post-1997 Bulgaria—were initiated by newly elected governments assuming power during a deep economic crisis and taking advantage of this crisis to build political reform coalitions. While provoking recessions and inflationary crises can hardly represent acceptable policy advice for neoliberal reformers in search of political consensus, the Bolivian and Bulgarian successes highlight the importance of taking advantage of the initial economic crisis not only in rhetorical terms but also to forge a more durable political coalition in support of economic reforms.

While—as illustrated by Argentina in the 1980s and Romania from 1997 to 2000—the importance of such coalitions is easy to ignore during the postelectoral honeymoon period, democratic governments that succumb to the temptation of insulated economic policy decision making have a much more difficult time sustaining economic reforms once their popularity is undermined by the sometimes sizable social costs of such reforms. Therefore, domestic reformers and their outside advisers would be well advised to adopt a more inclusive, consultative approach to economic decision making even if such an approach may entail some short-term delays in passing the required legislation.[7]

The statistical evidence from the two main crisis episodes has also emphasized the importance of well-functioning bureaucratic institutions for the successful initiation and implementation of IMF-style reforms, particularly in the post-communist context, where the legacy of underdeveloped state institutions was exacerbated by technically demanding structural reforms of IMF programs in the 1990s. While the Moldovan case suggests that financially motivated government commitments to IMF programs can temporarily compensate for weak bureaucratic capacity, the patterns of program initiation in both regions and of compliance during the debt crisis suggest that such state capacity deficits are particularly salient during extreme crisis situations, where less competent bureaucracies were much slower to respond. Therefore, if IMF-style neoliberal reforms are to succeed in the long run without creating inordinate social costs and political tensions, they must be accompanied by a sustained effort to build effective bureaucracies and states, which, as the last two decades have made abundantly clear, do not emerge spontaneously from the happy marriage of democracy and capitalism. The Fund's decision to establish the Poverty Reduction and Growth Facility in September 1999 in order to provide more comprehensive assistance and improve governance in its poorest members was definitely a step in the right direction. What is less clear, however, is how such institutions can be fostered, given the inadequacy of our current theoretical understanding of institution building for sustainable economic and political development (Dunning and Pop-Eleches 2005).

Finally, the analysis in this book holds a more general lesson for the design of IMF programs and of external policy conditionality more broadly: The remarkable context-specificity of economic and political dynamics of IMF programs in the three clusters of cases discussed in this book should make us extremely wary of broad generalizations about the politics of economic policy making in the developing world. Instead our attention should focus on identifying the particular constellations of political and economic factors that make sustainable economic reforms in a

---

[7] However, such an inclusive approach should not be confused with allowing special-interest groups to hijack the government's policy agenda, especially given the deleterious effects of corruption on the legitimacy of neoliberal reforms in Latin America (discussed in chapter 7).

democratic setting feasible. The country cases discussed in this book have revealed the extraordinarily delicate political balancing act required of democratic governments attempting to reconcile the conflicting demands of international financial markets and domestic political constituencies. In order to facilitate the long-term viability of such reforms, IMF conditionality should allow governments more flexibility in the timing and details of policy reforms. Even though in the short run such an approach may lead to slower reforms, the possible costs are likely to be greatly outweighed by the benefits of avoiding the disruptive effects of political failures that are usually triggered by overly ambitious targets. Finally, to the extent that the ultimate goal of reformers (in the IMF and elsewhere) is the long-term coexistence of pro-market economic policies and genuine democracy, neoliberal reformers will have to find a more effective way to ensure that the everyday lives of the world's poor are improved by these reforms in tangible ways. Otherwise, the political economy of neoliberal reforms and IMF programs will continue to fluctuate in line with international business cycles and to produce the costly political conflicts and partisan policy reversals that have been the norm in much of the developing world in recent decades.

APPENDIX

A Formal Model of IMF Program Initiation and Implementation

Model Setup

The model revolves around two main actors—the government and the IMF—who bargain over funding and policy reforms. There are two stages to the model: program initiation and program implementation. During program initiation, the government decides whether or not to approach the IMF to negotiate a program. If the government does not approach the IMF or if the two sides cannot agree on mutually acceptable program parameters, then nothing happens and both the IMF and the government get their status quo payoffs.[1] If the two sides reach an agreement, they establish a set of program parameters (M_p, q_p) consisting of a certain funding commitment M_p conditional on the fulfillment of a set of policy targets q_p. Throughout this analysis I will treat q as standing for one-dimensional policy reforms, with higher q meaning more reforms.[2] Once the program parameters are set, the game moves to the second stage—implementation.

During program implementation, the government decides on a policy target q_0, which it attempts to implement. Due to imperfect implementation, modeled as a random shock chosen by nature, the actual policy outcome q^* differs from the government's policy target. Having observed the outcome q^* of the government's policy choice (but not its intended policy target q_0), the IMF decides whether to disburse the promised funding to the government. International financial markets then react to the Fund's signal either by extending additional credit to the government (in the case of IMF approval) or by withdrawing existing credits (if the IMF withholds approval). Since the typical IMF loan is disbursed in several tranches, this game is repeated several times during the duration of a program. While I do not explicitly model this repeated-game aspect, I will discuss how tar-

---

[1] In practice the status quo payoffs are only achieved if the failed negotiations between the Fund and the potential borrower government are secret. If they are not, the country may incur audience costs, as discussed below.

[2] Of course, in reality, reforms are not one-dimensional, but including multidimensional reforms significantly complicates the model, and to a large extent we can think about IMF program bargaining as being over more or less adjustment.

get fulfillment at a given stage affects the model parameters for the next period, and implicitly the chances of future compliance.

Actors' Preferences and Utility Functions

The Government

The utility function of the program country government U^{gov} is assumed to take the same functional form throughout program initiation and implementation:

$$U^{gov} = E[-(q^* - q_{gov})^2 + \mu F - s(q^* - q_{opp})^2] \qquad (2.1)$$

where q^* stands for the implemented policy; q_{gov} and q_{opp} represent the partisan ideal points of the government and the opposition respectively; μ is a measure of financial need, which reflects how important IMF funds are for the government; F is the funding obtained in connection with the IMF program, s stands for political influence of the opposition. E () indicates that the government bases its decisions on the expected rather than actual utility, since it does not know the actual policy and program outcome due to uncertainty in policy implementation, which will be discussed below.

The government's utility function captures the three main components discussed in chapter 2. The first term, $-(q^*-q_{gov})^2$, indicates that a government's utility declines as a function of the distance between the implemented policy and its partisan ideal point (which reflects the ideal and material interests of the governing parties and their supporters). The second term, μF, implies that the government's financial considerations in evaluating IMF programs depend on the size of the expected funds (F) and on how badly the money is needed (μ). The overall funds F, which reflect not only direct IMF funding but also the financial implications of the Fund's policy signals, depend on the program status: if the country does not enter an IMF agreement, then $F = 0$; if the country enters a program but fails to comply, then $F = S_n < 0$, where S_n is the economic cost of the negative signal sent to third-party lenders by the IMF's unwillingness to disburse funding. If the country complies with IMF conditionality, then $F = M_p + S_p$, where M_p is the direct funding provided by the IMF in conjunction with the program, whereas S_p captures the positive signal of the Fund's approval of the country's policies. The third term, $-s(q^*- q_{opp})^2$, suggests that the government prefers to keep the opposition reasonably content in order to avoid domestic political challenges, and the intensity of this concerns is proportional to the intensity of political competition s. The government's decision making is also influenced by its incomplete control over the outcome of the program.

Due to this policy-making uncertainty, the implemented policy $q^* = q_0 + \theta$, where q_0 is the government's policy intention and θ is a random shock, uniformly distributed between $[-(k/2), (k/2)]$. As the degree of policy uncertainty k increases, the expected magnitude of the policy shock increases and the actual policy is more likely to deviate considerably from the government's target.

The IMF

The IMF faces slightly different utility considerations during program initiation and implementation. During *program initiation* the IMF's utility function is:

$$U^{MF} = -M_p(q_p - q^*)^2 + (\mu p_{sys} + p_{pol})M_p - \frac{j}{M_{tot} - M_p} \qquad (2.2)$$

where q_p is the program policy target, M_p represents the committed program funding; M_{tot} are the total undisbursed IMF funds available; p_{pol} stands for the political importance and p_{sys} for the systemic importance of the program country, and j is a parameter reflecting the relative "cost" to the IMF of providing funding.

The first term, $-M_p(q_p - q^*)^2$, reflects the logic of the IMF's role as a bank, which does not want to lend money to countries whose policies deviate from program targets, since this reduces the probability of timely repayment. Since defaults on IMF loans occur very infrequently, this cost can also be interpreted as the Fund's loss of credibility as a signaling device for international investors, which undermines its ability to leverage additional funding in support of its reform programs (Stone 2002). The second term, $(\mu p_{sys} + p_{pol})M_p$, captures the systemic and political objectives of IMF lending: The Fund has stronger incentives to lend to countries facing serious crises (high μ) especially when these countries are systemically important for international financial stability (high p_{sys}). Moreover, the Fund may derive utility from lending to allies of its largest Western shareholders (high p_{pol}). The final term, $-[j/(M_{tot}-M_p)]$, captures the Fund's budgetary limitations of IMF funds and implies that the Fund's generosity toward a given country is also affected by how badly those funds are needed elsewhere.

During the *implementation phase* the IMF observes the policy choice of the government q^* and decides whether to disburse the committed funds M_p for that period. At this stage the budget term is replaced[3] by the

---

[3] The exclusion of the budgetary constraint during the implementation phase is supported by Vreeland and Przeworski's (2000) findings that budget constraints are only important in explaining program initiation but not program renewal.

constraint that the disbursed amount M^* cannot exceed the total funding M_p committed by the initial letter of agreement $M^* \leq M_p$:

$$U^{IMF} = -M^* (q_p - q^*)^2 + (\mu p_{sys} + p_{pol}) M^* \qquad (2.3)$$

where the notation is the same as for expression (3) except for M^*, which represents the disbursed rather than the committed amount of funding.

Solving the Model

The game has a unique subgame perfect Nash equilibrium, characterized by the following strategies:

1. During program initiation, the IMF offers the government a set of program parameters (q_p, M_p), based on the f.o.c. of its initiation-stage utility function as defined in (2.2).
2. During program initiation, the government enters a program if and only if given the IMF's program parameter offer (q_p, M_p) there exists a policy q_{cond} so that $U^{gov} (q_{cond}) > U^{gov} (q_{SQ})$, where q_{SQ} is the policy the government would have chosen in the absence of an IMF program.
3. Once a program is in place, the government sets a policy target q_0 so as to maximize its utility function as defined in (2.1).
4. During implementation, the IMF disburses the full loan tranche M_p as long as the realized policy outcome $q^* \geq q_{min}$, where q_{min} is derived from the f.o.c. of the Fund's implementation-stage utility function in (2.3). If $q^* < q_{min}$, then the IMF withholds funding completely. Third-party lenders follow the Fund's cues and either extend additional funds S_p or withdraw existing funds S_n.

Since these strategies form a subgame perfect Nash equilibrium (from which neither party has the incentive to deviate unilaterally), the model can be solved through backward induction. Therefore, the analysis starts at the last stage of program implementation, in which the IMF decides how much of the committed funding to disburse to the program country.

The IMF's Disbursement Decision

In this part, the actors operate within the constraints of the program parameters (M_p, q_p) set during the program initiation stage. The first order condition for the IMF's utility maximization during implementation is:

$$\frac{\partial U_{\text{IMF}}}{\partial M^*} = -(q_p - q^*)^2 + \mu p_{\text{sys}} + p_{\text{pol}} = 0$$

We get two corner solutions, depending on the relationship between the deviation from program targets and the country's political importance: If $-(q_p - q^*)^2 + \mu p_{\text{sys}} + p_{\text{pol}} < 0$, then the IMF will not disburse any funds $(M^* = 0)$.

If $-(q_p - q^*)^2 + \mu p_{\text{sys}} + p_{\text{pol}} \geq 0$, then the IMF will disburse all the committed funds for the period $(M^* = M_p)$. Based on these conditions we can determine the minimum policy level, q_{min}, for which the IMF will be willing to disburse the funding:

$$q_{\text{min}} = q_p - \sqrt{\mu p_{\text{sys}} + p_{\text{pol}}}$$

At the borderline policy level (q_{min}) the IMF is indifferent between withholding and disbursing funding to the government. Notice, however that this borderline policy is lower than the initial policy conditions q_p, indicating that we would expect the IMF to tolerate small deviations from program targets, and that the extent of this tolerance increases with the country's political and systemic importance and the severity of its financial crisis.

The Government's Policy Choice during Implementation

Next, let us turn to the government's maximization task—here the government uses its knowledge of the expected course of action of the IMF to maximize its own utility subject to the constraints of the model. In a determinist world, the government could just choose to either implement q_{min} in order to obtain IMF funding at the lowest political cost, or alternatively to avoid IMF conditionality altogether and implement its status quo policy. However, as discussed above, in reality the government does not have sufficient information/capabilities to be able to set the policy at exactly the q_{min} level necessary to just make the IMF indifferent between disbursing and withholding funds. Once we introduce uncertainty about policy implementation, the government can no longer simply aim for q_{min} to minimize adjustment costs while still obtaining IMF funding since it runs the risk of losing IMF support if implementation falls short of expectations. Thus, intuitively it is easy to see the negative effects of uncertainty on the government's expected utility: Either implementation falls short $(q^* < q_{\text{min}})$ and the government receives no IMF funds despite partial reform efforts or the government implements more reforms than absolutely necessary to meet minimum IMF standards ($q^* > q_{min}$). In this case the government receives IMF funding but at a higher political cost than necessary.

To formalize this intuition, we will analyze the implications of uncertainty under the earlier assumption that the implemented policy q^* is the result of the government's policy intention q_0 and a random shock θ, so that $q^* = q_0 + \theta$. Thus, the government can set its target policy q_0, and it also knows the value of k (i.e., the extent of implementation uncertainty) but it cannot predict the actual realization of θ, which can be anywhere in the interval $[-(k/2), (k/2)]$. As long as the realized policy shock is sufficiently favorable $\theta > q_p - q_0 - \sqrt{\mu p_{sys} + p_{pol}}$, the government receives IMF funding, since the implemented policy is higher than the minimum required by the Fund $q^* = q_0 + \theta \geq q_{min}$.

The uncertainty about policy implementation affects not only the probability of IMF funding disbursement, but also the other components of the government's utility function (partisan and political competition). Thus, the expected utility of the government under uncertainty can be written as:

$$U^{gov} = E[-(q^* - q_{gov})^2] + E(\mu F) + E[-s(q^* - q_{opp})^2]$$

After some algebraic manipulation we can rewrite the government's utility function as:

$$U^{gov} = -(q_0 - q_{gov})^2 - \frac{1}{3}k^2 + \mu E(F) - s(q_0 - q_{opp})^2 - \frac{1}{3}sk^2 \qquad (2.4)$$

While the IMF's funding disbursement decision is a step-function with an abrupt breaking point at q_{min}, for the government the expected value of the funding under implementation uncertainty is a continuous function of the intended policy q_0. Based on the value of q_0 we can distinguish three intervals:

1. If $q_0 < q_p - \sqrt{\mu p_{sys} + p_{pol}} - k/2$, then the government receives no funding and incurs the cost of the negative signal S_n regardless of the realization of the policy shock θ. Based on the first-order condition for the government's utility function,[4] we find that the government's ideal policy target in the low-reform status quo case is $q_0^{LSQ} = [(q_{gov} + sq_{opp}) / (s + 1)]$. In other words, the status quo policy is a weighted sum between the government's and the opposition's preferences, and depends on the relative strength of their influence on the economic policy-making process.

Notice that under the current model setup, this situation would never occur because the government, knowing that it will not want to implement

---

[4] The f.o.c. is $([\partial U_{gov} / \partial q_0] = 0)$ where $U^{gov}(q_0) = -(q_0 - q_{gov})^2 - (1/3)(1 + s)k^2 + \mu S_n - s(q_0 - q_{opp})^2$.

the IMF program, would choose not to enter an agreement in the first place, in order to avoid the cost of the negative signal. However, in the context of a multistage game, the situation discussed here could occur in the later stages of the program: Thus, if during the first stage of the program the government complies with conditionality and receives IMF and third-party funding, we would expect that in subsequent stages its financial need would be lower ($\mu_2 < \mu_1$). This lower need would reduce the benefits of IMF funding and might induce the government to ignore IMF conditionality and instead implement the status quo policy q_0^{LSQ}. A similar effect would occur if the social costs of reforms were to radicalize the antireform opposition ($q_{opp2} < q_{opp1}$), thereby raising the political costs of reforms to the point where they outweigh the benefits of IMF funding. Finally, if a change in government occurs during an IMF program, and the new government is less reformist than its predecessor ($q_{gov2} < q_{gov1}$), then it is possible that the new government would be willing to bear the financial costs of non-compliance in order to fulfill its ideological priorities.

2. If $q_0 > q_p - \sqrt{\mu p_{sys} + p_{pol}} + (k/2)$, then the government receives funding regardless of the realization of the policy shock θ. In this case, the government's maximization task is very similar to the first case, in that the government sets $q_0^{HSQ} = [(q_{gov} + sq_{opp}) / (1 + s)]$. While the functional form of q_0 is identical to the low-reform status quo case, the implemented policy is obviously higher (i.e., more reformist), as is the government's utility (since it receives the funds associated with the IMF program).[5]

3. For the purpose of the current analysis, the most interesting scenario occurs when $q_p - \sqrt{\mu p_{sys} + p_{pol}} - (k/2) \leq q_0 \leq q_p - \sqrt{\mu p_{sys} + p_{pol}} + (k/2)$. In this interval the expected probability of funding disbursement increases with higher levels of the government's intended policy q_0. Thus, we can write the government's utility function as:

$$U_{cond}^{gov} (q_0) = -(q_0 - q_{gov})^2 - \frac{1}{3}(1+s)k^2 - s(q_0 - q_{opp})^2 + \qquad (2.5)$$

$$+ \mu \left[(M_p + S_p - S_n) \left(\frac{-q_p + q_0 + \sqrt{\mu p_{sys} + p_{pol}}}{k} \right) + \frac{1}{2}(M_p + S_p + S_n) \right]$$

Setting the first order condition $(\partial U^{gov} / \partial q_0) = 0$ and solving for q_0 we get the optimum value of the government's policy target q_0^{unc} in the uncertainty range:

$$q_0^{unc} = \frac{q^{gov} + \frac{1}{2}\mu(M_p + S_p - S_n)\frac{1}{k} + sq_{opp}}{1 + s} \qquad (2.6)$$

[5] More precisely, $U^{gov} = -(q_0 - q_{gov})^2 - (1/3)(1+s)k^2 + \mu(M_p + S_p) - s(q_0 - q_{opp})^2$.

Based on (2.6), we can analyze the factors driving the probability of program success (defined narrowly as the IMF's approval of the country's policies). The probability of compliance Pr*(comp)* can be written as:

$$\Pr(comp) = \frac{1}{2} + \frac{-q_p + \sqrt{\mu p_{sys} + p_{pol}}}{k} + \frac{q_{gov} + \frac{1}{2}\mu\,(M_p + S_p - S_n)\frac{1}{k} + sq_{opp}}{k(1+s)} \qquad (2.7)$$

The comparative statics of (2.7) can be used to derive the model's key predictions about the drivers of IMF program compliance. With respect to the financial incentives of IMF programs, the model supports the intuitive notion that compliance with IMF programs could be improved if the Fund could commit more financial resources to a given program (since $\{[\partial\Pr(comp)] / \partial M_p\} > 0$), and if third-party (official and/or private) lenders would be more responsive to IMF signals and thereby raise the indirect financing function of IMF programs and the costs of noncompliance (since $[\partial\Pr(comp)] / \partial S_p > 0$ and $[\partial\Pr(comp)] / \partial S_n > 0$).

Hypothesis 1 *Higher expected levels of direct and indirect IMF funding increase the probability of program compliance.*

Since $\{[\partial\Pr(comp)] / \partial\mu\} > 0$, greater financial need also raises the chance of compliance, both because it raises the benefit to the government of IMF funding and because it makes the IMF more lenient, given that $(\partial q_{min} / \partial\mu) < 0$. The other drivers of IMF lenience—the political and systemic importance of a given country—should also contribute to higher IMF program completion rates, $[(\partial\Pr(comp)) / \partial p_{sys}] > 0$; $[(\partial\Pr(comp)) / \partial p_{pol}] > 0$), since the IMF has a wider tolerance interval for deviations from the policy targets. Finally, since $[(\partial\Pr(comp)) / \partial\mu\partial p_{sys}] > 0$, the model also predicts that the effect of financial need should be stronger in systemically important countries and that systemic importance should matter more in crisis situations, because it is precisely this interaction of size and financial distress that has the greatest potential repercussions for international economic and political stability.

Hypothesis 2 *Higher levels of financial need by the program country raise the probability of IMF program compliance, especially in systemically important countries. Political importance also facilitates compliance but its effect does not depend on financial need.*

The expected impact of financial need on compliance is also mediated by domestic institutional factors. Thus, countries with high institutional policy uncertainty should react less resolutely to financial need while implementing IMF programs (since $[\partial \text{Pr}(comp) / \partial \mu \partial k] < 0$).

Hypothesis 3 *Higher financial need has a greater positive impact on compliance in countries with low institutionally driven policy uncertainty.*

The effects of institutionally driven uncertainty on the probability of compliance depend on the relative value of the government's policy target. Thus, if the government's policy target is sufficiently ambitious ($q_0 > q_{min} - [\mu(M_p + S_p - S_n) / 2k(1 + s)]$), then weak institutions undermine compliance with program targets ($[\partial \text{Pr}(comp) / \partial k] < 0$). On the other hand, for sufficiently modest reform efforts ($q_0 < q_{min} - [\mu(M_p + S_p - S_n) / 2k(1 + s)]$), institutionally driven policy uncertainty may actually improve the chances of IMF funding disbursement ($[\partial \text{Pr}(comp) / \partial k] < 0$). The greater the government's financial need, the more likely it is that countries are dealing with the first scenario, which means that the predominant effect of policy uncertainty on compliance is likely to be negative, particularly in situations where is financial need is high.

Hypothesis 4 *Higher institutionally driven policy uncertainty reduces the probability of IMF program implementation at least in situations where the government makes a significant reform effort due to high financial need.*

The effects of greater political competition (s) are also uneven. If the opposition is sufficiently pro-reformist compared to the government ($q_{opp} > q_{gov} - [\mu(M_p + S_p - S_n) / k]$), then higher degrees of political competition promote implementation ($[\partial \text{Pr}(comp / \partial s] > 0$). However, in the opposite partisan scenario ($q_{opp} < q_{gov} + [\mu(M_p + S_p - S_n) / k]$), more political competition undermines implementation ($[\partial \text{Pr}(comp) / \partial s] < 0$).

Hypothesis 5 *More intense political competition undermines program compliance when governments favor more reforms than the opposition, but facilitates compliance if the opposition is sufficiently more reformist than the government.*

Program Initiation

Using backward induction, we can now investigate under what conditions a government decides to enter an IMF program in the first place. To do so, the government compares the expected utility in the presence of IMF conditionality to that of its status quo policies without IMF involvement. Based on the relationship between the government's status quo policy target q_0^{SQ} and the minimum level of policy reforms q_{min} for which the IMF is willing to disburse funding, we can distinguish two broad categories of cases:

1. If $q_0^{SQ} > q_{min} + k/2$, then the government is strictly better off initiating an IMF program because it receives the benefits of IMF funding and signaling by simply pursuing its preferred status quo policy. The likelihood of this scenario can increase for several reasons: First, if the policy preferences of the main domestic political actors (q_{gov} and q_{opp}) are sufficiently pro-reform, then the domestic political process would produce policies compatible with IMF prescriptions even in the absence of conditionality. In this case, the IMF provides a bonus to a reformist government but does not actually influence the final policy choice. Nonetheless, a program may help sustain the reformist momentum past the initial stages, when political costs may lead to a reversal of reforms in the absence of the financial incentives provided by the IMF program. The other main driver of such "foolproof" IMF programs is a severe financial crisis in a systemically important country. Such a crisis creates an international imperative for IMF intervention, and thereby leads to a relaxation of conditionality (since $q_{min} = q_p - \sqrt{\mu p_{sys} + p_{pol}}$), which makes the program more attractive. Therefore, we would expect more frequent IMF programs in financially strapped countries, especially when the country question is sufficiently important in economic or political terms. However, it should be noted that for governments in this category, greater financial need or greater ideological commitment no longer affects the likelihood of program initiation, since such governments are already strictly better off entering IMF programs.

2. The theoretically more interesting scenario, however, occurs when the government's status quo policies are less reformist than the Fund's policy requirements ($q_0^{SQ} < q_{min} + k/2$). In this case the government faces a trade-off between the benefits of IMF funding and the political costs of complying with IMF conditionality. Moreover, given the uncertainty about the actually implemented policy, the government also needs to consider the possibility that despite its reform efforts it may fall short of IMF expectations and, therefore, have to bear both the political costs of partial reforms and the negative signal of a failed IMF program. Taking the parameters of the program (q_p and M_p) as exogenous, the net expected benefit of initiating an IMF program equals the difference between the expected utility of an IMF program and the expected utility of implementing status quo policies ($V = U_{cond}^{gov} - U_{sq}^{gov}$).

To derive the main theoretical predictions of the model, we can use the expression for U_{cond}^{gov} from (2.5) and the fact that $U_{sq}^{gov} = (q_0^{sq} - q_{gov})^2 - 1/3 (1 + s)k^2 - s(q_0^{sq} - q_{opp})^2$ to write V as:

$$V = -(q_0^{unc} - q_0^{sq})(q_0^{unc} + q_0^{sq} - 2q_{gov}) - s(q_0^{unc} - q_0^{sq})(q_0^{unc} + q_0^{sq} - 2q_{opp}) + \quad (28)$$

$$+ \mu \left[\frac{1}{2}(M_p + S_p - S_n) \left(\frac{-q_p + q_0^{unc} + \sqrt{\mu p_{sys} + p_{pol}}}{k} \right) + \frac{1}{2}(M_p + S_p + S_n) \right]$$

Since by definition we know that $\partial U_{cond}^{gov} / \partial U_0^{unc} = 0$ and $\partial U_{sq}^{gov} / \partial U_0^{sq} = 0$, we can apply the envelope theorem to analyze the comparative statics of (2.8). Given that $q_0^{sq} > q_p - \sqrt{\mu p_{sys} + p_{pol}} - k/2$, it is easy to see that program initiation is more likely when the direct and indirect financing potential of IMF programs is higher ($\partial V / \partial M_p > 0$, $\partial V / \partial S_p > 0$). However, whereas during program implementation, the threat of negative signals can serve as an incentive for higher compliance, in the case of initiation, higher noncompliance penalties act as deterrents for IMF programs (since $\partial V / \partial S_n > 0$).[6]

Hypothesis 6 *Program initiation is facilitated by the promise of higher direct and indirect funding but is undermined by the threat of negative IMF signals.*

With respect to other model parameters, it is easy to see that higher political and systemic importance should encourage governments to apply for IMF support ($\partial V / \partial p_{pol} > 0$, $\partial V / \partial p_{sys} > 0$), because the politically motivated leniency makes programs relatively easier to fulfill. However, we would expect the effect of systemic importance to be more pronounced for countries with high levels of financial need ($\partial V / \partial p_{sys} \partial \mu > 0$), because Western concerns about the welfare of important countries are likely to be amplified in crisis situations.

Hypothesis 7 *Systemically important countries are more likely to enter IMF programs, especially when experiencing significant financial need. Politically important countries are more likely to enter IMF program irrespective of financial need.*

Unlike its consistently positive predicted effect during implementation, more intense financial need does not necessarily increase the likelihood of IMF program initiation. Thus, the effect of monetary need μ depends on the parameters of the IMF program (M_p, q_p) and on the relative incentives offered by international financial markets (S_n, S_p). If the costs of non-implementation (S_n) are large in absolute terms compared to the implementation benefits ($M_p + S_p$), and the probability of failure is relatively high

---

[6] This is true because $q_0^{unc} \leq q_p - \sqrt{\mu p_{sys} + p_{pol}} + (k/2)$. The counterintuitive sign of the derivative is due to the fact that $S_n < 0$, i.e., stronger signals are more negative and reduce the initiation benefit and probability.

(i.e., the government's optimal policy target q_0^{unc} is significantly below the program target q_p), then it is possible that financially desperate governments may be less likely to resort to IMF programs in order to avoid the high noncompliance costs ($\partial V / \partial \mu < 0$). However, in the more likely scenario, where the financial benefits of IMF programs exceed the potential signaling costs of noncompliance, financial need should act as a catalyst for program initiation ($\partial V / \partial \mu > 0$). Moreover, the model predicts that under such circumstances, financial need matters more for systemically important countries ($\partial V / \partial p_{sys} \partial \mu > 0$) and pro-reform governments ($\partial V / \partial q_{gov} \partial \mu > 0$), but less for countries with weak institutions ($\partial V / \partial k \partial \mu < 0$).

Hypothesis 8 *Unless the likelihood and costs of failure are very high compared to the expected financial benefits, countries experiencing significant financial need are more likely to enter IMF programs, especially if they are systemically important and have pro-reform governments and low institutional policy uncertainty.*

The degree of policy uncertainty k also affects the likelihood of IMF program initiation in an uneven fashion. Thus, for governments committed to significant reform efforts ($q_0^{unc} > q_p - \sqrt{\mu p_{sys} + p_{pol}}$), policy uncertainty acts as a deterrent against program initiation ($\partial V / \partial k < 0$). This effect is likely to be exacerbated in situations of high financial need ($\partial V / \partial k \partial \mu < 0$). However, policy uncertainty may actually contribute to the proliferation of IMF programs with low likelihood of success, given that for $q_0^{unc} < q_p - \sqrt{\mu p_{sys} + p_{pol}}$ we get ($\partial V / \partial k) > 0$.

Hypothesis 9 *Higher policy uncertainty undermines IMF program initiation at least in situations where the government intends to make a significant reform effort (for ideological or financial reasons).*

With respect to the domestic political factors, it is easy to see that $\partial V / \partial q_{gov} > 0$ (because $q_0^{unc} - q_0^{sq} > 0$), which means that more reformist governments are more likely to initiate IMF programs. For domestic political constraints, the model predicts that $[\partial V] / [\partial s] < 0$ if $q_{opp} < [\mu(M_p + S_p - S_n) / 2k] + q_{gov}$, whereas when $q_{opp} > [\mu(M_p + S_p - S_n) / 2k] + q_{gov}$ we get ($\partial V / \partial s) > 0$.

Hypothesis 10 *Intense political competition reduces the likelihood of IMF program initiation unless the opposition favors significantly greater economic reforms than the government.*

It is important to remember that hypotheses 6–10 refer to governments in the conditionality zone, i.e., governments whose status quo policies in the absence of IMF financial incentives would be less reformist than what is required to ensure slippage-proof IMF policy approval ($q_0^{sq} < q_{min} +$

(1/2)). However, if enough governments in the region would implement IMF-style policies even in the absence of IMF conditionality, then it is conceivable that the direction of some of the predicted interaction effects could be reversed. Thus, hypothesis 8 predicts crisis-driven ideological policy divergence in the sense that financial need should matter more in countries with pro-reform governments. However, if pro-reform governments are largely setting IMF-style policies even in the absence of IMF pressures, then greater financial need could have a weaker impact on reformers than on their less reformist counterparts, for whom financial pressures could provide a crucial reform impetus (especially if their partisan preferences are not too intense).

This final point about the intensity of partisan preferences suggests an interesting extension of the formal model, which can help capture the idea that economic crises are filtered through the partisan preferences of domestic politicians. In the basic model, partisan policy considerations are assumed to be constant, and economic crises affect policy choices by raising the government's dependence on direct and indirect funding in conjunction with IMF programs. However, let us briefly consider the implications of allowing the intensity of partisan preferences to vary as a function of crisis intensity. One way to model this idea is to rewrite the first term of the government's utility function as $-\mu^{\lambda}(q^{*} - q_{gov})^{2}$. Notice that if $\lambda = 0$ the term reduces to the original assumption of crisis-independent partisan preference intensity $-(q^{*} - q_{gov})^{2}$. However, if $\lambda \neq 0$, then we can distinguish between two different partisan scenarios: If $\lambda > 0$ then partisan preferences are accentuated during intense economic crises, which implies that partisan policy differences between governments of different political orientations will be particularly visible during economic emergencies. If λ is sufficiently large (i.e., if partisan concerns are very salient) and if the government's policy differences q_{gov} are sufficiently far removed from the Fund's policy requirements, then it is conceivable that more intense economic crises no longer promote IMF program initiation since the economic benefits of using IMF funds to tackle the crisis are outweighed by the rising partisan political costs triggered by the economic crisis. If, however, $\lambda < 0$, then intense economic crises reduce the salience of partisan preferences, which implies that policy differences between governments of different political orientations will diminish during economic emergencies, as governments of all stripes recognize the necessity of securing IMF support to deal with the crisis.

Hypothesis 11 *Pro-reform governments should be more likely to initiate IMF programs but the salience of partisan preferences will vary as a function of crisis intensity.*

Setting the Program Parameters:
The IMF's Maximization Task

The IMF has to decide the loan size for a certain program and a set of policy targets that the government needs to meet in order to receive the funding. In reality, negotiations can and do cover both the amount of funding and the degree of conditionality. For reasons of brevity I will here discuss only the model's implications for the amount of funding attached to a given IMF program, while assuming conditionality q_p to be exogenously determined. The model can in fact be used to generate hypotheses about the factors affecting the strictness of the IMF conditionality but these predictions are quite similar in their logic to the discussion below and are omitted for space reasons.

The expected utility of the IMF during initiation can be obtained from expression (2.3), keeping in mind that the IMF does not actually observe the realized value of q^* but instead has to use the expected value of the policy realization in its calculations. However, the IMF has the advantage of being able to cut its losses during implementation, by refusing to disburse money to countries whose policies do not meet the q_{min} threshold. Thus we can write the IMF's utility as a function of the committed amount M_p and the probability of compliance $Pr(comp)$:

$$U_{IMF} = \left[- M_p \, (q_0^{unc} - q_p)^2 + \mu p_{sys} \, M_p + p_{pol} \, M_p - \frac{j}{M_{tot} - M_p} \right]$$
$$Pr(comp) + \left[- \frac{j}{M_{tot} - M_p} \right] [1 - Pr(comp)]$$

Setting the first order condition, we get:

$$\frac{\partial U_{IMF}}{\partial M_p} = -(q_0^{unc} - q_p)^2 \, Pr(comp) - M_p \, (q_0^{unc} - q_p) \frac{\mu}{k(1 + s)}$$
$$Pr(comp) - M_p \, (q_0^{unc} - q_p)^2 \frac{\mu}{2k^2(1 + s)} + (\mu p_{sys} + p_{pol}) \quad\quad (2.9)$$
$$Pr(comp) + (\mu p_{sys} + p_{pol}) \, M_p \frac{\mu}{2k^2(1 + s)} - \frac{j}{(M_{tot} - M_p)^2} = 0$$

Based on (2.9) we can determine how changes in the model components affect the optimal level of program funding. First, after rearranging the terms it is easy to see that for $q_0^{unc} < q_p - \sqrt{\mu p_{sys} + p_{pol}} = q_{min}$ we have $(\partial U_{IMF} / \partial M_p < 0)$, which yields the corner solution $M_p = 0$ implying that the IMF is not willing to commit funds to programs with very low chances of success. For $q_0^{unc} > q_p - \sqrt{\mu p_{sys} + p_{pol}} = q_{min}$ the relationship between the optimal M_p and the other variables in the model will be derived through implicit differentiation. Thus, politically and systemically more important countries should receive more generous loans relative to their size ($\partial M_p / \partial p_{pol} > 0$, $\partial M_p / \partial p_{sys} > 0$), whereas the effect of financial need on the size of the IMF loan commitments should be positive ($\partial M_p / \partial \mu > 0$), which confirms the intuition that the IMF should lend more to desperate countries, both because of the impact of such lending on global financial markets (by avoiding defaults and international contagion) and because governments facing severe crises are more likely to comply with external conditionality. With respect to the government's partisan position q_{gov}, we find that as long as we do not get a corner solution ($M_p = 0$) more reformist governments are expected to receive more generous loans ($\partial M_p / \partial q_{gov} > 0$). Within the context of this model the often cited "rightist bias" of the IMF can be explained without resorting to conspiracy theories but simply because IMF programs initiated by reformist governments are more likely to succeed ($\partial P_r(comp) / \partial q_{gov} > 0$).

BIBLIOGRAPHY

Acemoglu, Daron, and James Robinson. 2005. *Economic Origins of Dictatorship and Democracy.* New York: Cambridge University Press.

Acuña, Carlos. 1995. "Business Interests, Dictatorship and Democracy in Latin America." In *Business and Democracy in Latin America.* J. Bartell and Leigh A. Payne (eds.). Pittsburgh: University of Pittsburgh Press.

Acuña, Marcelo L. 1995. *Alfonsín y el poder económico: el fracaso de la concertación y los pactos corporativos entre 1983 y 1989.* Buenos Aires: Corregidor.

Adserà, Alicia, Carles Boix, and M. Payne. 2000. "Are You Being Served? Political Accountability and Quality of Government." *Inter-American Development Bank Research Department Working Paper* 438.

Aggarwal, Vinod K. 1996. *Debt Games: Strategic Interaction in International Debt Rescheduling.* New York: Cambridge University Press.

Alvarez R. Michael, Geoffrey Garrett, and Peter Lange. 1991. "Government Partisanship, Labor Organization, and Macroeconomic Performance." *American Political Science Review* 85:539–56.

Appel, Hillary, 2004. *A New Capitalist Order.* Pittsburgh, PA: University of Pittsburgh Press.

Armijo, Leslie Eliott, and Philippe Faucher. 2001. "We Have a Consensus: Explaining Political Support for Market Reforms in Latin America." *Latin American Politics and Society* 44(2):1–51.

Baldwin, David, ed. 1993. *Neorealism and Neoliberalism.* New York: Columbia University Press.

Barnett, Michael, and Martha Finnemore. 1999. "The Politics, Power, and Pathologies of International Organizations." *International Organization* 53(4): 699–732.

Bartell, Ernest J., and L. A. Payne. 1995. *Business and Democracy in Latin America.* Pittsburgh: University of Pittsburgh Press.

Beck, Nathaniel, Jonathan N. Katz, and Richard Tucker. 1998. "Taking Time Seriously: Time-Series-Cross-Section Analysis with a Binary Dependent Variable." *American Journal of Political Science* 42(4):1260.

Beck, Thorsten, Gregory Clarke, A. Groff, Philip Keefer, and Peter Walsh. 2000. *New Tools and New Tests in Comparative Political Economy: The Database of Political Institutions,* Washington DC: The World Bank.

Bercu, Vlad. 1997. "Dependenta economica—o sfidare la adresa societatii deschise." *Sfera Politica*—http://ziua.sfos.ro/PoliticalArena/economia.html.

Bernhard, William, and David Leblang. 1999. "Democratic Institutions and Exchange-rate Commitments." *International Organization* 53(1):71–97.

Beveridge, William, and Margaret Kelly. 1980 "Fiscal Content of Financial Programs Supported by Standby Agreements in the Upper Credit Tranches, 1969–78." *IMF Staff Papers* 27:205–49.

Bird, Graham. 1995. *IMF Lending to Developing Countries: Issues and Evidence.* London: Routledge.

Bird, Graham, Mumtaz Hussain, and Joseph P. Joyce. 2004. "Many Happy Returns? Recidivism and the IMF." *Journal of International Money and Finance* 23: 231–51.

Bird, Graham, and Timothy Orme. 1981. "An Analysis of Drawings on the IMF by Developing Countries." *World Development,* 9(6):563–568.

Birdsall, Nancy. 2005. "Why It Matters Who Runs the IMF and the World Bank." In Stephen Kosack, Gustav Ranis, and James Vreeland (eds.). *Globalization and the Nation State: The Impact of the IMF and the World Bank.* London: Routledge, 429–51.

Boix, Carles. 2000. "Partisan Governments, the International Economy, and Macroeconomic Policies in OECD Countries, 1964–93." *World Politics* 53:38–73.

———. 2003. *Democracy and Redistribution.* New York: Cambridge University.

Borzutzky, Silvia. 1987. "The Pinochet Regime: Crisis and Consolidation." In *Authoritarians and Democrats: Regime Transition in Latin America.* J. M. Malloy and M. A. Seligson (eds.). Pittsburgh: University of Pittsburgh Press.

Brady, Henry, and David Collier, eds. 2004. *Rethinking Social Inquiry: Diverse Tools, Shared Standards.* Lanham, MD: Rowman and Littlefield.

Bruno, Michael, and William Easterly. 1995. "Inflation Crisis and Long-Run Growth." National Bureau for Economic Research Working Paper WP 5209.

Buira, Ariel. 1983. "IMF Financial Programs and Conditionality." *Journal of Development Economics* 12(1/2)111–36.

Bunce, Valerie. 1995. "Comparing East and South." *Journal of Democracy* 6(3) 87–100.

———. 1998. "Regional Differences in Democratization: The East versus the South." *Post-Soviet Affairs* 14(3) 187–211.

———. 2001. "Democratization and Economic Reform." *Annual Review of Political Science* 4:43–65.

Callaghy, Thomas. 1989. "Toward State Capability and Embedded Liberalism in the Third World: Lessons for Adjustment." In J. M. Nelson (ed.). *Fragile Conditions: The Politics of Economic Adjustment,* New Brunswick, NJ: Transaction Books.

Canitrot, Adolfo. 1994. "Crisis and Transformation in the Argentine State." In William C. Smith, Carlos Acuña, and Eduardo Gamarra (eds.). *Democracy, Markets, and Structural Reform in Contemporary Latin America: Argentina, Bolivia, Brazil, Chile, and Mexico.* New Brunswick, NJ: Transaction Publishers.

Centeno, Miguel A., and Alejandro Portes. 2006. "The informal economy in the shadow of the state." In P. Fernández-Kelly (Ed) *Out of the Shadows: Political Action and the Informed Economy in Latin America,* pp. 23–48. University Park, PA: Pennsylvania State University Press.

Clark, William, U. N. Reichert, S. L. Lomas, K. L. Parker. 1998. "International and Domestic Constraints on Political Business Cycles in OECD Economies." *International Organization* 52(1):87–120.

Cojocaru, Gheorghe. 1997. "Stabilirea relatiilor Moldo-Americane si factorul militar in cadrul CSI." *Arena Politica*—available at http://ziua.sfos.ro/PoliticalArena/diplomatie.html.

Collier, Ruth Berins, and David Collier. 1991. *Shaping the Political Arena*. Princeton, NJ: Princeton University Press.

Conaghan, Catherine M., and James M. Malloy. 1994. *Unsettling Statecraft: Democracy and Neoliberalism in the Central Andes*. Pittsburgh: University of Pittsburgh Press.

Coppedge, Michael. 1997. "A Classification of Latin American Political Parties." *Kellogg Institute Working Paper 244*.

Cornelius, Peter. 1987. "The Demand for IMF Credits by Sub-Saharan African Countries." *Economics Letters* 23, 99–102.

Corsetti, Giancarlo, Bernardo Guimaraes, Nouriel Roubini. 2003. "International Lending of Last Resort and Moral Hazard: A Model of IMF's Catalytic Finance." *NBER Working Paper* No. 10125.

Cotler, Julio. 1995. "Political Parties and the Problems of Democratic Consolidation." In Scott Mainwaring and Timothy Scully (eds.). *Building Democratic Institutions: Party Systems in Latin America*. Stanford, CA: Stanford University Press.

Crowther, William. 1997. "Moldova: Caught between Nation and Empire." In Ian Bremmer and Ray Taras (eds.). *New States, New Politics: Building the Post-Soviet Nations*, 316–49. Cambridge: Cambridge University Press.

Czech News Agency National News Wire (CTK).

Daianu, Daniel. 1997. "Macro-Economic Stabilization in Post-Communist Romania." In Lavinia Stan (ed.). *Romania in Transition*. Brookfield, VT: Dartmouth Publishing Company.

———. 2000. *Incotro se indreapta fostele tari comuniste*. Iasi: Editura Polirom.

Damill, Mario, and Roberto Frenkel. 1996. "Democratic Restoration and Economic Policy: Argentina 1984–91." In Juan Antonio Morales and Gary McMahon (eds.). *Economic Policy and the Transition to Democracy: The Latin American Experience*. New York: St. Martin's Press.

David, Wilfred. 1985. *The IMF Policy Paradigm*. New York: Prager Publishers.

DeGrauwe, Paul, and Michelle Frattiani. 1984. "The Political Economy of International Lending." *Cato Journal* 4(1):147–65.

De Melo, Martha, Cevdet Denizer, Alan Gelb, and Stoyan Tenev. 1997. "Circumstance and Choice: The Role of Initial Conditions and Policies in Transition Economies." *World Bank Working Paper*.

Derksen, Wilfried. 2001. *Parties and Elections Around the World*. Available online at www.electionworld.org.

Deutsche Presse-Agentur. 1998. "IMF Chief Defends Policies, Liberalization." *Deutsche Presse-Agentur*, November 10.

Donovan, Donal. 1982. "Macroeconomic Performance and Adjustment under Fund-Supported Programs: The Experience of the Seventies." *IMF Staff Papers* 29:171–203.

Dreher, Axel, and Nathan Jensen. 2007. "Independent Actor or Agent? An Empirical Analysis of the Impact of US Interests on IMF Conditions." *Journal of Law and Economics* 50(1):105–24.

Dunning, Thad, and Grigore Pop-Eleches. 2005. "From Transplants ot Hybrids: Exploring Institutional Pathways to Growth." *Studies in Comparative International Development* 38(4)3–29.

Edwards, Martin S. 2001. "Sticking with Yes: Domestic Institutions and IMF Compliance." Paper prepared for delivery at the 2001 Annual Meeting of the American Political Science Association, San Francisco, August 30–September 2.

———. 2006. "Signalling Credibility? The IMF and Catalytic Finance." *Journal of International Relations and Development* 9:27–52.

Edwards, Sebastian. 1989. "The International Monetary Fund and the Developing Countries: A Critical Evaluation." In Karl Brunner and Allan Meltzer (eds.), *Carnegie-Rochester Conference Series and Public Policy.* Amsterdam: Elsevier Science Publishers.

———. 1995. *Crisis and Reform in Latin America: From Despair to Hope.* The World Bank. Oxford University Press.

Etchemendy, Sebastián. 2001. "Constructing Reform Coalitions: The Politics of Compensation in Argentina's Economic Liberalization." *Latin American Politics and Society* 43(3):1–35.

Etchemendy, Sebastián, and Ruth Berins Collier. 2007. "Down but Not Out: Union Resurgence and Segmented Neocorporatism in Argentina, 2003–2007." *Politics and Society* vol. 35, no. 3, 363–401.

Ffrench-Davis, Ricardo. 1999. *Entre el neoliberalismo y el crecimiento con equidad: tres décadas de política económica en Chile.* Caracas, Santiago de Chile: Dolmen Ediciones.

———. 2002. *Economic Reforms in Chile: From Dictatorship to Democracy.* Ann Arbor, MI: University of Michigan Press.

Fisher, Sharon. 1993. "The Slovak Arms Industry." *Radio Free Europe/Radio Liberty Research Report,* 24 September.

Fisher, Stanley. 1999. "On the Need for an International Lender of Last Resort." *Journal of Economic Perspectives,* v85.

Fisher, Stanley, Ratna Sahay, and Carlos Vegh. 1996. "Stabilization and Growth in Transition Economies: The Early Experience." *Journal of Economic Perspectives* v10, n2:45–66.

Franzese, Robert J. Jr. 2002a. "Electoral and Partisan Cycles in Economic Policies and Outcomes." *Annual Review of Political Science* 5:369–421.

———. 2002b. *Macroeconomic Policies of Developed Democracies.* New York: Cambridge University Press, 2002.

Frieden, Jeffrey. 1989. "Winners and Losers in the Latin American Debt Crisis: The Political Implications." In Barbara Stallings and Robert Kaufmann, *Debt and Democracy in Latin America.* Boulder, CO: Westview Press.

Frye, Timothy. 2002. "The Perils of Polarization: Economic Performance in the Postcommunist World." *World Politics* 54(3):308–37.

Gabanyi, Ute. 1996. "Moldova im Spannungsfeld zwischen Rußland, Rumenien und der Ukraine." *Bericht des BIOst,* n16.

Gamarra, Eduardo. 1994. "Crafting Political Support for Stabilization: Political Pacts and the New Economic Policy in Bolivia." In William C. Smith, Carlos Acuña, and Eduardo Gamarra (eds.). *Democracy, Markets, and Structural Reform in Contemporary Latin America: Argentina, Bolivia, Brazil, Chile, and Mexico.* New Brunswick, NJ: Transaction Publishers.

Gamarra, Eduardo, and James M. Malloy. 1995. "The Patrimonial Dynamics of Party Politics in Bolivia." In Scott Mainwaring and Timothy Scully (eds.). *Building Democratic Institutions: Party Systems in Latin America*. Stanford, CA: Stanford University Press.

Ganev, Venelin. 1997. "Bulgaria's Symphony of Hope." *Journal of Democracy* 8(4):125–40.

Garrett, Geoffrey. 1998. *Partisan Politics in the Global Economy*. Cambridge Studies in Comparative Politics. Cambridge, UK; New York: Cambridge University Press.

Gerloff, Axel. 2000. "Stylized Facts about Stabilization in Central and Eastern Europe." *International Advances in Economic Research* v6, n2:127.

Ghosh, Atish, and Steven Phillips. 1998. "Warning: Inflation May Be Harmful to Your Growth." IMF Staff Papers 45(4) 672–710.

Global Development Finance. 2005. Online edition.

Goldstein M., and P. Montiel. 1986. "Evaluating Fund Stabilization Programs with Multi-Country Data: Some Methodological Pitfalls." IMF Staff Papers 33:304–44.

Gopal Garuda, "The Distributional Effects of IMF Programs: A Cross-Country Analysis." *World Development* 28 no. 6. 2000): 1031–51.

Gould, Erica. 2003. "Money Talks: Supplementary Financiers and International Monetary Fund Conditionality." *International Organization* 57:551–86.

Gourevitch, Peter. 1978. "The Second Image Reversed: The International Sources of Domestic Politics." *International Organization* 32(4):881–912.

———. 1986. *Politics in Hard Times: Comparative Responses to International Economic Crises*. Ithaca, N.Y.: Cornell University Press.

Greene, William H. 1993. *Econometric Analysis*. New York: Maxwell Macmillan International Publishing Group.

Gregory, Ilya. 1998. "Indebted to Gazprom." *Central European*. September, v8, n7:78.

Greskovits, Bela. 1998. *The Political Economy of Protest and Patience*. Budapest: Central European University Press.

Grzymala-Busse, Anna. 2002. *Redeeming the Communist Past: The Regeneration of Communist Parties in East Central Europe*. New York: Cambridge University Press.

———. 2007. *Rebuilding Leviathan Party Competition and State Exploitation in Post-Communist Democracies*. New York: Cambridge Studies in Comparative Politics.

Gylafson, Thorvaldur. 1987. "Credit Policy and Economic Activity in Developing Countries with IMF Stabilization Programs." Princeton Studies in International Finance, n60.

Haggard, Stephan, Chung H. Lee, and Sylvia Maxfield. 1993. *The Politics of Finance in Developing Countries*. Ithaca: Cornell University Press.

Haggard, Stephan, and Robert Kaufmann, eds. 1992. *The Politics of Economic Adjustment*. Princeton: Princeton University Press.

———. 1995. The Political Economy of Democratic Transitions. Princeton, Princeton University Press.

Haggard, Stephan, and Steven Webb. 1994. "Introduction." In Haggard and Webb (eds.). *Voting for Reform: Democracy, Political Liberalization and Economic Adjustment.* Washington, DC: World Bank.

Henisz, Witold 2000. "The Institutional Environment for Economic Growth." *Economics and Politics* 12(1):1–31.

Herrera, Yoshiko M. 2005. *Imagined Economies: The Sources of Russian Regionalism.* New York: Cambridge University Press.

Hoffman, Kelly, and Miguel A. Centeno. 2003. "The Lopsided Continent: Inequality in Latin America." *Annual Review of Sociology,* 29:363–90.

Howard, Marc Morjé. 2003. *The Weakness of Civil Society in Post-Communist Europe.* New York: Cambridge University Press.

Huber, Evelyne, and John D. Stephens. 1989. "Partisan Governance, Women's Employment, and the Social Democratic Service State." *American Sociological Review* 65(3):323–42.

———. 2001. a. *Development and Crisis of the Welfare State.*
Chicago: University of Chicago Press.

Iguíñiz, Javier, Rosario Basay Vega, and Mónica Rubio. 1993. *Los ajustes: Perú 1975–1992.* Lima: Fundación Friedrich Ebert.

IMF Survey. 1990–2000.

Innes, Abby. 2002. "Party Competition in Postcommunist Europe—The Great Electoral Lottery." *Comparative Politics* 35 (1):85–104.

International Financial Statistics. 2001. CD-ROM Edition.

International Monetary Fund. 2001. a. "Conditionality in Fund-Supported Programs—Policy Issues." Policy Development and Review Department (available at www.imf.org).

———. 2001. b. "Romania: Selected Issues and Statistical Appendix." *IMF Country Report* 01/16.

———. 2004. *The IMF and Argentina, 1991–2001.* Washington, DC: International Monetary Fund, Independent Evaluation Office.

Ishihara, Yoichiro. 2005. "Quantitative Analysis of Crisis: Crisis Identification and Causality." *Policy Research Working Paper* 3958, Washington, DC: World Bank.

Ivanova, Anna, Wolfgang Mayer, Alex Mourmouras, and George Anayiotos. 2003. "What Determines the Implementation of IMF-Supported Programs?" *IMF Working Paper* 03/08.

Jacoby, Wade. 2004. *The Enlargement of the European Union and NATO: Ordering from the Menu in Central Europe.* New York: Cambridge University Press.

Janos, Andrew C. 1997. *Czechoslovakia and Yugoslavia: Ethnic Conflict and the Dissolution of Multinational States.* Berkeley: University of California Press.

———. 2000. *East Central Europe in the Modern World: The Politics of the Borderlands from Pre- to Postcommunism.* Stanford: Stanford University Press.

Johnson, Chalmers. 1987. "Political Institutions and Economic Performance: The Government Business Relationship in Japan, South Korea, and Taiwan." 136–65. In Fred C. Deyo (ed.), *The Political Economy of New Asian Industrialism.* Ithaca: Cornell University Press.

Jorge, Antonio. 1985. *External Debt and Development Strategy in Latin America.* New York: Pergamon Press.

Kahler, Miles. 1989. "International Financial Institutions and the Politics of Adjustment." In Joan Nelson (ed.). *Fragile Coalitions: The Politics of Economic Adjustment*. Oxford, UK: Transaction Publishers.

Karatnycky, Adrian, Alexander Motyl, and Boris Shor (eds.) 1998. *Nations in Transit. 1997: Civil Society, Democracy and Markets in East Central Europe and the Newly Independent States*. New Brunswick: Transaction Publishers.

Kaufman, Robert R. 1985. "Democratic and Authoritarian Responses to the Debt Issue: Argentina, Brazil, Mexico." *International Organization* 39(3):473–503.

Kaufman, Robert, and Barbara Stallings. 1989. *Debt and Democracy in the 1980s: The Latin American Experience*. In *Debt and Democracy in Latin America*, B. Stallings, R. Kaufman (eds.), 201–21. Boulder, CO: Westview.

Keohane, Robert, and Helen Milner (eds.). 1996. *Internationalization and Domestic Politics*. Cambridge, UK: Cambridge University Press.

Khan, Mohsin. 1990. "The Macro-Economic Effects of Fund-Supported Adjustment Programs." *IMF Staff Papers* 37(2).

Killick, Tony. 1995. *IMF Programmes in Developing Countries: Design and Impact*. New York: Routledge.

King, Gary, Michael Tomz, and Jason Wittenberg. 2000. "Making the Most of Statistical Analyses: Improving Interpretation and Presentation." *American Journal of Political Science* 44(2):347–61.

Klein, Hans S. 1992. *Bolivia: The Evolution of a Multi-Ethnic Society*. New York, Oxford University Press.

Knack, S. Keefer, P. 1995. "Institutions and Economic Performance: Cross-Country Tests Using Alternative Institutional Measures." *Economics and Politics* 7(3):207–27.

Kolsto, Pal. 1995. "Nation-Building in the Former USSR." *Journal of Democracy* 7:118–32.

Kopstein, Jeffrey, and David Reilly. 2000. "Geographic Diffusion and the Transformation of the Postcommunist World." *World Politics* 53(1):1–37.

Kornai, János. 1992. *The Socialist System: The Political Economy of Communism*. Oxford, UK: Oxford University Press.

Korner, Peter, Gero Mass, Thomas Siebold, Rainer Tetzlaff. 1986. *The IMF and the Debt Crisis*, translated by Paul Knight. London: Zeb Books.

Kurtz, Marcus. 2004. "The Dilemmas of Democracy in the Open Economy: Lessons from Latin America." *World Politics* 56(2):262–302.

Kurtz, Marcus J., and Andrew Barnes. 2002. "The Political Foundations of Post-Communist Regimes—Marketization, Agrarian Legacies, or International Influences." *Comparative Political Studies* 35(5):524–53.

Kurtz, Marcus, and Andrew Schrank. 2007. "Growth and Governance: Models, Measures, and Mechanisms." *Journal of Politics* 69(2):538–54.

Kwon, Hyeok Yong, and Jonas Pontusson. 2005. "The Rise and Fall of Government Partisanship: Dynamics of Social Spending in OECD Countries, 1962–2000." Unpublished manuscript.

Lake, David. 1996. "Anarchy, Hierarchy, and the Variety of International Relations." *International Organization* 50(1):1–34.

Levitsky, Steven. 2003. *Transforming Labor-Based Parties in Latin America: Argentine Peronism in Comparative Perspective*. New York: Cambridge University Press.

Lieberman, Evan S. 2005. "Nested Analysis as a Mixed-Method Strategy for Comparative Research." *American Political Science Review* 99:435–52.

Lodola, German, and Rosario Queirolo. 2005. *Ideological Classification of Latin American Political Parties*. Pittsburgh, PA: University of Pittsburgh.

Lora, Eduardo. 2001. "What Makes Reforms Likely? Timing and Sequencing of Structural Reforms in Latin America." *Inter-American Development Bank Working Paper #424*.

Malloy, James M., and Gamarra, Eduardo. 1988. *Revolution and Reaction: Bolivia, 1964–1985*. New Brunswick, NJ: Transaction Books.

Manzetti, Luigi, and Dell'Aquila Marco. 1988. "Economic Stabilisation in Argentina: The Austral Plan." *Journal of Latin American Studies*, 20:1–26.

McFaul, Michael. 1995. "State Power, Institutional Change, and the Politics of Privatization in Russia." "World Politics 47 (2):210–43.

McGuire, James. 1995. "Political Parties and Democracy in Argentina." In Scott Mainwaring and Timothy Scully (eds.). *Building Democratic Institutions: Party Systems in Latin America*. Stanford, CA: Stanford University Press.

Mearsheimer, John. 1994. "The False Promise of International Institutions." *International Security* 19 (3):5–49.

Meller, Patricio. 1996. *Un siglo de economía política chilena (1890–1990)*. Santiago, Chile: Editorial Andrés Bello.

Mercer-Blackman, Valerie, and Anna Unigovskaya. 2000. "Compliance with IMF Program Indicators and Growth in Transition Economies." IMF Working Paper 00/47.

Milner, Helen, and Benjamin Judkins. 2004. "Partisanship, Trade Policy, and Globalization: Is There a Left-Right Divide on Trade Policy?" *International Studies Quarterly* 48(1):95–120.

Milner, Helen, and Keiko Kubota. 2005. "Why the Move to Free Trade? Democracy and Trade Policy in the Developing Countries." *International Organization* 59:107–43.

Minton-Beddoes, Zanny. 1995. "Why the IMF Needs Reform." *Foreign Affairs* 74(3):123.

Morales, Juan Antonio. 1996. "Democratic Restoration and Economic Policy: Argentina 1984–91." In Juan Antonio Morales and Gary McMahon (eds.), *Economic Policy and the Transition to Democracy: The Latin American Experience*. New York: St. Martin's Press.

Moravcsik, Andrew. 1997. "Taking Preferences Seriously: A Liberal Theory of International Politics." *International Organization* 51:513–53.

Munteanu, Igor. 1996. "Moldovanism as a Political Weapon," *Transition* 4.

Murillo, Maria V. 2002. "Political Bias in Policy Convergence: Privatization Choices in Latin America." *World Politics* 54:462–93.

Murillo, Maria V., and Andrew Schrank. 2005. "With a Little Help of My Friends: Partisan Politics, Transnational Alliances and Labor Rights in Latin America." *Comparative Political Studies* 38(8):971–99.

Negru, Nicolae. 1997. "Neutralitatea trebuie sa fie neutra." *Arena Politica* http://ziua.sfos.ro/PoliticalArena/neutralitatea.html.

Nelson, Joan. 1990. *Economic Crisis and Policy Choice: The Politics of Adjustment in the Third World*, Princeton: Princeton University Press.

Nohlen, Dieter. 1993. *Handbuch der Wahldaten Lateinamerikas und der Karibik*. Opladen: Leske and Budrich.

Nordsieck, Wolfram. 2001. *Parties and Elections in Europe*. Available online at www.parties-and-elections.de.

O'Dwyer, Conor. 2006. *Runaway State-Building: Patronage Politics and Democratic Development*. Baltimore: Johns Hopkins University Press.

O'Donnell, Guillermo. 1994. "Delegative Democracy." *Journal of Democracy* 5(1):55–69.

Ozler, Sule. 1993. "Have Commercial Banks Ignored History?" *American Economic Review* 83(3):608–20.

Pacek, Alexander, Grigore Pop-Eleches, and Joshua Tucker. 2009. "Disenchanted or Discerning: Voter Turnout in Post-Communist Countries." *The Journal of Politics* (forthcoming).

Pastor, Manuel. 1987. *The International Monetary Fund and Latin America*. Boulder and London: Westview Press.

———. 1992. *Inflation, Stabilization, and Debt: Macroeconomic Experiments in Peru and Bolivia*. Boulder: Westview Press.

Pastor, Manuel, and Carol Wise. 1992. "Peruvian Economic Policy in the 1980s: From Orthodoxy to Heterodoxy and Back." *Latin American Research Review* 27:83–117.

Payer, Cheryl. 1975. *The Debt Trap: The IMF and the Third World*. New York: Monthly Review Press.

Pereira da Silva, Luiz. "The International Financial Institutions (IFIs) and the Political Lessons from the Asian Crises of 1997–1998." *International Social Science Journal* 53(170):551–68.

Persson, Torsten, Guido Tabellini, and Francesco Trebbi. 2003. "Electoral Rules and Corruption." *Journal of the European Economic Association* 1:4, 958–89.

Pierson, Paul. 2001. "Coping with Permanent Austerity." In *The New Politics of the Welfare State*, Paul Pierson (ed.), 410–56. Oxford: Oxford University Press.

Polak, Jacques, 1991. "The Changing Nature of Conditionality." *Essays in International Finance*, no. 84. Princeton, NJ: Princeton University Press.

Pop-Eleches, Grigore. 1999. "Separated at Birth or Separated by Birth? The Communist Successor Parties in Romania and Hungary." *East European Politics and Societies* 13(1):117–47.

———. 2007. "Historical Legacies and Post-Communist Regime Change." *The Journal of Politics* 69(4): 908–26.

Przeworski, Adam. 1991. *Democracy and the Market: Political and Economic Reforms in Eastern Europe and Latin America*. Cambridge: Cambridge University Press.

Przeworski, Adam, and James Vreeland. 2000. "The Effect of IMF Programs on Economic Growth." *Journal of Development Economics* 62:385–421.

Putnam, Robert D. 1988. "Diplomacy and Domestic Politics: The Logic of Two-Level Games." *International Organization* 42(3):427–60.

Ranis, Gustav, and Syed Mahmood. 1992. *The Political Economy of Development Policy Change*. Cambridge, MA: Blackwell.

Reichmann, T. and R. Stillson. 1978 "Experience with Programs of Balance of Payments Adjustments: Standby Arrangements in the Higher Credit Tranches, 1961–72." IMF Staff Papers, 25:278–92.

Remmer, Karen. 1994. "The Politics of Economic Stabilization: IMF Stand-by Programs in Latin America, 1954–1984." In *Money Doctors, Foreign Debts, and Economic Reforms in Latin America from the 1890s to the Present*. Paul Drake (ed.). Wilmington, DE: SR Books.

———. 1998. "The Politics of Neoliberal Economic Reform in South America: 1980–1994," *Studies in Comparative International Development* 33(2):3–29.

Roberts, Kenneth. 1995. "Neoliberalism and the Transformation of Populism in Latin America: The Peruvian Case." *World Politics* 48(1):82–116.

———. 2002a. "Social Inequalities without Class Cleavages: Party Systems and Labor Movements in Latin America's Neoliberal Era." *Studies in Comparative International Development* 36(4):3–33.

———. 2002b. "Party-Society Linkages and the Transformation of Political Representation in Latin America." *Canadian Journal of Latin American and Caribbean Studies* 27(53):9–34.

Robertson, Graeme. 2004. "Leading Labor: Unions, Politics and Protest in New Democracies." *Comparative Politics* 36(3):253–72.

Rodrik, Dani. 1994. "The Rush to Free Trade in the Developing World: Why So Late? Why Now? Will It Last?" In *Voting for Reform: Democracy, Political Liberalization, and Economic Adjustment*, S. Haggard and S. Webb (eds.). New York: Oxford University Press.

Roeder, Philip G. 1999. "Peoples and States after 1989: The Political Costs of Incomplete National Revolutions." *Slavic Review* 58, 854–82.

Rogowski, Ronald. 1989. *Commerce and Coalitions*. Princeton: Princeton University Press.

Sachs, Jeffrey. 1986. *The Bolivian Hyperinflation and Stabilization*. Cambridge, MA: National Bureau of Economic Research.

———. 1994a. "A New Blueprint: Beyond Bretton Woods." *Economist* 333(7883):23–25.

———. 1994b. "Towards Glasnost in the IMF; Russia's Democratization Policy; International Monetary Fund." *Challenge* 37(3).

Santaella, Julio. 1996. "Stylized Facts before IMF-Supported Macro-Economic Adjustment." IMF Staff Papers, 43(3).

Sheahan, John. 1987. *Patterns of Development in Latin America: Poverty, Repression and Economic Strategy*. Princeton: Princeton University Press.

Silva, Eduardo. 1996. *The State and Capital in Chile: Business Elites, Technocrats, and Market Economics*. Boulder, CO: Westview Press.

Simmons, Beth. 1994. *Who Adjusts? Domestic Sources of Foreign Economic Policy during the Interwar Years*. Princeton: Princeton University Press.

Smith, William C. 1990. "Democracy, Distributional Conflicts and Macroeconomic Policymaking in Argentina, 1983–89." *Journal of Interamerican Studies and World Affairs* 32(2):1–42.

Smith, William C., Carlos Acuña, and Eduardo Gamarra. 1994. *Democracy, Markets, and Structural Reform in Latin America: Argentina, Bolivia, Brazil, Chile, and Mexico*. New Brunswick, NJ: Transaction Publishers.

Socor, Vladimir. 1994. "Moldova's Political Landscape: Profile of the Parties." *Radio Free Europe/Radio Liberty Research Report* 3/11/1994.

Stallings, Barbara. 1992. "International Influence on Economic Policy: Debt Stabilization, and Structural Reform." In Stephan Haggard and Robert Kaufman (eds.). *The Politics of Economic Adjustment*. Princeton, NJ: Princeton University Press, 41–88.

Stallings, Barbara, and Robert R. Kaufman. 1989. *Debt and Democracy in Latin America*. Boulder, CO: Westview Press.

Stan, Lavinia. 2001. "Comparing Regime Performance—A Case Study." Prepared for delivery at the 2001 Annual Meeting of the American Political Science Association, San Francisco, 2001.

Steinwand, Martin, and Randall W. Stone. 2008. "The International Monetary Fund: A Review of the Recent Evidence." *Review of International Organizations* 3(2): 123–49.

Stiglitz, Joseph. 2000. "What I Learned at the World Economic Crisis." *New Republic* 4/17/2000.

———. 2002. "Globalism's Discontents." *American Prospect* 13(1):A16–A21.

Stiles, Kendall W. 1991. *Negotiating Debt: The IMF Lending Process*. Boulder, CO: Westview Press.

Stokes, Susan. 2001. *Mandates and Democracy: Neoliberalism by Surprise in Latin America*. New York: Cambridge Studies in Comparative Politics.

Stone, Randall W. 1999. "Credible Adjustment: A Time-Series Cross-Sectional Approach to IMF Programs for Post-Communist Countries." Annual Meeting of the American Political Science Association, Atlanta, 1999.

———. 2002. *Lending Credibility: The International Monetary Fund and the Post-Communist Transition*. Princeton: Princeton University Press.

Stone, Randall. 2004. "The Political Economy of IMF Lending in Africa." *American Political Science Review* 98:577–91.

Strange, Susan. 1996. *The Retreat of the State: The Diffusion of Power in the World Economy*. Cambridge, UK: Cambridge University Press.

———. *Economist*. 2005. "The Americas: Kirchner and Lula: Different Ways to Give the Fund the Kiss-Off; Argentina, Brazil and the IMF." *Economist*. 377(8458):65.

Tismaneanu, Vladimir. 1996. "The Leninist Debris or Waiting for Perón." *East European Politics and Societies* 10 (3):504–35.

Torre, Juan Carlos. 1993. "Conflict and Cooperation in Governing the Economic Emergency: The Alfonsin Years." In *Argentina in the Crisis Years, 1983–1990: From Alfonsin to Menem*. Colin M. Lewis and Nissa Torrents (eds.). London: Institute of Latin American Studies.

Tsebelis, George. 1995. "Decision Making in Political Systems: Veto Players in Presidentialism, Parliamentarism, Multicameralism and Multipartyism." *British Journal of Political Science* 25(3):289–325.

Tucker, Joshua. 2006. *Comparative Economic Voting: Economic Conditions and Election Results in Russia, Poland, Hungary, Slovakia and Russia 1990–99*. Cambridge; New York: Cambridge University Press.

Tussie, Diana, and Mirta Botzman. 1990. "Sweet Entanglement: Argentina and the World Bank 1985–89." *Development Policy Review* 8:393–409.

Vachudova, Milada Anna. 2005. *Europe Undivided: Democracy, Leverage, and Integration After Communism.* Oxford: Oxford University Press.

Vaubel, Roland. 1991. "A Public Choice View of International Organization." In *The Political Economy of International Organizations.* Roland Vaubel and Thomas Willett (eds.). 27–45. Boulder, CO: Westview Press.

Vosganian, Varujan. 1999. *Reforma pietelor financiare din Romania.* Iasi: Editura Polirom.

Vreeland, James. 2001. "The Institutional Determinants of IMF Programs." Annual Meeting of the American Political Science Association, San Francisco, 2001.

Vreeland, James. 2003. *The IMF and Economic Development.* Cambridge; New York: Cambridge University Press.

Weyland, Kurt. 1998. "Swallowing the Bitter Pill: Sources of Popular Support for Neoliberal Reform in Latin America." *Comparative Political Studies* 31:539–68.

———. 1999. "Neoliberal Populism in Latin America and Eastern Europe." *Comparative Politics* 31:379–401.

———. 2002. *The Politics of Market Reform in Fragile Democracies: Argentina, Brazil, Peru, and Venezuela.* Princeton: Princeton University Press.

———. 2004. "Neoliberalism and Democracy in Latin America: A Mixed Record." *Latin American Politics and Society* 46:1.

Williamson, John. 1990. "What Washington Means by Policy Reform." In *Latin American Adjustment: How Much Has Happened?* John Williamson (ed.). 7–38. Washington, DC: Institute for International Economics.

———. 1994. *The Political Economy of Policy Reform.* Washington, DC: Institute for International Economics.

Wood, Barry. 1996. "Romania: Eastern Europe's Second-Biggest Market Is Often Overlooked." *Europe* 356:26.

World Bank. 1994. *Moldova: Moving to a Market Economy.* Washington, DC: The World Bank.

INDEX

Milton Keynes UK
Ingram Content Group UK Ltd.
UKHW040951180824
447095UK00003B/254